SEEKING EL DORADO

African Americans in California

Constitutional Amendment Abolishing Slavery

In Legislature of California — Sixteenth Session 1865 & 1866.

SEEKING EL DORADO

African Americans in California

Edited by Lawrence B. de Graaf,
Kevin Mulroy, and Quintard Taylor

AUTRY MUSEUM OF WESTERN HERITAGE
Los Angeles

in association with

UNIVERSITY OF WASHINGTON PRESS
Seattle and London

The publication of
Seeking El Dorado: African Americans in California
has been made possible by a generous gift from Wells Fargo.

FRONTISPIECE: *Constitutional Amendment Abolishing Slavery.
In Legislature of California, Sixteenth Session, 1865 & 1866*
(Sacramento: L. Nagel Printer, c. 1866). This pictorial broadside, created
by noted artist Charles Nahl with the assistance of Louis Nagel,
announces the ratification by the legislature of California of the Thirteenth
Amendment to the U.S. Constitution. The signatures of each California
senator and assemblyman are printed, indicating who voted for or against
ratification. Autry Museum of Western Heritage, Los Angeles.

Contents

Contents

PART III
DEVELOPMENTS IN CULTURE AND POLITICS

Contents

PART IV
THE DREAM DEFERRED

Maps

Preface

Seeking El Dorado began in the winter of 1993. Those were heady days for the Gene Autry Western Heritage Museum (renamed the Autry Museum of Western Heritage in 1995). The museum had been open for five years and had built a record of solid achievement in its collecting, exhibitions, and educational programs. But the time seemed right to engage in new discourse, to follow the direction of the "new Western history" and extend the museum's interpretation of the American West.

Adopting a more inclusive approach within the permanent displays, by giving more coverage to issues of race, ethnicity, and gender, lay at the heart of the new initiatives. Each of the museum's seven galleries features a theme, arranged somewhat chronologically and named after the "spirits" of the Old West. Two galleries in particular—the Spirit of Community and the Spirit of Imagination—seemed to offer the strongest potential for substantive change, and these were targeted for new design and interpretation.

In the Spirit of Imagination gallery, the museum looks at how the West became a mythical place in the movies, radio, television, music, and advertising. New cases were built, artifacts selected, and label copy prepared. In the new design, the curators gave more attention and space to how women, American Indians, Asian Americans, Hispanics, and African Americans have been portrayed in Western film and TV shows, how stereotypes have developed, and how those stereotypes have influenced popular perceptions. Alongside displays on Tom Mix, John Wayne, and Clint Eastwood, the museum now interprets Western roles played by such African Americans as Bill

Pickett, Herb Jeffries, Woody Strode, Sidney Poitier, Danny Glover, Morgan Freeman, and Mario Van Peebles.

The curators chose to reorganize the Spirit of Community gallery into eight profiles: American Indians, European Americans, Mexicans and Mexican Americans, Europeans, Asians, African Americans, Canadians, and Latter-Day Saints. The gallery now provides introductions to communities in the West around 1890. Each profile comes equipped with an interactive educational component, allowing teachers and docents to gather groups of children for hands-on instruction. From the beginning the project was conceived as a collaborative effort. Scholars and museum professionals from the communities represented in the gallery consulted on the development of the space. It was out of these discussions that the idea came for a series of public programs on African American communities in the West for Black History Month 1994.

Since its inception, The Autry has sought to produce innovative and diverse black history programs. In February 1990, William Loren Katz spoke on "The Black West" and "Black Indians" to packed houses, a landmark event in the museum's early development. Since then Juneteenth celebrations, radio theater presentations on John Horse and Bass Reeves, screenings of documentary and fictional films with African American content, gospel, jazz, "cowboy soul" and rap concerts, and demonstrations and children's classes conducted by working black cowboys have drawn interested audiences. In 1994, the museum brought in four of the leading scholars of African American history in the West to lecture during the February weekends. Quintard Taylor began the series with "In Search of a Racial Frontier: An Overview of the Black West" and Kenneth Hamilton, author of *Black Towns and Profit: Promotion and Development in the Trans-Appalachian West, 1877–1915* (1991), followed with "Western Towns for Blacks." Lonnie Bunch lectured on "Black America and the California Dream," and Al Broussard concluded the series with "Black San Francisco: The Struggle for Racial Equality in the West, 1900–1954." Lawrence de Graaf commented upon each of the papers. The lectures were stimulating, attendance grew, and the question-and-answer sessions became more lively and thought provoking each week. California African Americans in the audience began to speak from personal experience of triumph and hardship; most still sought the dream, but many had experienced discrimination and disappointment. Suddenly the Autry had become a town hall for racial and gender issues.

We clearly needed to publish the papers. Ken Hamilton was over extended at that time and could not take on another publication, but the others committed to the project. De Graaf, who was familiar with all the presentations, Taylor, whose book *In Search of the Racial Frontier: African Americans in the American West, 1528–1990* (1998) was nearing completion, and I assumed the roles of editors. We agreed that the project should grow in size and scope and include only new and previously unpublished work to increase its potential contribution to the field. The museum's Los Angeles location factored into our thinking. In Bunch, Broussard, and de Graaf we already had three California specialists on board. These considerations, combined with the knowledge that California was the focus of exciting new studies, persuaded us to go into the recruiting business. Soon Willi Coleman, Doug Flamming, Gretchen Lemke-Santangelo, Kevin Leonard, Delores McBroome, and Shirley Moore, all early-career scholars pursuing important research, had signed on. Bette Cox, whose book on Los Angeles's Central Avenue had just been published, then joined the project. De Graaf and Taylor would coauthor an introductory overview, and de Graaf would also contribute an essay. Esteemed authors Jack Forbes, Gerald Horne, and Raphael Sonenshein completed the picture.

Anticipating that interest in the subject would be increased by the California sesquicentennial celebrations in 2000, the editors adopted a sweeping, holistic approach toward the project: we wanted a study of African Americans in California that took the story from its beginnings to the present day. The contributors were encouraged to think in big pictures, adopt comparative approaches, and explore racial, ethnic, and gender relations. We also sought to adopt one voice for the project. Although there are many contributors, we hope that this anthology reads as a unified whole.

The dominant theme that emerges from the essays is a ceaseless search for the American Dream, for the fundamental rights of life, liberty, and the pursuit of happiness supposedly guaranteed under the United States Constitution but denied African Americans in many parts of the Union. This led to the anthology's title. California's Spanish and Mexican heritage, the beauty of its landscape, the warmth of its climate, and a reputation for tolerance and inclusion make it an attractive place for almost everyone, but it holds a special appeal for the adventurer, the entrepreneur, the pioneer. It is the sense of almost limitless opportunity—whether it be gold or silicon, grapes or oranges, or a movie, recording, or sports contract—that has led many to move there. That pioneering spirit crosses racial, ethnic, and gender lines, and it transcends time. Within the African American community, it links Biddy

Mason with Magic Johnson. Yet it would be the more modest prospect of being able to find work, own a home, and raise a family relatively free of discrimination that would cause many unknown African American pioneers to try their luck in the Golden State. Both the search and its outcome are covered in these essays. It is a fascinating, moving, and ongoing story. For some, El Dorado has seemed frustratingly out of reach or, worse, an illusion: fool's gold. This helps explain the rise of the Black Panthers in Oakland and the outbreaks of civil unrest in Los Angeles in 1965 and 1992.

It has been a joy to work with my fellow editors on this project. Both have been unflinching in their dedication to its completion and success. They have passed along their wealth of experience and wisdom to the younger scholars, challenging them to raise the bar not only in their writing but in the field as a whole. Since our lecture series took place, Quintard Taylor has published two important books on the West. First came *The Forging of a Black Community: Seattle's Central District, from 1870 through the Civil Rights Era* (1994). Following the publication of *In Search of the Racial Frontier*, the Autry hosted a program titled "A Conversation with Quintard Taylor" in the summer of 1998. A departure for the museum, the program featured Taylor discussing issues raised in his book in open forum with Professor Juan Gómez-Quiñones of UCLA and Janet Clayton, an African American senior editor at the *Los Angeles Times*. Lawrence de Graaf is now professor emeritus after a long and distinguished career at California State University, Fullerton. A true pioneer historian, de Graaf was researching black urban history in the American West long before it became a recognized area of study. He here sets out a new agenda for the field in his essay on African American suburbanization in California.

In November 1998, The Autry celebrated its tenth anniversary. This and the impending end of the twentieth century gave rise to both retrospection and planning for the future. At the dawn of the new millennium, we join many other institutions whose leaders are reconsidering the role of museums within society. For The Autry, the time seems right to branch out into new areas of endeavor. The museum cannot yet boast of having a distinguished collection in the field of African American history. A new museum faces difficult challenges in building collections on underrepresented groups. Clearly, a flexible approach is required. The Autry may begin to collect in nontraditional areas, borrow rather than own materials, display items from private collections, provide catalog access to collections it does not own, or develop virtual exhibitions. It must also engage in cooperative networks and partner with community organizations. As a beginning, during Black History Month 1999, The Autry displayed items from the collection of the Western States Black Research Center, run by Dr. Mayme Clayton, a significant resource within the Los Angeles African American community but little known outside of it.

In 2001, the museum will collaborate with organizations in the Los Angeles African American community to present public programming supporting the publication of *Seeking El Dorado*. We expect to generate the level of interest shown during the 1994 sessions and the 1998 Taylor program. Can that energy be harnessed and channeled into the Autry's future development? *Seeking El Dorado* could become an engine, driving collecting initiatives and interpretive activities. In sponsoring this anthology, The Autry Museum is seeking its own El Dorado: an inclusive view of the West in which the importance of African American history is recognized, understood, and celebrated.

KEVIN MULROY
Los Angeles, October 2000

SEEKING EL DORADO

African Americans in California

Introduction

African Americans in California History,

California in African American History

LAWRENCE B. DE GRAAF & QUINTARD TAYLOR

The experience of African Americans in California offers significant insights into myriad facets of American life and history. Indeed, the history of African Americans in the state is a crucially important, if still only slightly known, episode in the larger saga of black America. It needs to be told because the state's African American population, as of the 1990 census, ranked second only to that of New York state. California's represented 7.5 percent of the nation's total black populace. But that history is also important because the experiences of those forebears of contemporary black California both parallel and differ considerably from the better-defined history of African Americans in other states and regions of the nation as well as from the experiences of other racial groups in that state's history.

Four themes have been especially evident in the lives of black Californians. First, there is the development of separate communities. Beginning in the 1850s, the first residents of San Francisco and Sacramento established a society and culture—the churches, social clubs, literary societies, fraternal orders, civil rights organizations—which embodied the legacy of their past, the values they shared, and their vision of a common destiny defined by social justice. That sense of community, often viewed intellectually as well as spatially, remains a common feature of black life in California even as African Americans move into suburban communities far from the urban centers that have historically been home to the vast majority of African Americans in the state.

Occupational opportunities are the second important theme in the history of California's African Americans. Blacks came in search of the same

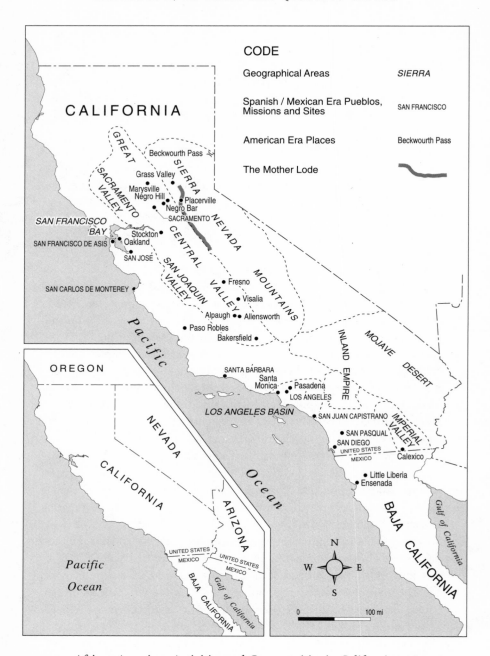

MAP 1. African American Activities and Communities in California, 1769–1930

jobs and dreams as other Americans, but the search often proved frustrating. In nineteenth-century cities, most found themselves confined to menial jobs. Farmwork was largely unavailable due to alternative sources of labor, and manufacturing jobs went almost exclusively to whites. Women frequently worked but for several decades largely as domestics. Their own communities offered some professional and business opportunities but mostly to a black clientele. World War II began a widening of occupational opportunities, but its breakthroughs were later minimized by the flight of many industries to suburbs. The 1960s expanded opportunities for middle-class blacks, but the plight of the "underclass" grew increasingly desperate. Occupational opportunities thus provide an insight into the discriminations blacks faced in California and show why many supported race leaders.

While usually giving a nod to "California exceptionalism," black leadership in the state throughout the nineteenth and twentieth centuries has consistently focused on achieving racial justice, the third major theme. This pursuit has remained paramount in the political discourse of blacks in the state, from the early abolitionist and civil rights activities of Mary Ellen Pleasant and Peter Lester in the 1850s through the early-twentieth-century efforts of the West Coast Improvement Association and the National Association for the Advancement of Colored People (NAACP) to the 1960s campaigns of the Congress of Racial Equality (CORE) and the Black Panther Party down to contemporary crusades of politicians such as San Francisco mayor Willie Brown and Los Angeles congresswoman Maxine Waters. The agendas of these leaders paralleled and, as with the Panthers, often anticipated similar struggles throughout African America.

Separate communities, limited occupational opportunities, and the importance of group leaders point to the fourth theme that pervades the saga of African Americans in California: the changing significance of race. Under Spanish and Mexican rule, race was not as decisive a factor in determining opportunities or legal status as it would later become. Anglo American rule, however, brought African slavery and related notions of racial inferiority as justifications for discriminating against Mexicans and Asians as well as blacks. Well into the twentieth century, black access to most public accommodations, housing, and jobs was restricted. The experience of being judged primarily by color would begin to change during World War II, though more slowly for African Americans than for other groups. Housing would remain widely restricted until the opening of suburbs in the 1970s.

But even as overt racial restrictions ended, many African Americans continued to feel that race was still a factor affecting their daily lives.

Persons of African ancestry have been present in the Golden State since its first non-Indian settlements, making their story an important part of the history of California. The patterns of migration and settlement and of experiencing discrimination and reacting to it parallel those of blacks in many other states. In that sense California offers a microcosm of black experiences nationwide. But African Americans were only one of several racial and ethnic groups to interact with the white majority in the state. Well into the twentieth century, the treatment and status of blacks were similar to those of other minorities, and this produced common experiences. Yet the story of African Americans in California is also unique. This has been especially so since 1960, as prominent black Californians became national figures and their quests and problems framed some of the weightiest issues of recent decades.

African American history in California began with the arrival of the first Spanish-speaking explorers and settlers from central Mexico. Those settlers, as Jack Forbes points out in the first essay in this anthology, "The Early African Heritage of California," were part of a multiracial population dating from the conquest of Mexico by Spanish conquistadors in 1521. Persons of African ancestry accompanied the naval and military expeditions that occupied San Diego and Monterey in 1769. Friar Junipero Serra wrote of two mulatto sailors he met after his arrival at Monterey in 1771, and the Juan Bautista de Anza expedition of 1775 included seven black soldier-settlers and their families among twenty-nine families emigrating to Alta California.[1]

Settlers of African, Indian, and Spanish ancestry founded Los Angeles in 1781. Spanish colonial officials recruited twelve families from a village in the province of Sinaloa, which was two-thirds mulatto. They left in February 1781 for a 500-mile journey to Alta California. Seven months later, on September 4, they founded Nuestra Señora la Reina de Los Angeles de Porciuncula. Colonial records indicate that twenty-six of the forty-six original settlers of Los Angeles were of African or part-African ancestry.[2]

Color presented no insurmountable barrier to fame and wealth on the California frontier. The mulatto Francisco Reyes, who arrived in Los Angeles from central Mexico in 1781, eventually became its alcalde (mayor), while Andres and Pio Pico, the grandsons of a mestizo and his mulatto wife, became prominent political leaders and wealthy ranchers in early-nineteenth-century California. Pio Pico served as governor twice, while Andres Pico was

6

military commander of the Mexican California militia at the battle of San Pasqual. In January 1847, Andres Pico represented California at the signing of the Treaty of Cahuenga, which ended the Mexican War in that area, and he subsequently served in the state legislature.3

The first English-speaking African Americans entered California between 1821 and 1848, having correctly concluded that Mexico imposed fewer racial restrictions than the United States. Some jumped ship while in the province's ports. Of the black sailors who settled in California before 1848, Allen Light became the most prominent. Light was a crew member of the *Pilgrim*, the ship whose California voyage was chronicled in Richard Henry Dana's *Two Years before the Mast* (1840). Light deserted the *Pilgrim* at Santa Barbara in 1835, acquired Mexican citizenship, and became a leading otter hunter along the Southern California coast. In 1839 Governor Juan Bautista Alvarado appointed Light *comisario-general* to serve as "principal representative of that national armada" assigned to halt illegal otter hunting in California's coastal waters, thus becoming the first U.S.-born black to serve as a Mexican official.4

The fur trader and trapper James Beckwourth was the best-known pre-1848 overland black immigrant. He made several trips to California and lived and worked there intermittently between 1835 and 1859. In his third trip in 1850, Beckwourth discovered the trail through the Sierra Nevada that now bears his name, which many gold-seekers used. He built a hotel and store that supplied California-bound migrants and anchored the town eventually named after him.5

West Indian-born William A. Leidesdorff became Mexican California's most prominent African American. Leidesdorff, of Danish-African ancestry, left the West Indies and became a successful merchant captain in New York and New Orleans before arriving in Yerba Buena (San Francisco) in 1841. Soon after his arrival, he sailed his commercial schooner, *Julia Ann*, on regular voyages between California and Honolulu. Leidesdorff also operated *Sitka*, the first steam-powered vessel on the San Francisco Bay. By 1844, he had become a Mexican citizen and had received a 3,500-acre land grant. Leidesdorff's commercial ties with the United States led to his appointment as American vice-consul in 1845 by President James K. Polk, who was probably unaware of the Californian's African ancestry. Leidesdorff was elected to the town council in 1847, helped establish its school system, and became city treasurer. His death in April 1848 came just months after the signing of the Treaty of Guadalupe Hidalgo, which transferred Alta California to U.S.

jurisdiction, and the discovery of gold near Sutter's Fort. These two events signaled the end of an era for the small population of African Americans in California. The Gold Rush rapidly "Americanized" California, and racially restrictive legislation and black slavery soon followed.[6]

The gold mining region stretched 400 miles along the western slope of the Sierra Nevada. An intrepid group of African Americans were among those who migrated to California in search of wealth. Between 1852 and 1860 California's African American population grew from 962 to 4,086. On the eve of the Civil War, California's African Americans constituted 75 percent of the free black population in the West.[7] Most black migrants trekked to California along the main route from Missouri through the Rockies across the Great Basin and over the Sierra Nevada to Northern California or went along the southern route from New Orleans or Fort Smith, Arkansas, across Indian Territory, the Texas Panhandle, New Mexico, Arizona, and the Mojave Desert into Southern California. Both routes tested the stamina of the strongest men and women regardless of race. Willi Coleman, in "African American Women and Community Development in California, 1848–1900," quotes Margaret Frink's description of a lone, unidentified black female migrant in 1850 near the Humboldt Sink, the desert just east of the Sierra Nevada, "carrying a cast-iron bake stove on her head, with her provisions and a blanket piled on top . . . bravely pushing on for California."[8]

The vast majority of African Americans migrated to California for economic reasons, pursuing the promise of quick wealth in the goldfields or in burgeoning San Francisco and Sacramento. Slightly over half of California's blacks in the early 1850s headed for the Mother Lode country. African American miners often worked in integrated settings, preferring the company of Chinese, Latin Americans, Europeans, or white New Englanders to the more prejudiced southerners and midwesterners. On occasion, black miners grew numerous enough to support a community. In 1852 a small, predominantly African American community called Little Negro Hill grew up around the lucrative claims of two Massachusetts-born black miners working along the American River. Little Negro Hill also attracted Chinese and Portuguese miners and eventually American-born whites.[9]

A few black gold seekers found wealth. In 1851 Peter Brown described his new life as a miner to his wife, Alley, in Saint Genevieve City, Missouri. "I am now mining about 25 miles from Sacramento City and doing well," he wrote. "I have been working for myself for the past two months . . . and have cleared three hundred dollars. California is the best country in the world to make money. It is also the best place for black folks on the globe. All a man has to do, is to work, and he will make money."[10]

But California soon proved to be much less than the utopia many African Americans had anticipated. Slavery remained the most immediate threat. The California Constitution of 1849 made slavery illegal, yet black bond servants lived there in the 1850s because officials were unwilling to challenge slaveholders who brought them into the state. Slaveholders interpreted the silence of California's leading officeholders as tacit support for the institution. Robert Givens admitted as much when he wrote to his father in Kentucky in 1852 that although the law made it impossible to hold "a slave . . . longer than the present year," he did not consider it a risk because "no one will put themselves to the trouble of investigating the matter." By that time, an estimated 300 slaves worked in the goldfields, and an undetermined but sizable number were house servants in California cities.[11]

Yet California slavery was undermined by an African American community willing to employ both legal and extralegal means to ensure the freedom of those enslaved. Mary Ellen Pleasant became famous in San Francisco's black community in 1858 when she sheltered Archy Lee. Peter Lester, a Philadelphian who arrived in San Francisco in 1850, invited slaves into his home to lecture them on their rights. "When they left," he declared, "we had them strong in the spirit of freedom. They were leaving [slavery] every day." The active role of blacks in challenging slavery prompted one contemporary German observer to remark, "The wealthy California Negroes . . . exhibit a great deal of energy and intelligence in saving their brethren."[12]

Black activists like Pleasant and Lester were supported by white abolitionists such as prominent attorneys Edward D. Baker and Edwin Bryan Crocker (brother of Charles Crocker) and merchants like Mark Hopkins. Moreover, antislavery legal activists sometimes found such sympathetic jurists as Judge Benjamin Hayes of Los Angeles, who established important legal precedents while freeing blacks in cases before their courts. Indeed, throughout the 1850s, in a series of cases including Robert and Carter Perkins, Archy Lee, and Bridget (Biddy) Mason, slavery was undermined by both blacks and whites who were determined that all people in California would be free.[13]

Most white Californians were unwilling to embrace slavery, yet they supported racially discriminatory legislation. Between 1849 and 1860 successive antebellum California legislatures built what Malcolm Edwards has called "an appallingly extensive body of discriminatory laws." These laws denied blacks voting rights, prohibited African American court testimony, and banned black homesteading, jury service, and intermarriage with whites. The most threatening was the ban on African Americans (as well as Indians and Chinese) testifying against white persons in court. This essentially denied blacks who were robbed by whites the right to be witnesses to the crime and to protect their property.[14]

Responding particularly to the testimony ban, the state's African American leaders called three Colored Conventions, in 1855 and 1856 in Sacramento and in 1857 in San Francisco. While their protests were not immediately acted upon, these meetings initiated the first civil rights campaign in the West. The first convention, organized by Mifflin Gibbs, William Newby, and Jonas Townsend, brought together at Sacramento's Saint Andrews African Methodist Episcopal (AME) Church forty-nine delegates representing ten of California's twenty-seven counties. Fully conscious of their history-making mission, Sacramento delegate Jeremiah B. Sanderson proclaimed the convention "the most important step [toward civil rights] on this side of the continent." Setting the model for subsequent gatherings, the first convention profiled the wealth of black California while debating ways to challenge the testimony ban and other discriminatory legislation. It concluded with a statement to white California urging that "justice . . . be meted out to all, without respect to complexion."[15]

The origins of California's black population partly explain the roots of these conventions and the willingness to fight for denied rights. The state's remarkably diverse Gold Rush-era population included members of the first significant voluntary African American migration to the West. In 1850 California had nearly 1,000 African Americans from north and south of the Mason-Dixon line as well as a foreign-born black population from Mexico, Peru, Chile, and Jamaica. Freeborn blacks from northern states such as Massachusetts and Ohio rubbed shoulders with slaves from Georgia and Texas. That mix, particularly with its leadership drawn disproportionately from New England abolitionist circles, produced a community willing and able to protect its interests.[16]

Latinos, Asians, and Native Americans also bore the burden of racial discrimination. Latinos were harassed in the goldfields and were subject, like the Chinese, to the Foreign Miner's Tax. The Gwin Land Act of 1852 stripped them of much of their land. The Chinese, who by 1870 formed 10 percent of California's population, were also driven from the goldfields and further restricted in their employment outside the Mother Lode. Ultimately California's anti-Chinese campaign would generate the first U.S. immigration legislation specifically targeting one nation, the Chinese Exclusion Act of 1882. American Indians suffered most of all, losing the vast majority of their land while their population declined to near extinction in some areas of the state. The practices of numerous European Americans reflected a belief in racial supremacy and unique destiny. Ironically, racism in California toward other groups of color may well have spared African Americans the harshest acts of repression. Nonetheless, black Californians, like other people of color, realized that California's golden image was tarnished by bigotry and discrimination.[17]

In the 1850s most black Californians worked in the goldfields. However, their political, intellectual, and cultural centers emerged in San Francisco and Sacramento. Those cities' 1852 populations, 464 and 338 respectively, understate their significance as points of arrival for newcomers destined for the gold country, as winter quarters, as entertainment centers for black miners, and as potential areas of retirement for both successful and unsuccessful argonauts. The goldfields provided a temporary home for African American miners, but black urban residents created permanent communities. San Francisco was the first indication of this trend. Between 1849 and 1855 most African American residents settled near the waterfront, and the group expanded inland slowly from there. In a single neighborhood of tents, shacks, saloons, hotels, and gambling houses, one of the earliest examples of cooperation among people of color was set by Mexican American, Chilean, and African American sailors, miners, and laborers who pooled their resources. In 1854, for example, Mexican Americans and African Americans organized a pre-Christmas masquerade ball.[18]

Middle-class African Americans lived throughout the city, often on the premises of their businesses. They created institutions that brought together blacks from throughout the city for spiritual and social support. Churches became the first permanent institutions. Saint Andrews A M E, organized by the Reverend Bernard Fletcher in Sacramento in 1851, was the first black church in California. The following year the Reverend John Jamison Moore, a former slave, founded the A M E Zion Church of San Francisco. Four years after its founding, the church occupied a brick building and had a library and a sabbath school with fifty pupils. The role of the African American church as a moral and spiritual base in an underdeveloped urban society was important in its own right, but these institutions also assumed other responsibilities. The congregations supported orphans and widows with food and financial assistance, aided victims of natural disasters such as the 1861 Sacramento flood, raised money to help sick and wounded black soldiers during the Civil War, and assisted both California Indians and southern freedmen immediately after 1865.[19] In smaller towns such as Los Angeles, blacks attended white churches, sometimes alongside whites, sometimes in segregated quarters. Once their population became large enough to sustain a separate church, however, they usually formed one. This was an early testimony to the uniqueness of black Christian beliefs and the centrality of the black church to the individual lives and sense of identity of African Americans, even in areas remote from most of the nation's black population.[20]

The African American population of Sacramento grew more slowly than that of San Francisco during the early 1850s. Most blacks in the California capital were cooks, barbers, or boardinghouse keepers. They were concentrated in residences along the banks of the Sacramento River, sharing their neighborhood with Mexican and Chinese settlers. All three groups were subject to random attacks by "rowdy young men and boys" who vandalized black- and Chinese-owned businesses. By 1860 Sacramento could boast of having the only two African American doctors in the Far West and its only African American engineer. Yet its black residents were less wealthy and educated and far more likely to be southern-born former slaves than their counterparts in San Francisco. The diverging growth of the two communities was best seen in their population increases. By 1860 San Francisco had 1,176 African Americans, compared to 394 in Sacramento.[21]

Marysville, Grass Valley, and Placerville in the Mother Lode country and Stockton in the Central Valley were the only other cities in antebellum Northern California that had a sizable black presence. Marysville and Grass Valley attracted former miners seeking permanent occupations. Many of these typically became barbers, porters, laborers, and servants. Stockton, however, reflecting its importance as an agricultural community, listed a few African Americans as farmers and vaqueros (cowboys). Marysville's 118 African American residents in 1860 maintained a community centered on the Mount Olivet Baptist Church. Founded in 1853, the church was supported not only by parishioners but also by committees of church women who conducted fund-raising "Ladies Festivals." Similar female-organized fund-raising activities also sustained small AME churches in Placerville, Grass Valley, and Stockton.[22]

Los Angeles had the only significant black population in Southern California through most of the nineteenth century. The first English-speaking black Angelenos were servants brought to California by white officers during the war between the United States and Mexico. Typical of this group was Peter Biggs, a former Missouri slave who became the city's first barber and bootblack. Biggs married a Mexican woman and during the 1860s had a monopoly on the barbering trade in the city. The small black Angeleno population also included the Owens family, which rode the post-Civil War Southern California real estate boom to become one of the wealthiest African American families in the state by the end of the century. Their saga began in Texas when Robert Owens earned his freedom and worked to purchase his wife and children. Bringing his family to Los Angeles in 1850, Owens held odd jobs and his wife took in washing until he received a government contract to supply wood for local military installations. By 1860 the Owens family had a flourishing livery business employing ten Mexican vaqueros to break wild horses and supply cattle to newly arriving settlers. The Owens and Biddy Mason families merged through the marriage of their eldest children. Their descendants continued to play prominent roles in Los Angeles's African American community through the end of the century.[23]

By the beginning of the Civil War, prospects for black Californians began to improve. Leland Stanford's election in 1862 as California's first Republican governor proved particularly encouraging. Sensing growing white support, San Francisco blacks created the Franchise League in 1862 to campaign for voting rights and an end to testimony restrictions. Meanwhile, the Republican-dominated legislature removed discriminatory barriers in education. But the crowning achievement was the legislative repeal of the testimony restriction in 1863.[24]

California's African Americans also challenged segregated public transportation during the Civil War years when William Bowen and Charlotte Brown initiated successful lawsuits. In May 1863, Bowen was ejected from a San Francisco streetcar. He filed a civil suit for $10,000, and in December 1864 a jury awarded him $3,199 in damages. The Charlotte Brown case began a month earlier when she was ejected from a streetcar and filed suit. Despite the judge's reminder that California law prohibited the exclusion of blacks from streetcars, the jury awarded Brown five cents in damages (the cost of the fare). But when she again was ejected from a streetcar and once more filed suit, a jury awarded her $500. These victories, however, did not abolish streetcar exclusion. The campaign for access to public transportation continued in San Francisco and other California cities, end-ing only in 1893 with the enactment of a state antidiscrimination law.[25]

California's African Americans waged a similar prolonged campaign to secure equal educational opportunities. Their earliest schools were private, all-black facilities created in the mid-1850s in Sacramento and San Francisco. In only a few cities did they receive any public funds. African American community groups demanded better schooling during the Civil War, and in 1866 they gained access to public schools throughout the state. However, this law included the proviso that any county could set up separate schools for "African, Indian, or Mongolian" children. African American newspapers and organizations campaigned against segregation, assisted by the fact that their small number often made separate black schools financially unfeasible. By 1875, when San Francisco ended segregation, most California communities had admitted blacks into integrated schools. A court case against Visalia in 1890 ended de jure school segregation for blacks in California.[26]

In February 1863, while the North and South did battle in the Civil War and the Emancipation Proclamation was less than two months old, Peter Anderson wrote an editorial in the *Pacific Appeal*, one of San Francisco's African American newspapers, that fused the destiny of former slaves with California and the West. Anderson called on "our leading men in the east" to initiate a "system of land speculation west of Kansas, or in any of the Territories, and endeavor to infuse into the minds of these freedmen the importance of agriculture, that they may become producers. By this means they can come up with the expected growth of the Great West."[27] Anderson envisioned a march of freed people westward to become farmers, but this did not happen. Between 1860 and 1910 the black population of California grew slowly from 4,086 to 21,645 and remained around 1 percent of the total population throughout the era. Some African Americans entered farming. They were a small presence in several Central Valley towns, and a few efforts were made to recruit them as farm laborers. Some black entrepreneurs tried to establish farming colonies, most notably Allensworth in the San Joaquin Valley and Little Liberia in Baja California. Insights on why so few blacks settled in these colonies or stayed with farming are offered by Delores Nason McBroome in "Harvests of Gold: African American Boosterism, Agriculture, and Investment in Allensworth and Little Liberia." But the majority migrated to the cities rather than to the countryside, ensuring that urban California would be the home to most of the state's African American residents, a trend clearly evident by 1910, as can be seen in table 1.[28]

TABLE 1. African American Population in California and Its Major Cities, 1880–1910

	1860		1880		1900		1910	
	Number of Blacks	Percentage of Total Population	Number of Blacks	Percentage of Total Population	Number of Blacks	Percentage of Total Population	Number of Blacks	Percentage of Total Population
California	4,086	1.1	6,081	0.7	11,045	0.7	21,645	0.9
Los Angeles	66	1.5	102	1.5	2,131	2.1	7,599	2.4
Oakland	18	1.7	593	1.7	1,026	1.5	3,055	2.0
San Francisco	1,176	2.1	1,628	0.7	1,654	0.5	1,642	0.4
Sacramento	394	2.9	455	2.1	402	1.4	486	1.1

The combined African American population of San Francisco, Los Angeles, and Oakland in 1910 totaled only 12,296, slightly less than one-eighth the total of the largest black urban community at the time, Washington, D.C. Such small numbers, however, did not prevent California's black urbanites from organizing a rich social and cultural life or battling against racial injustice. California's African American urban communities shared numerous characteristics. Blacks in every major city in the state performed surprisingly similar work; both men and women were employed as personal servants for wealthy households, while males also worked as hotel waiters, railroad porters, messengers, cooks, or janitors. Some entrepreneurial blacks operated barbershops, restaurants, and boardinghouses. By 1910 San Francisco and Los Angeles had a few African American doctors, lawyers, and newspaper editors, who, along with ministers and schoolteachers, constituted the local "elite."29

Despite their small numbers, black urban Californians created fraternal organizations, social clubs, newspapers, and literary societies. These fledgling nineteenth-century institutions addressed the spiritual, educational, social, and cultural needs of the local inhabitants. But "race organizations" also provided African Americans with a respite from a hostile world, a retreat where they could lose their anonymity and gain some control over their lives. While such goals were hardly peculiar to black Californians, the importance of these organizations was magnified by the small population and the vast distances between major cities and from the South. As early as 1862, the *Pacific Appeal* suggested their significance when it called upon its readers to create political, religious, and moral organizations "wherever there are half a dozen Colored people." Lonnie Bunch's essay, "'The Greatest State for the Negro': Jefferson L. Edmonds, Black Propagandist of the California Dream," assesses the work of one important black intellectual who was instrumental in suggesting race strategies. 30

With 1,330 residents in 1870 and 1,654 three decades later, black San Francisco grew slowly during the post-Civil War period. Nonetheless it remained the model for urban community life for African Americans from British Columbia to Southern California and as far east as Utah, until the rise of black Los Angeles shortly before World War I. Black San Francisco's reputation as the most cosmopolitan and sophisticated African American community in the West stemmed from various sources. First, it could uniquely lay claim to antebellum antecedents. Moreover, with northern and southern blacks as well as a foreign-born population, the city was far more diverse than other urban centers in the state. The foreign-born population constituted 13 percent of the city's blacks in 1860 and 11 percent in 1900, second only to New York City. West Indians, and particularly Jamaicans, dominated.[31]

Black San Francisco's leadership also flowed from its wealth. The resources of businesswoman Mary Ellen Pleasant are well known. Pleasant, however, should be viewed as merely the leading example of a remarkable group of resourceful entrepreneurs. The Gold Rush generated short-lived prosperity for a few fortunate black miners, but true wealth lay in successful real estate and stock speculation in a booming urban economy. By 1870, Richard Barber, despite his occupation as a porter, had amassed $70,000 in real estate, making him the city's richest African American. George Washington Dennis's story, however, encouraged and inspired blacks far beyond San Francisco. Arriving in California as a slave in 1849, Dennis purchased his and his mother's freedom while working as a janitor at a San Francisco gambling saloon. After 1865 Dennis operated a variety of businesses while buying and selling property. By 1890 his holdings were worth $50,000.[32]

Yet black San Francisco's prosperity rested precariously on a weak economic foundation. As Albert Broussard describes in his essay, "In Search of the Promised Land: African American Migration to San Francisco, 1900–1945," most of the city's black residents survived on the margin of the urban economy. San Francisco in 1910 offered the same types of service jobs that it had in 1860. Most black workers were coachmen, butlers, cooks, maids, and porters. If sailors, ship stewards, and dock workers gave that community a more varied workforce, their meager wages did little to raise overall prosperity.[33]

Despite the community's poverty, fraternal orders, cultural associations, social clubs, and literary societies abounded. These included the Young Men's Union Beneficial Society, the Prince Hall Masons, the West Indian Benevolent Association, the Amateur Literary and Drama Association, and the Elliott Literary Institute. In her essay, "'Your Life Is Really Not Just Your Own': African American Women in Twentieth-Century California," Shirley Moore discusses the organizations black women created to generate a sense of community. Not surprisingly, much of black social life derived from the city's churches. The three largest in 1880 were Powell Street (formerly Saint Cyprian) AME, the AME Zion Church, and the Third Baptist Church. Carpets, bells, cushioned seats, and an artificial pool for baptism in the Third Baptist Church suggested a sophistication that surprised visitors. New Yorker William P. Powell, who attended Powell Street AME in 1874, was moved to remark, "Well, I never! In all my travels I never saw the like—colored worshipers *rung* to church and *bell'd* to prayers."[34]

Faced with the high cost of housing, nineteenth-century black San Franciscans settled in Oakland and other East Bay communities. Oakland, founded in 1852, first attracted African Americans after the completion of the transcontinental railroad in 1869. Many of the initial settlers were railroad construction and repair workers lured to the city as the terminus of the Central Pacific, Southern Pacific, and Western Pacific Railroads. But the Oakland settlers also included Pullman porters, who emerged following the Pullman Company's 1869 decision to require an African American male porter on each of its cars. Some black sailors, most notably William T. Shorey, the Barbados-born captain of a whaling vessel, also sought out the East Bay city in the 1880s because of its lower housing costs. By the 1890s many African American newcomers settled in Oakland rather than San Francisco, with East Bay residents now using ferries and trolleys to travel between communities. The 1906 earthquake, which made thousands of San Franciscans temporarily homeless, accelerated the trend; by 1910 nearly twice as many African Americans lived in Oakland as in San Francisco.[35]

Los Angeles, though still second in size to San Francisco in total population in 1910, nonetheless had the largest African American urban concentration west of Texas. Modern black Los Angeles began with the land boom of the late 1880s, which propelled the African American population from 102 in 1880 to 2,131 twenty years later. That boom increased the entire city's populace from slightly more than 11,183 to 102,479, allowing a few early settlers to profit immensely from the increase. Among the most successful was Biddy Mason, who purchased her family homestead between Spring Street and Broadway for $250 in 1866 and sold part of her property for $1,500 eighteen years later. Mason established the First A M E Church in 1872, the oldest church in the city, and single-handedly supported it during the crucial first years by paying all of its taxes and expenses "to hold it for her people." Mason's descendants continued to profit from the growing value of Southern California real estate. Her grandson, Robert C. Owens, whom the *Colored American Magazine* in 1905 called "the richest Negro west of Chicago," became the friend and confidant of Booker T. Washington and a major contributor to the Tuskegee Institute.[36]

The prosperity of the Mason/Owens family was not typical of most nineteenth-century black Angelenos. Many newcomers found jobs as construction and repair workers for the Southern Pacific and Santa Fe Railroads or as porters, cooks, waiters, and maids. J. Max Bond described late-nineteenth-century black Angelenos as "without leadership . . . poor . . . scattered [but] with no restrictions against them." Like their counterparts in San Francisco, Los Angeles's African Americans were not residentially segregated, but their employment prospects were limited by biased employers and unions.37

African American Los Angeles continued to grow rapidly in the first decade of the twentieth century. The population jumped from 2,131 in 1900 to 7,599 in 1910. In 1903, the Southern Pacific Railroad brought in nearly 2,000 black laborers to break a strike by Mexican American construction workers. This corporate decision doubled the size of the African American community and initiated intense interracial rivalry that would continue long after the strike. Soon hundreds of black Texans migrated to the Los Angeles area, independent of the Southern Pacific's recruiting efforts, induced by their naive belief that "there [was] no antagonism against the race." Familial networks also encouraged migration: "We came here back in 1902," declared a Tennessee couple in a 1934 interview. "We were doing pretty well, so we sent back home and told cousins to come along. When the cousins got here, they sent for their cousins. Pretty soon the whole community was made up of Tennessee people." Others were enticed by urban boosters like E. H. Rydall, who wrote in 1907, "Southern California is more adapted for the colored man than any other part of the United States [because] the climate of Southern California is distinctively African. . . . This is the sunny southland in which the African thrives."38

Early twentieth-century black Angelenos also established organizations and institutions that defined and defended the community. By 1910 there were twelve churches, seven major fraternal organizations, the Union Literary Society in Boyle Heights, and the Sojourner Truth Industrial Club, founded by African American females in 1904 to "establish a . . . safe refuge" for the hundreds of young working women streaming into the city. The Women's Day Nursery, building on Biddy Mason's earlier efforts to assist poor families, provided day-care facilities for children of working parents. Although black women did not yet have the right to vote, their voices were prominently heard in the Women's Civic League, which sponsored candidate debates and held rallies for office seekers they endorsed. Three newspapers, the *Los Angeles New Age,* the *Liberator,* and the *California Eagle,* served the community, with the last paper surviving until 1966.39

In 1903, the Reverend J. E. Edwards, pastor of the First AME Church,

Jefferson Lewis Edmonds, editor of the *Liberator*, and Frederick Roberts, an attorney, created a local civil rights organization known simply as the Forum. This organization was predicated on two strategies: first, to incorporate new residents into the local community and second, to challenge white Angelenos who chose to discriminate. The Forum, open to every African American Angeleno, provided scholarships for ambitious community youth. The organization also became a vehicle for the discussion of various local issues until its demise in 1942. In 1913, Los Angeles's black leaders established the first state branch of the NAACP, which became the main instrument of legal protest against a growing array of segregation and discriminatory practices. Oakland and Pasadena soon did the same, and by 1940 there were NAACP branches in eighteen California cities.[40]

The growth of these civil rights defense organizations was prompted, in part, by the rise of discriminatory practices and policies against all people of color because of the growing anti-Asian movement in the state and the growing visibility of African Americans and Latinos. For African Americans in California this institutionalized discrimination, manifested in segregated housing, public accommodations, and transportation, arose because the state seldom enforced the 1893 antidiscrimination statute. Of course, employment discrimination prompted by both union exclusion and employer bias had been evident in the state since 1848 and continued almost unabated until World War II.[41]

One of the strongest indications of a growing black population and community in California in the early twentieth century was the proliferation and activities of churches. By 1906, there were 63 black churches in the state; ten years later, 95; by 1926, 192. This was probably an underenumeration, for most of those were mainline black churches. Often overlooked were "storefront" churches, whose significance is seen in the rise of Pentecostalism. While forms of this fundamentalist, emotional form of Christianity date back to the nineteenth century, its formal origins are usually attributed to the "Azusa Street Revival" that began in Los Angeles in 1906. A black holiness preacher, W. J. Seymour, came to town and set up meetings in an abandoned church on that street. At first he attracted a mixed white and black audience, partly by his practice of speaking in tongues and his claim of being under the power of the Holy Ghost and partly by accepting and targeting the working class. Within four years, Los Angeles had at least twenty-five Pentecostal churches, and the faith would spread to 30,000 churches and 5.5 million worshippers in the United States alone by 1991. Its interracial nature was short-lived, however, as whites broke off in 1908, and the two races established Pentecostal churches under different names.[42]

California's black churches were as widespread as they were numerous. By 1922, the Baptists alone had churches in twenty Southern California towns and cities besides Los Angeles, and pastors from larger cities often visited outlying ones, providing a vital link among isolated African American communities. They continued to provide a major source of social control and positive contacts as well as various services that were especially important to newly arriving migrants. Several of Los Angeles's black social organizations were begun as church projects, and churches provided early meeting places for the local NAACP and Urban League. During the Great Depression, most larger churches had a welfare department. Some became increasingly like businesses, either in raising funds and members for the church or in sponsoring African American enterprises, especially housing, in cities like Santa Barbara that had few blacks. California's most successful black enterprise of this period, the Golden State Mutual Life Insurance Company, built up its clientele by advertising through race churches.[43]

Yet, as Manning Marable has observed, the black church could be controversial. The need to build new churches or expand old ones to serve the growing population made the pursuit of funds for such purposes paramount. In 1923, a group mainly composed of whites raised a modest $10,000 in Los Angeles to support an antilynching bill, while black pastors collected a dollar per Sunday from each member of their congregations for a Baptist convention. This contrast brought charges that the church was a source of political apathy, its emphasis on the hereafter serving as an opiate to civic action. Furthermore, the proliferation of storefront churches was accompanied by a growing number of uneducated and unscrupulous "jack-leg" preachers. Such persons led some black residents of Los Angeles to characterize church leaders en bloc as "all a bunch of racketeers."[44] Overall, however, African Americans continued to look to the church for community leadership.

After 1910, Los Angeles became the center of black population, politics, and business in California, eclipsing San Francisco and Oakland, as can be seen in table 2.[45] This transition was symbolized by the 1918 election of Frederick Roberts as the first African American assemblyman in the state. Black Los Angeles also had high-profile businesses that generated enormous pride within the city's African American community and caused comment from outsiders. Chandler Owen, Harlem resident and editor of *The Messenger*,

TABLE 2. African American Population in California and Its Major Cities, 1920–40

	1920		1930		1940	
	Number of Blacks	Percentage of Total Population	Number of Blacks	Percentage of Total Population	Number of Blacks	Percentage of Total Population
California	38,763	1.1	81,048	1.4	124,306	1.8
Los Angeles	15,579	2.7	38,894	3.1	63,774	4.2
Oakland	5,489	2.5	7,503	2.6	8,462	2.8
San Francisco	2,414	0.5	3,803	0.6	4,846	0.8

declared Central Avenue a "veritable little Harlem in Los Angeles" after a 1922 speaking tour. Along a twelve-block section of Central Avenue could be found black-owned theaters, savings and loan associations, automobile dealerships, newspaper offices, and retail businesses. The avenue was also home to the Golden State Mutual Life Insurance Company, the largest black business in the West, and the Hotel Somerville (later the Dunbar Hotel), which became nationally famous after NAACP delegates stayed there during the organization's 1928 national convention. In 1929, Dr. H. Claude Hudson, a prominent dentist and president of the local NAACP, built the Hudson-Liddell Building at 41st and Central. This building, designed by African American architect Paul Williams, soon became the "symbol to black Angelenos of what was possible in Los Angeles."[46]

Nineteenth-century urban employment patterns continued virtually unchanged until World War II. In 1930, most African Americans in San Francisco, Oakland, and Los Angeles worked as servants. This was especially true of women, over 80 percent of whom were confined to domestic service. C. L. Dellums, vice president of the Brotherhood of Sleeping Car Porters, recalled the nature of work opportunities soon after he came to the San Francisco Bay Area from Texas in 1923: "I had been around here long enough to realize there wasn't very much work Negroes could get." African American workers could either "go down to the sea in ships or work on the railroads."[47]

One occupation—motion picture actor—was almost exclusively Californian. By the second decade of the twentieth century, the American motion picture industry was situated in Hollywood, as Los Angeles-area studios gained nationwide control over the production and distribution of films. African Americans had been film actors in the pre-California days of motion pictures and often had sensitive, nonstereotypical roles in pre-World War I films. African Americans hoped to continue working in the industry after it moved to Southern California, but film moguls relegated black employees to service jobs and black actors to roles that reflected their subservient status in the workforce. From 1915 to 1920, roughly half of the black roles reviewed by *Variety* consisted of maids, butlers, and janitors. In the 1920s, menial roles reached 80 percent and remained there until the 1930s, when such performers as Lena Horne, Cab Calloway, and Louis Armstrong played themselves in films directed toward black audiences. Art ruthlessly imitated life in the nation's film capital.[48]

Virtually no one inside the studios challenged those stereotypes, forcing black actors to accept demeaning roles to "build ourselves into" the movie industry, as law student turned actor Clarence Muse described it. A few actors, such as Paul Robeson, pursued careers abroad, while Louise Beavers and Hattie McDaniel plunged into community service or sponsored lavish parties to distance themselves from their portrayals as faithful servants. Yet the era's most successful black actor, Stepin Fetchit (Lincoln Theodore Monroe Andrew Perry), embraced Hollywood's negative characterizations of African Americans.[49]

Meanwhile, hundreds of black extras seeking careers in film lived precariously. Each day they clustered along Central Avenue waiting for a casting director to drive by and choose an especially attractive woman or man to try out as an extra—often a slave in a plantation musical or a native in a jungle adventure. The prospect of earning up to $3.50 per day in a feature film drew hundreds of bit players into motion pictures with negative or stereotypical images of blacks, ranging from D. W. Griffith's *The Birth of a Nation* (1914) through David O. Selznick's *Gone with the Wind* (1939).[50]

The Great Depression ravaged California's African American communities. As early as 1931, one out of every three black workers in Los Angeles was unemployed, but statistics alone cannot convey the sense of loss and despair. William Pittman, a San Francisco dentist, unable to continue his practice, worked for $80 per month as a chauffeur. His wife Tarea, a 1925 University of California graduate, concluded that race discrimination added to the family's declining economic fortunes. "I am unable to find work," she wrote, ". . . on account of my race."[51]

Black Californians initially turned to community self-help projects. Churches collected clothing and food and provided the homeless with temporary shelter. Father Divine and Daddy Grace helped some of Los

Angeles's destitute. In Richmond, Beryl Gwendolyn Reid single-handedly cooked "big pots of beans" to "feed all the people who were hungry." Despite these heroic efforts, New Deal programs were ultimately more effective in providing help to California's African Americans. Black workers throughout the state were particularly successful with the Works Progress Administration and the National Youth Administration (NYA) programs. Much of the success in the latter agency stemmed from the activities of Vivian Osborne Marsh, who headed the state Division of Negro Affairs. Marsh, a friend of Mary McLeod Bethune, the national director of the NYA's Division of Negro Affairs, used the network of the California Federation of Colored Women's Clubs to attract more than 2,000 black youths into the NYA between 1935 and 1941. Marsh's efforts allowed 400 African American college and graduate students to complete their education. Moreover, the California NYA provided more than 1,000 women and men with training in working with sheet metal and machinery, in radio, and in aircraft production and repair, which would serve them well in the state's World War II defense plants.⁵²

Like African American voters in the East, Depression-era black Californians embraced the Democratic Party. As Douglas Flamming describes in his essay, "Becoming Democrats: Liberal Politics and the African American Community in Los Angeles, 1930–1965," California's black voters began gravitating toward the Democratic Party in the late 1920s through political organizing by Titus Alexander, John W. Fowler, and Dr. J. Alexander Somerville. In 1934, when Republican Frederick Roberts, who had served sixteen years in the state assembly, was defeated by a twenty-seven-year-old Democrat, Augustus Hawkins, a new political era began in the state. Hawkins represented the South Central Los Angeles assembly district until 1962, when he became the first African American congressman from California. With his ties to unions and liberal politicians, Hawkins personified an emerging political nexus of white liberals, organized labor, and blacks in President Franklin Roosevelt's New Deal coalition.⁵³

Despite their low occupational status, a number of California's pre-World War II African Americans purchased homes. Compared with the Northeast and Midwest, California cities (with San Francisco the notable exception) could boast of high levels of black homeownership. Los Angeles led the way with a "bungalow boom" during the first two decades of the twentieth century. Along Central Avenue four- or five-bedroom "California cottages" were advertised for $900 to $2,500 and usually sold for a $100 down payment plus monthly payments of $20. By 1924, black realtors advertised Los Angeles as having one of the nation's highest percentages of homeowners. Realtor and land developer Hugh Macbeth, profiled in this anthology by McBroome, used the high rate of homeownership to proclaim, "The opportunity, the welcome, the hope . . . which free California, its hills and valleys . . . and always sunshine offer to the American Negro."[54]

Some black Angelenos gravitated to the independent community of Watts, seven miles southeast of downtown Los Angeles. Established in 1903, the town soon became attractive to white working-class families who were drawn to its low rents and housing prices. However, Watts was unique among Los Angeles suburbs; from its founding, black, Latino, and white migrants purchased homes and small farms there. By 1920, 14 percent of Watts was African American, the highest percentage in any California community. Arna Bontemps, whose family arrived in 1906 from Alexandria, Louisiana, recalled the integrated setting that greeted early black migrants: "We moved into a house in a neighborhood where we were the only colored family. The people next door and up and down the block were friendly and talkative, the weather was perfect . . . and my mother seemed to float about on the clean air." By the 1920s, Watts was an attractive, increasingly African American suburb, the reputation of which reached the East. When the leading black Los Angeles realtor, Sidney P. Dones, relocated in this suburb in 1923, the *Pittsburgh Courier* announced, "Watts . . . is the coming Negro town of California." Watts's black population continued to grow after it was annexed to Los Angeles in 1926, and by World War II, the town had become mostly African American.[55]

Although some suburban home opportunities existed in Watts, Pasadena, Santa Monica, and Sierra Madre, most blacks resided in the Central Avenue district. African American Angelenos, like their counterparts across urban America, faced restrictive covenants that insured residential segregation. These covenants prohibited blacks, Asians, Native Americans, Latinos, and, on occasion, Jews from occupying certain neighborhoods. One Los Angeles resident in 1917 described these agreements as "invisible walls of steel. The whites surrounded us and made it impossible for us to go beyond these walls." A 1927 covenant covered the residential area between the University of Southern California and the suburb of Inglewood, placing it off limits for people of color for ninety-nine years. In order to ensure convenient domestic help, the covenant exempted "domestic servants, chauffeurs, or gardeners [who live] where their employer resides." The California Supreme Court in 1919 and 1928 upheld such agreements and ruled that even when blacks lived in neighborhoods before the restrictions were established, they must vacate properties under covenants. The most famous challenge of residential exclusion involved the family of realtor Booker T. Washington Jr., which in the 1920s retained its home in the San Gabriel Valley.[56]

Housing segregation was generally condemned by most African American Californians. Yet as Bette Yarbrough Cox describes in "The Evolution of Black Music in Los Angeles, 1890–1955," segregation brought together African American musicians who created a vibrant culture in the racially separate neighborhoods of Los Angeles, Oakland, and San Francisco in the 1920s and 1930s. Urban jazz grew from a variety of musical traditions, including southern blues and ragtime. However, it was developed and refined as dozens of black bands crisscrossed California, freely borrowing and changing musical styles as they worked in Prohibition-era nightclubs, cabarets, and speakeasies. These clubs, located primarily in African American urban communities, provided employment to hundreds of black musicians while entertaining thousands of people of all racial backgrounds.[57]

By the 1920s, the West Coast's jazz culture was headquartered along Los Angeles's Central Avenue. Southern-born musicians, such as Edward "Kid" Ory, migrated to Los Angeles during the World War I era and helped create West Coast jazz. These "creoles" were soon joined by growing numbers of Texans, Oklahomans, and midwesterners as well as talented local musicians, all of whom contributed to black Los Angeles's role in shaping America's most popular music. Central Avenue became, by 1925, the vital pulse of West Coast jazz with its "hot-colored" nightclubs—the Kentucky Club, the Club Alabam (known in the 1920s as the Apex), and the Savoy. The Cotton Club in Culver City attracted white and black celebrities, including Mae West, Orson Welles, Joe Louis, and William Randolph Hearst. After the advent of sound films, some bands played "mood music" for movie studios or appeared in productions directed toward black audiences. As the studios recognized the market for these black-oriented films, such performers as Louis Armstrong, Lena Horne, Bill "Bojangles" Robinson, and Duke Ellington supplemented their income by arranging local club dates, while such aspiring actresses as Carolynne Snowden and Mildred Washington sang and danced in the clubs "between roles."[58]

West Coast jazz, however, was not synonymous with Los Angeles. San Diego's Creole Palace Night Club became, by the 1930s, the most famous West Coast cabaret outside of Los Angeles. Built with the Douglas Hotel in 1924 by black entrepreneurs Robert Lowe and George Ramsey, by the 1930s, the Palace had become well known in the national black community of entertainers. Its nightclub and hotel employed African American and Latino band members, showgirls, waiters, cooks, and busboys and attracted Duke Ellington, Lionel Hampton, and Joe Louis as well as local black, white, and Latino patrons. Moreover, California musicians traveled a circuit that included Honolulu, the major West Coast ports, and southwestern cities such as Phoenix and Albuquerque in the 1920s, but that expanded during the 1930s to embrace Yokohama, Shanghai, Hong Kong, and Manila.[59]

The rise of an active jazz network in California symbolized white recognition of black influence on popular entertainment. In many other ways, however, African Americans by 1940 were a little-noticed part of California's population. Their numbers had grown to more than 124,000, but that was considerably below the number of Asian American or Mexican American inhabitants.[60] Moreover, those other groups of color were commonly associated with California, while the absence of African Americans from much of the Far West led observers to ignore their substantial presence in the Golden State. Few had gained public notice, and none of the issues associated with their unequal status had yet become important politically. Only in later decades would African Americans become a greater part of California's population and produce cultural and political figures who gained statewide and national stature and made their rights a major subject of civic discourse and action.

The growing significance of African Americans in California began with World War II, the pivotal period in their history in the state. As the nation's leading area of aircraft manufacturing, one of its major shipbuilding centers, and the location of numerous military bases, the Golden State entered into an employment boom before the bombing of Pearl Harbor. Although African Americans did not come to the state in large numbers until the spring of 1942, once their migration started, it grew rapidly. By mid-1943, Los Angeles alone was receiving 10,000 black migrants a month. By the end of the war, their number had more than doubled in the four major cities, Los Angeles, San Francisco, Oakland, and San Diego, from 81,225 in 1940 to 215,546 by 1946. This wartime movement initiated three decades of black migration to California, primarily to its large cities. By 1950, the state's African American population had grown from 124,306 in 1940 to 462,172.[61] This influx was especially striking in the Bay Area, as Broussard relates in his essay in this anthology, for those cities had small black populations before the war.

Most migrants came from southern states, challenging the urban western culture that older resident blacks had established and, in the Bay Area especially, overwhelming and replacing it.[62] The southern non-urban cultural ways, coupled with their huge increase in migrant population, made African Americans the most conspicuous minority group in the state and contributed to making racial friction a continuous problem during and long after the war. But those numbers would also make African Americans significant for the first time in California's labor force and ultimately in its politics. Such a change in their number and influence also made World War II the beginning of significant changes in the legal status and condition of blacks in California and throughout the United States. One leading historian of the twentieth-century West has concluded that the war "did much to hasten integration . . . , acting as a catalyst to break down various barriers in the way of racial equality."[63]

These changes did not come quickly or without considerable struggle. In 1941, the first year of the defense boom, black workers were not hired in many plants, particularly in the aircraft industry. One executive remarked that the employment of "Negroes" was "against Company policy." Shipyard unions relegated blacks to "auxiliary unions" where they were the last to be hired and then only for low-skill jobs. Training programs like the United States Employment Service (USES) augmented these discriminations, denying blacks entry with the assertion that they could not be hired, which allowed employers to reject them for lack of training. By 1942, acute labor shortages, persistent protests by African American organizations, and pressure from the Fair Employment Practices Commission (FEPC), which ran a vigorous West Coast office, opened jobs in most defense industries. African American women played a key role in this change, having suffered job restrictions due to fears of race mixing and their image of being suited only for domestic work. When a USES employee remarked that black women "were no problem since they showed a lack of interest in war work training," they marched on that agency's office. A few months later, the *California Eagle* reported that "the steps taken by the women of our community have broken down completely the barriers against the training of Negro women and Negro men" and set a new pattern for hiring in California defense plants.[64] By 1943, more than 30,000 blacks had been hired in Southern California war plants, and they made up 12 percent of that area's enrollees in training programs. Bay Area shipyards employed nearly 16,000, more than the prewar black populations of San Francisco and Oakland combined. By

1945, the exclusion of blacks from skilled shipyard jobs had also ended, and some unions were helping African Americans make unprecedented occupational breakthroughs.[65]

African American migrants also hoped to escape segregation and subordination by leaving the South, but here, too, California offered a mix of fulfillment and frustration. The state had few laws mandating discriminatory actions against blacks (an exception being suburban cities that prohibited their presence after dark), but in many situations African Americans encountered negative stereotypes and hostile actions. Prewar patterns of exclusion from public accommodations changed slowly. Many store managers responded to the growing black presence by posting "White Trade Only" signs. Wartime pressures and the sometimes rowdy behavior of southern blacks led to occasional racial clashes, such as the Twelfth Street "riot" in Oakland in 1944. The local press and police interpreted such incidents as threatening "crime waves," and they responded with efforts at social control.[66] Police shootings and beatings of blacks, though not unknown before the war, increased, usually without apology or punishment. Los Angeles's "Zoot Suit" riots in June 1943, though primarily aimed at Mexican American youth, also involved arrests of more than one hundred African Americans and have been seen by some scholars as an effort to suppress the growing mood of wartime reform. Black servicemen often were confined to segregated entertainment facilities near military bases. The indignities they suffered were highlighted by the Port Chicago "Mutiny," which grew out of the Navy's practice of relegating African Americans to laborer jobs with little concern for their safety. The result was an explosion that killed 320 men, including 202 blacks, and led others to refuse to return to work until conditions improved.[67]

The greatest general difficulty came in housing. Prior to the war, African Americans had been excluded from most suburban communities and limited by restrictive covenants to a few areas of older housing. These failed to match the demands of thousands of black migrants for shelter. A few African Americans were able to occupy neighborhoods from which Japanese Americans had been sent to internment camps, but far more were forced into makeshift arrangements. In Richmond, where the African American population grew nearly fifty-fold, vacant land was filled with trailers, shanties, and tents. In Los Angeles, more than 100,000 blacks were concentrated in an area that before the war had housed less than 40,000. As a result, blacks often occupied garages, sheds, and even chicken coops.[68]

Regular housing frequently was occupied by multiple families or unrelated lodgers, with densities as high as fourteen to a room. Nearly all migrants rented, and both black and white landlords used the shortage to extract rents that often amounted to half of workers' incomes. The deputy mayor of Los Angeles commented on such emerging slum conditions in African American neighborhoods: "You will see life as no human is expected to endure it."[69]

Housing for defense workers was primarily the responsibility of various federal government public-housing projects, but here, too, blacks faced widespread discrimination. Only a small portion of the units was open to African Americans, due partly to segregation and partly to racial quotas that unrealistically assumed all races had equal access to private housing. Sometimes units were left vacant rather than being made available to blacks. Entire projects were closed by the federal policy of following "local customs" in selecting the population of an area. But the most tragic consequences of housing discrimination came after the war, when the policy of segregating the majority of wartime worker housing from other housing as well as separating blacks from whites laid the foundations for ghettos in newer African American communities and intensified adverse conditions in older ones.[70]

Throughout the nation, World War II brought out a spirit of militance among African Americans, sparked by their awareness that they were resisting at home ideas and practices similar to those their country claimed to be fighting abroad. This "Double V" spirit—victory over fascism at home and abroad—produced new protest organizations and leaders and invigorated existing ones in several California black communities. The membership in long-standing civil rights organizations such as the NAACP and the Urban League grew as they fought employment restrictions and sought to improve living conditions for migrants. Job discrimination also led to a series of ad hoc protest organizations in several cities. Some, like the Los Angeles Shipworkers Committee for Equal Participation, were created by workers themselves. An outstanding example of one worker overcoming entrenched discriminatory practices was the career of Joseph James in San Francisco. Hired as a shipyard worker in 1942, James formed the Committee Against Segregation and Discrimination to end the "Jim Crow" locals in the boilermakers' union. His campaign included non-payment of union dues, FEPC hearings, and a lawsuit. Toward the end of the war, a series of court decisions led by *James v. Marinship* essentially ended segregated locals in California shipyards.[71]

Equally important within African American communities were organizations led by the black elite, often church or civic leaders. One of the most effective was the Negro Victory Committee, formed in Los Angeles by the Reverend Clayton Russell, pastor of the People's Independent Church of Christ. Russell had first become prominent during the Depression by using his church as a center for cooperative markets and job relief. In 1941, he united a group of public officials, professionals, union leaders, and NAACP members to create the Negro Victory Committee with the aim of gaining blacks jobs in defense plants. One of its earliest successes was the women's march on USES. Russell subsequently challenged the location of training centers in areas hostile to blacks, exclusion of blacks from streetcar jobs, Jim Crow shipyard locals, and other wartime problems. But many black pastors criticized his secular focus, despite Russell's Martin Luther King-like response: "I consider it a sin to stand up in the pulpit and preach to hungry people and not help them to get a job or to get some food." When his bid for county supervisor failed, his support declined, and the Negro Victory Committee, like many other wartime organizations, disappeared.72

A more conservative form of wartime protest involved various interracial organizations, usually formed and run largely by whites. In San Francisco, the Bay Area Committee Against Discrimination was formed in 1942 to investigate and lobby against racial, religious, or ethnic discrimination. Though the committee was predominantly composed of whites, Walter Gordon, a black attorney from Alameda County, served as its chair. In 1944 it was succeeded by the Council on Civic Unity, which set up branches in several California cities by the late 1940s. A Southern California counterpart was the Los Angeles County Committee (later Commission) on Human Relations, which grew out of the 1943 riots and likewise spawned counterparts in other cities. Even the tradition of a racially exclusive black church was modified, most notably in San Francisco, when Dean Howard Thurman of Howard University came to the city in 1943 to establish the Church for the Fellowship of All Peoples. Hailed as the first "fully integrated" church in America, it launched an ambitious array of services, but it never succeeded in attracting a large segment of the black community.73

One of the most potentially significant forms of protest saw efforts by blacks to establish links with other minority groups, white liberals, and labor unions. Kevin Leonard, in his essay "'In the Interest of All Races': African Americans and Interracial Cooperation in Los Angeles during and after World War II," discusses such attempts. This effort illustrates the realization by some African Americans that California was a multiracial society and that their fate was linked to that of other minorities. Blacks also worked with the Congress of Industrial Organizations (cio) and leftist groups, forming a coalition of the working class that challenged the political establishment in several cities. Although they ultimately broke up, these coalitions helped to make such issues as fair employment and housing important topics in California politics and in the national civil rights movement.74

The economic gains made by California's African Americans during World War II were threatened by the retrenchment in most defense industries immediately after the war. Even before V-J Day, shipyards and aircraft plants began laying off workers. Since they had been predominantly employed in such defense industries, blacks were disproportionately affected. As most black migrants remained in California cities, the shrinking work opportunities, combined with the return of servicemen and Japanese American evacuees, made unemployment an acute problem. By the end of 1946, one-third of all African Americans in the Bay Area and 40 percent of black women there were unemployed. Discrimination continued to limit the entry of blacks into civilian employment. The termination of the FEPC and reduced reliance by employers on uses denied blacks two agencies that had opposed discrimination. In 1946 the United States Employment Service in Los Angeles reported that 70 percent of job requests were earmarked for whites only. One writer estimated that "the Negro employment situation one year after V-J Day in San Diego is about where it was in 1940. Firms not employing Negroes [then] do not employ them now." Moreover, African Americans tended to be placed in low-paying, unskilled jobs, guaranteeing their continued poverty. In this desperate situation Chico farmers hired more than 200 blacks from Richmond as seasonal workers.75

But African Americans still found many reasons to regard California as a land of opportunity from the late 1940s through the 1950s. While the number of manufacturing jobs shrank, blacks were able to hold onto many wartime gains, largely with the help of unions. As a result, one-third of black workers secured positions in manufacturing. While many employers continued to refuse to hire blacks, most barriers to unions and training programs fell. As a result of these gains, a Bay Area survey in 1948 concluded that blacks there "were spread much more widely through the occupational and industrial structure than before the war," though not as widely as whites. Government positions, especially on military bases, in the post office, and in local governments, also provided expanding work opportunities.76 Blacks

TABLE 3. African American Population in California and Its Major Cities, 1940–60

	1940		1950		1960	
	Number of Blacks	*Percentage of Total Population*	*Number of Blacks*	*Percentage of Total Population*	*Number of Blacks*	*Percentage of Total Population*
California	124,306	1.8	462,172	4.4	883,861	5.6
Los Angeles	63,774	4.2	171,209	8.7	334,916	13.5
Oakland	8,462	2.8	47,562	12.4	82,618	22.8
San Diego	4,143	2.0	14,904	4.5	34,435	6.0
San Francisco	4,846	0.8	43,402	5.6	74,383	10.0

also gained greater entry to some professional occupations. At the start of World War II, there were fewer than 150 African American schoolteachers in the state, most of them confined to the few schools with predominantly black enrollment. By the 1950s, African Americans were being hired in interracial districts, and by the end of the decade California would have nearly 3,000 black teachers. One "race" magazine concluded in 1947 that the economic opportunities of Los Angeles and San Francisco made those cities two of the ten best for blacks in the nation.[77] The contrast between these conditions and the continued poverty and oppression in the South led nearly all wartime migrants to stay in California, despite long periods of unemployment, and soon revived the wartime exodus to West Coast cities, as can be seen in table 3.[78]

Race relations outside the workplace presented a similar pattern of continuing inequity and gradual progress. Immediately after the war some observers feared that California was on the verge of interracial conflict. The arrival of thousands of black migrants, often southerners new to urban life and anxious to assert the freedom they felt in California, mixed poorly with the fears of many whites unaccustomed to encountering African Americans except as servants. Laurence Hewes summarized this situation in San Diego by noting that African Americans and Mexicans suffered from "inequality in income, employment opportunity, educational opportunity and housing" while whites exhibited "ignorance, prejudice, insecurity and a thousand and one personal frustrations."[79] Such attitudes were manifested in Ku Klux Klan activity (such as cross burnings) in Los Angeles suburbs, race riots in some high schools, and numerous complaints about police brutality. The

Oakland NAACP claimed that the killing of a black man in 1947 was "only the worst in a long series of cases of Oakland police brutality and terrorism." In such cities as San Diego and smaller towns, most restaurants and dance halls continued to refuse to serve blacks. But in downtown Los Angeles, leading restaurants changed their policies during the war, and by the late 1940s many nightclubs accepted black patrons as well as performers. San Francisco prided itself on similarly open accommodations. To many, the change from prewar conditions seemed more impressive than lingering discriminations. Carey McWilliams observed in 1948, "[T]here is probably less miscellaneous Jim Crowism in Los Angeles than in any city in the West, and certainly, there is less discrimination in places of public accommodation than in 1940."[80]

This image of racial progress could not conceal the continuing crisis in housing, however. Through the late 1940s and the following decade, only a few additional areas were opened to black residence. The most striking advances came in Los Angeles, where blacks moved into homes in the west-central district that whites vacated. A few suburban cities adjacent to the spreading Los Angeles ghetto, most notably Compton, were also opened. But in the vast majority of the state, communities remained closed to blacks, particularly because of race-restrictive covenants. In the San Fernando Valley, property owners and realtors hired public relations firms to promote blanket agreements for whole tracts. Except for the celebrated Sugar Hill case in Los Angeles, in which prominent African American residents won a court victory over efforts to expel them, these covenants were upheld in the courts until 1948. When they did not work, violence was used. In Fontana, an African American family entering a white neighborhood in 1945 was burned to death in an arson attack, and outside of Richmond in 1952, a lone black family in a new tract needed state and local police protection to secure a home.[81]

This confinement to longtime boundaries made once interracial communities increasingly African American, as it did schools within them. The hope that public projects would increase the housing supply and facilitate integration soon died. Richmond razed hundreds of acres of wartime structures, while in Los Angeles and Oakland, efforts to build public homes were defeated by "anti-socialized housing" campaigns. In San Diego and Pasadena, public housing projects remained either exclusively white or heavily segregated. In San Francisco, the NAACP won a suit that ended the exclusion of African Americans from public housing in white neighborhoods, but the number of units opened neither met the need of black residents nor significantly changed the overall pattern of residential segregation.[82]

African Americans did not accept job or housing discrimination without protest. The activism that World War II had stimulated continued into the postwar period in several forms. The black press, especially the *California Eagle* and *Los Angeles Sentinel*, campaigned against restrictive covenants. Editorials denounced promoters of covenants as "fascists," or linked covenants to the formation of ghettos, ghettos to slums, and slums to crime.[83] The NAACP remained active in the housing campaign. Between 1945 and 1948, the Los Angeles branch alone filed more suits against restrictive covenants than were filed by blacks in the rest of the nation. Local attorney Loren Miller was part of the team that lobbied the Supreme Court to declare the enforcement of restrictive covenants illegal in a series of cases culminating in the *Barrows v. Jackson* decision in 1953.[84]

The growing African American population made political activity a logical avenue of reform. Blacks were also encouraged by the rise of "race liberalism" during and after the war, with its promise of realizing equality through electoral victories and antidiscrimination legislation. In the Bay Area, C. L. Dellums urged blacks to join with labor unions to seek expanded job opportunities, better education and civic services, and public housing. In Los Angeles, several prominent members of the African American community sought public office, including Charlotta Bass, who ran for a city council seat in 1945 and for Congress and the vice presidency in the 1950s. But most race candidates were defeated, and the dream of a black-labor coalition foundered on the sensitive issue of housing integration. Similar fates befell attempts to pass fair employment laws in the legislature and by initiative. As of 1958, the only significant victories blacks had won were a few local offices and the election of W. Byron Rumford to an assembly seat in Berkeley. As Flamming details in his essay in this anthology, Rumford and Augustus Hawkins were relentless in their advocacy of civil rights issues, ranging from desegregating the state National Guard to fair employment and housing laws, throughout the 1950s.[85]

Political defeats and segregated housing notwithstanding, many African Americans regarded California in the 1950s as a land of opportunity. The growing number of celebrities and entrepreneurs who were accepted by white society promised similar success for other blacks. Los Angeles's Norman O. Houston, of Golden State Mutual Life Insurance Company, was active in general civic functions. The city had at least two African American savings and loan associations in the late 1940s, one led by the venerable civil rights activist H. Claude Hudson. In San Francisco, journalist Carleton Goodlett was a comparable symbol of community success. Other members of the black elite gained prominence in appointive or local elective government positions. These included San Francisco attorney Cecil Poole, Los Angeles Judge Edwin Jefferson, and Fay Allen of the Los Angeles Board of Education. The arrival of major league baseball in San Francisco and Los Angeles in the late 1950s brought black athletes who joined local basketball and football stars as celebrities to their cities.[86]

Other African Americans gained notice as heads of interracial organizations that in the 1950s tended to overshadow black activist groups. John Buggs was a longtime head of the Los Angeles County Commission on Human Relations (LACCHR), a government body that studied and mediated relations among all resident ethnic groups. In 1947, George Thomas founded the Los Angeles County Conference on Community Relations (LACCCR), which similarly worked with all religious, racial, and ethnic groups in the area and by 1960 embraced sixty-five organizations. Both agencies prided themselves on quietly resolving incidents before they became crises. In 1962, Buggs attributed the attractiveness of Los Angeles to black migrants to the fact that "he [the black migrant] has heard about race riots in Chicago, Detroit, and Philadelphia, but he hasn't heard about them here." Three years later these words would haunt Buggs, but at the time they seemed appropriate for a city that the National Urban League would rank in 1964 as first among sixty-eight as a desirable place for blacks to live.[87]

But the 1950s were also the time when trends in housing and jobs for African Americans in major cities that had started during the war and immediate postwar years began to be recognized as serious problems. Most basic was the increasing isolation of most blacks in a few large urban ghettos. As Gretchen Lemke-Santangelo describes in "Deindustrialization, Urban Poverty, and African American Community Mobilization in Oakland, 1945 through the 1990s," Oakland and Los Angeles began to suffer an exodus of industries and jobs, leaving growing black populations with shrinking employment opportunities. Automobile and tire companies, once prevalent in and adjacent to Los Angeles, either folded or moved to suburban locations in the early 1950s, and some of Oakland's largest employers moved south to suburban cities. Continued exclusion from suburbs discouraged blacks from following the exodus of jobs; many more were left in old, deteriorating housing, often close to undesirable surroundings, and their neighborhoods were sometimes split by freeways. Public housing, once seen as a potential solution to these problems, more and more often was occupied by low-income African American tenants, and its expansion suffered from its being seen as a black cause.[88] These structural changes contributed to other growing problems within large black communities. As early as 1947, San Francisco reported an upsurge of crime by African Americans, mostly against other blacks. By the late 1950s, increasingly segregated inner city schools were reporting rising dropout rates. Studies noted that in unemployment and income, minority communities in some inner cities, "far from advancing, are steadily sinking below previous levels," and that the gap between whites and blacks was widening. An early effort to address these problems would be the liberal acceptance of antidiscrimination legislation long promoted by black politicians.[89]

The initial effort at equality through the law came after the 1958 election, when the Democratic Party's takeover of state government led to the passage of a state Fair Employment Act and the establishment of a Fair Employment Practices Commission (FEPC). The Unruh and Hawkins acts, which offered limited authority over housing discrimination, were also passed that year. In 1961, Assemblyman Hawkins introduced a more comprehensive fair housing law, which ultimately was steered through the legislature on the last day of the 1963 session by Assemblyman Rumford.[90] That year also witnessed the end of the gerrymander in Los Angeles that had excluded African Americans from the city council. Three black Angelenos, including Tom Bradley, subsequently gained seats. The next year saw the first African American on the San Francisco board of supervisors and the election of Willie L. Brown Jr. to the state assembly.[91] A third area of complaint—de facto school segregation—began to be addressed when the American Civil Liberties Union (ACLU) filed a suit against the Los Angeles City board of education and the state supreme court declared Pasadena's segregated system unconstitutional. The following year, Berkeley inaugurated the nation's first non-court-ordered busing plan.[92] The long-sought hope of middle-class black leaders to integrate into the California Dream in coalition with white liberal allies seemed about to be realized.

The civil rights movement in the South carried over to California, where, by the early 1960s, some younger African Americans believed that race liberalism had brought only belated and token victories, necessitating a shift from legal and political activities to direct action. One key organization was the Congress of Racial Equality (CORE), which had established small branches in Los Angeles, San Francisco, and Berkeley in the late 1940s. By the 1960s, these chapters were picketing chain stores and supermarkets and protesting segregated schools. In the Bay Area, they used sit-in tactics to gain blacks jobs in department stores, hotels, and car dealerships. In 1963, they staged a sit-in at the state capitol during debate over the Rumford Act. Their militant tactics led to hundreds being arrested and jailed. With only minimal other gains, this led by the mid-1960s to increasing black nationalist rhetoric, the exodus of white members, and the decline of CORE activities.[93]

In Los Angeles, the NAACP and the recently formed United Civil Rights Committee held similar demonstrations against housing and de facto school segregation. Another sign of changing attitudes was the rapid growth of the Black Muslims, whose fiery rhetoric led to growing friction with police. In one such incident, Los Angeles police officers killed one Muslim and wounded six others in front of a mosque in 1962. Finally, the intransigence and apparent racism of local white officials and the public, epitomized by the passage in 1964 of Proposition 14, which invalidated all fair-housing laws, increased black resentment.[94] Even as it was winning historic legislative victories on the national level, race liberalism in California was under fire from both civil rights activists and their white opponents.

These trends culminated in the Watts uprising of August 1965, which continued for six days, leaving thirty-four dead, more than 1,000 injured, and 3,952 arrested. "Watts," as the uprising was popularly called, transformed the ideology of black activists and more than any prior event made the world aware of California's African American presence. To most contemporary observers, Watts came as a complete surprise. Only five days earlier, President Johnson had signed the Voting Rights Act of 1965, a key goal of the civil rights movement. But civil rights laws did not deal with the immediate needs of African Americans in inner cities. Their rates of unemployment and poverty levels, far beyond those of surrounding areas, were attributable to structural causes, similar to those in Oakland that Lemke-Santangelo describes. These were exacerbated by deteriorating low-income housing and the impact of the uprising, which contributed to the flight of some of the community's higher-skilled and better-educated residents and a marked rise in the number of people not even seeking employment. Federal programs designed to uplift such areas indirectly contributed to the uprising, as Mayor Yorty's efforts to preempt federal funds delayed and reduced their flow to the black community.[95] The deeper causes of the attitudes of participant youth and the way in which police handling of the riot epitomized what shaped those attitudes are detailed in "Black Fire: 'Riot' and 'Revolt' in Los Angeles, 1965 and 1992," by Gerald Horne.

The most enduring legacy of Watts was less the four years of "riots" that it inaugurated nationwide than the California-born black nationalist thought and movements it inspired. Malcolm X had already articulated an alternative to civil rights and integration: a program of black unity, self-determination, and community control in which African American history and culture were seen as key components. A few months after the uprising, Maulana Ron Karenga, a social worker and Ph.D. student in Los Angeles, founded United Slaves (u s). Karenga developed a philosophy of cultural nationalism, replete with special holidays such as Kwanzaa, education in African history and Swahili, and the basic tenet that African Americans constituted a separate "alien Nation/Race" whose progress was being suppressed by the "internal colonialism" of the ghetto. To promote this philosophy, in 1966 he founded the Watts Summer Festival, an annual display of African and African American art, crafts, and music. Though plagued by internal schisms and gang violence, this event continued until the mid-1980s. Some contend it was supported by local white officials in part because it seemed a more benign version of black nationalism than the organization that was established later that year: the Black Panthers.[96]

Formed in October 1966 by Huey Newton and Bobby Seale, the Black Panther Party for Self Defense advocated that African Americans control their own communities and destinies. The Panthers regarded police power and white capitalism as the main obstacles to those ends and so emphasized military preparedness and Marxism. This military posture quickly gained the organization media attention, especially in 1967, when party members entered the California state capitol in their black garb, with weapons and cartridge belts. By 1970, the Panthers had branches in thirty-five cities in nineteen states. They also cooperated with white radical organizations, as when their minister of information, Eldridge Cleaver, ran for president of the United States in 1968 for the Peace and Freedom Party.[97] The Panthers' derision of u s for its emphasis on African culture led to a deadly shootout in 1969 at u c l a, but that proved to be mild compared with the reaction of local police and the Counterintelligence Program (c o i n t e l p r o) campaign of the f b i. In 1968, Newton, Seale, and Cleaver were arrested or forced into exile, and in 1969 alone, twenty-seven Panthers were killed and 749 jailed. While New Left admirers denounced these acts as repressing an organization that brought food services and voter registration to inner city neighborhoods, some observers like David Horowitz contended that the Panthers also engaged in murder, drug dealing, and extortion and were essentially "a criminal gang that preyed on the black ghetto itself."[98]

The spirit of black nationalism permeated California in other ways in the late 1960s and early 1970s. The killing of an African American youth by a white policeman at Hunter's Point in 1966 led to a five-day uprising in San Francisco that reflected the contempt poorer blacks showed for both white and black leaders. The appointment of Angela Davis, Eldridge Cleaver, and George Murray, all associated with the Black Panthers, to college teaching positions suggests the extent to which black nationalist ideas were being accepted as representing the feelings of the African American population. Black studies programs were established in many universities, and, along with black research centers, they continued to promote a program of pride in African heritage through the '70s and '80s. The historical significance of black nationalism remains a subject of debate. Some have noted that beneath the rhetoric, few of the movement's stated goals were met. Others contend that they left a cultural legacy that has influenced African American art and literature to the present.[99] But one point is undeniable: many of the most important figures and organizations of black nationalism in the United States came from California.

The publicity given to black power in the late 1960s and early 1970s did not stop middle-class activists from seeking reforms through legal or administrative action. Two of the most controversial, which became major state issues from the 1970s to the 1990s, were school desegregation by busing and affirmative action in employment and higher education. Busing tried to remedy the de facto school segregation that frequently resulted in inferior educational resources and left black students poorly equipped when they entered integrated high schools or colleges. The obvious solution seemed to be the mandatory reassignment of a certain portion of black and white children to schools previously racially exclusive. One of the earliest integration programs took place in Berkeley in the 1960s. It immediately drew the wrath of white parents, whose organized opposition fueled black student hostility and soured many African American parents on busing. This scenario was replayed during the 1970s in Los Angeles, where the case of *Crawford v. Los Angeles* (1970) secured a court order requiring desegregation in much of that school district. But opponents continued the fight through school board elections, and the physical strain of transporting students as much as fifty miles each way led most black parents by the early

1980s to seek a more limited integration through "magnet" schools. The withdrawal of many white children from the various Los Angeles public schools, or "white flight," often so shrank the pool of students that desegregation became impossible.[100] Desegregation efforts had similarly mixed results in other California communities, and only the onset of residential integration would put an end to most segregated schools.

By the 1970s, the quality of education had become a greater concern than segregation. Gang activity, high dropout and absentee rates, an exodus of experienced teachers, and tight budgets resulted in inner city schools having some of the lowest achievement scores in the state. Some blacks responded by establishing independent schools that emphasized strict discipline and curricula that focused on pride in African heritage. School personnel criticized standardized tests and curricula as culturally biased and tried to adapt their teaching to the culture of the inner city. The epitome of this trend was the short-lived requirement in the mid-1990s that Oakland schools teach Ebonics, a form of Black English.[101]

Many African Americans hoped that affirmative action programs would improve their condition. Affirmative action originated as a federal employment program to encourage the hiring of minorities and quickly assumed urgency in the wake of the Watts uprising. The limited authority of the Equal Employment Opportunities Commission (EEOC) was expanded in 1974 by the adoption of "pattern and practice" suits that were particularly significant against some California police departments, resulting in considerable expansion of the numbers of black as well as Latino and female police officers.[102] Defense contractors and other large companies generally complied with this policy from the late 1960s on, leading to substantial improvement in the occupational profile of employed African Americans. Affirmative action in higher education aimed to raise the enrollment of African Americans by increasing the exceptions to admission requirements, establishing Educational Opportunity Programs (EOP) to provide financial support, and launching "outreach" recruitment programs in minority communities. These efforts increased black enrollments at the University of California from 2.1 percent in 1968 to 5.2 percent in 1972, but they declined to 3.8 percent by 1978. These programs provoked opposition, especially in the case of *Bakke v. the Regents of the University of California* (1978). But the Supreme Court distinguished between the racial quotas at the University of California, Davis, which it declared unconstitutional, and the basic principle of minority preferences, which it left intact, so the African American presence continued to grow in some state universities and community colleges into the 1980s.[103]

Minority preference programs proved to be of most use to African Americans who already had the skills to enter the job market or college. Another set of government programs was enacted at the same time to try to meet the needs of the "hard-core" unemployed and the poor. By 1968, the city of Oakland received more than $50 million for federal programs that were primarily designed to provide income, jobs, housing, food, or special education for those in need. Since African Americans constituted a large portion of the eligible residents, these programs invited the charge of being "give-aways" of (white) taxpayers' funds to blacks and of ineffectiveness in solving the problems of poverty and high unemployment. The reality was more complex. Some programs were continuations of urban-renewal or area-planning policies of the 1940s and 1950s that had destroyed low-income housing to create industrial or commercial redevelopment, with little concern for or representation from the minority poor. In other cases, local officials unsympathetic to antipoverty or community-control goals tried to minimize their impact. In Oakland, this led to the use of federal agencies by representatives of the black poor that paved the way for African Americans' taking over much of that city's government in the late 1970s, as is detailed by Lemke-Santangelo.[104] Yet even victories like those of Lionel Wilson in Oakland and Tom Bradley in Los Angeles would prove hollow, as both administrations continued to focus on downtown redevelopment projects that seemed to have little impact on the problems of low-income blacks. Moreover, the Reagan administration in 1981 inaugurated an era of sharp cuts in federal funds for training, economic development, and low-income housing. Those realities help explain the mixed reaction to those programs by many blacks. Officeholders have defended such federal funds as essential replacements for the flight of jobs from the inner city, but the failure of these programs to bring dramatic change left its intended beneficiaries with the feeling that "if you're poor and you're black, everything is against you."[105]

By the 1960s, the success, wealth and celebrity of some black sports and entertainment figures challenged images of universal African American poverty and alienation. Nowhere was this more evident than in athletics, and California contributed in several ways to opening college and professional sports to blacks. Jackie Robinson, whose publicized breaking into major league baseball marked the beginnings of African American participation in professional sports, was a product of Pasadena and UCLA, which also produced the first two blacks to play in the National Football League (NFL). In 1946, both Woody Strode and Kenny Washington were hired by the Los Angeles Rams. Bill Russell led the University of San Francisco to National Collegiate Athletic Association (NCAA) titles in 1955 and 1956. He went on to help make professional basketball as popular as other sports and became the first African American coach of a professional team. Willie Mays, who came west with the Giants in 1958 when major league baseball ended its exclusion of the West, and Elgin Baylor, who brought professional basketball to Southern California with the Lakers in 1960, did not associate themselves with racial protest, even though they endured prejudiced coaches and discriminatory practices within their sports and were treated as blacks, not stars, if they tried to purchase housing in white neighborhoods.[106]

By the late 1960s, African American athletes in California were becoming more celebrated—and controversial. The University of Southern California (USC) produced two winners of college football's coveted Heisman trophy, Michael Garrett in 1965 and O. J. Simpson in 1968. Lew Alcindor (after 1971, Kareem Abdul-Jabbar) led a host of black stars in making UCLA the nation's premier college basketball team for many years. The Los Angeles Rams' African American "Fearsome Foursome," meanwhile, terrorized NFL quarterbacks. But professional athletes complained of the near total absence of African American managers and coaches and the policy of "stacking" blacks in certain positions, while college athletes were feeling exploited by all-white coaching staffs who seemed indifferent to their education. Harry Edwards of San Jose State University tried to publicize these grievances by organizing an African American boycott of the 1968 Olympic Games. While the nation got a sense of black power's anger from the image of Tommie Smith and John Carlos raising black-gloved fists, the boycott fizzled, and the ultimate effect of localized protests became "reforms [that] more often took the form of gestures rather than substance."[107]

By the 1970s, black athletes had less to protest. The proportion of African American players rose sharply to more than one-quarter in baseball, over one-third in football and nearly three-fourths in basketball, national levels that were reflected in most California teams and that would endure into the early 1990s. The salaries of top stars became spectacular, epitomized by Earvin "Magic" Johnson's receiving a twenty-five-year, $25 million contract from the National Basketball Association's (NBA) Los Angeles Lakers in 1981 and Shaquille O'Neill's receiving a six-year, $120 million deal from that same team in 1996. At the college level, USC produced two more Heisman winners,

Charles White and Marcus Allen, in 1979 and 1981 respectively. UCLA's Cheryl Miller, acclaimed "the best female athlete in the history of the sport," meanwhile, began to put women's basketball into the limelight. The absence of African American coaches and managers was countered somewhat when Alvin Attles became head coach of the NBA's Golden State Warriors in 1970, Art Shell the state's first black NFL coach in 1989, and "Dusty" Baker the state's first black Major League Baseball manager in 1993. There was also a notable increase in black assistant coaches in the late 1980s and early 1990s.[108] Besides bringing attention to African Americans in the Golden State, the success of these and many other athlete-celebrities carried, as Arthur Ashe suggested, a "psychic value [that] was and is higher in the black community than among any other American subculture."[109]

Many African Americans have viewed as a mark of progress the post-World War II ascendance of blacks into celebrity status in the entertainment media. Black actors and actresses, particularly Sidney Poitier and Dorothy Dandridge, first became public celebrities in the 1950s. In 1954, Dandridge's role in *Carmen Jones* made her only the second African American performer nominated for an Academy Award (Hattie McDaniel earlier had won for her supporting role in the 1939 epic *Gone with the Wind*). A few films of this era, especially *A Raisin in the Sun* (1961), realistically portrayed the despair and oppression of black ghetto life. But the experiences of Poitier and Dandridge also suggest the limitations on film celebrities into the late 1960s. Poitier's popularity stemmed from his appearance as an "integrationist hero" who met white standards and middle-class black values. Dandridge's suicide in 1965, on the other hand, revealed the personal anguish of seldom-employed black actresses. Both, therefore, demonstrated that until the late 1960s, white perceptions of reality and audience desires heavily influenced acting opportunities for African Americans. Producers' attitudes were succinctly summarized by the creators of the television show *Julia*: "Who wants to see poverty and despair week after week?"[110]

But such restrictions on films began to change in the late 1960s, as Hollywood discovered the different trends sweeping through African American communities. Former football star Jim Brown typified a new breed of African American actor not afraid to depict black power or male sexuality. Producer-director Melvin Van Peebles, in films like *Sweet Sweetback's Baadasssss Song* (1971), advanced the idea that the lifestyle of the ghetto was the essence of blackness, a theme followed in a series of films through the early 1970s that were among Hollywood's biggest hits. While these celebrities provided African Americans with a new set of heroes, some critics doubted that such "blaxploitation" films did much to answer the needs of the community in realistic terms.[111]

Hollywood continued to produce African American celebrities through the 1980s and 1990s. Richard Pryor, Eddie Murphy, and Chris Rock brought a less stereotyped genre of black comedy, while films like *The Color Purple* (1985) depicted the writings of African American authors (in this case, adoptive Californian Alice Walker) and featured performers like Oprah Winfrey and Whoopi Goldberg. Directors and independent producers have portrayed African American heroes and conditions more candidly, as when John Singleton debuted with *Boyz N the Hood* (1991), a film set in gang-ravaged South Central Los Angeles, and became the youngest director ever nominated for an Oscar. Melvin Van Peebles's son Mario, an actor, also became a director, making the films *New Jack City* (1991), *Posse* (1993), and *Panther* (1995). Former athletes, O. J. Simpson among them, joined Jim Brown in pursuing film careers. In music, black celebrities, like adoptive Californians Michael Jackson and Quincy Jones, became some of the nation's top stars and producers. Behind the scenes, music industry professionals, such as Motown's Suzanne de Passe and singer Kenneth "Babyface" Edmonds, moved to California and branched out into film and TV production. Yet in television, particularly, many observers felt that the perspectives and values of black characters were indistinguishable from those of whites. Furthermore, the number of African Americans in the film industry remained well below their proportion of California's population.[112]

African Americans also made great gains in elective office after the mid-1960s and could boast of having the largest number in significant posts of any minority group in the state. Up to 1961 only two blacks, assemblymen Rumford and Hawkins, had served in the California state legislature and none in the state senate. Moreover, African Americans held no statewide office or mayorships, and none served as councilmen of major cities. This began to change after blacks gained city council seats in Berkeley, Richmond, Los Angeles, and Oakland between 1961 and 1964. In the latter year, Willie Brown became the third African American elected to an assembly seat. In 1969 Compton elected the state's first black mayor. By 1970, African Americans held seventeen significant positions in California, including two congressional seats (held by Hawkins and Ron Dellums), and gained their first statewide elective office when Wilson Riles defeated Max Rafferty for Superintendent of Public Instruction.[113]

Blacks made even more striking gains in the 1970s, winning mayorships in Los Angeles (Tom Bradley) and Oakland (Lionel Wilson) and the post of lieutenant governor (Mervin Dymally). By 1980, African Americans held twenty-eight significant posts, more than 60 percent of all minority-held elective offices in the state, and Willie Brown began his record sixteen-year tenure as speaker of the assembly. In 1982, Tom Bradley was nominated for governor and lost by barely 100,000 votes out of more than 7.6 million cast. Through the late 1980s and early 1990s, blacks continued to hold four congressional seats, from seven to nine state legislative seats, and several mayoral positions in the Bay Area and around Los Angeles. Two blacks were appointed to the state supreme court in the 1970s and 1980s, and by 1990, California had seventy-five African American judges and councilmen in twenty-five cities. The coalition politics responsible for Bradley's 1973 mayoral victory and twenty-year tenure in Los Angeles are discussed by Raphael Sonenshein in "Coalition Building in Los Angeles: The Bradley Years and Beyond." In 1995, Willie Brown became the first African American mayor of San Francisco.[114]

But even as the pivotal victories of the 1970s and 1980s made California's African Americans a formidable political presence, changes were underway that threatened their political power and cohesiveness. Migration from the South declined rapidly after 1970, and a number of Golden State African Americans returned to that region. The state's black population continued to grow, but at a much slower pace than that of either Latinos or Asians, whose numbers were augmented by higher rates of birth and immigration. By 1990, both Latinos and Asians were more numerous in California than African Americans. Latinos had grown to 26 percent of the population, more than three times the size of black California. Asians constituted 9.6 percent of the state and had a population 30 percent larger than that of African Americans. These trends continued into the 1990s, when a serious recession contributed to a net out-migration of blacks in 1993 and 1994. State projections forecast that by 2020 Hispanics will outnumber African Americans six to one, while the number of "others" (mostly Asian Americans) will surpass the number of blacks by two and one-half million. These trends can be seen in table 4.[115]

The political implications of these demographic changes are suggested in Sonenshein's essay, and they became evident in elections by the mid-1990s. The Hispanic vote in California drew more public attention than the black vote in the 1996 election. The following year, the Los Angeles suburb of Lyn-

TABLE 4. Actual and Projected African American
Populations in California, 1970–2020

	Number of Blacks	*Percentage of Total Population*
1970	1,400,143	7.0
1980	1,818,660	7.7
1990	2,208,801	7.4
2000	2,470,721	6.8
2020	3,118,197	6.4

wood became the first California city to replace a black-controlled government with one under Latino control. The 1998 election especially underscored the shift in racial influence, as the two major parties nominated four Latinos and two Asians but no African Americans to statewide office. Both parties selected a Hispanic to lead them in the assembly, and Cruz Bustamante completed his succession to positions formerly held by Willie Brown and Melvin Dymally.[116]

Beyond the dazzling array of sports and entertainment celebrities and the growing body of public officeholders, those who feel that African Americans are closer to realizing the California Dream as the twenty-first century begins can cite some impressive race enterprises. California could boast of having ten of the nation's one hundred largest black businesses by 1987. The movement from inner cities to suburbs also continued through the 1990s. Between 1990 and 1996, nearly 40,000 African Americans moved into San Bernadino and Riverside Counties, while Orange County continued to receive a modest increase of blacks in all but one of its cities. Much of this represented the flight of African Americans from south Los Angeles, whose population declined 20 percent during the 1980s and continued dropping through the 1990s.[117]

Changes within the African American community in the late twentieth century were even more significant than its shifting demographic position. A black middle class has grown substantially since 1970, and the economic gap and physical distance between it and the impoverished lower classes has steadily increased. For many African Americans, the years since the Watts uprising have marked a road to frustration and despair. Between 1970 and

1990, a continued exodus of manufacturing plants from inner cities coupled with growing competition from immigrants fueled by employers' preferences reduced the job opportunities for blacks in low-skill occupations. Increasing numbers of black men with limited education became unemployed or dropped out of the job market entirely. By early 1992, the problems of the inner city—gangs, crime, crack cocaine, poverty, lawlessness, and racial and ethnic tension—had come to dominate the lives of a great many residents of Los Angeles. These problems were exacerbated by continuing demographic change, especially Mexican Americans moving into south Los Angeles and some adjacent black suburbs, resulting in sporadic racial clashes at schools. Many African American families who wanted to keep their children away from the influence of gangs, crime, and possible death shunned the communities they had once flocked to and moved to outlying suburbs. Police reaction and stiffening penalties made prison time much more common for black males than for whites, further increasing resentment of the law, as Horne details in his essay. By 1992, South Central Los Angeles had become "a tinderbox ready to explode at the striking of a single match."[118]

That "match" was the acquittal of four Los Angeles Police Department (LAPD) officers in April 1992 accused of beating African American motorist Rodney King a year earlier. The frequently televised videotape of King's beating reminded African Americans of numerous other occurrences of police brutality, including the death of several blacks from chokeholds, and led many to hope that the officers would be convicted. A not-guilty verdict from the all-white suburban jury, coupled with the killing of Latasha Harlins, a teenage black girl, by a Korean grocer who received a six-month suspended sentence, provided the immediate impetus for civil unrest that in two days left 52 dead, 2,383 injured, and more than 16,000 arrested, and caused nearly $1 billion dollars in property damage.[119]

The wide area covered by looting and the fact that Latinos constituted a greater number of arrestees than African Americans suggests that the uprising was also class-based, a reaction to years of deterioration in poorer areas of the city that cut across racial lines. The impact of the decline in high-wage manufacturing jobs in Los Angeles was worsened by the cutting of social services by state and federal administrations and government's acquiescence in allowing companies to relocate plants outside the country. The dearth of jobs fueled a despair among inner-city black youth that manifested itself in high rates of crime, gang affiliation, and school dropouts. Horne offers a detailed analysis of the background to the 1992 uprising in his essay. The twenty-year tenure of Mayor Bradley did not appreciably combat this deterioration.[120] After April 1992, it was clear that a significant part of California's African American population felt angry, frustrated, and alienated.

For more fortunate black Californians, the last decades of the twentieth century were a mixture of prosperity and frustration. One event that increased their concerns was the celebrated murder trial of O. J. Simpson, who was arrested in June 1994 on suspicion of murdering his former wife, Nicole Brown Simpson, and her friend Ron Goldman, both white. Simpson first was tried on criminal charges in downtown Los Angeles and acquitted by a predominantly black jury in October 1995. He then was ordered to pay $33 million in damages to the Brown and Goldman families by a largely white Santa Monica jury in a civil suit in early 1997. In the first case, Simpson's attorneys were widely criticized for playing the "race card," that is, focusing upon the demonstrated racist attitudes of L A P D detective Mark Fuhrman, one of the investigating officers. Other commentators emphasized the association between the racial mix of the two juries and the outcome of the respective cases. Both observations provided grim indicators of the extent to which race still pervaded popular thought. The fact that Simpson earlier had epitomized the "colorblind dream" of some successful African Americans and many white liberals—that blacks could escape association with race and be accepted solely on their merits—made his case especially devastating.[121]

Many middle-class blacks were also concerned by the political campaign against one of their most successful public programs, affirmative action, in the mid-1990s. Led by an African American, Ward Connerly, the University of California Board of Regents in 1995 voted to end its policy of admitting minority students with lower examination scores than some whites who were turned away. This program had significantly increased black and Latino enrollments since the late 1960s, but it was criticized for bringing them into a milieu for which many were unprepared, leading to high dropout rates. A similar decision came in 1996 when California voters approved Proposition 209, ending all "racial preferences" in higher education and in state employment. These two actions reduced African American enrollment at all but one campus by as much as 45 percent in 1997 and resulted in no blacks attending Boalt Hall School of Law at the University of California at Berkeley that year. Dire forecasts of few blacks but athletes in the university and a tidal wave of repeals of affirmative action up to the federal level

were lessened when outreach programs by both state university systems stabilized black enrollments and the Clinton administration maintained a policy of "mending but not ending" affirmative action in employment.[122]

Despite setbacks, an increasing majority of the population was entering
the middle class. Between 1970 and 1990, blacks with education were increasingly hired by large private firms while continuing to hold a substantial share of public-sector jobs. They became integrated into the general
economy and entered higher occupations to an unprecedented extent. Black
men had the largest percentage increase in income during those two
decades of males in any racial group in Los Angeles. Women fared even better, reaching income parity with white women by 1980, and entering the
labor force in larger numbers than black men by 1990. Residential segregation also notably declined, enabling many who could afford to do so to leave
central cities for suburbs and increasing spatial integration, as Lawrence de
Graaf discusses in his essay, "African American Suburbanization in California, 1960 through 1990." Between 1980 and 1990, the number of African
Americans in the Inland Empire increased 116 percent, making it the fastest-
growing black population in the nation, and black businesses multiplied in
that area. Other middle-class African Americans moved to more fashionable
parts of central cities and similarly expanded black enterprise. By 1992, Los
Angeles was home to 32,645 African American businesses with annual receipts of more than $3.5 billion, double those of black firms in any other
American city. The opening of the Crenshaw Mall near Baldwin Hills in the
1980s and its embellishment in 1994 with the addition of the Magic Johnson
Theaters epitomized the growing affluence of this group of blacks in Los
Angeles and throughout much of California.[123]

This growing affluence is part of a widening economic gap between
classes, provoking the question: Did African Americans in California still
have one cohesive black community, in the sense of sharing a common set
of desires and experiences? Despite the trends toward integration, African
Americans retained strong desires for cultural identity and a racial community. Even as many moved into new, mixed neighborhoods, they established
organizations that united race members or preserved unique cultural activities. They often returned to central cities for cultural or religious activities.
Crises revealed the number and strength of black organizations, as in the
wake of the 1989 Bay Area earthquake and the 1992 Los Angeles civil unrest.[124] Middle-class blacks also found they shared vestiges of discrimination
with the poor. These ranged from general insults and racial slurs, to such a

prominent individual as Willie Brown encountering housing discrimination, and other celebrities being detained by police. In 1991, a *Los Angeles Times* poll found that 8 percent of affluent African Americans and 54 percent of college-educated blacks reported experiencing discrimination at work or on campus. The trials of O. J. Simpson in 1995 and 1997 were evidence of the deep influence that race and discrimination had on many blacks. Even as they came closer to realizing the California Dream, many African Americans seemed to doubt its validity.[125]

The civil rights protests, black power movements, celebrities, and elected officials of the postwar years had one thing in common: they were secular. What became of the institution that earlier had been central in African American communities, the black church? While still many in number, black churches across the nation, particularly in the second half of the twentieth century, lost some of their historic importance. The increased role of public agencies in meeting many community needs has reduced the necessity of uniquely black organizations—secular or religious—to fill those roles. In an increasingly educated and professional African American population, the preacher has become less often a community leader. A few outstanding preachers in California continued to serve in community leadership roles, for example, the Reverend H. H. Brookins, head of the Los Angeles chapter of the Southern Christian Leadership Conference, and the Reverend Cecil Williams of San Francisco's Glide Memorial Chapel. But more often they were only one part of community action, appearing in protest meetings in the company of leaders from secular organizations or black public officials. Their diminished influence was evident during the Watts uprising of 1965, when the predominantly storefront churches of that area had little impact on its residents or the course of events. When these factors are added to the trend in the early 1960s toward interracial unity, the leadership role of the uniquely black church appeared to be shrinking.[126]

Yet at the end of the twentieth century, the black church continued to be an important institution in the personal and community lives of California's African Americans. Its historic emphasis on freedom for all humans, as God's children, has been carried from earlier causes to modern issues of social, political, and economic justice. Its continuation of unique styles of worship has retained much of the growing black middle class in an era of renewed emphasis on racial identity and heritage. Service as a pastor remains an important training ground for future black leaders. And in a time of diaspora from urban ghettos, black churches remain one of the main places where African Americans can reunite. The importance of that feature is seen in such suburban churches as Fellowship Baptist in Orange County. Located in Yorba Linda, a city with a tiny black population, it has attracted on a weekly basis more than 1,000 mostly middle-class blacks from several counties.[127] In such ways, the black church continues to be not only a religious establishment but also a reminder of the importance of racial heritage to African Americans in California.

The church also persists as a powerful force in organizing and mobilizing the black community. A striking example is Los Angeles's First African Methodist Episcopal (FAME) Church. FAME, founded in 1872, is the city's oldest black congregation, and, with more than 17,000 members in 1999, one of its largest. Led by the Reverend Cecil L. Murray, it maintains a diverse array of programs, such as a school, a free legal clinic run in partnership with Temple Isaiah and UCLA, housing for the elderly, and drug and AIDS counseling services. The entrepreneurial Reverend Mark Whitlock directs the FAME Renaissance organization, whose many dynamic programs include a multi-million-dollar project funding small businesses. As FAME exemplifies, black churches large and small continue to play a crucial role in spiritual and social leadership for African Americans throughout the state.

One cannot review the long history of African Americans in California without asking: Is it a history of progress? Many have looked back nostalgically at the tightly knit pioneer settlements of the nineteenth century, at Central Avenue and similar multiclass urban communities of the early twentieth century, or at creative colonies of black musicians, and bemoaned the loss of their social unity and cultural uniqueness.[128] Yet these communities existed on the margins of society and represented the relegation of African Americans to much more segregated and subordinate positions than many have attained in recent decades. Some have portrayed the African American experience through the lives of outstanding persons who might serve as role models for contemporary blacks. Unfortunately, many prominent individuals in recent experience have been celebrities whose value as role models has been questioned. One former athlete and current jurist has commented,

> Every day, in any given community, there are hundreds of decent black Americans who provide real opportunities for creating and sustaining hope for the future. These are not the heroes who offer hope with promises of winning the lottery, becoming a rap star, or pulling down backboards

and endorsements with the NBA. They are simply men and women who get up every morning and do the things that citizens do.[129]

This observation captures the strongest feature of the black experience in California: that African Americans have had to confront overwhelming odds in their pursuit of the California Dream, yet have seldom lost faith that they could attain it. Despite the negative racial attitudes of many whites and the frustratingly slow pace of change, African Americans continued to migrate to California in search of freedom and work; they formed colonies in hopes of creating utopias; and they strove to form political coalitions to bring equality through the law. Their dreams were supported by their dogged persistence, whether they be women establishing community organizations or male politicians seeking civil rights laws. Such determination has often borne fruit. This timeless and fervent search for El Dorado, more than any other single factor, has defined the history of African Americans in California.

NOTES

1. See "Mestizaje: The First Census of Los Angeles, 1781," in David J. Weber, ed., *Foreigners in Their Native Land: Historical Roots of the Mexican Americans* (Albuquerque: University of New Mexico Press, 1973), 33–35; Jack D. Forbes, "Black Pioneers: The Spanish-Speaking Afroamericans of the Southwest," *Phylon* 27 (1966): 235–42; Gloria E. Miranda, "Racial and Cultural Dimensions of *Gente de Razón* Status in Spanish and Mexican California," *Southern California Quarterly* 70 (1988): 265–78; and A. Odell Thurman, "The Negro in California before 1890," *Pacific Historian* 19 (1975): 324–25. Rudolph Lapp reminds us, however, that the first four blacks to land in California, three men and one woman, arrived with Sir Francis Drake when he reached the San Francisco Bay in 1579. See Lapp, *Blacks in Gold Rush California* (New Haven: Yale University Press, 1977), 2.

2. For a rich discussion of the role of blacks in the settlement of Los Angeles, see Antonio Rios-Bustamante, "Los Angeles, Pueblo and Region, 1781–1850: Continuity and Adaptation on the North Mexican Periphery" (Ph.D. diss., University of California, Los Angeles, 1985), 56–59, 71–72; and Lonnie G. Bunch III, *Black Angelenos: The Afro-American in Los Angeles, 1850–1950* (Los Angeles: California Afro-American Museum, 1988), 10–12. Rios-Bustamante describes the settlers'

background in Sinaloa, including the reasons for the heavy concentration of mulattos in the province.

3. See Forbes, "Black Pioneers," 238, 244. On color in California and New Spain, see Magnus Morner, *Race Mixture in the History of Latin America* (Boston: Little, Brown and Company, 1967), 56; and Miranda, "Racial and Cultural Dimensions of *Gente de Razón* Status," 266–67, 269–70, 272–76. For an account of Pio Pico's life, see Martin Cole and Henry Welcome, eds., *Don Pio Pico's Historical Narrative* (Glendale, CA: Arthur H. Clark Company, 1973), 12–15, 19–21.

4. Light moved to San Diego in the early 1840s but was last reported in the California gold country in the 1850s. See David J. Weber, "A Black American in Mexican San Diego: Two Recently Discovered Documents," *Journal of San Diego History* 20 (1974): 29–32; Lapp, *Blacks in Gold Rush California*, 4.

5. *The Life and Adventures of James Beckwourth as Told to Thomas D. Bonner* (1856, reprint, Lincoln: University of Nebraska Press, 1972), 98–99, 122–41, 456–65, 518–20; Delmont R. Oswald, "James P. Beckwourth," in LeRoy Hafen, ed., *The Mountain Men and the Fur Trade of the Far West* (Glendale, CA: Arthur H. Clark Company, 1968), 37–60; David J. Weber, *The Mexican Frontier, 1821–1846: The American Southwest under Mexico* (Albuquerque: University of New Mexico Press, 1982), 101–2. For a brief discussion of Beckwourth's California years, see Lapp, *Blacks in Gold Rush California*, 35.

6. See Mary Lee Spence and Donald Jackson, eds., *The Expeditions of John Charles Frémont,* 2 vols. (Urbana: University of Illinois Press, 1973), vol. 2, xxv, 63. See also W. Sherman Savage, "The Influence of Alexander Leidesdorff on the History of California," *Journal of Negro History* 38 (1953): 322–32; and Lapp, *Blacks in Gold Rush California*, 9–11.

7. U.S. Bureau of the Census, *Seventh Census of the United States, 1850* (Washington, DC: Robert Armstrong, Public Printer, 1853), xxxiii; U.S. Bureau of the Census, *Eighth Census of the United States, 1860, Population* (Washington, DC: Government Printing Office [G P O], 1864), 33; *Governor's Message and Report to the Secretary of State on the Census of 1852* (Sacramento: George Kerr, State Printer, 1853), 6–7. See also Quintard Taylor, *In Search of the Racial Frontier: African Americans in the American West, 1528–1990* (New York: W. W. Norton, 1998), chap. 3.

8. The quote appears in Margaret A. Frink, *Adventures of a Party of California Gold Seekers* (Oakland: Ledyard Frink, 1897), 92.

9. Lapp, *Blacks in Gold Rush California*, 50–52.

10. See P. Brown to Alley Brown, December 1851, California-Oregon Collection, Missouri Historical Society, Saint Louis.

11. The estimate is from Lapp, *Blacks in Gold Rush California*, 65. Givens is quoted on p. 131.

12. The Lester quote appears in the *Pennsylvania Freeman*, 5 December 1850, 2. The quote of the German observer is in Ruth Frye Ax, ed., *Bound for Sacramento* (Claremont, CA: Saunders Studio Press, 1938), 144. See also Lapp, *Blacks in Gold Rush California*, 120–21, 137–39, 155–56.

13. For a discussion of the California antislavery campaign, see Lapp, *Blacks in Gold Rush California*, chap. 6, and Taylor, *In Search of the Racial Frontier*, chap. 2.

14. Malcolm Edwards, "The War of Complexional Distinction: Blacks in Gold Rush California and British Columbia," *California Historical Quarterly* 56 (1977): 36; Howard H. Bell, "Negroes in California, 1849–1859," *Phylon* 28 (1967): 155–57; Rudolph Lapp, *Afro-Americans in California* (San Francisco: Boyd and Fraser, 1979), 7–8.

15. See *Proceedings of the First State Convention of the Colored Citizens of the State of California* (Sacramento: Democratic State Journal Printer, 1855) 27.

16. Lapp, *Blacks in Gold Rush California*, 49.

17. There is a vast literature on racism toward people of color in California. See, for example, Tomás Almaguer, *Racial Fault Lines: The Historical Origins of White Supremacy in California* (Berkeley: University of California Press, 1994); Roger Daniels and Spencer C. Olin Jr., eds., *Racism in California: A Reader in the History of Oppression* (New York: Macmillan, 1972); Robert F. Heizer and Alan F. Almquist, *The Other Californians: Prejudice and Discrimination under Spain, Mexico, and the United States to 1920* (Berkeley: University of California Press, 1971); and Charles Wollenberg, ed., *Ethnic Conflict in California History* (Los Angeles: Tinnon-Brown, 1970). See also Howard A. DeWitt, *The Fragmented Dream: Multicultural California* (Dubuque, IA: Kendall/Hunt Publishing Company, 1996); and Ronald Takaki, *Strangers from a Different Shore: A History of Asian Americans* (New York: Penguin Books, 1989).

18. Lapp, *Blacks in Gold Rush California*, 103–4. For a discussion of white attitudes toward black Gold Rush-era San Franciscans, see Roger W. Lotchin, *San Francisco, 1846–1856: From Hamlet to City* (New York: Oxford University Press, 1974), 129–33.

19. For a discussion of the crucial religious, cultural, and political role of early African American churches in San Francisco, see Philip M. Montesano, "San Francisco Black Churches in the Early 1860s: Political Pressure Group," *California Historical Quarterly* 52 (1973): 145–52; and Larry George Murphy, "Equality before the Law: The Struggle of Nineteenth-Century Black Californians for Social and Political Justice" (Ph.D. diss., University of California, Berkeley, 1973), 3.

20. Michael E. Engh, *Frontier Faiths: Church, Temple, and Synagogue in Los Angeles, 1846–1888* (Albuquerque: University of New Mexico Press, 1992), 106–7; C. Eric Lincoln and Lawrence H. Mamiya, *The Black Church in the African American Experience* (Durham, NC: Duke University Press, 1990), 3–4, 7–8.

21. Lapp, *Blacks in Gold Rush California*, 108–11; Clarence Caesar, "The Historical Demographics of Sacramento's Black Community, 1848–1900," *California History* 75 (1996): 198–213.

22. Lapp, *Blacks in Gold Rush California*, 111–17, 163–65.

23. See Dolores Hayden, "Biddy Mason's Los Angeles, 1856-1891," *California History* 68 (1989): 86–99. The Owenses' only son, Charles, married Ellen, Biddy Mason's eldest daughter, a few weeks after Mason was freed from slavery by Judge Hayes.

24. Robert J. Chandler provides a rich and fascinating account of Republican efforts to assist the black community during this period. See Chandler, "Friends in Time of Need: Republicans and Black Civil Rights in California during the Civil War Era," *Arizona and the West* 24 (1982): 319–40. See also James A. Fisher, "The Struggle for Negro Testimony in California, 1851–1863," *Southern California Quarterly* 51 (1969): 313–24; and Gerald Stanley, "Civil War Politics in California," *Southern California Quarterly* 64 (1982): 115–32. On the Franchise League, see James A. Fisher, "A History of the Political and Social Development of the Black Community in California, 1850–1950" (Ph.D. diss., State University of New York at Stony Brook, 1971), 95.

25. The Bowen and Brown cases were followed by other streetcar segregation cases involving Mary Ellen Pleasant and Emma J. Turner. In October 1866, Pleasant was removed from an Omnibus Railroad Company streetcar. She charged racial discrimination but later withdrew her claim when company officials assured her that "negroes would hereafter be allowed to ride on the car." Two years later Pleasant and Turner filed separate lawsuits against the North Beach and Mission Railroad Company and won in a lower court. However, both women lost on appeal in the California Supreme Court. For background on the Pleasant cases, see the San Francisco *Daily Alta California*, 18 October 1866, 1; Lynn M. Hudson, "A New Look, or 'I'm Not Mammy to Everybody in California': Mary Ellen Pleasant, a Black Entrepreneur," *Journal of the West* 32 (1993): 37; and Albert Broussard, "The New Racial Frontier: San Francisco's Black Community, 1900–1940" (Ph.D. diss., Duke University, 1977), 26–27. On Turner, see Chandler, "Friends in Time of Need," 332–34. California's 1893 antidiscrimination statute is profiled in Nathaniel S. Colley, "Civil Actions for Damages Arising out of Violations of Civil Rights," *Hastings Law Journal* 17 (1965): 190.

26. Lapp, *Blacks in Gold Rush California*, 148–52. See also Susan Bragg, "Knowledge Is Power: Sacramento Blacks and the Public Schools, 1854–1860," *California History* 75 (1996): 215–21.

27. *Pacific Appeal*, 14 February 1863, 2.

28. Table 1 is drawn from the following: U.S. Bureau of the Census, *Eighth Census of the United States, 1860, Population*, 29–32; U.S. Bureau of the Census, *Population of the United States, 1880*, vol. 1 (Washington, DC: G P O, 1883), 416–25; U.S. Bureau of the Census, *Twelfth Census of the United States, 1900*, vol. 1, *Population*, part 1 (Washington, DC: G P O, 1901), 609–46; U.S. Bureau of the Census, *Negro Population, 1790–1915* (Washington, DC: G P O, 1918), 95–105. Sacramento was no longer a "major city" by 1900 in terms of population, but it is included here due to its prominence in earlier decades.

29. U.S. Bureau of the Census, *Twelfth Census of the United States, 1900, Population*, part 1, cxix–cxxi; Willard B. Gatewood, *Aristocrats of Color: The Black Elite, 1880–1920* (Bloomington: Indiana University Press, 1990), 129–38.

30. *Pacific Appeal*, editorial, 7 June 1862, 2. See also Douglas H. Daniels, *Pioneer Urbanites: A Social and Cultural History of Black San Francisco* (Philadelphia: Temple University Press, 1980), 106.

31. Daniels, *Pioneer Urbanites*, 106–7. Throughout the late nineteenth century, San Franciscans who were foreign-born or of foreign-born parentage constituted more than half of the city's population and at times more than 70 percent. See ibid., 17, 82; and William Issel and Robert W. Cherny, *San Francisco, 1865–1932: Politics, Power, and Urban Development* (Berkeley: University of California Press, 1986), 55.

32. For a balanced, scholarly appraisal of Mary Ellen Pleasant, see Lynn M. Hudson, "When 'Mammy' Becomes a Millionaire: Mary Ellen Pleasant, An African American Entrepreneur" (Ph.D. diss., Indiana University, 1996). See also Daniels, *Pioneer Urbanites*, 29–30, for a discussion of other prosperous San Francisco African Americans.

33. Daniels, *Pioneer Urbanites*, 15–17, 31.

34. Powell is quoted in ibid., 119.

35. On the lack of employment opportunities in the Bay Area, see Albert S. Broussard, *Black San Francisco: The Struggle for Racial Equality in the West, 1900–1954* (Lawrence: University Press of Kansas, 1993), 38–39. Black Oakland is described in Lawrence P. Crouchett, Lonnie G. Bunch III, and Martha Kendall Winnacker, *Visions toward Tomorrow: The History of the East Bay Afro-American Community, 1852–1977* (Oakland: Northern California Center for Afro-American History and Life, 1989), 1–18. William T. Shorey's life is detailed in E. Berkeley

Tompkins, "Black Ahab: William T. Shorey, Whaling Master," *California Historical Quarterly* 51 (1972): 75–84.

36. Owens is described in F. H. Crumbly, "A Los Angeles Citizen," *Colored American Magazine* 9 (1905): 482–85; and Bunch, *Black Angelenos*, 17–19. See also Lawrence B. de Graaf, "The City of Black Angels: Emergence of the Los Angeles Ghetto, 1890–1930," *Pacific Historical Review* 39 (1970): 327; Hayden, "Biddy Mason's Los Angeles," 95–99; Charlotta A. Bass, *Forty Years: Memoirs from the Pages of a Newspaper* (Los Angeles: C. A. Bass, 1960), 8; and Gatewood, *Aristocrats of Color*, 132.

37. See J. Max Bond, "The Negro in Los Angeles" (Ph.D. diss., University of Southern California, 1936), 11–14. The quote appears on p. 13. See also Hayden, "Biddy Mason's Los Angeles," 86, 97; and Bunch, *Black Angelenos*, 19–20.

38. The Texas quote appears in de Graaf, "City of Black Angels," 330; see also 334–35. For the interview of Tennessee migrants, see Bond, "Negro in Los Angeles," 14–15, 65. For the Rydall quote, see E. H. Rydall, "California for Colored Folk," *The Colored American Magazine* 12 (1907): 386.

39. The Sojourner Truth Club quote appears in Lonnie G. Bunch III, "A Past Not Necessarily Prologue: The African American in Los Angeles," in Norman M. Klein and Martin J. Schiesl, eds., *20th Century Los Angeles: Power, Promotion, and Social Conflict* (Claremont, CA: Regina Books, 1990), 108. The Women's Day Nursery Association, founded in January 1907 at the Wesley Chapel A M E Church, was profiled in the *Los Angeles Times*, 12 February 1909, section 3, 4. On black politics in the first two decades of the twentieth century, see Douglas Flamming, "African Americans and the Politics of Race in Progressive-Era Los Angeles," in William Deverell and Tom Sitton, eds., *California Progressivism Revisited* (Berkeley: University of California Press, 1994), 203–28. On Los Angeles black newspapers, see Fisher, "A History of the Political and Social Development of the Black Community," 163, 174–75.

40. See the *Los Angeles Times*, 12 February 1909, section 3, 2, for an account of the history of the Forum. See also Emory J. Tolbert, *The U N I A and Black Los Angeles: Ideology and Community in the American Garvey Movement* (Los Angeles: U C L A Center for Afro-American Studies, 1980), 27, 33; E. Frederick Anderson, *The Development of Leadership and Organization Building in the Black Community of Los Angeles from 1900 through World War II* (Saratoga, CA: Century Twenty One Publishing, 1980), 59–60, 73; Flamming, "African Americans and the Politics of Race," 205, 208; Bunch, "Past Not Necessarily Prologue," 107–8; and Gloria Harrison, "The National Association for the Advancement of Colored People in California" (Master's thesis, Stanford University, 1949), passim.

41. For examples of the growing discrimination against various people of color at the beginning of the twentieth century, see Roger Daniels, *Asian America: Chinese and Japanese in the United States since 1850* (Seattle: University of Washington Press, 1988), chap. 4; John Modell, *The Economics and Politics of Racial Accommodation: The Japanese of Los Angeles, 1900–1942* (Urbana: University of Illinois Press, 1977), chap. 1; Albert Camarillo, *Chicanos in a Changing Society: From Mexican Pueblos to American Barrios in Santa Barbara and Southern California, 1848–1930* (Cambridge: Harvard University Press, 1979), chaps. 7–8; Ricardo Romo, *East Los Angeles: History of a Barrio* (Austin: University of Texas Press, 1983), 78–88; Broussard, *Black San Francisco*, 38–42; and Taylor, *In Search of the Racial Frontier*, 222–25.

42. U.S. Bureau of the Census, *Census of Religious Bodies, 1906*, part 1, *Summary and General Tables* (Washington, DC: G P O, 1910), 544; *Census of Religious Bodies, 1916, Summary and General Tables* (Washington, DC: G P O, 1919), 558; *Census of Religious Bodies, 1926, Summary and Detailed Tables* (Washington, DC: G P O, 1930), 728; George E. Sampson, "Black Pentecostals in the United States," *Phylon* 35 (1974): 203–4; Sherry S. DuPree, "Church of God in Christ," in Jack Salzman, David L. Smith, and Cornel West, eds., *Encyclopedia of African-American Culture and History*, vol. 1 (New York: Macmillan Library Reference, 1996), 544–45; Russell Chandler, "Pentecostals: Old Faith, New Impact," *Los Angeles Times*, 11 January 1976, section 1, 22. Ironically, the year the Azusa Street Mission closed was the one in which Los Angeles's most celebrated Pentecostal preacher, Aimee Semple McPherson, dedicated Angelus Temple.

43. *California Eagle*, 25 March 1916, 1–2; 3 June 1922, 4; 15 November 1919, 8; 22 November 1919, 4; Bond, "Negro in Los Angeles," 89–92, 219–23; *California Eagle*, 10 February 1923, 3; *Los Angeles Times Sunday Magazine*, 18 June 1933, 4–5, 10; *California Eagle*, 15 November 1919, 8; 22 November 1919, 4; Victor Nickerson, "Golden State: Early History" (typescript, 1946), Golden State Mutual Life Insurance Company Archives, Los Angeles.

44. Florence K. Robertson, "Problems in Training Adult Negroes in Los Angeles" (Master's thesis, University of Southern California, 1929), 44; Bond, "Negro in Los Angeles," 222; *California Eagle*, 12 May 1923, 10; 19 May 1923, 10; E. Franklin Frazier, *The Negro Church in America*, 214 (New York: Schocken Books, 1964), 58; *California Eagle*, 24 February 1917, 1, 8. The charge that black churches stifled civic activism was reiterated during the civil rights era; see Wesley Marx's Los Angeles–based study, *Protest and Prejudice*, rev. ed. (New York: Harper and Row, 1969).

45. Table 2 is drawn from the following: U.S. Bureau of the Census, *Fourteenth Census of the United States*, vol. 2, *Population, 1920* (Washington, DC: G P O, 1922),

47; U.S. Bureau of the Census, *Sixteenth Census of the United States, 1940, Population*, vol. 2, *Characteristics of the Population* (Washington, DC: G P O, 1943), part 1, 629, 636, 657, 787; part 5, 1041; part 6, 1026, 1044, 1053; part 7, 400.

46. See Bunch, *Black Angelenos*, 29–34. Black Los Angeles's eclipse of the Bay Area communities is described in Fisher, "Political and Social Development," 161, 170–73. See also Tolbert, U N I A *and Black Los Angeles*, 72. Chandler Owen's quote appears in Owen, "From Coast to Coast," *The Messenger* 4 (1922): 409. On the Hotel Somerville, see *Crisis* 35 (1928): 309, 317–18. Williams's quote appears in Bunch, *Black Angelenos*, 31.

47. U.S. Bureau of the Census, *Fifteenth Census of the United States, 1930, Population*, vol. 4, *Occupations by States* (Washington, DC: G P O, 1933), 199–210, 244–46, 1370–72, 1585–87, 1593–96, 1709–11. Dellums is quoted in Broussard, *Black San Francisco*, 40.

48. For background on the concentration of blacks in the motion picture industry, see Thomas Cripps, *Slow Fade to Black: The Negro in American Film, 1900–1942* (New York: Oxford University Press, 1977), 90–94, 112.

49. Ibid., 108–9.

50. Ibid., 99–102, 241, 275, 360–66.

51. The Pittman quote appears in Broussard, *Black San Francisco*, 118; see also 117, 119; and Crouchett, *Visions toward Tomorrow*, 35.

52. Bunch, *Black Angelenos*, 37; Crouchett, *Visions toward Tomorrow*, 35–36. On California's N Y A, see Olen Cole Jr., "Black Youth in the National Youth Administration in California, 1935–1943," *Southern California Quarterly* 73 (1991): 385–402; and Broussard, *Black San Francisco*, 120–27.

53. On Augustus Hawkins, see Fisher, "Political and Social Development," 228–35.

54. The Hugh Macbeth quote appears in the *California Eagle*, 26 December 1924, 1. See also Bunch, "Past Not Necessarily Prologue," 103–4; and de Graaf, "City of Black Angels," 345–47.

55. The Bontemps quote appears in "Why I Returned," Arna Bontemps, *The Old South: "A Summer Tragedy" and Other Stories of the Thirties* (New York: Dodd, Mead and Company, 1973), 5–6. The quote from the *Pittsburgh Courier* appeared in the 29 September 1923 edition, 13. For a history of Watts between its founding and annexation to Los Angeles, see Mary Ellen Bell Ray, *The City of Watts, California: 1907 to 1926* (Los Angeles: Rising Publishing, 1985), chaps. 4–5; and Patricia Rae Adler, "Watts: From Suburb to Black Ghetto" (Ph.D. diss., University of Southern California, 1977), 48–50, 309.

56. The quote appears in Bond, "The Negro in Los Angeles," 35. The entire re-

strictive covenant affecting southwest Los Angeles appears in Bass, *Forty Years*, 97. On the Booker T. Washington Jr. episode, see the *Los Angeles Times*, 17 February 1924, part 2, 6. The long history of the Los Angeles black community's campaign against housing discrimination is described in Bunch, "Past Not Necessarily Prologue," 106–19. Clement Vose, *Caucasians Only: The Supreme Court, the NAACP, and the Restrictive Covenant Cases*, 2d ed. (Berkeley: University of California Press, 1967), remains the best study of both restrictive covenants and the long and ultimately successful legal struggle against them. See especially chaps. 1, 3, and 8.

57. On the evolution of jazz, see LeRoi Jones, *Blues People: Negro Music in White America* (New York: William Morrow and Company, 1963), 109–21; Thomas J. Hennessey, *From Jazz to Swing: African American Jazz Musicians and Their Music, 1890–1935* (Detroit: Wayne State University Press, 1994), chaps. 1–2; Eileen Southern, *The Music of Black Americans: A History* (New York: W. W. Norton, 1971), 389–90; and Tom Stoddard, *Jazz on the Barbary Coast* (Chigwell, England: Storyville Publications, 1982), 6, 98, 126, 131–33, 143. Stoddard argues that San Francisco's Barbary Coast during the first two decades of the twentieth century had most of the conditions that encouraged the rise of jazz in New Orleans's Storyville district, including an active (if smaller) cadre of African American musicians.

58. See Bette Yarbrough Cox, *Central Avenue—Its Rise and Fall, 1890–c. 1955* (Los Angeles: BEEM Publications, 1996), 10–14, 30–36; Ted Gioia, *West Coast Jazz: Modern Jazz in California, 1945–1960* (New York: Oxford University Press, 1992), 3–9; Hennessey, *From Jazz to Swing*, 58–60, 114–15; Cripps, *Slow Fade to Black*, 100–101; and Bunch, *Black Angelenos*, 33–34. For one black musician's experiences with the Hollywood studios, see Joe Darensbourg, *Jazz Odyssey: The Autobiography of Joe Darensbourg* (Baton Rouge: Louisiana State University Press, 1988), 61–63.

59. Michael Austin, "Harlem of the West: The Douglas Hotel and Creole Palace Nite Club" (Master's thesis, University of San Diego, 1994), 3–7. Tom Stoddard reports that black jazz musicians played in Yokohama, Japan, as early as 1925. See Stoddard, *Jazz on the Barbary Coast*, 140.

60. Davis McEntire, *The Population of California* (San Francisco: Parker Printing, 1946), 138.

61. Lawrence B. de Graaf, "Negro Migration to Los Angeles, 1930–50" (Ph.D. diss., University of California, Los Angeles, 1962), 318, 333.

62. This idea is especially propounded by Marilynn S. Johnson, *The Second Gold Rush: Oakland and the East Bay in World War II* (Berkeley: University of California Press, 1993); and Gretchen Lemke-Santangelo, *Abiding Courage: African*

American Migrant Women and the East Bay Community (Chapel Hill: University of North Carolina Press, 1996).

63. Gerald D. Nash, *The American West Transformed: The Impact of the Second World War* (Bloomington: Indiana University Press, 1985), 152.

64. Lester Granger, "Negroes and War Production," *Survey Graphic* 31 (1942): 470; de Graaf, "Negro Migration," 166–72; *California Eagle*, 16 July 1942, 1A, 8B; 24 September 1942, 2A.

65. Broussard, *Black San Francisco,* 144–45; *California Eagle,* 24 February 1943, 4A, 7B; Bass, *Forty Years,* 87–89. Wartime discrimination in San Francisco is well covered in Broussard's essay in this anthology as well as in his book *Black San Francisco,* especially chap. 8. For Southern California's employment problems, see Alonzo Smith and Quintard Taylor, "Racial Discrimination in the Workplace: A Study of Two West Coast Cities during the 1940s," *Journal of Ethnic Studies* 8 (1980): 35–54; Josh Sides, "Battle on the Home Front: African American Shipyard Workers in World War II Los Angeles," *California History* 75 (1996): 251–63.

66. Johnson, *Second Gold Rush,* 167–69; Keith Collins, *Black Los Angeles: The Maturing of the Ghetto, 1940–1950* (Saratoga, CA: Century Twenty One Publishing, 1980), 48; Laurence C. Hewes, *Intergroup Relations in San Diego: A Report to the City Council and the Board of Education in the City of San Diego* (San Francisco: n.p., 1946), 20.

67. Bruce M. Tyler, "The Zoot-Suit Riots and the Double V during World War II" (unpublished ms. in possession of Lawrence de Graaf); Lawrence B. de Graaf, "Significant Steps on an Arduous Path: The Impact of World War II on Discrimination against African Americans in the West," *Journal of the West* 35 (1996): 24–25. For a full account of the Port Chicago incident and trials, see Robert L. Allen, *The Port Chicago Mutiny* (New York: Amistad, 1993).

68. De Graaf, "Significant Steps," 29–30; Crouchett, et. al., *Visions toward Tomorrow,* 49; Harold Draper, *Jim Crow in Los Angeles* (Los Angeles: Workers' Party, 1946), 3; Statement of Howard R. Holtzendorf, Hearings on Congested Areas, Records of Committee on Congested Production Areas, Los Angeles Congested Area file, Housing folder, National Archives, Washington, DC.

69. Quote from Arthur C. Verge, *Paradise Transformed: Los Angeles during the Second World War* (Dubuque, IA: Kendall/Hunt Publishing Company, 1993), 52–53. See also Nash, *West Transformed,* 98.

70. Johnson, *Second Gold Rush,* 83–84, 104–6, 110–11; Hewes, *Intergroup Relations,* 21–22.

71. De Graaf, "Significant Steps," 31–32; Sides, "Battle on Home Front," 255–62; Broussard, *Black San Francisco,* chap. 10.

72. Anderson, *Development of Leadership*, 83, 85, 88–89, 92–95, 97–98, 102–3. See also Harlan Unrau, "The Double V Movement in Los Angeles during World War II" (Master's thesis, California State University, Fullerton, 1972).

73. Broussard, *Black San Francisco*, chap. 11; Los Angeles County Commission on Human Relations, "Notes on the History and Activities of the Human Relations Commission" (October 1965, mimeographed), 1; Broussard, *Black San Francisco*, 187–89.

74. Johnson, *Second Gold Rush*, chap. 7; Taylor, *In Search of the Racial Frontier*, 345–46.

75. De Graaf, "Negro Migration," 274–77; Johnson, *Second Gold Rush*, 198–99; U.S. Fair Employment Practices Committee, "Impact of Reconversion on Minority Workers" (Washington, DC: n.p., n.d.), 9–11; Wilson Record, "Willie Stokes at the Golden Gate," *Crisis* 56 (1949): 176–79; *California Eagle*, 28 February 1946, 20; Wilson Record, "The Chico Story: A Black and White Harvest," *Crisis* 58 (1951): 95–101, 129–33; Hewes, *Intergroup Relations*, 13.

76. De Graaf, "Negro Migration," 273–74, 276; Lemke-Santangelo, *Abiding Courage*, 64; Davis McEntire, *Labor Force in California: A Study of Characteristics and Trends in Labor Force, Employment, and Occupations in California, 1900–1950* (Berkeley: University of California Press, 1952), 65; *California Eagle*, 6 June 1946, 2.

77. Wilson Record, "Dimensions of Discrimination in Negro Teacher Employment," *Teacher* (1961): n.p.; Laurence A. Maes, "A Survey of Post-War Negro Employment Patterns in the San Francisco Bay Area" (Master's thesis, University of California, Berkeley, 1948), 64–65.

78. Table 3 is drawn from the following: U.S. Bureau of the Census, *Census of Population: 1940*, vol. 2, *Characteristics of the Population* (Washington, DC: G P O, 1943), 516–17, 541; U.S. Bureau of the Census, *Census of Population: 1950*, vol. 2, *Characteristics of the Population*, part 5, *California* (Washington, DC: G P O, 1953), tables 14, 34; U.S. Bureau of the Census, *Census of Population: 1960*, vol. 1, *Characteristics of the Population*, part 6, *California* (Washington, DC: G P O, 1963), tables 14, 21.

79. "Introduction," in Lloyd H. Fisher, *The Problem of Violence: Observations on Race Conflict in Los Angeles* (San Francisco: American Council on Race Relations, 1947), 2; Testimony of Orville Caldwell, Hearings on Congested Areas, 1764.

80. Delores Nason McBroome, *Parallel Communities: African Americans in California's East Bay, 1850–1963* (New York: Garland Publishing, 1993), 134–35; *California Eagle*, 20 March 1947, 1, 8; Hewes, *Intergroup Relations*, 20–21; Ruth Tuck, *Not with the Fist: Mexican Americans in a Southwest City* (New York: Harcourt Brace, 1946), 46–47; John Anson Ford, *Thirty Explosive Years in Los Angeles County*

(San Marino, CA: Huntington Library, 1961), 26–27; Cox, *Central Avenue*, 88; Broussard, *Black San Francisco*, 240; Carey McWilliams, "Los Angeles: An Emerging Pattern," *Common Ground* 9 (1949): 8 (McWilliams quote).

81. See also Brief of the State of California Amicus Curiae, *McGhee v. Sipes*, 334 US 1; Charles B. Spaulding, "Housing Problems of Minority Groups in Los Angeles County," *Annals of the American Academy of Political and Social Science* 248 (1946): 222; *Los Angeles Times*, 18 December 1945; *California Eagle*, 17 July 1947, 8.

82. Johnson, *Second Gold Rush*, 209, 218–21, 226–27, 232–33; Hewes, *Intergroup Relations*, 21–22; *California Eagle*, 17 July 1947, 8; Broussard, *Black San Francisco*, 222–26. For an analysis of the Fontana case, see Mike Davis, *City of Quartz: Excavating the Future in Los Angeles* (New York: Vintage Books, 1992), 397–403.

83. Elizabeth De Kam, "'A Home to Call Our Own': Textual Analysis of the Story of Residential Race-Restrictive Covenants in the *California Eagle* and *Los Angeles Sentinel*" (Master's thesis, California State University, Northridge, 1993), 72, 90–94, 161–62.

84. De Kam, "A Home," 32–33; McWilliams, "Los Angeles," 5–6; Brief of California, *McGhee v. Sipes*.

85. Johnson, *Second Gold Rush*, 194–207; Broussard, *Black San Francisco*, 236–38; Bass, *Forty Years*, 132–33, 144–53; Lawrence P. Crouchett, "Assemblyman W. Byron Rumford: Symbol for an Era," *California History* 66 (1987): 15–17, 23.

86. Broussard, *Black San Francisco*, 182–83, 235–36; Ford, *Thirty Explosive Years*, 138–39; Lawrence F. LaMar, "Los Angeles—The Negro Image," *Negro History and Neighborhood Business Annual Year Book Edition: 1964* (Los Angeles: Negro Achievement League, 1964), 47; Bunch, "Past Not Necessarily Prologue," 111, 119.

87. Los Angeles County Commission on Human Relations (LACCHR), "Notes on the History and Activities of the Human Relations Commision" (mimeographed report), October 1965, 3–4; *Los Angeles Examiner*, 22, 23 February 1960; Buggs quote is from Wesley Marx, "The Negro Community: A Better Chance?" *Los Angeles* 3 (1962): 38; *Violence in the City—An End or a Beginning? Report by the Governor's Commission on the Los Angeles Riots*, 2 December 1965, 3.

88. Johnson, *Second Gold Rush*, 231–32; Larry Ford and Ernest Griffin, "The Ghettoization of Paradise," *Geographical Review* 69 (1979): 147–49; Paul Jacobs, *Prelude to Riot: A View of Urban America from the Bottom* (New York: Random House, 1967), 156–57.

89. Broussard, *Black San Francisco*, 232, 240; *The Urban Reality: A Comparative Study of the Socio-Economic Situation of Mexican Americans, Negroes, and Anglo-Caucasians in Los Angeles County* (Los Angeles: LACCHR, June 1965), 18;

127. Lincoln and Mamiya, *Black Church*, 4, 15, 234–35; interview of the Reverend James Carrington by Noah Kimbwala, May 1994, Oral History Program, California State University, Fullerton.

128. A good example of this view is Bunch, "Past Not Necessarily Prologue."

129. Alan C. Page, "We Become What We Emulate," *Los Angeles Times*, 23 February 1996, B9.

PART I
FORMING THE COMMUNITY

The Early African Heritage of California

JACK D. FORBES

W hat is an African American? To many, the answer seems obvious: anyone of African descent living in the United States. But what if that person is also partly of European and/or Native American ancestry? With which group does he identify? In much of their experience in the United States, African Americans have been singled out because of color—and concepts of race associated with it—for conspicuously different treatment than most Americans. Slavery is the most striking example. Was such a different set of experiences always true of blacks in California, or were there periods in which persons of African descent shared much of the culture and life of other Californians? These questions resonate throughout the experience of African Americans in the Golden State. When we ask them with respect to the period of Spanish and Mexican rule, they produce some interesting answers that lead to deeper questions about the role of race in American history.

California and African American history enjoyed a symbiosis from the initial appearance of nonindigenous people. The name "California" is derived from a Spanish tale of chivalry written around 1508 that described an island by that name "at the right hand of the Indies . . . which was inhabited by black women without any man being among them, so that their way of life was almost Amazon-like." The island was ruled by a giant queen, Calafia, possibly the origin of the state's name. This name appeared on maps of Baja California before the Spanish discovery of Alta California in 1542, and while the idea that it was an island quickly disappeared, the name was extended to the north and remained.[1]

The story of people of African descent in California (and other areas col-onized by Spain) is important because it is quite different from African American experience in areas where English was spoken. The Spanish Em-pire made full use of its free subjects of African origin, and the Mexican re-public, after 1821–24, extended full legal equality to all citizens regardless of color. Many Mexicans of African ancestry were able to achieve successes that would have been undreamed of in the United States of America. At least twice, in 1830–31 and 1845–46, the Mexican governor of California was al-leged to be of partially African background. This contrasts with a situation in the United States in which 90 percent of all blacks were slaves and the re-mainder were second-class citizens who could not even vote in more than a few states.

It is often forgotten that the struggles between the United States of the North and the Mexican United States had as one of their bases the racial an-tagonism existing between a republic marred by slavery and antipathy to-ward both Africans and Original Americans and the predominantly non-white population of Mexico, with its Original American majority and large numbers of persons of racially mixed and African ancestry.[2] Today African Americans and Mexican Americans are interacting in neighborhood after neighborhood throughout much of the United States. Sadly, neither group is usually acquainted with the history of Mexicans of African ancestry or of the close relationship between African Americans and persons of the in-digenous American race generally. Mexican Americans are often unaware of their own African heritage, and African Americans are often unaware of the African heritage of the Spanish-speaking world generally or of their own part–Native American racial heritage. It is hoped that this study will help to fill in some of those gaps.

Several lists of names from California census records offer empirical ev-idence of the presence of African Americans in Hispano-Mexican Califor-nia and illustrate the wide extent of interracial marriage. Unfortunately, the subjects of California's early African heritage and extensive interracial mix-ture both remain controversial among nonscholars. Public school curricula and widely used texts continue to exclude both subjects.[3]

The social position of African Americans, like that of other racial mi-norities, has been a matter of contention through much of California's history. But although its citizens immediately wrote Anglo American views toward blacks into law when California joined the United States in 1850, in many ways the African heritage of California prior to statehood had more in common with the historical development of Spanish America than with the United States. In Spanish California, the social system allowed Africans and their descendants to be defined and redefined more flexibly than did the increasingly rigid dichotomies of black and white in Anglo America. Moreover, slavery, though a common status of many of the earliest blacks in the Spanish Empire, was much more easily escaped and finally became illegal in the era of Mexican independence, even as it became increasingly defended in the southern United States.

The Spanish Empire was largely dependent upon the labor of Africans and First Americans in South and Central America, the Caribbean Islands, and Florida. Spain sent relatively small numbers of men to control new societies in the Americas. The presence of few European women led to extensive intermarriage with other peoples, and the mixed children of these unions, "outnumbering Spaniards in New Spain as early as 1650, were to play a large role in the later stages of colonization and conquest." The smaller percentage of Europeans also meant greater dependence on black and Native alliances; for example, Spaniards relied extensively on maroons and Seminoles in their competition with the British and Anglo Americans for Florida, beginning in the late eighteenth century. The Spaniards also used Africans as artisans and supervisors of Original American slaves in colonial Mexico, which enhanced the status of many blacks. As David Weber has noted,

> Throughout the Spanish empire, an individual's social status correlated strongly with his or her racial and ethnic origins. . . . Españoles scorned mestizos, mulattos, Indians, and blacks, as much for their presumed social inferiority as for their race. . . . But colonizers embarking from New Spain could not be choosy. . . . Mixed bloods, together with blacks and Hispanicized Indians, composed the vast majority of New Spain, and, therefore, of immigrants to New Mexico, Texas, Arizona, and California. . . . Inevitably, the frontier population became "whiter" as Indians and mulattos declared themselves mestizos, and mestizos described themselves as españoles. . . . Whitening occurred throughout Spain's empire, for a person's social status, or *calidad*, was never fixed solely by race, but rather defined by occupation and wealth as well as by parentage and skin color.

Although African blood remained an impediment in Spanish American society, it was much more easily overcome than in Anglo America.[4]

Tolerance toward Africans and part-Africans may also have been greater because of the heterogeneous ethnic heritage of the Spanish. Significantly, the Spaniards who invaded the Americas in and after 1492 were themselves a mestizo (mixed) people of part-African descent, being of native Iberic (Basque or Basque-related), Celtic, Carthaginian-Phoenician, Greek, Roman-Italian, and German ancestries, mixed with large elements of North African Mauritanian (Moro), Egyptian, Middle Eastern, Jewish, and sub-Saharan African ancestry. Since the 1200s, large numbers of slaves had been brought into Spain and Portugal from areas as diverse as Senegal, the Canary Islands, North Africa, Russia, the Ukraine, Abkhazia, and Circassia. Thus, black, brown, and white slaves were common in Iberia, and all were essentially absorbed into the Spanish and Portuguese populations. Furthermore, Spaniards had experienced "incessant contact with dark-skinned Muslims over centuries of Islamic expansion into Spain," which "created continuous racial blending and a mingled civilization."[5] Their national history had prepared Spaniards for a society composed of many races (but not necessarily of diverse religions!).

When the Spanish Empire expanded to the Caribbean, many persons of African origin were included. Diego the Black accompanied Christopher Columbus on his fourth voyage (1502–4). In 1501, Andrés García *de color loro* (of brown color), a former servant, and Cristobal de Palacios, also a brown man and a resident of Trigueros in Spain, went to Haiti on four-year work contracts. In 1502, black slaves from Seville who were *ladinos* (Spanish-speaking) were sent to Haiti. Many soon joined Original American rebels on the island, a phenomenon that would be replicated in region after region in subsequent years.

In the Caribbean as well as in Mexico, incoming Africans (usually male) tended to intermarry with indigenous people, producing offspring generally known to the Spaniards as *mulatos* but also as *zambos* or *zambahigos* (from Peru to Panama) and *lobos* (in Mexico). Many of the *zambos* and *lobos* lived in independent communities and were a freedom-loving, troublesome element to the Spaniards. This growing red-black mulatto population married in turn with unmixed Americans and with mestizos (children of Spaniards and Original Americans), eventually producing huge numbers of persons known variously as *pardos*, *grifos*, *morenos*, *de color quebrado*, *mestizos pardos*, and dozens of other names.

As they intermarried and their numbers grew, persons of African ancestry acquired varying roles in different parts of the Spanish Empire. In many areas, they found that their social status remained strongly related to racial or ethnic origins. But on the frontiers of the Spanish Empire, colonizers could not afford to make race a mandatory badge of subordinate status. By the end of the sixteenth century, and even more so by the mid-eighteenth century, persons of mixed blood, along with blacks and Hispanicized Native Americans, composed a large majority of the population of New Spain and particularly of regions adjacent to the present-day United States. Therefore, they would play a major role in the occupation of northern Mexico, New Mexico, Texas, and California. Relatively few Spaniards were available for service in that region, and the often unwelcome role of soldiers and laborers fell heavily on American Indians, Africans, and persons of mixed ancestry. Africans who had been converted to Christianity and who spoke Spanish were especially helpful in supervising missionized Indians and in developing pueblos devoted to mining.[6]

African Americans and other nonwhites in the Spanish Empire suffered from many injustices, but nonetheless it was possible for them to rise to positions of importance, especially in frontier regions. By the eighteenth century, virtually every description of a Spanish town in Chihuahua, Durango, or Sonora referred to the presence of mulattos. Adventurous African Americans also appear in the record, such as a mulatto who traveled from the Hopi villages to southern Arizona in 1720, by all available evidence the first non–Native American to pass through that region in more than a century.[7]

By 1744, the Marquis de Altamira noted that many troops along the northern frontier of the Spanish Empire, especially in Texas, were not Spaniards but mixed bloods or other nonwhites. In 1760 another Spaniard asserted that most of the frontier soldiers were mulattos. Spaniards often looked down on these mulatto, mestizo, and Indian soldiers, but without their presence Spain could not have held northern Mexico or the North American Southwest. Spain also used black troops in Florida in the eighteenth and early nineteenth centuries, many of whom were especially motivated to fight in order to avoid reenslavement in British colonies or the United States.[8]

In the early 1530s, Hernán Cortés ordered an expedition up the west coast of Mexico, primarily to find a strait through North America but also in search of an island "inhabited only by women without any men." Possibly he had read *Las sergas* and was in search of the land of Queen Calafia. This expedition included 300 Africans, some of whom might have remained in California after Cortés retreated. The Otondo expedition to California from

1683 to 1685 included a mulatto boy, while the 1697 expedition included Juan, a Peruvian mulatto. In the 1720s, American Indians continued to resist the invaders, aided by mulattos and mestizos who had grown up among them. The leaders of a major rebellion against the Spaniards from 1733 to 1736 included Chicori and Botón, both part-African. Nonetheless, most of the African Americans in California became miners and soldiers and remained loyal to the crown. In 1790, the population of Baja California included 844 Spanish-speaking persons of whom 183, or 22 percent, were mulattos, mostly concentrated at the mines of Santa Ana. The province also contained 418 *castas* (persons of unclassified mixed ancestry), or almost 50 percent of the population, and 243 persons classified as *español* (Spanish). Many of the *castas* and some of the Spaniards probably were part-African, and it is therefore likely that at least one out of every four Spanish-speaking Baja Californians was part-African.[9]

In 1769, the Spanish Empire expanded to include much of coastal Alta California. Because Sonora, Sinaloa, and Baja California included so many part-Africans among their Spanish-speaking residents, African Americans played an important role in the occupation of Alta California. The Portola expedition, which founded San Diego and Monterey and explored the coast, numbered among its members at least one mulatto soldier, Juan Antonio Coronel (a *soldado de cuera*, or "leather jacket," a member of the crack frontier troops used to fight and control Indians). Several mulatto mule drivers also served with the expedition, including one who traveled alone through the region in February 1770.

The Juan Bautista de Anza expedition of 1775, important in the annals of California settlement, included seven mulatto soldiers out of a total of twenty-nine. These and other early African Americans in California blazed trails, fought natives, suffered from near starvation, and finally settled down to help found communities and build ranches. All of the early African pioneers in California were free men and women, serving either as soldiers or civilian settlers. Later, in the 1790s and early 1800s, convicts were sent to California to serve out their sentences. Of one such group sent out in 1798, 18 percent were mulattos. Such persons usually had been convicted of petty crimes and soon became free. Overall, at least 20 percent of the Spanish-speaking settlers and soldiers in California in the 1790s were of African or part-African descent. Since the Spaniards' position was at best precarious, with perhaps 200,000 Californians to conquer and control, the African Americans' contribution in terms of manpower was essential.[10]

Several Spanish settlements in California could not have been established without Africans. This was certainly the case with the founding of Los Angeles in 1781. Of the first forty-six *pobladores* (settlers), twenty-six were African or part-African. The remainder further demonstrates the city's multiracial beginnings: one was a Chinese from Manila, two were *español,* and the rest were Indian or part-Indian. The first alcalde (mayor) was José Vanegas, a Native American, while Francisco Reyes, a mulatto married to a Spanish-Indian woman, served as alcalde during the 1790s. The families settling Los Angeles were racially mixed, revealing that intermarriage was already absorbing the African stock. Of the eleven original families, seven involved couples of different racial backgrounds, while two couples were already mulatto. Only two families' members were both of the same race, and that was Indian. At least nine children were of mixed Indian-Spanish-African ancestry, constituting 20 percent of the population. Some of the "mulattos" may have had Indian, Spanish, and African blood, since the children of a mulatto and a Native American were often classified as mulatto in California, as were the children of mestizos and mulattos. These early Angelenos were also residentially integrated, since house lots were distributed to the settlers without reference to racial characteristics.[11]

By 1790, some significant changes had occurred in Los Angeles. The total population had increased to 141, of whom 73 were classified as *españoles*, 39 as mestizos, 22 as mulattos, and seven as Indians. These figures are inaccurate, however, because many of the original settlers of 1781 had undergone a "change" of race in the intervening years. The following list illustrates this process:

Name	Race in 1781	Race in 1790
Pablo Rodríquez	Indian	*coyote* (3/4 Indian)
Manuel Camero	mulatto	mestizo
José Moreno	mulatto	mestizo
María Guadalupe Pérez	mulatto	*coyote*
Basilio Rosas	Indian	*coyote*
José Vanegas	Indian	mestizo
José Navarro	mestizo	*español*
María Rufina Navarro	mulatto	mestizo (or Indian)

The changes in racial classification were all away from Indian or mulatto and toward *español*; that is, everyone acquired some Caucasian ancestry and shed African background, becoming, in effect, lighter upon moving up the social scale.

Despite this process of reclassification, it is still possible to trace additional persons of part-African background who came to Los Angeles between 1781 and 1790. These settlers included five part-African families, illustrating a complex process of hybridization. Significantly for an understanding of the place of part-Africans in California society, the head of one family, Francisco Reyes, a mulatto married to a mestiza, became the alcalde of the community, and the descendants of Santiago Pico became prominent political leaders and wealthy ranchers.[12]

Of the twenty-five families whose characteristics can be ascertained from the 1790 census, the following marriage pattern can be derived: fourteen of the families involved new forms of hybridization, while only nine were composed of persons classified as nonhybrids. This latter figure must be regarded with skepticism, however, as the following census entry indicates:

> José Sinova, *español*, 40, from Mexico City; married to María Gertrudis Bohorques, *mestiza*, 28; their Spanish daughters: Josefa Dolores, 12; Casilda de la Cruz, 9; María Julia, 4; and María Sefernia, 1.

Many persons classified as *español* were actually the progeny of *españoles* and mestizos, and were, therefore, at least one-quarter Indian. Many may also have been part-African, because a census summary of 1792 reduced the number of *españoles* in Los Angeles from 73 to 59, while the mulatto class increased from 22 to 57, the total population increasing from 141 to 148. In 1792, therefore, the recorded part-Africans constituted 39 percent of the population of Los Angeles.[13]

The records of Santa Barbara are also of considerable interest, especially in view of the contemporary romanticization of the Spanish heritage evident in that community. In 1785, Santa Barbara included sixteen families of African American descent. Of the 191 persons whose racial identity is listed in the census, at least 37 were part-African, while more than half were officially classified as non-Spanish (Indians, mestizos and *coyotes*). Of the total 45 families, only 24 did not involve new hybridization, while just 18 possessed unmixed lineages. Between 1785 and 1792, a strong tendency existed at Santa Barbara, as elsewhere, to reclassify many mixed-bloods as *españoles*. Thus, in spite of a 25 percent increase in total population during those years, the number of non-Spaniards remained uniform.[14]

A similar example of an African presence in the population, and the subsequent reclassification thereof, can be seen in the census for San José in 1790. Of the fifteen families constituting the total population, only seven did not involve hybridization or hybrid lineages. Of the total number of settlers, 24.3 percent were part-African and 55.5 percent were non-*español*. Four years later, the part-African proportion had been reclassified to form less than 15 percent, while the non-*español* had increased to 60 percent, thus indicating that some *pardos* (people of Indian, African, and Caucasian heritage, the progeny of a mulatto and a mestizo) and mulattos had become mestizos.[15]

Similar developments occurred at Monterey, where, in 1790, mulattos constituted 18.5 percent of the population and *castas* an additional 50 percent. The latter included part-Africans as well as mestizos. The total non-*español* proportion at Monterey was almost 75 percent of the population. Within one year, however, at least twenty-eight non-*españoles* were reclassified as *españoles* in the Monterey region.[16]

San Francisco repeated the theme of how Africans in early California and their descendants were allowed the flexibility, sometimes within the same generation, to reclassify their race. Ignacio Linares, for example, changed his status from mulatto to Indian between 1782 and 1790. This might not seem particularly advantageous, but it made it possible for his son Ramón Linares and eight other children to become mestizos, since his wife, Gertrudis Rivas, was an *española*. The status of mestizo evidently was preferable to that of mulatto. One-half of the families, in fact, involved hybrid lineages or new hybridization. Of the total population, close to 15 percent possessed African ancestry, while 47 percent were classified as non-*español*.[17]

It is difficult to synthesize all of the records cited above, for the same categories are not always utilized. Nevertheless, an estimate is provided here of the racial character of Spanish-speaking California (excluding San Diego) in 1790:

españoles	364
mestizos and *coyotes*	127
mulattos	127
Indians	60
pardos	16
castas	106 (includes mestizo and other mixtures)
unknown	4
Total	804

Persons of part-African ancestry constituted at least 18 percent of the population, and in addition, the *castas* group (13 percent) undoubtedly included
many African Americans. Altogether, 55 percent of Spanish-speaking Californians were classified as non-*español*, although that percentage would be
much higher if it were possible to trace back the various lineages for several
generations. At least 20 percent of the Hispanic Alta Californians were part-
African in 1790, while probably 25 percent of the Hispanic Baja Californians
possessed African ancestry. Subsequent additions to the population of
Spanish-Mexican California probably did not greatly alter its genetic heritage, since the bulk of the later immigrants were Mexicans of mixed ancestry. After about 1800, their racial makeup was no longer recorded.

The physical appearance of the Spanish-speaking Californians did not
remain static, however. From the earliest intrusion of Spanish settlers in
1769, intermarriage with native Californians was encouraged by the Spanish
government, although the scarcity of Spanish-speaking women also contributed to that end. Over the years, therefore, the immigrants became more
Indian, genetically speaking. In addition, the Spanish-speaking people of
Caucasian, Native American, and African ancestry readily mixed, producing
what amounted to a new people.

While there was a substantial presence of persons of African ancestry in
several California pueblos with potential for upward mobility one must be
careful not to exaggerate the extent of that mobility or their sense of African
identity. First, the vast majority were only part-African and were formally
designated as persons of mixed race. Spanish California's population included a substantial number of persons of solely African ancestry, or individuals who identified themselves as such, but many, in fact, took steps to
avoid any such identification. Second, the Spanish system imposed strict
ceilings on how high persons of mixed ancestry could rise. European-born
Spaniards dominated Californian society before 1821, with American-born
Spaniards and light-skinned mixed bloods holding down the higher ranks
within the army. African Americans and other non-Spaniards were seldom
able to rise above the level of *cabo* (literally, "corporal," but actually a more
important rank) in the Spanish army, but they were able to advance in terms
of civilian activities. Examples include Manuel Nieto, the first rancher in the
area to the east and southeast of Los Angeles, a mulatto soldier who was the
son of an African man and an *española* woman and who acquired the use of
some 167,000 acres of grazing land. Juan José Dominguez, an Indian or mestizo, became the first rancher in the area south of Los Angeles, while José

Bartolomé Tapia, the son of a mulatto soldier and a mestiza, became the owner of the scenic Rancho Malibu along the Pacific Ocean. Tapia served as majordomo of the San Luis Obispo Mission, a type of supervisory post frequently held by mulattos.[18]

The children of Santiago de la Cruz Pico (mestizo) and María de la Bastida (mulatto) achieved considerable success during the Spanish period, 1769–1821. José María Pico, a son of Santiago de la Cruz Pico, served as a soldier and in 1798 became *cabo* at San Luis Obispo Mission, in charge of the soldiers stationed there. From 1805 to 1818, he served as sergeant, a high achievement for a mixed blood, and may have been promoted to *alferez* (ensign) upon his retirement. José María had three sons, one of whom became Governor Pio Pico, and seven daughters. José Dolores Pico, another son of Santiago de la Cruz Pico, while still a common soldier married Gertrudis Amezquita (mulatto*)* in 1791. After her death, he transferred north to the Monterey garrison, married Isabel Cota, an *española* from an important family, and by 1811 had become a sergeant. José Dolores led campaigns against Indians and acquired a ranch in the Salinas area a few years later. His widow died in 1869, leaving more than 100 part-African and part-American Indian descendants.

African American successes during the Spanish period had the potential to multiply after 1821, for Mexican independence brought into California new ideas of republicanism, overthrowing the European Spaniards, and breaking up the large mission estates. Mixed bloods found it easier to secure land grants, wealth, and higher military rank. However, the forces working toward greater social mobility have been obscured by the disappearance of most racial records by the early nineteenth century and the tendency simply to designate persons in California as *indio* (Indian) or *gente de razón* ("rational persons" or Spanish-speaking).[19] The main examples of persons of African ancestry achieving success in the Mexican era come first from successors to families that had already achieved prominence before 1821.

The successes of Tiburcio Tapia and the Picos illustrate this process. Tapia, born in 1789, was the son of José Bartolomé Tapia. He was at least one-eighth African and one-eighth Indian. He became a soldier at Santa Barbara and by 1824 had risen to be head of the Purísima Mission escort. He later entered business as a merchant, served in the provincial legislature, became a judge, and served twice as mayor of Los Angeles. The daughters of the Tapia family married prominent men and helped to disperse African and Indian ancestry widely, though in ever more minute quantities.

The Picos achieved greater success and social prominence than any other family of part-African descent in California. Two of the sons of José María Pico serve as good examples of African "upward mobility." Andrés Pico, born in 1810, rapidly acquired wealth and prominence by accumulating a long string of ranchos in the San Diego area. He achieved the rank of captain, served as a government official in numerous capacities, became an official delegate to Mexico City, and functioned as a military commander in several factional rebellions within California. But his greatest fame came in 1846, when he became third in command of the Mexican forces resisting the United States and helped defeat General Stephen Watts Kearny at the Battle of San Pasqual. In January 1847 Andrés Pico represented the Californians at the treaty discussions with John C. Frémont. Still later, he served as a member of the California State Legislature.

Andrés's older brother, Pio Pico, also rose rapidly after 1821. Pio Pico acquired ranches, obtained government appointments, and aspired early to the governorship. In 1834 he married María Ignacio Alvarado, a wise marriage in view of the power of the Alvarado family. María came from a "white" (Spanish) family, one of whose scions, Juan Bautista de Alvarado, dominated California politics during the 1830s and early 1840s. Pio Pico became governor in 1845, officiating until United States forces overran the province in 1846.[20] The daughters of the Pico family tended to marry socially prominent, lighter-skinned Californians or entered into unions with foreigners coming into the province.

The rise of such mixed bloods into the upper strata of Mexican Alta California society was facilitated by the increasing tendency to omit racial designations other than Spanish or Indian or by the lack of careful recording of other racial types in census records. While some scholars contend that priests and census takers continued to record racial classifications into the nineteenth century, such designations are generally missing from California pueblos after 1800. The trend toward "whitening" accelerated, as Indians and mulattos declared themselves mestizos and mestizos described themselves as *españoles*.[21] The increasing uncommonness and irrelevance of racial designations may also have reflected widespread mixing, as the lower half of the Spanish-speaking population, especially, became thoroughly hybridized. In a blending of Native American, African, and European strains, Indian descent assumed dominance due to the large number of natives in the missions, while the African influence became less conspicuous and was less often recorded.

Meanwhile, the more elite half of the Spanish-speaking population continued throughout the Mexican period to "marry light" and thus tone down any Indian or African features. This tendency was a heritage of the *calidad*, or social status, in the Spanish Empire, which had been based on race, color, occupation, and wealth, but evidence of racial origin was often the most lasting factor. Whitening was common throughout the Spanish Empire as mulattos, free blacks, and free Hispanicized Indians sought to improve their *calidad*. Such lightening intermarriage was facilitated by the willingness of the few resident European-born Spaniards to intermarry with light-skinned mixed bloods because of the shortage of Spanish women. The mixed bloods were also lightened by the settlement in California of several hundred foreign men, mostly British and Anglo American, who often married women from wealthier families. As the Picos and Tapias show, even when dark-skinned families rose to the upper strata of society during the Mexican period, they tended to "marry light" and thus gradually became "white."[22]

Thus, the early African Americans in California tended to disappear into the general population after 1800. They lost their identity as Africans, becoming *californios* or, after 1821, Mexicans. But occasionally, new individuals of African background entered the province and, for at least a generation, were identified as Africans or mulattos. One slave of unknown race was baptized at San Francisco in 1793 and was still recorded as a slave in 1798. In 1831, an African slave from Peru was brought to California. She must have soon become free, because slavery was then illegal in the Republic of Mexico. From 1838 to 1844 a Mexican African American, Ignacio Maramotes, served as *cabo* of the San Francisco military garrison. The most important Spanish-speaking African to enter California in this period was Lieutenant Colonel Manuel Victoria, the "black" governor. Victoria served as *comandante* of Baja California and was "an honest and energetic officer." In 1830 and 1831, he attempted to restore order in California and prevent a disruption in the mission system. His efforts earned him many enemies, resulting in a rebellion that led him to leave California at the end of 1831.[23]

While Spain still controlled California, but increasingly after 1821, a new chapter in the history of African Americans in the area was opened by the arrival of black settlers from the United States. The most prominent were usually of mulatto background and became accepted in Mexican society. The first known black settler from the United States, "Bob," arrived on the *Albatross* in January 1816, probably out of Boston. Baptized in 1819 as Juan

Cristobal, Bob settled in Santa Barbara and became absorbed into the California population.[24]

In 1818, several African Americans arrived in California as members of the Bouchard expedition, an Argentinean effort to liberate the Americas from Spain. Norris or Fisher [Bancroft uses both names] was captured by the Spanish at Monterey, pardoned, and served at San Juan Capistrano as a cook but later left California. Mateo José Pascual, probably an African or mulatto Argentine, was captured by Spaniards near Santa Barbara but was later exchanged for Californians taken prisoner by the Argentines. Still later, Pascual deserted the expedition and stayed in California. Francisco, an African American from the United States, meanwhile, was also captured at Monterey, later released, and also remained in California.[25]

Other African Americans undoubtedly arrived in California between 1821 and 1848, many of them escaping from U.S. vessels. One ran away from the warship *Cyane* in 1842. He took refuge among the Pomos at Clear Lake, only to be killed by Mexicans when they massacred a large number of the Indians. An African American runaway who became prominent was Allen B. Light, who probably deserted from the *Pilgrim* in 1835 and thereafter became a successful hunter along the California coast. Light participated in several California rebellions between 1836 and 1838 and became a Mexican citizen during this time. In 1839 he was appointed by Governor Alvarado to the post of *comisario general* in charge of the suppression of illegal otter hunting. Subsequently, Light settled in the San Diego area.[26]

Advancing toward the Far West from 1800 to the 1840s were numbers of English- and French-speaking fur trappers, hunters, and adventurers, sometimes called "mountain men." These rugged frontiersmen were often of racially mixed ancestry, and a number were African American. Some of these reached Mexican Territory. In 1826 Jedediah Smith led the first overland party of Anglo Americans to reach California, including Peter Ranne (or Ranee), a "man of color." The expedition traveled from the Great Salt Lake to Los Angeles. Leaving the rest of the party near Los Angeles, Smith and Ranne traveled to San Diego for an interview with Governor Echeandia. Then the entire expedition journeyed north to the Great Central Valley of California. Some of the men, including Ranne, spent the winter of 1826/27 in California while Smith returned to the Great Salt Lake. In the latter year Smith returned to California with a new group, half of which were killed by Mojave Indians on the Colorado River. Among the dead was Polette Labross, a mulatto. The balance rejoined the party left in California the previous winter, and the combined group trekked north to Oregon. There the Umpqua River Indians killed all but three of the trappers, among them Peter Ranne.[27]

Jim Beckwourth, the famous mulatto mountain man and scout, never became a permanent settler in California, but he was a frequent visitor. After spending many years as a fur trapper and leading man among the Crow Indians, Beckwourth from 1838 to 1840 joined "Peg Leg" Smith and Ute and Shawnee Indians in stealing large herds of horses in Southern California. In 1840 he married a Mexican woman in New Mexico. From 1844 to 1846 Beckwourth was back in California, taking part in a rebellion in 1845. During the next two years he served as a scout for the U.S. Army, operating between California and Missouri, and as the mail carrier from Monterey to Southern California. He took part in the California Gold Rush and became one of the first settlers in Plumas County. In 1857, however, he returned to the New Mexico-Colorado region and finally died among the Crow Indians in 1866.[28]

One of the most successful African Americans to arrive late in the Mexican period was William Alexander Leidesdorff, whose mother was a mulatto from St. Croix, Virgin Islands. From 1841 to 1845, Leidesdorff operated between San Francisco and Hawaii as a ship's captain and trader. The wealth he accumulated allowed him to purchase extensive property in still-undeveloped San Francisco. In 1844, Leidesdorff became a Mexican citizen and acquired a rancho grant in the Sacramento Valley. The following year he became the U.S. vice-consul, serving under Thomas Larkin. In 1846, he built the City Hotel at Clay and Kearny streets in San Francisco, and in 1847 he launched the first steamship ever to cruise San Francisco Bay. Bancroft notes that Leidesdorff "was not only one of [San Francisco's] most prominent businessmen, but a member of the council, treasurer, and a member of the school committee, taking an active part in local politics. . . . He was an intelligent man of fair education, speaking several languages; active, enterprising, and public-spirited." He died as a young man in 1848, one year before "descendants of Africans" were disfranchised in California.[29]

Other African Americans entered California with overland parties coming from the East. For example, one came with Joseph B. Chiles's party in 1843, settling at Sonoma. Jacob Dodson, a free black from the United States, was a volunteer member of the Frémont exploring expeditions in California from 1843 to 1845. From 1846 to 1847, Dodson took part in many campaigns against the Californians, and John C. Frémont appears to have relied upon him heavily.[30]

By the close of the Mexican era, the descendants of Africans had been al-most completely absorbed into the population of California as a whole. As of 1848 the *californio* was a complex mixture of American, European, and African, with some additional Hawaiian, Chinese, Aleut-Eskimo, Russian, British, French, and Anglo American elements also represented. Most African Americans who entered California between 1816 and 1848 were also absorbed, and thus no "black" community existed prior to the Gold Rush. Tens of thousands of descendants of those early African Americans still re-side in the state, primarily as members of the Mexican American commu-nity or the English-speaking "white" population.

The number of African Americans in California was augmented during the Gold Rush beginning in 1848. These newcomers did not at first suffer any serious discrimination. The mining districts were not overly crowded, gold was relatively abundant, and even Native Americans were allowed to pan or dig for the metal, either on their own or in the employ of others. But in 1849, white Americans became dominant in the gold region, and the intense ri-valry for riches led to antipathy toward all nonwhites. Native Americans, Mexicans, and other groups became targets for assault, and a discriminatory society rapidly emerged. The California Constitutional Convention of 1849 marked the formal close of the era of Mexican racial tolerance. In spite of the partial objections of a few Mexican American and Anglo American dele-gates, the convention voted to disfranchise "Indians, Africans, and descen-dants of Africans."[31]

Ironically, at least one of the delegates to the Constitutional Conven-tion, Antonio María Pico, was a mixed blood, but he apparently kept his silence, anticipating perhaps that the wealthy would remain able to exercise their political rights. In that he was correct, since Spanish-speaking mixed bloods were able to hold political office for several decades, especially in Southern California. In that region also, persons of African descent were sometimes able to mingle with the still dominant American indigenous and Mexican populations, at least until the opening of the railroads in the 1870s and 1880s brought in a flood tide of Anglo Americans from the East and the South.

This Anglo American migration ushered in a new era for persons of African descent in California—one that defined them rigidly and restric-tively as blacks. From then on, they would have to fight as a group for any measure of legal and social assimilation. Spanish and Mexican societies, by contrast, took race into account but allowed more rights on an individual basis. This was prompted largely by the demands of empire and later by the ideals of Mexican republicanism and egalitarianism.

The small number of Africans who entered Mexican California did not alter the fact that throughout the Mexican era there was no "black" community there, as there would be after 1850. Most persons of African ancestry were absorbed into a more general identity as *californios*. By the 1840s, a few blacks like Jacob Dodson arrived with U.S. expeditions and remained aloof or even hostile to the *californios*, but such individuals were exceptions.

The acquisition of California by the United States and the subsequent influx of thousands of white settlers during the Gold Rush marked an end to persons of African ancestry blending into the population and sometimes attaining significant social status. As was nearly universal in the antebellum United States, black people were now widely denied rights enjoyed by whites. In some western territories and states, including California during the 1850s, efforts were made to bar blacks from residing there at all. Hundreds lived in slavery despite California's formal ban on that institution.[32] Intermarriage by anyone "one-quarter or more Negro" with whites was banned in 1866, thus denying blacks, including most mulattos, the option to "whiten" that had been an escape route from the inferior status assigned to them during the Spanish and Mexican eras.[33] Instead, subjugation in various forms would be the lot of most black Californians for the next century. While the Spanish and Mexican eras were hardly free of racial discrimination, and while color played an important role in determining social and economic position, before 1848 race was not the insurmountable barrier it would become for most African Americans under U.S. rule.

The experiences of Africans in California fall into two distinct periods: before and after 1848. Before the U.S.-Mexican War, Spain and Mexico tended to accommodate, absorb, and sometimes erase Africanness. After the Treaty of Guadalupe Hidalgo, the more racially conscious United States sought to enforce a stricter system of classification. Seemingly overnight, people of African descent arriving in California entered a society where their rights were denied, their opportunities were limited, and their social position was set firmly apart. Yet, the Spanish and Mexican periods established a California legacy that would shape the lives of blacks into the twenty-first century. Central to California's appeal for African Americans were its multiracial heritage and its absence of an extended history of slavery. To be sure, black people were attracted to the state for the same reason as others: the opportunity for economic advancement. But the chance for greater social freedom and equality also resonated strongly, for black Americans in particular. The opportunities, as well as the challenges, that they encountered had deep roots in the Spanish and Mexican heritages of California.

NOTES

1. Donald C. Cutter, "Sources of the Name 'California,'" *Arizona and the West* 3 (1961): 233–36. The novel was *Las sergas de Esplandian*, written by Garcia Ordonez de Montalvo. The quote is from a nineteenth-century translation by Edward Everett Hale. Cutter regards this novel as an example of early sixteenth-century belief in "fabulous" characters (233). Therefore, the portrayal of California's inhabitants as black may have been as mythical as their depiction as Amazons, or it may reflect the extensive experiences Spaniards had with persons of African background.

2. See Jack D. Forbes, *Azteca del Norte: The Chicanos of Aztlán* (New York: Fawcett, 1973), for discussions of Mexican republican ideals. The terms African American and black will be used for persons of African and part-African descent born in the Americas (many of whom were part-American by race as well as by place of birth). American, Native American, First American, Original American, indigenous people, and Indian will be used interchangeably for persons of Americanoid (American racial) or pre-Columbian ancestry. During the colonial era, Native Americans were the only persons known generally as Americans.

3. Texts used in California that focus on the Spanish and Mexican periods generally ignore the presence of African ancestry and racial mixture. New history and social science curriculum standards for grades K–12 of California schools totally ignore an African presence and interracial marriage in California history.

4. Gary B. Nash, "The Hidden History of Mestizo America," *Journal of American History* 82 (1995): 951 (first quote); Kevin Mulroy, *Freedom on the Border: The Seminole Maroons in Florida, the Indian Territory, Coahuila, and Texas* (Lubbock: Texas Tech University Press, 1993), introduction and chap. 1; David J. Weber, *The Spanish Frontier in North America* (New Haven: Yale University Press, 1992), 326–28 (second quote). See also David J. Weber, *The Mexican Frontier, 1821–1846: The American Southwest under Mexico* (Albuquerque: University of New Mexico Press, 1982), chap. 11; and William M. Mason, *The Census of 1790: A Demographic History of Colonial California* (Menlo Park: Ballena Press, 1998). For a discussion of California's racial policy involving Native Americans, see Jack D. Forbes, *Native*

Americans of California and Nevada, rev. ed. (Happy Camp, CA: Naturegraph Publishers, 1982).

5. Nash, "Hidden History," 951; Julián Marías, *Understanding Spain* (Ann Arbor: University of Michigan Press, 1990), chap. 10; Jack D. Forbes, *Africans and Native Americans: Color, Race, and Caste in the Evolution of Red-Black Peoples.* 2d ed. (Urbana: University of Illinois Press, 1993), 39–47, 106–15. For the converse of this argument, i.e., that England had been isolated from most nonwhite peoples and therefore was especially intolerant of them, see Gary Nash, *Red, White, and Black: The Peoples of Early America* (Englewood Cliffs, NJ: Prentice-Hall, 1974); and Winthrop D. Jordan, *White over Black: Historical Origins of Racism in the United States* (New York: Oxford University Press, 1974).

6. Weber, *Spanish Frontier*, 326–27; Jack D. Forbes, *Apache, Navaho, and Spaniard* (Norman: University of Oklahoma Press, 1960), 22, 42, 76, 135, 138–39, 148, 162, 183, 189, 189 n, 214.

7. Juan Antonio Baltasar, "De Nuevos Progresos . . . ," in *Apostólicos Afanes* (Mexico: Layac, 1944), 339.

8. See Jack D. Forbes, "Black Pioneers: The Spanish-speaking Afroamericans of the Southwest," *Phylon* 28 (1966): 233–35; Mulroy, *Freedom on the Border*, 9–17.

9. Forbes, "Black Pioneers," 235–36; "Resumen General de la Población de Ambas Californias," 13 July 1795, Bancroft Library, University of California, Berkeley, C-A50, 148; Weber, *Spanish Frontier*, 39–40.

10. Jack D. Forbes, *Afro-Americans in the Far West* (Berkeley: Far West Library, 1967), passim; "Padrones y extractos . . . ," Bancroft Library, C-R9, carton 3; "Memorial of Junipero Serra, March 13, 1773," in Francisco Palou, *Historical Memoirs of New California*, Herbert E. Bolton, ed., 4 vols. (Berkeley: University of California Press, 1926), vol. 3, 33.

11. The first settlers in Los Angeles in 1781 included the following African American and part-African families:

(1) Antonio Mesa, Negro, 36, from Los Alamos; married to Ana Gertrudis López, mulatto, 27; two children: Antonia María, 8; and María Paula, 10.

(2) Manuel Camero, mulatto, 30, from Chiametla; married to María Tomasa, mulatto, 24.

(3) José Nabarro (Navarro), mestizo, 42, from El Rosario; married to María Rufina Doretea, mulatto, 47; three children: José María, 10; José Clemente, 9; and María Josefa, 4.

(4) José Moreno, mulatto, 22, from Rosario; married to Guadalupe, mulatto, 19.

(5) Basilio Rosas, *indio*, 67, from Nombre de Dios, Durango; married to María

Manuela Calistra, mulatto, 43; six children: José Maxim, 15; Carlos, 12; Antonio Rosalino, 7; José Marcelino, 4; Esteban, 2; and María Josefa, 8.

(6) Luís Quintero, Negro, 65, from Guadalajara; married to Petra Rubin, mulatto, 40; five children: María Gertrudis, 16; María Concepción, 9; Tomás, 7; Rafaela, 6; and José Clemente, 3.

Two of the adult males were classified as Negro but their wives were mulattos and their children, therefore, also were mulattos. The wives also could have possessed either American or European ancestry. One of the adult males listed above was Indian, while another was mestizo. In both cases, the wives were mulattos and the nine children, or 20 percent of the population, were American-African-Caucasian hybrids.

An examination of all of the families in Los Angeles reveals the following marriage pattern:

Negro-mulatto—2 families

Indian-Indian—2 families

mulatto-mulatto—2 families

español-Indian—2 families

Mestizo-mulatto—1 family

Indian-mulatto—1 family

Indian-coyote (3/4 Indian)—1 family

Of the eleven Los Angeles families, only the two all-Indian marriages did not involve race mixture.

Sources: "Padrones y extractos . . . ," Bancroft Library, C-R9, carton 3; "Padrón de Los Angeles," 17 August 1790, Bancroft Library, C-A5, 159–64. See also John M. Weatherway, *The Founders of Los Angeles* (Los Angeles: Bryant Foundation, 1954); and William Mason, "Tracking the Founders of Los Angeles," *Museum Alliance Quarterly* 6 (1967): 26–28, 30.

12. These post-1781 settlers included the following families:

(1) José Ontiveras, mestizo, 47, from Real del Rosario; married to Anna María Carrassca, mulatto, 36; one child: María Encarnación, mulatto, 7.

(2) Santiago de la Cruz Pico, mestizo, 60, from San Javier de Cavasón; married to Jasinta de la Bastida, mulatto, 53; two children living with them: Javier, mulatto, 23; and Patricio, mulatto, 27.

(3) Domingo Aruz, *español*, 43, from Gerona, Spain; married to Gertrudis Quitero, mulatto, 26; two mestizo children from a previous marriage: José and Domingo; three children of present marriage: Martín, mulatto, 7; José, mulatto, 14; and Domingo, mulatto, 12.

(4) Francisco Reyes, mulatto, 43, from Pueblo of Spotlan; married to María

del Carmen Dominguez, mestiza, 23; three children: Antonio Faustin, mulatto, 4; Juana Inocencia, mulatto, 3; and José Jasinto, mulatto, 2.

(5) Faustino José de la Cruz, mulatto, 18, from San Blas; single.

Source: "Padrón de Los Angeles," 17 August 1790, Bancroft Library, C-A5, 159–64.

13. The twenty-five Los Angeles families of the 1790 census showed the following marriage pattern:

español-español—7 families
español-mestizo—4 families
mestizo-mulatto—4 families
español-coyote—3 families
Indian-Indian—2 families
mulatto-mulatto—2 families
español-Indian—1 family
español-mulatto—1 family
Indian-mulatto—1 family

Sources: "Padrón de Los Angeles," and "Estado del Censo y Castas," 31 December 1792, Bancroft Library, C-A50, 103–4.

14. The sixteen part-African families of Santa Barbara included the following:

(1) José Gonzalez, mulatto, 35; married to Tomasa, mulatto, 13.

(2) Felipe Moreno, mulatto, 46; married to Loreta, Indian, 22.

(3) Josef Hores, *español*, 33; married to María de la Concepción, mulatto, 14; one child.

(4) José Orchaga, mulatto, 29; married to María, *español*, 21; two children.

(5) José Patiño, mulatto, 45; married to María Victoria, *coyote*, 28.

(6) Agustín Leyva, mulatto, 45; married to María Guadalupe, *español*, 42; five children.

(7) José Velarde, mulatto, 40; married to Juliana, Indian, 45.

(8) José Ontiveras, mestizo, 39; married to Ana María, mulatto, 34; two children.

(9) Eugenio Valdéz, *español*, 30; married to Sebastiana, mulatto, 19; two children.

(10) Joaquín Rodríquez, mestizo, 25; married to Catrina, mulatto, 20; one child.

(11) Rosalino Fernández, mulatto, 28; married to Juana, mulatto, 22; three children.

(12) Mariano Pina, mulatto, 25; single.

(13) José Cisneros, mulatto, 26; married but wife not with him.

(14) José Acevedo, mulatto, 30; single.

(15) Luciano Masauegas, mulatto, 30; widower.

(16) José Lorenzo Valdés, *lobo*, 19. [In my 1966 article, "Black Pioneers," I define *lobo* as "an Indian-Negro mixed-blood, perhaps with some Caucasian ancestry."]

The marriage pattern of all forty-five Santa Barbara families is as follows:

español-español—17 families
español-mestizo—5 families
español-mulatto—4 families
español-Indian—3 families
mulatto-mulatto—3 families
mestizo-mestizo—3 families
Indian-*coyote*—2 families
mestizo-mulatto—2 families
mulatto-Indian—2 families
mulatto-*coyote*—1 family
Indian-Indian—1 family
mestizo-*coyote*—1 family
español-coyote—1 family

Sources: "Padrón de la Población de Santa Barbara," and "Estado del Censo y Castas," 31 December 1792, Bancroft Library, C-A50, 6–10, 103.

15. San José's part-African families in 1790 included:

(1) Antonio Romero, *pardo*, 40, from Guadalajara; married to Petra Acevez, 28, *parda*; one son.

(2) Manuel González, Indian, 70, from Valle de San Bartolo (Durango); married to Gertrudis Acevez, *parda*, 20; two sons: ages 18 and 13 (by a previous marriage).

(3) Bernardo Rosales, mulatto, 46, from Parras (Durango); married to Mónica, 28, Indian; four children.

(4) Manuel Amesquita, mulatto, 38, from Terrenate (Sonora); married to Graciana, mulatto, 26; four children.

(5) Antonio Acevez, mulatto, 50, from San Bartolomé (Durango); married to Feliciana Cortes, mestiza, 50; two children.

The marriage pattern among the total population of San José was as follows:

español-español—6 families
pardo-pardo—1 family
coyote-Indian—1 family
Indian-*pardo*—1 family
mulatto-Indian—1 family

mulatto-mulatto—1 family

mestizo-*español*—1 family

Indian-*español*—1 family

mulatto-mestizo—1 family

Indian-Indian—1 family

Sources: "Padrón de Vecinos de San José," 5 October 1790, Bancroft Library, C-A50, 61–64; and "Padrón del Pueblo San José," 31 December 1790, Bancroft Library, C-A8, 91.

16. "Estada que manidiesta el número de Vasallos y habitantes," 31 December 1791, Bancroft Library, C-A50, 101.

17. The 1782 census for San Francisco, listing only adult males, included the following part-Africans:

(1) J. A. Amesquita, mulatto, 43, from Metape.

(2) Ignacio Linares, mulatto, 37, from Orcasitas.

(3) Justo R. Altamirano, mulatto, 37, from Aguage.

(4) Juan A. Vásquez, mulatto, 47, from Agulalco.

(5) Antonio Aceves, mulatto, 42, from San Bartolomé (at San José in 1790)

(6) Felipe Tapía, mulatto, 37, from Culiacán

The 1790 San Francisco census expanded on the above by adding these individuals:

(1) Nicholas Galindo, mestizo, 47, from Real de Santa Eulalia (Durango); married to María Teresa Pinto, mulatto, 34; six children.

(2) José María Martínez, mestizo, 35, from Tapague (Sonora); married to María García, mulatto, 18.

(3) José Acevez, mulatto, 26, from San Bartolomé (Durango), single.

(4) Pablo Acevez, mulatto, 18, from Culiacán, single.

The marriage pattern in San Francisco in 1790 was as follows:

español-español—11 families

español-mestizo—6 families

mestizo-mulatto—2 families

español-Indian—1 family

español-mulatto—1 family

Indian-Indian—1 family

mestizo-Indian—1 family

mestizo-mestizo—1 family

Sources: "Padrón de San Francisco," 21 August 1782, Bancroft Library, C-R9, carton 3; and "Padrón de San Francisco," 2 October 1790, Bancroft Library, C-A50, 86–90. For a discussion of Spanish-speaking persons living throughout the Bay Area during the colonial period, see Jack D. Forbes, "Hispano-Mexican Pioneers of the San Francisco Bay Region: An Analysis of Racial Origins," *Aztlán* 14 (1983): 174–89.

18. Sources for this discussion of African American pioneers are summarized in note 25.

19. See Lisbeth Haas, *Conquests and Historical Identities in California, 1769–1936* (Berkeley: University of California Press, 1995), 30.

20. The last Mexican governor of California is overdue a book-length biography. For accounts of Pio Pico's life, see Martin Cole and Henry Welcome, eds., *Don Pio Pico's Historical Narrative* (Glendale: The Arthur H. Clark Company, 1973), 12–21; and Marian G. Cannon, "Pio Pico: The Last Don," *Westways* 73 (1981): 49–51, 80.

21. Weber, *Spanish Frontier*, 328.

22. For further discussion of this period, see Jack D. Forbes, *The Indian in America's Past* (Englewood Cliffs, NJ: Prentice-Hall, 1964), 147–51; Forbes, "Black Pioneers," 243ff. Much of the discussion is based upon research in the *padrones* (censuses) of the California Archives, Bancroft Library; Hubert Howe Bancroft, *History of California, 1769–1848*, 7 vols. (San Francisco: History Company, 1886), vols. 1 and 2; Hubert Howe Bancroft, *California Pastoral* (San Francisco: History Company, 1888); and Hubert Howe Bancroft, *Pioneer Register* [and Index] *1542–1848* (San Francisco: History Co., 1886). See Forbes, "Hispano-Mexican Pioneers," for additional sources; and see also Jack D. Forbes, "The Founders of Los Angeles," *Simi Valley News-Advertiser*, 25 August 1960, 4; *The Northridger*, 9 February 1962; *The Flatlands* (Oakland) 2 (1967): 3; "California's Non-White Governors," *The Flatlands*, 2 (1967): 7; *Oakland Post*, 10 January 1968, 2; and "California's Black Pioneers," *Liberator* 8 (1968): 6–9.

23. Victoria had made a name for himself as a lieutenant colonel in Baja California before being named governor in March 1830. He quickly gained enemies for his executions of several Indians charged with crimes and by 1831 was widely called "a cruel, blood-thirsty monster . . . as well as others asserting that he was a full-blooded negro [sic]." In December of that year he was overthrown by armed rebellion. Hubert H. Bancroft, *History of California*, vol. 2, 181, 189–93, 198 (quote). This is Bancroft's only reference to why Victoria should have been described as of African ancestry, and it could be seen as a pejorative rather than an accurate racial designation. More likely, Victoria, like the second governor, Pio Pico, had some African features, which became the focus of negative innuendo.

24. Bancroft, *History of California*, vol. 2, 277, 277 n, 722.

25. Ibid., vol. 2, 230–32, 231 n, 237, 241; Bancroft, *California Pastoral*, vol. 1, 283. Bancroft's is the most detailed work on these early California settlers of African

ancestry, but he lumps them together as "foreign Africans" or "Negroes" without a clear designation of their nationality. Bob, having come from a U.S. ship, was almost certainly an African American; whether any of the others were is uncertain. Bancroft, *History of California*, vol. 2, 248, 393.

26. Dr. Sandels, "King's Orphan," Bancroft Library, C-E 105, 7; Bancroft, *History of California*, vol. 4, 302, 311, 314, 362–63. For other works on Light, see David J. Weber, "A Black American in Mexican San Diego: Two Recently Discovered Documents," *Journal of San Diego History* 20 (1974): 29–32; and Rudolph M. Lapp, *Blacks in Gold Rush California* (New Haven: Yale University Press, 1977), 4.

27. Dale L. Morgan, *Jedediah Smith and the Opening of the West* (Indianapolis: Bobbs-Merrill, 1953), 194–95, 204, 210, 236, 240, 257, 267, 278.

28. Juan Francisco Dana, *The Blond Ranchero* (Los Angeles: Dawson's Bookstore, 1960), 30; and see James P. Beckwourth, *The Life and Adventures of James P. Beckwourth, as Told to Thomas D. Bonner* (1856; reprint, Lincoln: University of Nebraska Press, 1972), 466–76, 504–29. See also Dellmont R. Oswald, "James P. Beckwourth," in LeRoy Hafen, ed., *The Mountain Men and the Fur Trade of the Far West*, vol. 6 (Glendale, CA: Arthur H. Clark Company, 1968), 37–60; and David J. Weber, *The Mexican Frontier*, 101–2.

29. Bancroft, *History of California*, vol. 4, 711. See also W. Sherman Savage, "The Influence of Alexander Leidesdorff on the History of California," *Journal of Negro History* 38 (1953): 322–32.

30. Bancroft, *History of California*, vol. 4, 394 n; Bancroft, *Pioneer Register*, 129; Allan Nevins, *Frémont, the West's Greatest Adventurer*, 2 vols. (New York: Harper and Brothers, 1928), vol. 1, 139.

31. Robert F. Heizer and Alan F. Almquist, *The Other Californians* (Berkeley: University of California Press, 1971), 92–115, et seq. See also Lapp, *Blacks in Gold Rush California*, especially chaps. 4, 6–9.

32. Tomás Almaguer, *Racial Fault Lines: The Historical Origins of White Supremacy in California* (Berkeley: University of California Press, 1994), 34–40. Discrimination against blacks in nineteenth-century California is detailed in essays in this anthology by Lawrence de Graaf and Quintard Taylor and by Willi Coleman.

33. Elliot G. Mears, *Resident Orientals on the American Pacific Coast: Their Legal and Economic Status* (New York: Institute of Pacific Relations, 1927), 149–50.

African American Women and Community
Development in California, 1848–1900

WILLI COLEMAN

Traditional U.S. frontier history has taken little notice of population groups other than Native Americans and European Americans, and it has long neglected the role of women. Even popular images of the white female pioneer "have almost always emphasized her gentility and passivity. Painting after painting features a woman in a wagon, babe in arms, being led across the plains. Metaphorically carrying American civilization westward as she literally cradles the next generation, the pioneer woman has little opportunity to act as an individual in her own right." [1]

The traditional portraits of the inhabitants of the American West have been challenged during the last two decades, however, by new historical narratives that have more deeply explored the lives of European American women and added other faces—Native Americans, Asian Americans, Chicanos and Chicanas, and African American men—to the western historical saga. Black women have lagged behind, however. As recently as 1987, an important anthology with the inclusive title *The Women's West*—a book clearly informed by the "new social history"—commented on the importance of including African Americans in "jointly interpreting our interrelated histories" but did little more than suggest that black women had been present. Unlike African American women in other regions of the United States, whose history had to be rescued from stereotype, in the West they have remained largely invisible. Whether in movies, textbooks and novels, or on television, images of females voyaging westward did not raise the specter of race; these women were portrayed as white as they traveled to the Golden State, to the West, and into history. Even in W. Sherman Savage's pioneer work on African

Americans, *Blacks in the West* (1976), brief mentions of but a few celebrated individuals represent most of the discussion of black women.[2]

But by the mid-1980s, black women began to assume their place in the historical narrative, adding layers of meaning to western history, and the process has accelerated in the 1990s. Quintard Taylor's sweeping 1998 survey of African Americans in the West, *In Search of the Racial Frontier*, updated Savage's work and added a significant emphasis on women. When an entire issue of *California History* was devoted to African Americans in 1996, the consulting editor chosen was Shirley Ann Wilson Moore, a leading historian of black women of the West. William Loren Katz's 1997 annual banquet address to the Western History Association was titled "Black Western Women: Images and Realities." Indications that black women's history in the West was being taken seriously could be subtle, as when the Library of Congress introduced to its classifications the subject heading "Afro-American Women Pioneers" in 1996. But the new inclusivity could also be clearly announced, as in the mission statement of the landmark Women of the West Museum in Boulder, Colorado, which promises to "trace and interpret the multicultural history and contributions of women in the American West," in part through an exhibit of the "five major cultures in the American West"—one of which will be African American.[3]

Women of African ancestry held a place in California history long before the area became part of the United States. As many studies are beginning to illustrate, the black presence began in the Spanish colonial era. When settlers from Sonora and Sinaloa arrived at the site that would become Los Angeles in 1781, there was already a population of African and part-African residents in Alta California. That more than half of the Los Angeles pueblo's first settlers were of African ancestry is well known; less familiar is the fact that half of those individuals were female. Spanish censuses documented descriptions of female settlers by using designations such as *mulata*, meaning a Spanish and African mix, and *morisca*, meaning a light-skinned *mulata*. For some there was the catch-all category "race unknown." An apparently wide range of decidedly African (or Indian) physical features among women elicited a revealing comment from one census taker: "Most of the women were mixed-bloods of somewhat doubtful affiliations." Such racially "doubtful" women included various mixtures of Indian, Spanish, and African bloodlines. Thus it is little wonder that at least 70 percent of the pueblo's first children had mothers defined as *mulatas*. This increasingly multiracial population inhabited all of Spanish-speaking California.[4]

By the time of the war between Mexico and the United States, the Pico family had become a powerful force in California. The Picos, who had been a part of eighteenth-century Spanish Mexico's history, remained economically and politically powerful throughout Mexican independence. During the nineteenth century, Pio Pico served as the last governor to preside over Mexican California, while his brother Andrés served as a general, successfully engaging in battle against American forces. After the signing of the Treaty of Guadalupe Hidalgo in 1848, members of the Pico clan retained their influence and wealth and became part of a more homogeneous California society. The fact that María Jacinta de la Bastida, the grandmother of Pio and Andrés, was described in the 1790 census of Los Angeles as *mulata* appeared to be of little consequence in the lives of her descendants. As a result, by the time the United States took a census of California—1850—*californios* listed as black had virtually disappeared. While intermarriage had almost completely hidden most evidence of African ancestry in California's population by 1825, "Negro" characteristics among both the elite and the general population remained visible. Class, money, personal ambition, and the desire of the ruling classes for Native American and black allies produced a flexibility toward accommodating people of color within California.5

While those Africans who arrived in California prior to 1848 blended with Indian, Mexican, and even Spanish peoples, post–Gold Rush immigrants would not be so easily assimilated. Admission to the United States also inducted California into a society where racial lines were more rigidly drawn than in the Spanish and Mexican eras, though the state held the promise of greater freedom and opportunity for black people than elsewhere in the Union. With the discovery of gold luring people from around the world, women and men of African descent began to arrive in noticeable numbers, drawn by the goal of economic opportunity and the belief that one could have, in California, a life free from racial bigotry. By 1849, free blacks as far away as New York and Massachusetts read newspaper articles announcing that "the merest Negro could make more than our present governor." Former Missourian Peter Brown, who worked a mining claim near Sacramento in 1851, wrote to his wife, Alley, in Sainte Genevieve, Missouri: "This is the best place for black folks on the globe. All a man has to do is work, and he will make money."6

A poignant image of black migration to California during the Gold Rush era is provided in Margaret Frink's description of an African American woman she encountered in 1850 near the Humboldt Sink, the desert just east of the Sierra Nevada. Frink recalled the woman "carrying a cast-iron bake stove on her head, with her provisions and a blanket piled on top . . . bravely pushing on for California." Yet for most black women, travel to California was a family affair—they crossed the western United States as wives, mothers, daughters, or some other designation within a kinship network. Occasionally women and children were left behind as "father pioneered the way through various states, and when he found a place which he felt would be prosperous, he sent for his family." For African Americans, there was a particularly touching twist to the traditional scenarios in which men traveled ahead of their families into frontier areas in search of a better life. Both women and men saw California as a place that could provide the means for freedom not only for themselves but also for family members still enslaved in the South or living in conditions closely approximating slavery. On occasion, female relatives "sent for" women and children. In other instances, black California women relied upon community donations to "secure the purchase" of enslaved family members living elsewhere. In one striking illustration of the role the family could play, the life of sculptor Edmonia Lewis was changed irrevocably when her brother, a California gold miner, financed her education at Oberlin College, thus launching her subsequent successful career in art.7

The African Americans who populated California by 1860 represented a unique segment of both the American and the African diaspora. Forty-one percent of San Francisco's blacks had come from northern states; 37 percent came from the South. Seven percent had arrived from such distant locations as England, Chile, France, Hawaii, and Africa, as well as from neighboring Mexico. As might be expected, most of those who identified themselves as foreign-born were men living in San Francisco, the gateway to the rest of the state. But even among tiny Calaveras County's four black females in 1852, one claimed to be a native of Africa and a second was from Chile. Scattered through the other counties were black women who had arrived from such far-off places as the Sandwich Islands and the Virgin Islands.8

No matter their place of origin, nineteenth-century black Californians disproportionately chose cities as their place of settlement after reaching the state. In 1852, San Francisco and Sacramento accounted for 33 percent of the state's black inhabitants, with 20 percent of the total in San Francisco alone. The balance—a majority through most of the 1850s—settled in the gold-mining counties. Eight years later, San Francisco and Sacramento were home to 40 percent of the state's black population. African American females shared with their male counterparts a preference for the city; indeed, black women concentrated in urban areas in larger percentages than either black men or white women. Yet they could also be found in outlying gold-mining hamlets such as Strawberry and Rough and Ready, or coastal communities such as Santa Cruz.9

Throughout the nineteenth century, California's African American women formed a distinct minority. In 1850, they constituted 9 percent of the total black population. The gender ratio improved by 1860, when 31 percent of African Americans in California were female. San Francisco's black population was particularly imbalanced; in 1860 there were 261 males for every 100 females. Sacramento shows a greater balance. In 1850, nearly 19 percent of its black population was female. By 1860, the male-female ratio was not more than two to one in three of its four wards. As one scholar has observed, "Given the overwhelmingly male population of Sacramento in the early 1850s, the number of black women, though small, reflected as much parity with its male population as any other group. These figures suggest that the black migration to Sacramento was remarkably family-oriented." By the end of the century, this characteristic was statewide, as females grew to 48 percent of the state's African American population.10

Research into census data reveals a group of African American women who differed from other black women across the nation and from nonblack women in California. Besides being older, having fewer children, and congregating in cities, these women possessed a remarkably high rate of literacy. In 1860, when the overwhelming majority of African Americans were illiterate, 74 percent of California's black female population could read and write. Three decades later, a larger percentage of black than white girls attended school for six or more months per year. This high degree of literacy produced cultural tastes, social life, and a concern for education that collectively gave a majority of blacks in cities like San Francisco a middle-class upbringing by 1880. It is little wonder that these African Americans have been described as "a select class of blacks already living in the North, or southern blacks who were able and willing to break with their traditional culture." 11

Although California had entered the Union as a free state in 1850 with a constitution that had specifically outlawed slavery the year before, the social and legal status of enslaved blacks remained unclear for the rest of the decade. Not only were there loopholes in the laws governing the holding of slaves, but slaveholders also seemed convinced that they could keep their

TABLE 1. African American Women in California, 1850–1900

| | | African American Population | | |
| | | | | Percent |
Year	Total Population	Total	Female	Female
1850	92,597	962	90	9
1860	379,994	4,086	1,259	31
1870	560,247	4,272	1,758	41
1880	864,694	6,018	2,551	42
1890	1,208,130	11,322	4,975	44
1900	1,485,053	11,045	5,279	48

bond servants because "no one [would] put themselves to the trouble of investigating the matter." Masters used newspapers to post notices about runaway blacks and to sell the services of slaves, as indicated in an advertisement for "a valuable Negro Girl . . . a good washer, ironer, and cook."[12]

Agitating for freedom and freeing those still enslaved were among the first battles fought. Joining with abolitionist whites, blacks both free and unfree refused to accept slavery in any guise. In the words of one contemporary observer, "The Negroes exhibit a great deal of energy and intelligence in saving their brothers."[13] Women were among the rescuers and the rescued, using both legal and extralegal means to attain freedom. One "old colored woman" was accused of "stealing" a young Mary Ann Harris from her master for the sole purpose of setting her free. An equally heroic act succeeded through the combined efforts of a courageous slave woman, free blacks, and a white sheriff willing to "arrest" slaves to prevent their removal from the state. Bridget "Biddy" Mason and her children were brought to San Bernardino in 1851 as slaves. With encouragement from free African Americans in Los Angeles, she challenged her owner's attempt to move her family to Texas in 1855. When it became apparent that the owner, who was illegally holding the Mason family in bondage, might try to remove them forcibly from the state, the Los Angeles County sheriff placed them under his protection in the county jail. Mason then petitioned the local court for freedom for herself and her family. Los Angeles District Court Judge Benjamin Hayes, citing California's prohibition of slavery, ruled that "all of the said persons of color are entitled to their freedom and are free forever."[14]

Along with their resistance to slavery, California's African Americans also waged a battle to have their voices heard in the state's courts. In April 1850, a new law introduced legal limitations on all residents of color by barring anyone with "one-eighth part or more of Negro blood . . . and every person who shall have one-half Indian blood" from testifying for or against any white person. African Americans, however, challenged their legal status as defenseless victims. One of the earliest attempts to overcome the prohibition of testimony came in 1850 from an unlikely source—a legal suit by an African American woman against her European American common-law husband. In Sacramento, Sarah Carrol filed a charge of grand larceny against one H. Potter. Demanding redress for the loss of $700 in gold pieces and other valuable items, Carrol revealed yet another side of California Gold Rush history:

> I have lived with the defendant for some time past. I have never said I was his wife but others have said that we were husband and wife. . . . The money in the trunk was partly his and partly mine but no part of the $700 was his. The defendant kept no part of his clothes in the trunk and he was not permitted to have access to it. . . . He told me he had taken the money. I asked him to return it. I never gave him permission to use my money. I paid my own expenses.

Sarah Carrol's attempt to regain her funds through the court system took a disappointing turn when the accused Potter, establishing his identity as a white man, brought the proceedings to a halt, since there was "none but Colored testimony against him."[15]

Women who attempted to challenge the imbalance of power upon which the testimony law was based risked more than simply having their lawsuits thrown out of court. Such was the case when the owner of a millinery shop witnessed a thief removing money from her cash drawer. Outraged because the woman had followed him into the street shouting and identifying him as a thief, the culprit returned the next day and shot her brother to death. During the trial, a witness to the crime, described as Portuguese, was disqualified when it was discovered that he had a certain "kink" in his hair. Accused of having a trace of African blood, the witness was ruled unqualified to testify against a white defendant. It was not until a white witness was found that the defendant was charged with second-degree murder. Although black women in such cases were unable to predict the consequences that might result from forcing themselves upon a reluctant judicial system, they continued to thrust themselves into the public arena to air their grievances.[16]

The precarious legal standing of black Californians led to a series of conventions in which African Americans heralded their economic progress while challenging the testimony ban and the denial of their civil rights. In November 1855, the First Convention of the Colored Citizens of California was held at the Colored Methodist Church in Sacramento. This mostly male assembly did not address questions of gender, but the presence of a lone woman among more than fifty men became a matter of official record when "a resolution was placed in the hands of the business committee by . . . a lady from Tuolumne County." Mrs. Alfred J. White not only received an effusive and flowery welcome but also was assured, "Where the ladies are with us, and approve, we are satisfied that we are right." When the second convention met in Sacramento the next year, California's leading black male political activists had become accustomed to accepting financial support from "ladies . . . in support of the cause."[17]

Such activist women lived in a state where various racial groups lived in close proximity and constantly faced the challenges of discrimination.[18] A vibrant black community developed in California by 1860, with women playing an important role. In part, the state may have tolerated their activism because African Americans did not present some of the problems that other groups did. Unlike Native Americans, blacks did not need to be pushed from lands that whites coveted, be settled elsewhere, or be provided for after their land and resources had been appropriated. Unlike many Chinese and Mexicans, they spoke English, and they did not immigrate in threatening numbers. But African Americans had struggles of their own. The desire of white Californians to prohibit slavery in their new state had owed less to abolitionist moral sentiment than to the "free-soil" argument: that a society free of slavery, and the blacks that slavery brought with it, offered greater freedom and opportunity for the common white man.[19]

As California passed statutes that mimicked southern discrimination in such matters as segregation and the right to testify, black women took a prominent role in challenging these restrictions and exploring economic opportunities. A number sought to emulate Victorian standards of ladyhood, as one of the major goals shared by former slaves, however fruitlessly, was to free wives from work outside the home. California's former slaves, male and female, had shared with others "the rough 'equality' of powerlessness" during their bondage, but "with freedom came developments that strengthened patriarchy within the black family and institutionalized the notion that men and women should inhabit separate spheres."[20] But women were also bolstered in their activism and economic pursuits by a long tradition of free black women working in cities and of slave women who often had to build families and communities without men, who had been sold away or who lived on different farms or plantations. As in other states, the California African American community was shaped by a tradition of free and slave women assuming active leadership roles.

California's 4,086 African American citizens, as of 1860, represented less than 1 percent of the state's total population, yet evidence of their social institutions could be found throughout the state. Areas with the largest urban populations could boast of having their own Masonic lodges, billiard saloons, bathhouses, and brass bands.[21] A tradition of pioneering black newspapers in the West began with *The Mirror of the Times* in San Francisco in 1855. Within the next decade, there was a strong and steady line of information regularly transferred not only between blacks within the state but also nationally.[22] Even as other arrivals attempted to find ways to remove, ignore, or neutralize the black presence among them, African Americans relentlessly continued the work of carving out a place for themselves in California.

Although few communities were able to publish their own newspapers, even those with the smallest populations could establish formal or informal churches. While San Franciscans could boast of an African Methodist Episcopal (AME) Zion Church holding services in a building large enough to accommodate 800 worshipers in 1864, smaller congregations managed to survive in pockets throughout the state. Before purchasing a synagogue to convert to its own uses in 1860, the congregation of Sacramento's Siloam Baptist Church convened for several years with a borrowed minister in a Chinese chapel. Equally tenacious congregations could be found in Marysville and Stockton.[23] In buildings complete with "bells, belfry, and organ," or in shacks adapted to serve a higher cause, the role of African American women in the church most frequently followed traditional patterns already established "down south" or "back east." By holding "ladies' festivals," tea parties, picnics, and food fairs, African American women made it possible to buy, construct, or rent church buildings. Once these churches were established, women provided a substantial portion of the monetary and physical resources required to support them.[24]

Most of California's African American women attained their accomplishments in obscurity. Two exceptions to what has amounted to historical invisibility are Biddy Mason and Mary Ellen ("Mammy") Pleasant. By 1866, Mason had purchased the first in a series of properties that eventually would make her one of the richest self-made women in the state. Her financial genius was balanced by strong philanthropic sensibilities. She ran what amounted to a social service agency and regularly paid grocery bills for hungry families, found work for the unemployed, and provided shelter for the homeless. In addition to maintaining her own family, Mason became known as "a resource for settlers of all races." The first black church in Los Angeles began with meetings in her home. Even though she did not attend the First A M E Church after the membership moved into its own building, Mason paid its property taxes on more than one occasion.[25]

Known as a "good and pious" slave woman who rose to unimaginable heights in nineteenth-century California, Biddy Mason had a counterpart in the north of the state, another former slave, whose life offers a second view of an exceptional black woman. Unlike Mason, who had reached California on foot, Mary Ellen Pleasant arrived in San Francisco by ship as a free woman of mysterious but independent means. As if setting the stage for great things to come, "Before she had so much as left the wharf at which her ship had docked . . . [she] sold her services at auction for five hundred dollars a month, with the stipulation that she would do no washing, not even dishwashing."[26]

From that beginning, Pleasant became immersed in the social and political life of both the black and white communities in California. Like Mason, Pleasant invested money in real estate, continued to work in traditional female caretaker roles among whites, and found ways to address problems that plagued the black community. In spite of her suggested involvement in helping runaway slaves and offering financial support to the abolitionist John Brown, Pleasant's image as a social activist paled beside more titillating descriptions of a bordello-running voodoo queen imbued with the power to cloud the minds of San Francisco's wealthy power brokers. Whatever funds she may have gained from such enterprises were often used to provide employment to San Francisco's growing African American population. One writer claims that Pleasant put some fifty people to work during the 1850s and set up several in businesses. The black press praised her as a noble-hearted and philanthropic woman, viewing her support of black ministers as "strengthening the arms of God's servant." She was an active church participant who could chair committees with both male and female members, make "neat little speeches," or donate funds.[27]

By the 1860s, California's African American women began to demonstrate publicly their resistance to the status quo through their pursuit of civil rights. Within communities that perceived themselves as being constantly under siege, women stepped into the fray in a variety of ways. The treatment of black passengers on California's public transportation lines caused particular outrage. Vulnerable to the mood and temperament of white operators and passengers, black women and children, in particular, risked verbal insult and bodily injury on streetcars and trains. They were regularly denied entry, forcibly separated from other passengers, or physically removed from moving vehicles. Black California women, denied even the most minimal forms of deference and protection reserved for white women in the Victorian era, took particular offense at such public forms of discrimination.[28]

When Charlotte Brown filed a suit against San Francisco's Omnibus line in 1863, after being ejected from a car, she entered the ranks of pioneers who used the legal system to gain access to public transportation. Brown, the daughter of civil rights activist James E. Brown, won her case in the county court. Within days of the judgment, however, she and her father were forced from a streetcar when they demanded the right to sit inside the vehicle rather than stand on an outside platform. Again, a ruling in Brown's favor did not protect her from public humiliation. As she repeatedly returned to the courts, San Francisco's white newspapers criticized her for her persistence, prompting a rebuttal from the local black press. The *Pacific Appeal*, for example, objected to San Franciscans who "pretend to be interested in our elevation and coldly permit us to suffer these indignities." Although Charlotte Brown waged a two-year battle, winning judgments in both county and district courts, African American rights in streetcars remained tenuous.[29]

In October 1866, one year after Brown's most significant victory, Mary Ellen Pleasant followed her in seeking redress in the courts after being removed from an Omnibus Railroad Company streetcar. Pleasant charged racial discrimination, but she later withdrew her claim when company officials assured her that "negroes would hereafter be allowed to ride on the car." Two years later Pleasant filed another lawsuit that entered the annals of California's legal history as *John J. Pleasant and Mary E. v. North Beach and Mission R.R. Company* after one of the company drivers refused to take the San Francisco businesswoman aboard. Pleasant's lawsuit paralleled another legal action against the North Beach Railroad by Emma J. Turner. Although both

Pleasant and Turner won their respective suits in the county court, with Pleasant receiving a $500 judgment, the California Supreme Court over-turned both rulings. The legal campaigns initiated by Brown, the Pleasants, and Turner continued until 1893, when California's state assembly enacted an antidiscrimination statute prohibiting streetcar segregation and exclusion.[30]

African Americans in nineteenth-century California also sought access to public schools, initiating a campaign in the 1850s that would last well into the twentieth century. Their efforts initially focused on obtaining education by any means. California's first law authorizing public schools left both funding and the inclusion of nonwhites up to local officials. San Francisco, Sacramento, and most other communities followed the pattern of many northern states in excluding African Americans from public schools and leaving the funding of any "colored" school to private charity. This policy led blacks to found the first two African American schools in California in 1854, in Sacramento and San Francisco. The Sacramento school was orga-nized in the home of Elizabeth Thorn Scott, an African American woman originally from New Bedford, Massachusetts. San Francisco's first black school met in Saint Cyprian A M E Church. By 1855, Sacramento's school board assumed support for the city's "colored school," and two years later San Francisco's board of education followed the state capital's lead. But public funds proved inadequate, so black women again assumed a signifi-cant role, especially in Sacramento, by forming school committees to raise funds to supplement meager public revenues. Such activities continued until 1866, when the state legislature again presented California's black com-munity with a "half loaf" in the form of a school bill that provided full pub-lic funding but even more explicitly mandated segregated schools for chil-dren of black, "Mongolian," or Indian descent. Segregated facilities proved inadequate, as indicated in an 1862 petition calling attention to the appalling conditions faced by the 300 African American children in San Francisco's black school. In one school, fifty black boys and girls were taught in a single room in a basement below the street where "the air came laden—foul and unhealthful," study was disturbed by noise from a military band in the room above, and "the plastering is broken and falling from the ceiling, so that the water from above runs through the floor upon the desks and floor of the schoolroom beneath."[31]

Not all African American families accepted the separate black schools. In 1857, fifteen-year-old Sarah Lester, the daughter of Peter Lester, a well-known, politically active black businessman, became the center of attention when attempts were made to remove her from the city's only high school. Lester had been accepted into the high school because she was very light skinned as well as intelligent, traits that explain much of the sympathy and pressure for her to be allowed to stay. But a pro-slavery newspaper, the *San Francisco Herald*, pressured the school board to enforce the law and keep all black students—however light—away from whites. In the ensuing citywide debate, parents and students entered the fray; both those who favored her staying and those who were opposed threatened a boycott. Several African American families joined the fight by attempting to register their children in the high school. The superintendent "agonized" over enforcing the decision of the majority of the board to remove her from the school. The issue was still pending when the Lesters moved to Victoria, Canada.[32]

Education remained a major concern of California's blacks in the early 1870s; an editorial in the *Pacific Appeal* in 1871 declared, "The proper education of our children is paramount to all other considerations." But the black press was also upset at the inequities of the state's segregated schools. The *San Francisco Elevator* charged in 1874 that black schools received only two-thirds of the per-student appropriation that white schools obtained and that in twenty counties funds designated for colored schools had been diverted to whites.[33] It was in this milieu that Mary Frances Ward's parents filed a lawsuit that became the first legal challenge to public school segregation. *Ward v. Flood* eventually reached the California State Supreme Court. In testifying before the state's highest court on behalf of her daughter, Harriet Ward voiced the aspirations of an entire community when she declared, "We are all of African descent . . . residents of San Francisco, . . . [and] have a right to be received . . . at the school nearest their residence." Mary Ward lost her case, but economic pragmatism eventually accomplished what the legal system would not. In 1875, Ward was enrolled in an integrated school when the San Francisco Board of Education declared it could no longer afford the practice of separating the city's school children by race.[34] Such protests and boycotts supplemented the economic argument and contributed in 1880 to the California legislature's striking the word "white" from the law requiring that schools be open for all students and repealing provisions mandating separate schools for blacks and Indians. Visalia's continued segregation of blacks led to an 1890 case that effectively ended legal segregation of African Americans in California's public schools.[35]

While Charlotte Brown, Mary Ellen Pleasant, and Harriet Ward were clearly not typical of any race or class during the nineteenth century, it cannot be assumed that most African American women left the public sphere to men, either within their own or the dominant society. Within the broader and more traditional framework of female support for male leadership, women were both visible and involved in a variety of ways. When the "colored citizens of San Francisco" assembled to celebrate the Emancipation Proclamation, "lady" participants were present throughout both the day and evening sessions. Praise for "neat and elegant" dresses was no less effusive than praise for the talent of the only woman to grace the platform. So taken were the members of the audience with Miss Emma Harding's speech on Abraham Lincoln, they appeared "spellbound" into silence as if "charmed." "The subsequent burst of glowing eloquence brought everyone to their feet, and three cheers [were] given for the President and three for Miss Emma."36

As in other regions of the country, African American women in the Golden State created formal and informal "uplift" organizations. The earliest such women's group on record was formed in Placerville in 1859. By the early 1860s, San Francisco women had formed the Ladies' Benevolent Society and the Ladies' Pacific Accommodating and Benevolent Society. Sacramento formed the first women's auxiliary to a male fraternal order, an Eastern Star chapter, in 1861. In addition to rendering medical aid, burial services, and general charity, some of these groups were important supporters of the first black newspapers in the state. African American women also conducted fund-raising and charitable activities through churches, where they held "ladies' festivals" to solicit funds from whites as well as blacks. Throughout the state, women used traditional events such as tea parties, fairs, and "evenings of literature" to support political and social agendas. With most African American men apparently accepting and depending upon "ladies in full force . . . willing to contribute their aid," there was no lack of opportunity for women in "many a glorious enterprise."37

Although black Californians numbered only slightly more than 11,000 by the end of the nineteenth century, African American women's organizations continued to flourish. Oakland's clubs were typical of this organizational growth. The first groups, such as the Colored Citizens' Library Association and the Literary and Aid Society, both founded in the 1870s, were not specifically female, even though women provided much of the leadership. By 1884, the House of Ruth, the women's auxiliary of the Odd Fellows lodge, was founded. Shortly afterward, the Ladies Beneficial Society, run by African American women and independent of any fraternal order, was established to aid sick members of the Oakland community. The Daughters of Samaria, a women's chapter of the Independent Order of Good Samaritans, promoted temperance. In 1899, the Fanny Jackson Coppin Club, the "mother" of the black women's club movement in California, was founded by members of Beth Eden Baptist Church. The construction and operation of the Home for Aged and Infirm Colored People, which opened in east Oakland in 1897, was the most ambitious nineteenth-century undertaking of black women in the state up to that time. Under the leadership of Emma Scott, they launched a five-year fund-raising campaign that resulted in the acquisition of a custom-built, two-story, sixteen-room Victorian home. The home became the final residence for a number of California's most prominent African American citizens. The turn of the century would see a new wave of women's organizations, especially in Los Angeles, partly as a sequel to the formation of national black women's organizations in the 1890s and partly in reaction to open exclusion of blacks from white women's clubs. By 1912, Los Angeles was "considered the greatest center of colored women's club activity in California."[38]

California black women often fit social and organizational activities into a schedule of paid employment, for they held jobs outside the home to a greater degree than any other population group. By 1900, more than one-fourth of California blacks who were gainfully employed were women, compared to less than 17 percent for native whites, 11 percent for foreign whites, and 2.4 percent for Chinese and Japanese. Through the late nineteenth century, black women made only limited occupational gains. Despite the optimism engendered by the Gold Rush decade, black workers soon discovered that they were clustered into job categories they had occupied as unpaid laborers during slavery. At the heart of their economic problems remained racial discrimination. In the 1860s and 1870s, the rapid growth of Northern California cities assured a growing number of service positions, such as hairdresser, seamstress, and domestic servant. But even these positions could be jeopardized, as when a "colored gentleman" in San Francisco who apprenticed his daughter to a dressmaker saw her fired "because all the customers had run away at the sight of a colored apprentice." The anti-Chinese campaigns of white trade unions in the Bay Area were followed in the 1880s by antiblack actions and led some prominent hotels to fire all African American maids. Discrimination became so widespread that, by the turn of the century, a Los Angeles newspaper was urging its readers to boycott stores that did not employ blacks, in order to "open hundreds of opportunities for your sons and daughters" and "aid in breaking the senseless color prejudice that is injuring both races."[39]

In this atmosphere, the vast majority of employed black women in California worked in some form of domestic and personal service, especially as house servants. To some extent this was true of women of all races throughout the nation. In 1870, more than half of all employed women in the West were domestic servants; in 1890, more than one-third. The smaller percentage of women and the decline of the Chinese servant population as a result of exclusionary law created an "insatiable demand" for female servants in California and made their wages the highest in the country. It is little wonder that African American newspapers joined white labor agents in urging southern black women to come west as servants, though some voiced this appeal in resigned tones, as in an 1866 editorial: "For the colored servants there are few other occupations open, and from the effects of generations of servitude, we are compelled to acknowledge the humiliating fact that a majority of our people are better fitted for that kind of labor than any other."[40] The concentration of black women in domestic service is graphically seen in comparison with women in other racial groups (see table 2).[41]

Within these occupational limits, black women were able to fashion occasionally remunerative careers. "Domestic and personal service" extended to hairdressing, and black women had established parlors in several California cities by 1900. By the early 1860s, many an astute African American businesswoman advertised her services as a dressmaker, midwife, or milliner. In the 1870s, San Francisco women were assured that Mrs. A. C. Buckner provided a wide array of services that included "pressing, crimping, weaving, and hair dyed in all colors." At least one black seamstress in Los Angeles became a recognized modiste for the rich of that city, while another built a lucrative business as a caterer to the wealthy. The small number of professionals included several teachers, who had been present in black communities since the early days of the Gold Rush. While most of them taught in the early "colored" schools, at least one, Sarah Mildred Jones, was retained by Sacramento after desegregation and became the principal of a predominantly white school. This isolated triumph, however, probably facilitated by her very light complexion and marred by several attempts to fire her, underscores the difficulty that African American women would continue to have breaking into teaching in California well into the twentieth century.[42]

A few African American women achieved wealth and fame. By far the

TABLE 2. Occupations of White, Black, and Asian Women in California, 1900

Sector	Native White		Foreign White		Black		"Other Colored"*	
	Number	Percentage	Number	Percentage	Number	Percentage	Number	Percentage
Agriculture	314	4.9	1,569	7.5	17	1.3	138	10.5
Professional	12,306	19.1	1,207	5.8	22	1.6	5	0.4
Domestic and personal service	20,813	32.4	13,015	62.0	1,161	86.1	702	53.4
Trade and transportation	11,425	17.8	1,665	7.9	11	1.4	24	1.8
Manufacturing and mechanical pursuits	16,598	25.8	3,518	16.8	130	9.6	435	33.9

*Chinese and Japanese

most noted was Pleasant, who transformed a small inheritance from her first husband into a financial empire that, by the 1870s, included urban real estate as well as mining and bank stock, making her one of the wealthiest women in the state. But Pleasant was not alone in her success. Salina Williams, a steward on a river steamer, wisely invested her salary of approximately $120 per month in San Francisco real estate and, by 1870, owned $12,000 in property. African American women who began work as domestic servants sometimes attained considerable wealth, as was the case with Harriet Owens-Bynum. Coming to Los Angeles in 1887, she tired of the long walk to her jobs and opened first a hand laundry, then a bakery and a dairy. She finally became a successful real estate agent, selling more than sixty-five houses to African Americans. Biddy Mason's property in rapidly growing Los Angeles generated a modest fortune for her and an even larger estate for her heirs, including a grandson who, by 1900, was reputed to be the wealthiest African American west of Chicago.[43]

Equally enterprising, if less spectacularly successful, were women advertising the availability of "pleasant lodging rooms." As in other parts of the country experiencing an influx of African American migrants, housing became a major issue. The sharing of dwellings with extended family members and unrelated "boarders" helped meet the need for additional housing, while also producing income. Black women ran dining and hotel enterprises in such remote areas as Julian, in northern San Diego County, where the Robinson Hotel thrived for forty years. This was an exception, however, for various configurations of shared accommodations did little more than provide a survival income for female entrepreneurs. But no matter how spartan their surroundings and meager the return, these women were determined to find a way to supplement their income and maintain a degree of independence rarely possible for working women employed outside the home. The centrality of both issues with the African American community continued into the next century. In 1906 the *Colored American* magazine described Los Angeles as "one vast encampment devoted to the industry of 'furnished room.'"[44]

A more unusual occupational group consisted of talented African American women who commanded public attention as artists and entertainers. The sculptor Edmonia Lewis, acclaimed as "the only colored professor who ever attained eminence in . . . fine arts," was introduced to Californians when pictures of her statues were displayed in the offices of San Francisco's black newspapers. The positive reaction to her work culminated in 1873 in her first major exhibition, in San Francisco. Afterward her marble statues sold to both public and private collectors.[45] More African American women gained prominence as entertainers. Anna Pindell, billed as "The Black Nightingale," toured the state in the late 1850s and early 1860s with a troupe of black actors, performing comic and dramatic routines. San Francisco residents Anna and Emma Hyer, noted opera singers, made their debut before 800 people in Sacramento in 1867. For the next fifteen years, their careers took them throughout the United States and overseas to Europe, the Hawaiian Islands, and Australia.[46]

No account of the economic roles of black women would be complete without noting the occupation that probably included the second largest group of wage-earning employed women in California in the nineteenth century: prostitution. This is one occupation that the Census Office largely omitted, so its incidence must be conjectured from narrative sources. Accounts of black prostitutes during the Gold Rush era are rare and seem to corroborate the observation by Delilah Beasley that "very few of the free women of color went astray during the wild days of the gold rush," remarkable in light of "the lawlessness among the men and women of the opposite race." Toward the end of the century, more notices appear of black prostitutes in major California cities, especially San Francisco and west Oakland. But overall, prostitution among California's African Americans was not a widespread pursuit, though it loomed as a potential image that the black press feared could be imposed on all black women.[47]

Seen in this light, the image of the "bad" black woman was only part of a greater contradiction between the rhetoric that sought to define African American women's roles and the realities of those roles in daily life. The overall tone set by the African American press in the West perpetuated an idealized version of women's place in society. In a style that was "stuffy, moralistic, and Victorian," female existence was tied to the domestic sphere. Regular "household" columns, as well as articles reprinted from other publications, defined women within the context of home, husband, and children. Hints for preparing nutritious meals and efficient methods of cleaning were stressed. Unmarried women were helped with the pursuit of a husband, while males were advised that "mute wives are a rare treasure." Replicating the trend already established by the eastern press, emphasis was placed on female grooming and personal attire, but women were also warned that excessiveness in any area would prove disastrous.[48]

Yet alongside such traditionally defined gender roles, at least one black

California newspaper included remarkably advanced viewpoints on women. In August 1872, the "Household" column of the *San Francisco Elevator* challenged readers to reconsider the conventional wisdom that women had a "natural" affinity for housework: "People generally think that all women young and old, whatever their taste or talent . . . ought to like housework." Moreover, the writer pointed out that while men were encouraged to pursue anything that interested them, "Custom [assigned] one vocation for women [and] that is housework." It was suggested that such a social mandate was insulting to women. The *Elevator* was also liberally sprinkled with quips and jokes that offered another view into the lives of single women: "A maiden lady being asked why she had never married replied that she had never seen the man for whom she was willing to get three meals a day for forty years," and, "A cynical lady rather inclined to flirt, says most men are like a cold, very easily caught, but very hard to get rid of." In a somewhat more serious vein, the editors assumed a novel position for African American newspapers in the 1860s. Rather than following the established trend of either ignoring or opposing the question of women's suffrage, readers were encouraged to consider the idea "a noble enterprise."[49]

Another aspect of this apparent liberalism surfaced in 1891 in an advice book written "for the young women of the race" by R. C. O. Benjamin, a black male lawyer and journalist. *Don't: A Book for Girls* contained many of the usual bromides of the day. Girls were advised, "Don't lose your temper, be gentle . . . look pleasant; you have no right to render other people miserable by your long face and dolorous tones." Chapters were devoted to a series of other "don'ts," including cautionary tales against associating with women of less than spotless reputation, sneezing in public, or "having around you the arm of a man who may be a profligate, and not possess the first instinct of a gentleman." Nevertheless, presenting the traditional life of refined womanhood as the key to both individual and racial pride did not prevent the author from considering other issues. While marriage is presented as a standard goal throughout the book, Benjamin includes a chapter in which he explains why marriage is not necessary for women. Being warned against the "pitfalls of a hasty marriage," young women are counseled to consider the institution a matter of choice. The time was past for regarding a woman who chose to remain single a "blighted being"; an unmarried woman not only commanded respect but, "far from being a subject of contempt or pity, she is more likely the object of open or secret envy on the part of most of her married acquaintances." These views were unusual, although Benjamin was not alone in advocating another progressive idea, the education of girls. At the core of his beliefs was the idea that education could provide women with much needed choices: "Every girl should receive [an] education with the idea of utilizing it." Claiming that he had "yet to learn of a spirited, well-informed woman losing anything [by] the knowledge that renders her independent," Benjamin urged his female readers to agitate for a place beside men in the male professions.[50]

By the dawn of the twentieth century, California's women of African descent were well on their way to carving out a place for themselves in what was no longer a new frontier. First arriving in significant numbers half a century before, they, like the larger stream of immigrants, were pioneers in search of new lives on the Pacific shore. In a land of many races and ethnicities, their opportunities and challenges differed from those of other women of color; the black/white model of eastern race relations would have to be adjusted in the Golden State. Their difficulties bore some resemblance to the struggles of other black females in the United States, but California offered such hope that many were willing to journey thousands of miles to try their luck. Its opportunities, ironically, sometimes threatened the ideal of separate spheres for the genders to which many black men and women aspired, but their families also benefited from a chance to earn money and the freedom to struggle for civil rights. As much as California's opportunities in the nineteenth century have been associated with white male miners and entrepreneurs, its promise perhaps was even more golden for African American women.

NOTES

1. Corlann Gee Bush, "The Way We Weren't: Images of Women and Men in Cowboy Art," in *The Women's West*, Susan Armitage and Elizabeth Jameson, eds. (Norman: University of Oklahoma Press, 1987), 21. See also William H. Goetzmann and William N. Goetzmann, *The West of the Imagination* (New York: W. W. Norton, 1986); and Ann F. Hyde, "'Cultural Filters': The Significance of Perception in the History of the American West," *Western Historical Quarterly* 23 (1993): 351–74.

2. See Sucheng Chan, ed., *Peoples of Color in the American West* (Lexington, MA: D. C. Heath and Company, 1994); Annette Kolodny, *The Land before Her:*

Fantasy and Experience of the American Frontiers, 1630–1860 (Chapel Hill: University of North Carolina Press, 1984); and Sandra L. Myers, "Mexican Americans and Westering Anglos: A Feminine Perspective," *New Mexico Historical Review* 57 (1992): 317–33. On popular portrayals of Western women, see Bush, "The Way We Weren't," 19–33; Beverly J. Stoeltje, "A Helpmate for Man Indeed: The Image of the Frontier Woman," *Journal of American Folklore* 88 (1975): 25–41; and June O. Underwood, "Western Women and True Womanhood: Culture and Symbol in History and Literature," *Great Plains Quarterly* 5 (1985): 93–106. For examples of the growing body of literature on African American women in the nineteenth-century West, see Lawrence B. de Graaf, "Race, Sex, and Region: Black Women in the American West, 1850–1920," *Pacific Historical Review* 49 (1980): 285, 313; Glenda Riley, "American Daughters: Black Women in the West," *Montana* 38 (1988): 14–27; Quintard Taylor, "The Emergence of Black Communities in the Pacific Northwest, 1864–1910," *Journal of Negro History* 64 (1979): 346–51; Taylor, *In Search of the Racial Frontier: African Americans in the American West, 1528–1990* (New York: W. W. Norton, 1998), chaps. 3 and 7. For pioneer attempts to include those from the West in the literature on African American women, see Delilah L. Beasley, *The Negro Trail Blazers of California* (Los Angeles: *Times-Mirror*, 1919); Delilah L. Beasley, "California Colored Women Trail Blazers," in Hallie Q. Brown, ed., *Homespun Heroines and Other Women of Distinction* (Xenia, OH: Aldine Publishing Company, 1926); and A. W. Hunton, "The Club Movement in California," *Crisis* (December 1912).

3. See Taylor, *In Search of the Racial Frontier* and *California History* 75 (1996); William Loren Katz, "Black Western Women: Images and Realities," annual banquet address, Western History Association, 37th Annual Conference, 1997; and Women of the West website, www.hga.com/wow/wowmain.htm (May 1997).

4. Spanish census records and lists of settlers in San Francisco are reprinted in Jack D. Forbes, "Hispano-Mexican Pioneers of the San Francisco Bay Area: Analysis of Racial Origins," *Aztlán* 14 (1983): 183 (quote), 188; *History of Santa Clara County* (San Francisco: Alley, Bowen, 1881), 63; and Charles Dwight Willard, *The Herald's History of Los Angeles City* (Los Angeles: Kingsley-Barnes and Neuner Company, 1901), 88. See also Jack D. Forbes, "Black Pioneers: The Spanish Speaking Afro-Americans of the Southwest," *Phylon* 27 (1966): 239–43; William M. Mason and James Anderson, "Los Angeles' Black Heritage," *L.A. County Museum Alliance* 70 (1969): 4–5; "Deed of Emancipation of a Negro Woman Slave, Dated Mexico, September 14, 1585," *Hispanic American Historical Review* 11 (1930): 51–57; Jack D. Forbes, "The Early African Heritage of California," essay in this anthology.

5. Helen Tyler, "The Family of Pico," *Southern California Quarterly* 25 (1953):

221–38; Rudolph M. Lapp, *Blacks in Gold Rush California* (New Haven: Yale University Press, 1977), 2; Mason and Anderson, "Los Angeles' Black Heritage," 4–5.

6. The first quote is from the *Albany Argus,* 18 January 1849, cited in Lapp, *Blacks in Gold Rush California,* 12. See also P. Brown to Alley Brown, December 1851, quoted in Taylor, *In Search of the Racial Frontier,* 84.

7. The first quote appears in Margaret A. Frink, *Adventures of a Party of California Gold Seekers* (Oakland: Ledyard Frink, 1897), 92. The second quote appears in *History of Black Americans in Santa Clara Valley* (San Jose, CA: Garden City Women's Club, 1978), 116, 174. See also Beasley, *Negro Trail Blazers,* 107–38, 232, 242; Lapp, *Blacks in Gold Rush California,* 23–24; Dorothy Sterling, *We Are Your Sisters: Black Women in the Nineteenth Century* (New York: W.W. Norton, 1984), 71; and Ernest V. Siracusa, *Black 49ers: The Negro in the California Gold Rush, 1848–1860,* research paper, n.p., 1969, microform (Berkeley: University of California, Library Photographic Service, n.d.), 33. On Lewis, see Lynda R. Hartigan, "Edmonia Lewis," in Darlene Clark Hine, ed., *Black Women in American History: From Colonial Times through the Nineteenth Century,* 4 vols. (Brooklyn: Carlson Publishing, 1990), vol. 2, 616.

8. Manuscript Census, 1860, cited in Douglas H. Daniels, *Pioneer Urbanites: A Social and Cultural History of Black San Francisco* (Philadelphia: Temple University Press, 1980), 17–19; "Aggregate List of Negro Population for 1852, Foreign Born," in Siracusa, *Black 49ers,* appendices A and B.

9. See James A. Fisher, "The California Negro, 1860: An Analysis of State Census Returns," San Francisco Negro Historical and Cultural Society, *California History Series* 4 (1965): 1–7. See also J. Max Bond, "The Negro in Los Angeles" (Ph.D. diss., University of Southern California, 1936), 19–20; Robert L. Carlton, "Blacks in San Diego County: A Social Profile, 1850–1880," *Journal of San Diego History* 2 (1975): 16; Michael S. Coray, "Blacks in the Pacific North West, 1850–1860: A View from the Census," *Nevada Historical Society Quarterly* 28 (1985): 90–121; Lapp, *Blacks in Gold Rush California,* 9; Siracusa, *Black 49ers,* appendix B.

10. Clarence Caesar, "The Historical Demographics of Sacramento's Black Community, 1848–1900," *California History* 75 (1996): 208. Table 1 is drawn from U.S. Bureau of the Census, *Seventh Census of the United States, 1850* (Washington, DC: Robert Armstrong, Public Printer, 1853), 969; U.S. Bureau of the Census, *Eighth Census of the United States, 1860, Population* (Washington, DC: Government Printing Office [G P O], 1864), 28; U.S. Bureau of the Census, *Ninth Census of the United States, 1870* (Washington, DC: G P O, 1872), 606–7; U.S. Bureau of the Census, *Eleventh Census of the United States, 1890, Population* (Washington, DC:

G P O, 1895), 4; U.S. Bureau of the Census, *Twelfth Census of the United States, 1900, Population*, part 1 (Washington, DC: U.S. Census Office, 1901), xviii.

11. Francis Lortie, *San Francisco's Black Community, 1870–1890* (San Francisco: R and E Publishers, 1973), 29–30; de Graaf, "Race, Sex, and Region," 289 (quote) 293–95.

12. The first quote appears in Taylor, *In Search of the Racial Frontier*, 77–78, the second in Lapp, *Blacks in Gold Rush California*, 132. For background on California's antiblack legislation, see Eugene Berwanger, "The 'Black Law' Question in Ante-Bellum California," *Journal of the West* 6 (1967): 214; Malcolm Edwards, "The War of Complexional Distinction: Blacks in Gold Rush California and British Columbia," *California Historical Quarterly* 56 (1977): 36; Lapp, *Blacks in Gold Rush California*, 131–33.

13. Quoted in Lapp, *Blacks in Gold Rush California*, 137. See also Beasley, *Negro Trail Blazers*, 9; and Taylor, *In Search of the Racial Frontier*, 78–80.

14. Quoted in Dolores Hayden, "Biddy Mason's Los Angeles, 1851–1891," *California History* 68 (1989): 91. On Harris, see Beasley, *Negro Trail Blazers*, 91.

15. The two quotes are included in David L. Snyder, *Negro Civil Rights in California, 1850* (Sacramento: Sacramento Book Collectors' Club, 1969), n.p.

16. See Elizabeth L. Parker and James Abajian, *A Walking Tour of the Black Presence in San Francisco during the Nineteenth Century* (San Francisco: African American Historical and Cultural Society, 1974), 11–12; and Remarks of Thomas H. Kuchel, 90th Cong., 2d sess., *Congressional Record* (3 October 1968), 8–9.

17. The first quote appears in Philip S. Foner and George E. Walker, *Proceedings of the Black State Conventions, 1840–1865,* 2 vols. (Philadelphia: Temple University Press, 1979–1980), vol. 2, 113. See also 128, 146, 150. The second quote is from the *San Francisco Elevator,* 25 May 1872.

18. For a discussion of California's multiracial origins, see the essay by Jack Forbes in this anthology. For good studies of peoples of color other than African American in California, see Albert Camarillo, *Chicanos in California: A History of Mexican Americans in California* (Sparks, NV: Materials for Today's Learning, 1990); Vicki L. Ruiz, *From Out of the Shadows: Mexican Women in Twentieth-Century America* (New York: Oxford University Press, 1998); Sucheng Chan, *Asian Californians* (San Francisco: MTL/Boyd and Fraser, 1991); Shih-Shan Henry Tsai, "Chinese Immigration, 1848–1882," in Chan, et. al., eds., *Peoples of Color,* 110–16; Linda Peavy and Ursula Smith, *Pioneer Women: The Lives of Women on the Frontier* (Norman: University of Oklahoma Press, 1998), 115; Albert L. Hurtado, *Indian Survival on the California Frontier* (New Haven: Yale University Press, 1988), 75;

Sharon Malinowski and Anna Sheets, eds., *The Gale Encyclopedia of Native American Tribes*, vol. 4 (Detroit: Gale, 1998), 6-8; Sherburne F. Cook, *The Conflict between the California Indian and White Civilization* (Berkeley: University of California Press, 1976); *Handbook of North American Indians*, vol. 8, *California*, ed. Robert F. Heizer (Washington, DC: Smithsonian Institution, 1978); Victoria D. Patterson, "Evolving Gender Roles in Pomo Society," in Laura F. Klein and Lillian A. Ackerman, eds., *Women and Power in Native North America* (Norman: University of Oklahoma Press, 1995).

19. The standard work on the free-soil movement is Eric Foner, *Free Soil, Free Labor, Free Men: The Ideology of the Republican Party before the Civil War* (New York: Oxford University Press, 1995).

20. Eric Foner, *Reconstruction: America's Unfinished Revolution, 1863–1877* (New York: Harper and Row, 1988), 85–87 (quote, p. 87).

21. Lapp, *Blacks in Gold Rush California*, 102.

22. Savage, *Blacks in the West*, 129; Daniels, *Pioneer Urbanites*, 70.

23. See Lapp, *Blacks in Gold Rush California*, 102, 161–63; Savage, *Blacks in the West*, 129; and Daniels, *Pioneer Urbanites*, 70.

24. See Daniels, *Pioneer Urbanites*, 119; Philip M. Montesano, *The Black Churches in Urban San Francisco, 1860–1865: Their Educational, Civic, and Civil Rights Activities* (P. Montesano, 1969), 14; Lapp, *Blacks in Gold Rush California*, 164; *Pacific Appeal*, 30 March 1862, 2 January 1864; *San Francisco Elevator*, 14 April and 19 May 1865.

25. Hayden, "Biddy Mason's Los Angeles," 89; "God and Us," brochure sponsored by the First A M E Church, Los Angeles, n.d. Copy in author's possession.

26. Lynn M. Hudson, "A New Look, or 'I'm Not Mammy to Everybody in California': Mary Ellen Pleasant, a Black Entrepreneur," *Journal of the West* 32 (1993): 36.

27. *Pacific Appeal*, 7 December 1867, 10 September and 17 November 1870; *San Francisco Elevator*, 14 April 1865; Helen Holdredge, *Mammy Pleasant* (New York: G.P. Putnam's Sons, 1953), 39–43.

28. See Robert J. Chandler, "Friends in Time of Need: Republicans and Black Civil Rights in California during the Civil Rights Era," *Arizona and the West* 24 (1982): 332–34; Philip S. Foner, "The Battle to End Discrimination against Negroes on Philadelphia Streetcars," in Philip S. Foner, ed., *Essays in Afro-American History* (Philadelphia: Temple University Press, 1978), 28–30, 35–37, 60. Beasley, *Negro Trail Blazers*, 65.

29. See *Pacific Appeal*, 31 May 1862; *San Francisco Elevator*, 7 April 1865; Chandler, "Friends in Time of Need," 333–34. For background on the particular role of

African American women in the campaign to end streetcar exclusion, see Sterling, *We Are Your Sisters,* 223; Willi Coleman, "Black Women and Segregated Transportation: Ninety Years of Resistance," in Hine, *Black Women in American History: The Twentieth Century,* vol. 5–8 in *Black Women in United States History,* 16 vols. (Brooklyn: Carlson, 1990), vol. 5, 295–301; Foner, "Battle to End Discrimination," 55, 65.

30. *John J. Pleasant, and Mary E. v. North Beach and Mission R.R. Company,* State of California, Supreme Court, no. 1380 (San Francisco: Alta California Printing House, 1867), Transcript on Appeal. See also Brief for the Appellant and Brief of Respondents, 13 January 1868. For studies of these cases see Chandler, "Friends in Time of Need," 333–34, 340; and Nathaniel S. Colley, "Civil Actions for Damages Arising Out of Violations of Civil Rights," *Hastings Law Journal* 17 (1965): 190.

31. Quoted in Lapp, *Blacks in Gold Rush California,* 175. See also ibid., 167; and Susan Bragg, "Knowledge Is Power: Sacramento Blacks and the Public Schools, 1854–1860," *California History* 75 (1996): 216–17.

32. Lapp, *Blacks in Gold Rush California,* 167–171; *Mirror of the Times,* 12 December 1857.

33. *Pacific Appeal,* 25 November 1871; *San Francisco Elevator,* 21 February 1874. For school conditions and black concern, see also *Pacific Appeal,* 15 March, 17 May, 30 August, 15 November, and 22 November 1873. For a discussion of the national debate among African Americans over segregated versus integrated public school education, see William M. Banks, *Black Intellectuals: Race and Responsibility in American Life* (New York: W.W. Norton, 1996), 25–28.

34. The quote appears in *Ward v. Flood* in Helen T. Catterall, ed., *Judicial Cases Concerning American Slavery,* vol. 5 (Carnegie Institute of Washington, 1937; reprint, New York: Octagon Books, 1968), 338. For background on the court case and the challenge to segregated education, see Charles Wollenberg, *All Deliberate Speed: Segregation and Exclusion in California Schools, 1855–1975* (Berkeley: University of California Press, 1976), chap. 1. See also Rudolph M. Lapp, *Afro-Americans in California* (San Francisco: Boyd and Fraser Publishing Company, 1979), 20. For a similar case in Stockton, California, see A. Odell Thurman, "The Negro in California before 1890," *Pacific Historian,* 19 (Winter 1975): 321–345.

35. James Fisher, "A History of the Political and Social Development of the Black Community in California, 1850–1950" (Ph.D. diss., State University of New York at Stony Brook, 1971), 132–35; Gilbert Thomas Stephenson, *Race Distinctions in American Law* (1910; reprint, New York: Negro Universities Press, 1969), 177–78. Ironically, the 1880 statute and 1890 case (*Wysinger v. Crookshank,* 82 Cal. 588) that ended segregated education for blacks institutionalized it for the Chinese, and

"oriental schools" would continue in parts of California into the twentieth century. Charles A. Mangum Jr., *The Legal Status of the Negro* (Chapel Hill: University of North Carolina Press, 1940), 83–84.

36. *Pacific Appeal,* 2 January 1864.

37. Quoted in the *Pacific Appeal,* 5 July 1862; and see also 2 January 1864. On Los Angeles, see Mikel Hogan Garcia, "Adaptation Strategies of the Los Angeles Black Community, 1883–1919" (Ph.D. diss., University of California, Irvine, 1985), 86–89; James de T. Abajian, comp., *Blacks in Selected Newspapers, Censuses, and Other Sources: An Index to Names and Subjects,* 3 vols. (Boston: G. K. Hall, 1977), vol. 2, 441; *San Francisco Elevator,* 20 October 1865, 2; 22 May 1868, 2; Caesar, "Historical Demographics," 210; Lapp, *Negroes in Gold Rush California,* 164, 231.

38. Lawrence P. Crouchett, Lonnie G. Bunch III, and Martha Kendall Winnacker, *Visions toward Tomorrow: The History of the East Bay Afro-American Community, 1852–1977* (Oakland: Northern California Center for Afro-American History and Life, 1989), 14; Gerda Lerner, ed., *Black Women in White America* (New York: Pantheon, 1972), 436, 440–41; *Los Angeles Liberator,* April 1901, 1; Hunton, "Club Movement" 90–91; *Pacific Appeal,* 5 July 1862 (quote).

39. Quotes from *San Francisco Elevator,* 7 March 1874, 2, and *Los Angeles Liberator,* May 1901, 5; Lortie, *San Francisco's Black Community,* 11–12; Caesar, "Historical Demographics," 211–12.

40. *San Francisco Elevator,* 16 March 1866, 2 (quote); David M. Katzman, *Seven Days a Week: Women and Domestic Service in Industrializing America* (New York: Oxford University Press, 1978), 55–56, 206–7; T. A. Larson, "Women's Role in the American West," *Montana* 24 (1974): 5, 6.

41. Table 2 is drawn from the *Twelfth Census, Occupations,* 154–65.

42. The quote is from *Pacific Appeal,* 30 March 1872. See also ibid., 12 April 1862; 30 March 1872; *San Francisco Elevator,* 7 April 1865; 3 July 1886; de Graaf, "Race, Sex, and Region," 301–2; Beasley, *Negro Trail Blazers,* 121, 173–78, 230, 242; *Los Angeles Liberator,* December 1902, 5; *California Eagle,* 6 March 1925, 1; Caesar, "Historical Demographics," 205–6.

43. On Pleasant, see Lynn M. Hudson, "When 'Mammy' Becomes a Millionaire: Mary Ellen Pleasant, an African American Entrepreneur" (Ph.D. diss., Indiana University, 1996). On Williams, see Daniels, *Pioneer Urbanites,* 29; and on Owens-Bynum, see Joan M. Jensen and Gloria Ricci Lothrop, *California Women: A History* (San Francisco: Boyd and Fraser Publishing Company, 1987), 32; and Beasley, *Negro Trail Blazers,* 244. Mason's wealth is profiled in Hayden, "Biddy Mason's Los Angeles," 95–99; and Taylor, *In Search of the Racial Frontier,* 206.

44. The quote from *Colored American Magazine* appears in Garcia, "Adapta-

tion Strategies," 50. Ads for "pleasant lodging room" appeared in the *Pacific Appeal*, 26 December 1863 and the *San Francisco Elevator*, 7 April 1865. See also Coray, "Blacks in the Pacific West," 109–10; Elizabeth H. Pleck, *Black Migration and Poverty: Boston 1865–1900* (New York: Academic Press, 1979), 191. Dick Carlson, "Women in San Diego: A History in Photographs," *Journal of San Diego History* 14 (1978): 317.

45. Philip M. Montesano, "Some Aspects of the Free Negro Question in San Francisco, 1849–1870" (Master's thesis, University of San Francisco, 1967), 68–70; Hartigan, "Edmonia Lewis," in Hine, *Black Women in American History*, vol. 2, 621.

46. On Anna Pindell, see Daniels, *Pioneer Urbanites*, 16. The career of the Hyer sisters is described in Hine, *Black Women in American History*, vol. 2, 1162; and in Lapp, *Blacks in Gold Rush California*, 116.

47. De Graaf, "Race, Sex, and Region," 303–5; Larson, "Women's Role in the American West," 6; Beasley, "California Colored Women Trail Blazers," in Brown, ed., *Homespun Heroines*, 240.

48. *San Francisco Elevator*, 24 August 1872; 2 May 1874; *San Francisco Vindicator*, 16 February 1889; and *Pacific Appeal*, 16 January 1864; 7 December 1872. See also Frankie Hutton, *The Early Black Press in America, 1827–1860* (Westport, CT: Greenwood Press, 1993), 68–69.

49. *San Francisco Elevator*, 24, 31 August 1872; 7 March 1874; see also Bess Beatty, "Perspectives on American Women: The View from Black Newspapers, 1865–1900," in Frances Richardson Keller, ed., *Views of Women's Lives in Western Tradition: Frontiers of the Past and the Future* (Lewiston, NY: E. Mellen Press, 1990), 581.

50. R. C. O. Benjamin, *Don't: A Book for Girls* (San Francisco: Valleau and Peterson Book and Job Printers, 1891), 18, 29, 33, 41–42, 47.

PART II
PURSUING THE DREAM

"The Greatest State for the Negro"

Jefferson L. Edmonds, Black Propagandist

of the California Dream

LONNIE G. BUNCH III

In May 1913 W. E. B. Du Bois, the lone African American officer in the National Association for the Advancement of Colored People (NAACP) and the editor of the *Crisis* magazine, arrived in Los Angeles hoping to increase the participation of black Californians in the activities of that civil rights organization. But Du Bois also used this, his first trip to Southern California, to satisfy his curiosity about race relations in this land "of roses and orange blossoms." During his visit, Du Bois was feted by an elite group of middle-class black Angelenos that included representatives of such pioneering families as that of Robert C. Owens, members of the new professional class such as dentists John and Vada Somerville, and intellectuals and activists such as newspaper editor Jefferson Lewis Edmonds.

Although most of his time was spent delivering lectures at civic sites and on the campuses of Pomona and Occidental Colleges and the University of Southern California, Du Bois was able to visit black churches and businesses, explore the living conditions of the diverse African American community, and take "automobile rides all about the surrounding country and city." So impressed was Du Bois that, upon his return to New York City, he wrote, "Los Angeles is wonderful. Nowhere in the United States is the Negro so well and beautifully housed, nor the average efficiency and intelligence in the colored population so high." Though Du Bois recognized that Los Angeles was not a paradise free of racial hatred and bigotry, he nevertheless wrote, "Out here in this matchless Southern California there would seem to be no limit to your opportunities, your possibilities."[1]

Du Bois's comments resonated strongly with Jefferson Lewis Edmonds because they echoed much of what he believed and wrote about the opportunities for African Americans in the Los Angeles region. Edmonds felt that the conditions in Southern California in the early twentieth century were ripe for "advancing the race." What was needed was a clear vision of what was possible, a continuing influx of black migrants who were willing to work hard and vote often, and a means to communicate regularly and effectively to both black and white Angelenos. No one had more to contribute to the articulation, dissemination, and implementation of this effort than Edmonds. The editor of the *Liberator*, a Los Angeles newspaper so named in the hope that it would become as influential and as uncompromising as William Lloyd Garrison's nineteenth-century antislavery organ, Edmonds believed that his periodical "devoted to the cause of good government and the advancement of the Afro-American" could be an instrument for racial uplift in a rapidly changing and expanding Los Angeles.[2]

Du Bois's visit to Los Angeles confirmed the notion that the burgeoning city had replaced San Francisco and Oakland as the center of African American life in California. Throughout much of the latter half of the nineteenth century, black migration to the state had focused on San Francisco with its more established community, its transportation links to the East, and the economic opportunities of an urban center. That growth, however, was eventually limited by several factors, including improved access to Southern California and the devastating impact of the San Francisco earthquake of 1906. As a result of that natural disaster, many black San Franciscans relocated to the East Bay communities of Oakland and Berkeley, and potential migrants sought other places to settle. During that same period, Los Angeles slowly evolved from a Mexican pueblo to a United States city, with its black presence increasing from 12 African Americans in 1850 to 102 in 1880 and to more than 1,200 just a decade later. As the twentieth century began, the black population of Los Angeles (7,599 residents in 1910) quickly outpaced that of both San Francisco (1,642) and Oakland (3,055).[3]

Du Bois's words celebrating the "possibilities" of Southern California legitimized and helped to turn national attention toward the notion of a "California Dream" for African Americans. While the appeal of this dream was universal, drawing thousands of white and black Americans to the region, its offer of economic opportunity (or even prosperity), the chance for home ownership, and the potential for more individual freedom had an even greater appeal to those whose choices were circumscribed by race. It was the lure of this California Dream that drew thousands of African Americans to

Los Angeles from 1900 until the end of World War I, changing both the complexity and the complexion of the city.4

For more than a decade at the dawning of the twentieth century, Edmonds was the leading proponent and propagandist of the California Dream for African Americans. He believed that Southern California "was a place where Negroes could enjoy all the rights of citizenship." Using the *Liberator*, he effectively crafted an optimistic, middle-class vision of what black life could become in Los Angeles. But Edmonds was not simply a dreamer and a booster. His importance stems from his coupling the dream with a coherent and practical strategy for racial improvement that played out on the pages of his newspaper. Edmonds was thoroughly steeped in the sentiments of Progressive Era reform: regulated economic growth, good and efficient government, and a fairer society for all. He used these beliefs to undergird his struggle for racial equality in the region. Edmonds understood that many aspects and characteristics of Progressive Era reform, not to mention the prejudices of many of the individual reformers, did little to bridge the racial divide in America. Yet he realized that this broad-based movement to bring order and scientific rationality to the excesses of capitalism and society did provide some frameworks and ideological insights that could, in skilled hands, be applied to issues of race. Embracing the era's spirit of public protest and education, he, like many influenced by Progressivism, believed that an aroused and informed public would compel action against racial discrimination.5 As a leader and visionary in the struggle against racism in Southern California, Edmonds deserves the scholarly attention and reputation garnered by his contemporaries William Monroe Trotter, editor of the *Boston Guardian*, and Robert Abbott, publisher of the *Chicago Defender*.

The life of Jefferson Edmonds, who was born in 1845, was profoundly shaped by the twenty years he spent in bondage, working from a young age in the tobacco and cotton fields of Virginia. He never forgot how precious liberty was and how important it was to fight to protect it. More than forty years after gaining his freedom, Edmonds recalled how, upon hearing that they were emancipated, some slaves shouted, "I'm free, I'm free and I don't care who knows about it."6 This need to declare one's independence and demand the rights of freedom regardless of the consequences became the central theme in his life. After the Civil War, Edmonds migrated to Crawfordsville, Mississippi, where he received his formal education in a series of "freedman schools." From 1875 to 1888, he taught in the "colored" schools of

Mississippi. Becoming frustrated with the restrictions he experienced teaching in segregated schools, Edmonds purchased a small farm located thirty-five miles south of Memphis, Tennessee.

In addition to his duties as a farmer, Edmonds served two terms in the state legislature of Mississippi. As a state assemblyman, Edmonds lashed out at the growing violence and discrimination faced by blacks in the region. As white southerners struggled to throw off the yoke of Reconstruction and reestablish control over their former slaves, they crafted a system that sought to strip blacks of most legal and human rights, using violence as a primary means of enforcement. Blacks found themselves prevented from voting or testifying in courts and were left to labor as sharecroppers. When African Americans seemed to test the limits of the system, the reaction was swift and extreme. For example, in 1886, shortly before Edmonds left for California, Mississippi whites, concerned that blacks were attempting to enter the courthouse in Carrollton County, opened fire on an unarmed group, leaving twenty dead. From 1882 to 1901 more than two thousand African Americans were lynched in the South. The racial violence in the postbellum South was so severe that one historian has written that "lynchings continued as weekly phenomena, and mob assaults, comparable to European pogroms, against black communities were commonplace." It is easy to understand why this willingness to publicly combat the racism that permeated the state earned Edmonds both acclaim and violent condemnation. Reacting to a number of death threats against his family, Edmonds found his southern experience so distasteful that he once wrote that "the only thing that we are proud of in connection with the fact that we were born in the South, is that we left it."7

The Los Angeles that Edmonds encountered upon his arrival was both a place of possibility and one where opportunities were limited and shaped by the same racial discrimination that permeated the rest of the nation. The small African American community had grown in the years following the Civil War from a few individuals, most of whom were servants or domestics living with white families, to a diverse, yet cohesive, settlement of 1,258 residents that by 1890 constituted 2.5 percent of the population—up from 0.9 percent in 1880. These black Angelenos settled throughout the city—in Pico Heights, on Alameda Street between First and Third, along Central Avenue (north of First Street), near Azusa and Weller streets, and along West Adams Boulevard—which suggests that it was not until after 1910 that restrictive housing covenants would force the consolidation and overcrowding of the black community into specific parts of the city. Yet during this period, it was clear that the color line was sharply drawn. At various times during the century, laws were passed that sought to limit the legal, political, and economic rights of African Americans in California. Often schools and housing were segregated, many businesses and restaurants catered only to a white clientele, and most employment opportunities were restricted to poorly paid, low-status jobs such as laborers, porters, bootblacks, and domestics. Notions of the inherent inferiority of African Americans were so commonly accepted that black Angelenos were denied many common courtesies, routinely referred to as "Nigger Pete" or "Auntie Winnie," forced to bear beatings and public jostlings, and expected to accept a "second-class citizenship."[8]

Yet in spite of the racial conditions they faced, blacks in nineteenth-century Los Angeles created a vibrant community that crafted strategies, mutual assistance programs, political organizations, and religious institutions geared to providing practical and spiritual support. Former slaves Robert Owens and Biddy Mason were able to use their political and business acumen to achieve middle-class status through the acquisition of city real estate and to provide effective leadership for the African American community until their deaths (Owens in 1865 and Mason in 1891). While not every member of the community achieved middle-class status (in fact, in the 1860 census only five of the sixty black residents owned any property), the economic changes that were reshaping Los Angeles—the coming of the Southern Pacific and Santa Fe Railroads, the rise of citrus and truck farming, and the construction and real estate opportunities that accompanied urban development—contributed to greater employment possibilities for the city's African American residents. Black Angelenos created a series of sophisticated educational and cultural organizations like the Sojourner Truth Club ("dedicated to racial uplift through education"); political groups like the Los Angeles Men's Forum (founded in 1903), whose stated goal was "to encourage united effort on the part of Negroes for their advance"; and newspapers like John Niemore's the *Owl*, created in 1892 and later renamed the *Eagle*, all of which point to the presence of a significant African American community, poised for change, at the time Edmonds moved west.[9]

In 1896, within a few years of his arrival in California, Edmonds began publishing a weekly newspaper, the *Pasadena Searchlight*. This venture was short-lived because of his unwillingness to fit his viewpoints into current political fashions. During the presidential election of 1896, Edmonds championed the candidacy of William Jennings Bryan. Many black and white Republicans chastised him for "abandoning the party of Lincoln." The outcry against Edmonds was so great that his partners in the publishing venture relieved him of his editorial duties in order to keep the newspaper viable. For the next several years he joined a variety of community organizations, including the Los Angeles Forum, and served as an officer in some of them, thus demonstrating that he was a willing and effective participant in the struggle to "uplift the race."[10]

In 1900, Edmonds finally found his "bully pulpit" when he established the *Liberator* as a monthly "news magazine." Like many black newspapers nationally—whether the *San Francisco Elevator*, the *Washington* (D.C.) *Bee* or the *Chicago Defender*—the *Liberator* reflected the personality, style, and politics of its editor. And as with many other black periodicals, financial considerations initially limited the paper to one monthly edition. While Edmonds would have preferred to publish a weekly or daily edition, the costs associated with the publication of a polished, photographically filled newspaper, as well as the daily editorial rigors, were too great for what was essentially a small family business. Edmonds's son, Jefferson Lewis Edmonds Jr., served as the paper's editorial assistant whenever school and work allowed. Ultimately, Edmonds's decisions concerning the look of the periodical reflected both his financial burdens and his editorial vision. The smaller, magazine-like format of the *Liberator* helped to reduce the production and mailing costs, and the size also made the periodical more likely to be saved, reread, and shared with others, all part of the editor's plan.[11] By March 1911, Edmonds decided that the income from advertising and increased local and national subscriptions as well as the help provided by an assistant editor, Noah Thompson, would make the publication of a weekly edition of the *Liberator* possible.

For fourteen years, Edmonds published the paper out of a small office (room 210) in the Thorpe Building, located at the corner of Broadway and Franklin Street. From there he used the columns of the *Liberator* to encourage migration to Southern California by articulating, and occasionally embellishing, the lure of Los Angeles to African Americans and to express a coherent political and economic strategy that would allow black Angelenos to combat racism in the city. In Edmonds's view, his newspaper had to be of service to the Los Angeles African American community; he proclaimed that the "paper is against any man who is against the Negro; and friend of any man who is friend of the Negroes." Coupled with this was the editor's desire to "give the people a first-class, up-to-date newspaper, containing all original matter, dealing in a fearless, independent way with all local and public questions." Edmonds hoped that his publication would be a catalyst for change, a vehicle for exposing racial inequalities and government misconduct, and an educational forum that would provide information that the African American community would find useful in its daily struggles.[12]

Though Edmonds wanted the *Liberator* to be "read and supported by all classes of people," he was not afraid to prod, criticize, or be controversial. He proudly proclaimed that the paper "is a molder of public opinion, not a slave of it." Responding to those who thought the editor was unnecessarily incendiary, Edmonds wrote, "If denouncing those as enemies who are taking every advantage to encourage lawlessness, murder and brutality; if pleading for the supremacy of law, equal rights and equal opportunity for all regardless of color is incendiary, then the Liberator is incendiary to the core. . . . The Liberator will fight in the ranks of those who stand for law and order and equal opportunity for all." The *Liberator* gave Edmonds a forum, one that he used unhesitatingly with great passion and skill. Yet the question is, how large was this forum? While accurate subscription records for the *Liberator* no longer exist, Edmonds claimed three thousand weekly subscribers in 1912 at the yearly rate of $1.50 or $.20 per month. This would mean that nearly half of black Los Angeles subscribed to the paper. More important than the numbers, however, was the paper's influence among black Angelenos. At a time when the white media, like the *Los Angeles Times* or the *Los Angeles Star*, ignored or often misrepresented the concerns of the city's African American residents, middle-class blacks looked to newspapers like the *Liberator* to find a fuller, more accurate depiction of their needs, achievements and struggles.[13]

While other black newspapers like *Colored American* or the *New Age* celebrated the lure of "colored California" in the early twentieth century, only the *Liberator* consistently championed Los Angeles's "possibilities" and explored the complex and interrelated elements that composed the "dream." In 1911, Edmonds wrote one of his clearest articulations of the appeal of Los Angeles:

> Only a few years ago, the bulk of our present colored population came here from the South without any money, in search of better things and were not disappointed. The hospitable white people received them kindly, employed them at good wages, treated them as men and women, furnished

their children with the best educational advantages offered anywhere. . . . They were treated absolutely fair in courts. . . . Feeling perfectly safe, the colored people planted themselves . . . [A]ll the Negroes [*sic*] wants is an opportunity to develop himself.

Two years later, he commented, "We are here like other people, to share these splendid conditions found in California." To Edmonds, then, California provided a better chance for African Americans to enjoy economic growth, educational opportunities for their children, legal protection, and the respect of their peers.[14]

To better understand Edmonds's vision, one must view the California Dream through a southern prism. The inequalities and brutalities that African Americans experienced in the Jim Crow South made the rough edges of race relations in California seem smoother. While discrimination was an everyday occurrence in Los Angeles, the capricious use of violence in the South meant that on a daily basis black southerners faced not just a loss of their dignity and their humanity, but the loss of their lives, their homes, and their livelihood. The almost total disregard for black legal and political rights in the South meant that there were few restraints on white rage and racism that African Americans could rely upon. Even sophisticated southern cities like Atlanta and New Orleans experienced unchecked racial violence in the early twentieth century. Thus Edmonds's interpretation of the opportunities and possibilities of "colored California," when juxtaposed with the realities of southern life, seems less naive and more understandable.[15]

At the center of Edmonds's vision of the California Dream was freedom from the extralegal violence—the lynchings, burnings, and mob actions— that shaped and limited African American life in the South. Nearly every edition of the *Liberator* carried examples of this violence, such as the story about "the murder of Betsy McCray . . . by blood thirsty [*sic*] mob of 500." Edmonds believed that until the "mobocrats and nigger burners" were punished and the rule of law was reestablished in the region, African Americans should view Southern California as an alternative to the violent South because the legal system afforded the black Californian protection that limited the incidents of mob action. This notion was amplified in an editorial Edmonds wrote in 1911: "It is important to note that the Negroes of California are treated as citizens and are allowed to enjoy unmolested whatever he has [*sic*] honestly acquired." For many African Americans, access to a legal system that protected them from the violence rampant in the South provided the foundation that supported the other elements of the California Dream.[16]

Another reason why African Americans found California attractive was the possibility of providing an effective education for their children, especially when compared to the lack of such opportunities in the South. While some southerners believed that African Americans should be minimally trained so that they would be more effective members of the workforce, most white politicians and educators echoed the sentiments of a southern governor who, when asked to support an increased educational allotment for blacks, replied, "Why should we pay money to educate mules?" This attitude was difficult for African Americans to accept, since their thirst for education had led to the establishment of an array of black institutions from freedman schools to colleges like the Hampton and Tuskegee Institutes. As this desire for education was stifled in the South, African Americans looked for places where opportunities were available. Some turned to Los Angeles. In 1911, Edmonds championed this alternative when he wrote, "The opportunities offered by Los Angeles to acquire an education are unsurpassed by any city in the country. . . . Under the circumstances, what a crime it is to be ignorant." What made the schools in Southern California so appealing in the early twentieth century was that they were integrated. To many African Americans, integrated schools seemed to ensure that black children would finally receive an education equal to that of whites. As a former teacher in segregated schools, Edmonds trumpeted the fact that "all the schools of this state are open to the colored children. . . . Colored citizens in this city come here to get rid of the separate schools . . . that made life intolerable in the South." Black families, only a generation removed from bondage, found the educational opportunities in Southern California a strong reason to move to the region.[17]

But relocating to Southern California would occur only if employment opportunities were available to African Americans. Recognizing the limited job possibilities in the South, Edmonds chronicled the chances for work in Los Angeles. "The demand for colored help cannot be supplied," Edmonds wrote in 1903. "Wages are good and the treatment is . . . just." This chance to improve one's economic circumstances in Los Angeles was a constant refrain in the columns of the *Liberator*. Edmonds wrote of a city that had "plenty of room for every honest and industrious man and woman." For those who were unafraid of hard work, "the colored man has a better opportunity to become self-supporting and independent." To Edmonds, as well as to thousands of African Americans who migrated to the city, Los Angeles was not an economic paradise but a place where former sharecroppers—men and women who had been forced to labor in the South under economic exploitation barely one step removed from slavery—could obtain more meaningful and lucrative employment.[18]

In many ways, Edmonds's clarion call of economic opportunity was simply a reflection of the burgeoning prosperity of the region. During the first two decades of the twentieth century, Los Angeles experienced a period of rapid growth and economic expansion that stemmed from an array of circumstances. The growth of the city, reflected in its population's increase to more than 319,000 residents in 1910, led to increased opportunities in agriculture, transportation, the construction trades, and the service industries. This boom would continue through the next two decades, with the population reaching 576,673 by 1920. African American migrants were able to participate in the new economic opportunities, though not on equal terms with whites who had recently arrived. Black Angelenos often found themselves competing with Asians and Mexicans for low-level employment in the expanding agricultural sector, on the railroads, and in the service industries. That competition typically ensured that wages remained low.[19]

Yet for many southern migrants the region's prosperity brought opportunities impossible to imagine in the South. The economic possibilities in the area also appealed to African American businessmen from around the country. The increased size of the black community, coupled with the rapid growth of the region's economy, provided an expanding market that seemed accessible to entrepreneurs of color. In the years prior to World War I, an array of black-owned businesses graced the streets of Los Angeles. Businessmen like Robert C. Owens built grand edifices to house their activities and showcase their success. Smaller enterprises like the Canadian Second Hand Furniture Store, the Golden West Hotel ("the largest colored hotel on the Pacific Coast"), Donnell's Blacksmith Shop, and the Los Angeles Van and Storage Company all epitomized the growing economic activity of the African American community. With each passing year, the columns of the *Liberator* celebrated the achievements of black businessmen and women. Edmonds wrote, "The year 1913 opens auspiciously for the colored people in this city. The number of business establishments conducted by Negroes have [*sic*] increased. . . . The Negroes are represented in nearly every department of the city's business and industries." Thus the opportunity to participate in the economic growth of Los Angeles, however unequally, became central to attracting African Americans to the area.[20]

An underappreciated aspect of the lure of California was the opportunity for African Americans to purchase homes and property in the state. In his newspaper, Edmonds championed both the possibility and the importance of homeownership. As early as 1903, he claimed that "the opportunity for the colored people to acquire homes in Southern California was never greater." Three years later he wrote, "Perhaps in no other city are the colored people so admirably situated. . . . Having prudently refused to segregate, their homes are to be found on every street and in every quarter of the city." To Edmonds, the quality and number of homes owned by black Californians separated Los Angeles from other American cities: "It has been repeatedly said by people who have traveled extensively that the colored people in Los Angeles are the best housed of any city. . . . Tenement houses and alley life, such as exists in New York, Chicago and Philadelphia is practically unknown here." Edmonds equated homeownership with citizenship. The more blacks were able to own property, the more likely they were to receive the protection and freedoms that accompanied citizenship.[21]

Edmonds was not alone in championing black homeownership. Other leading black Angelenos like Owens and the future state legislator Fred Roberts stressed the ties between homeownership, citizenship, and middle-class respectability. At the national level, leaders as diverse as Booker T. Washington, William Monroe Trotter, and Ida B. Wells all recognized the symbolic and practical value of a large class of African American homeowners. In each edition of the *Liberator*, Edmonds listed the acquisitions of black Angelenos ("Mr. C. W. Brooks bought five acres. . . . J. L. Thorton purchased a nice lot at 1455 E. 21st"); ran real estate advertisements, including that of his own company ("for sale to colored people, 1/2 acre in Sierra Madre"); and celebrated the acquisition of property ("The Negro population continues to purchase homes in this city, which indicates that there is no immediate danger of Los Angeles being depopulated soon by Negro people"). The dream of homeownership struck a responsive chord with many African Americans and contributed mightily to the appeal of Southern California. Yet, while Los Angeles had a higher percentage of African American homeownership than many other cities in the early years of the twentieth century, most black migrants still faced significant economic challenges that made owning a home just a dream. Nevertheless, just the greater prospects that Los Angeles offered were enough for many people of all economic classes to move west.

The final component of the lure of California to African Americans was access to its political system. At a time when nearly all African Americans in the South were prevented from exercising their franchise through violence, intimidation, and the law, black Angelenos "had the full right of citizenship, including the right to vote." To Edmonds, the right to vote was central to any success that blacks could enjoy in America. Thus the franchise was one of the primary reasons Edmonds claimed that "California is the greatest state for the Negro," and it was the key factor in his program for black advancement.[22]

Jefferson Edmonds's interpretation of the California Dream for African Americans was born out of a Progressive Era optimism that, in contrast to the violence, oppression, and racial limits of the South, Southern California could be seen as a place of great "possibility and opportunity." But Edmonds was not simply a naive propagandist who oversold the promise of California; he recognized that "no race ever dreamed itself to affluence." To ensure that Los Angeles became a place that treated "the race fairly," he developed a strategy of racial uplift based on activism, racial pride, political acumen, and the columns of the *Liberator*. The key to Edmonds's strategy was the effective use of the vote by the African American community. He believed in the Progressive Era notion of an efficient government and judiciary composed of independent and fair men, held accountable for their actions by voters, and he extended it to the view that black voting was essential for "the elevation of the race."[23]

Edmonds preached that by using the vote effectively "colored voters have taught office holders that they will have to treat the Negroes as men or encounter their deadly opposition at the polls." To help blacks become more effective participants in the political arena, Edmonds counseled the voter to "pause before casting his ballot long enough to ask himself what he hopes to accomplish by voting." Beginning in 1905, the *Liberator* published sample ballots and formally endorsed candidates that Edmonds believed would help guarantee the legal and political rights of black Angelenos. Throughout the fourteen-year existence of the newspaper, politicians from judges to mayors appeared in the columns to solicit the black vote and to court the paper's endorsement. This increased the political clout of both the African American voter and the *Liberator*.[24]

To make the black vote count in the often closely contested elections in the city, Edmonds believed that African Americans should not allow the Republican Party to take their votes for granted. He believed that "political ills of the negroes were due to the fact that they voted solidly for one party regardless of the issues. [I] advocate a division of the Negro vote." According to Edmonds, this lack of independence limited black political influence. He hoped that "the colored voter would discover that he can advance his interest better as an independent than as a partisan." While the majority of black voters remained Republican, Edmonds's effort to increase the political profile and power of African Americans was successful. The most striking evidence of these efforts came in 1918, when local journalist Fred Roberts became the first African American elected to the state legislature, a position he would hold through 1934.[25]

Another element in Edmonds's strategy was the need to attract and promote a black middle-class community. Using the *Liberator*, Edmonds encouraged those who were "industrious," "hardworking," "serious," "law abiding," and "looking to improve" to resettle in Los Angeles. With both pictures and words, the articles in the *Liberator* focused on businessmen, prosperous doctors, and others in the African American middle class in order to demonstrate to the city's white residents that black Angelenos were worthy of their respect and the rights of citizenship. Equally important to Edmonds was the need to create and display black role models. By recognizing middle-class aspirations and achievement, he hoped to encourage and inculcate values that he believed would better serve the African American community.

But the most important tool that Edmonds possessed was the *Liberator* itself. For more than a decade, Edmonds kept his promise "to keep hammering until no man is discriminated against on account of race, color or creed." The *Liberator* became the guardian of the African American community in Los Angeles. Any form of bigotry or discrimination was attacked in the paper's columns. Whether condemning racial violence in the South, protesting the discrimination "faced by the colored tenants of a downtown office building," chastising racist politicians, championing women's suffrage, or attacking hair and skin products that "encourage some to believe that manhood depends entirely on the color of the skin or the texture of hair," the newspaper sought to improve the lives and prospects of African Americans in Los Angeles.[26]

An example of the *Liberator*'s leadership role involves the controversy surrounding the "Shenk Decision." In the summer of 1912, a prominent

African American businessman, Caleb Holden, was invited by a white associate to have a late afternoon drink. In the saloon, Holden was charged one dollar for his beer, while his white companion was told that his drink cost a nickel. After asking about the inequity, the two were told that "if a colored man wanted to drink in this establishment, he must pay a higher price." Eventually the mayor was asked to intercede. He asked his city attorney, John Shenk, to investigate. Shenk issued a ruling that businesses had the right to charge whatever they desired and could change their prices at will. To Edmonds, this decision effectively repealed the civil rights laws of California. Using his newspaper, Edmonds reported that as a result of the "Shenk Decision," blacks experienced unprecedented discrimination throughout the city. He wrote, "Many soda fountains now charge colored patrons one dollar for a glass of soda water." For the next six months he continued to attack the decision, and when John Shenk ran for mayor in 1913, Edmonds urged all African Americans to vote against him. When Shenk was defeated by a small margin, Edmonds claimed "another great victory for the *Liberator*."[27]

The defeat of Shenk was one of the paper's last great victories. Less than nine months later, on 4 January 1914, Jefferson Lewis Edmonds died.[28] Near the end of his life Edmonds became much more pessimistic about the possibilities of racial equality in Southern California. He believed that for "colored citizens, there is danger ahead. . . . There has never been a time in the history of the city when the lives of Negroes were so cheap." He despaired of the increase in violence against blacks, he worried that even the politicians African Americans supported soon forgot their commitments to the race, he wondered whether "Colored California" could achieve all that he hoped, and he feared that much of the *Liberator*'s efforts had been in vain.[29]

Edmonds was correct in his assessment of the declining state of black Los Angeles. As the African American population in the city increased to 15,579 by 1920, so too did the restrictions and racism that blacks experienced. While the middle class continued slowly to expand, most blacks found that they were unable to find the quality of life or security that many white laborers enjoyed. And as more African Americans entered the city, older residents found themselves in competition with new arrivals for the same low-paying jobs. This increased influx also caused more of the city's public services to become exclusive: black Angelenos could only swim at certain beaches, use municipal pools at specified times (usually the day before the pool was to be cleaned), and attend movies and concerts at certain theaters or sit in segregated seats (often called "nigger heaven"). The discriminatory precedent of the "Shenk Decision" quickly spread to local transportation with the rise of jitney buses that refused to serve blacks and enjoyed considerable support from the white population for that policy.[30] Du Bois perceptively acknowledged Los Angeles's silent segregation in the same article in the *Crisis* in which he had praised the city: "Los Angeles is not a paradise. . . . [T]he color line is there and sharply drawn. Women have difficulty in having shoes and gloves fitted at the stores, the hotels do not welcome colored people, and the restaurants are not for all who hunger."[31]

Other black Angelenos worried about the increased discrimination they were encountering. In the same year that Du Bois visited the city, a group of prominent African American citizens petitioned the NAACP to establish a branch in Los Angeles, warning that "problems and grievances arise constantly demanding attention and action by someone on behalf of the race."[32] Soon after, one of the most cherished qualities of Los Angeles—the ability of blacks to acquire homes in many parts of the city—was threatened. As early as 1917, one resident noted that as a result of a growing number of houses being covered by race-restrictive covenants, his tract was "encircled by invisible walls of steel. The whites surrounded us and made it impossible for us to go beyond these walls." Two years later, the California Supreme Court ruled that covenants could be enforced by courts to prevent non-whites from occupying or using property. Within a decade, residential segregation would define a tightly restricted African American community around Central Avenue. That area would become a vibrant community of black hotels, businesses, nightclubs, and educational organizations, such as the 28th Street Young Men's Christian Association (YMCA). But it also became overcrowded, as the continuing influx of southern migrants found few other parts of the city open to them.[33]

Despite all of his skill, passion, and hammering, Edmonds could not make Los Angeles a "place free of discrimination." But his impact and his importance should not be underestimated. First, his vision for the region did encourage many African Americans to move to Los Angeles, changing both the tenor and the color of the city. Much like the *Chicago Defender*, the *Liberator* painted a picture of what was possible in the West. Yet this was an unvarnished picture that revealed both the challenges and opportunities that African Americans would find in Los Angeles. Edmonds's frank portrayals were part of the reason that he was more than simply a black booster for the region. Edmonds realized that Los Angeles had possibilities that had to be made concrete through an effective use of the political system and the media. His strategy for racial change may ultimately have had limited success in early twentieth-century California, but his marriage of political acumen, middle-class aspirations, and the creative use and manipulation of the media was a model that future generations of African American leaders and visionaries would use to good effect. Edmonds was not simply a naive newspaperman who uncritically championed the California Dream. Rather, he was an effective leader whose concrete and creative strategy for racial equality changed Los Angeles.

A year after Edmonds's death, African Americans were in the throes of a "Great Migration" out of the South. Between 1910 and 1920, more than 450,000 blacks would leave for other regions, and during the 1920s nearly 750,000 more would join them. To be sure, the vast majority went to cities in the Northeast and Midwest, yet Edmonds would have been pleased that Los Angeles stood out as the only western metropolis to approach the swelling black populaces of eastern cities, its African American population growing to 38,898 by 1930. Perhaps even more reflective of Edmonds's thinking was the rationale often given for this mass exodus: that cities outside the South, whatever their problems, were a "Promised Land" by comparison to the "Egypt" from which they were fleeing. Thus, not only did Edmonds's activism and creativity make Los Angeles more responsive, even if for a brief period, to the needs and aspirations of its black residents, but he also articulated a dream that would continue to entice thousands of African Americans to the Golden State throughout much of the twentieth century.[34]

NOTES

1. W. E. B. Du Bois, quoted in *Crisis* (August 1913), 192–93; *Liberator*, 16 May 1913, 1, provides an examination of the importance of the visit of Du Bois to the black residents of the city.

2. The desire to emulate William Lloyd Garrison is conveyed in family lore: interview of Edmonds's grandson Chase Edmonds by Bunch, January 1987, Los Angeles, California. Edmonds's use of the motto "devoted to the cause of good government and the advancement of the Afro-American" on the masthead trumpeted his Progressive Era belief in the important role that good government must play in race relations. The masthead with motto appears in *Liberator*, September 1901, 1.

3. Douglas H. Daniels, *Pioneer Urbanites: A Social and Cultural History of Black San Francisco* (Philadelphia: Temple University Press, 1980), though dated, still provides an excellent examination of early black San Francisco. For an introduction to the black community in Oakland, see Lawrence P. Crouchett et al., *Visions toward Tomorrow: The History of the East Bay Afro-American Community, 1852–1977* (Oakland: Northern California Center for Afro-American History and Life, 1989). The population figures are drawn from U.S. Bureau of the Census, *Negro Population in the United States, 1790–1915* (1918; reprint, New York: Arno Press, 1968), 87–107. It is important to note that the lure of Southern California was not restricted to African Americans. The massive influx of white migrants into Los Angeles swelled the city's population to 319,198 in 1910. A good source for understanding this era of Los Angeles history is Kevin Starr, *Material Dreams: Southern California through the 1920s* (New York: Oxford University Press, 1990).

4. See Kevin Starr, *Americans and the California Dream, 1850–1915* (New York: Oxford University Press, 1986).

5. *Liberator*, May 1902, 1; 1 September 1911, 4. Among the many solid works on Progressivism is the old but still valuable George Mowry, *The California Progressives* (Berkeley: University of California Press, 1951), especially chap. 4; and the more recent William Deverell and Tom Sitton, eds., *California Progressivism Revisited* (Berkeley: University of California Press, 1994). Especially instructive on issues of race and reform are John Dittmer, *Black Georgia and the Progressive Era, 1900–1920* (Urbana: University of Illinois Press, 1977); and Joe W. Trotter, ed., *The Great Migration in Historical Perspective* (Bloomington: Indiana University Press, 1991).

6. Edmonds recounted this story to the editors of "The Negro Section" of the *Los Angeles Times* special edition commemorating the centennial of Abraham Lincoln's birth. *Los Angeles Times,* 12 February 1909, 1.

7. Edmonds often spoke and wrote about his life in the South. See the *Liberator*, March 1901, 3; and the *Los Angeles Times*, 12 February 1909, special section, 1. Discussions of racial violence in the South are numerous. Among the works that informed this essay are Herbert Shapiro, *White Violence and Black Response: From Reconstruction to Montgomery* (Amherst: University of Massachusetts Press, 1988), 35–93; Monroe Work, ed., *Negro Year Book, 1931–32* (Tuskegee: Tuskegee Institute Press, 1931), 293; and the *Liberator*, September 1901, 15.

8. For a discussion of nineteenth-century black Los Angeles, see Lonnie Bunch, *Black Angelenos: The Afro-American in Los Angeles, 1850–1950* (Los Angeles: California Afro-American Museum, 1988); and Dolores Hayden, "Biddy Mason's Los Angeles, 1856–1891," *California History* 68 (1989): 86–99.

9. See Bunch, *Black Angelenos,* and Hayden, "Biddy Mason's Los Angeles."

Also helpful is Delilah L. Beasley, *The Negro Trail Blazers of California* (1919; reprint, New York: Negro Universities Press, 1969); and Mikel Hogan Garcia, "Adaptation Strategies of the Los Angeles Black Community, 1883–1919" (Ph.D. diss., University of California, Irvine, 1985), chap. 2.

10. *Liberator*, 15 November 1912, 1. See Bunch, *Black Angelenos*, for an account of Edmonds's attending the Los Angeles Men's Forum, 21–24. Edmonds initially settled with friends in Pasadena, but within a year he relocated to the city of Los Angeles.

11. For insights into the challenges faced by African American newspapers, refer to Penelope L. Bullock, *The Afro-American Periodical Press, 1838–1909* (Baton Rouge: Louisiana State University Press, 1981), chap. 4; Charlotta A. Bass, *Forty Years: Memoirs from the Pages of a Newspaper* (Los Angeles: California Eagle Publishing, 1960); interview with Chase Edmonds, January 1987.

12. *Liberator*, October 1902, 5; 31 March 1911, 5.

13. Ibid., November 1901, 4; April 1902, 7; 15 November 1912, 4; interview with Chase Edmonds, January 1987.

14. Los Angeles supported several black newspapers from the late nineteenth to the early twentieth century. Preceding Edmonds were the *Owl*, which later was renamed the *California Eagle* and became an important chronicler of black Los Angeles from the 1920s to the 1950s, and the *New Age*. The *Liberator* was one of the most sophisticated African American newspapers in America. *Liberator*, 21 April 1911, 6; 31 January 1913, 1.

15. Three works that illuminate the violence and discrimination that southern blacks faced are Stewart E. Tolnay and E. M. Beck, *A Festival of Violence: An Analysis of Southern Lynchings, 1882–1930* (Urbana: University of Illinois Press, 1995); David Oshinsky, *Worse Than Slavery: Parchman Farm and the Ordeal of Jim Crow Justice* (New York: Free Press, 1996), chaps. 2 and 3; and Eric Foner, *Reconstruction: America's Unfinished Revolution* (New York: Harper and Row Publishers, 1988), chaps. 3 and 12.

16. *Liberator*, September 1901, 9; 1 September 1911, 4; November 1901, 3.

17. *Liberator*, 21 April 1911, 3; November 1901, 6. So strong was the desire for integrated schools that black Californians rallied against a "Tuskegee Institute-like" vocational school that was to be built in the Central Valley in 1914–15. While most African Americans recognized the need to enhance black educational opportunities, they feared that an all-black educational institution might lead to the resegregation of California schools. For a discussion of this controversy, see Eleanor Mason Ramsey, "Allensworth—A Study in Social Change" (Ph.D. diss., University of California, Berkeley, 1977), 170–89.

18. *Liberator*, November 1903, 4; January 1904, 4; May 1901, 5.

19. U.S. Bureau of the Census, *Thirteenth Census of the United States, 1910,* vol. 2, *Population, Reports by the States* (Washington, DC: Government Printing Office [GPO], 1913), 180; U.S. Bureau of the Census, *Fourteenth Census of the United States, 1920,* vol. 3, *Population, Composition, and Characteristics of the Population* (Washington, DC: GPO, 1922), 118. One of the best works to explore the economic growth of early-twentieth century Los Angeles is Robert Fogelson, *The Fragmented Metropolis: Los Angeles, 1850–1930* (1967; reprint, Berkeley: University of California Press, 1993), chaps. 4 and 7. The importation of black workers and their competition with Mexicans for unskilled jobs is covered in Charles Wollenberg, "Working on El Traque: The Pacific Electric Strike of 1903," *Pacific Historical Review* 42 (1973): 358–69.

20. These businesses are explored in Bunch, *Black Angelenos,* 21–22; and the *Liberator,* 17 January 1913, 2.

21. *Liberator,* December 1903, 3–4.

22. Ibid., May 1902, 6.

23. Ibid., January 1903, 4.

24. Edmonds realized that closely contested elections increased the value of the black vote. He began listing his preferred candidates as early as 1901. See ibid., December 1901, 1. Edmonds claimed his endorsement meant success for political candidates, for example, Harry Rose's defeat of John Shenk in 1913; see ibid., 6 June 1913, 1; November 1902, 4.

25. Ibid., November 1901, 4; 15 November 1912, 1. For a detailed account of Roberts's legislative career, see the essay by Douglas Flamming in this anthology.

26. *Liberator,* April 1902, 7; December 1903, 5; 17 January 1913, 5.

27. This episode is explored in Bunch, *Black Angelenos,* 22–23. The Shenk Decision dominated the columns of the *Liberator* for weeks; see *Liberator,* April–June 1913. The practice of excessively charging black patrons slowly faded after 1913, as businesses awoke to the profits that could flow from the increased spending power of the rapidly expanding African American community.

28. For examples of the sentiment for Edmonds at the time of his death, see Bunch, *Black Angelenos,* 28; and Beasley, *Negro Trailblazers,* 259. A poem written during Edmonds's life also captures the meaning of his death; see *Liberator,* 6 December 1912, 2.

29. *Liberator,* 14 June 1912, 4–5.

30. Lawrence B. de Graaf, "City of Black Angels: Emergence of the Los Angeles Ghetto, 1890–1930," *Pacific Historical Review* 39 (1970): 341–42; Rick Moss, "Not Quite Paradise: The Development of the African American Community in Los Angeles through 1950," *California History* 75 (1996): 229–30.

31. *Crisis*, August 1913, 195.

32. Emory Tolbert, *The UNIA and Black Los Angeles: Ideology and Community in the American Garvey Movement* (Los Angeles: Center for Afro-American Studies, 1980), 33–34. Interestingly, Edmonds was not among the black leaders who formed the NAACP chapter.

33. Quote from J. Max Bond, *The Negro in Los Angeles* (Ph.D. diss., University of Southern California, 1936; reprint, San Francisco: R and E Research Associates, 1972), 69; de Graaf, "City of Black Angels," 328, 337–38. Job discrimination also became a growing problem, which the local NAACP chapter challenged in cases like *George Cushnie v. City of Los Angeles*, Board of Playground and Recreation Commissioners, Case #180780, Records of the County Court of Los Angeles.

34. See Lawrence B. de Graaf, *Negro Migration to Los Angeles, 1930–1950* (Ph.D. diss., University of California, Los Angeles, 1962; reprint, San Francisco: R and E Research Associates, 1974). Several studies of the Great Migration have been published in recent years. See especially James R. Grossman, *Land of Hope: Chicago, Black Southerners, and the Great Migration* (Chicago: University of Chicago Press, 1989); and Carole Marks, *Farewell—We're Good and Gone: The Great Black Migration* (Bloomington: Indiana University Press, 1989). For an overview of the Central Avenue community, see Bette Yarbrough Cox, *Central Avenue—Its Rise and Fall, 1890–c. 1955* (Los Angeles: BEEM Publications, 1996); and the essay by Cox in this anthology.

Harvests of Gold

African American Boosterism, Agriculture,

and Investment in Allensworth and Little Liberia

DELORES NASON MCBROOME

D uring his visits to Los Angeles in 1903 and 1914, Booker T. Washington urged his African American audiences to promote their communities through free enterprise. Washington's support for all-black towns and land development schemes for economic self-sufficiency encouraged several African American entrepreneurs in California to participate in business ventures that they hoped would foster economic growth. Allen Allensworth, a lieutenant colonel newly retired from the U.S. Army, and Hugh E. Macbeth, an attorney appointed in 1914 as special counsel to the Los Angeles district attorney's office, were two such entrepreneurs who actively promoted farming and real estate ventures for black Californians as a means to achieve economic self-sufficiency and investment opportunities. Allensworth and Macbeth espoused values of middle-class culture and lifestyle and a view that in California blacks could attain them. Their ideas were shared by many California boosters; for a while, each man enjoyed support from California's black communities.[1] This support itself mirrored the diverse motives behind California agriculture, as it ranged from the romance of returning to the soil to visions of speculative wealth without engaging in farming.

Agriculture was California's most significant economic activity in the late nineteenth and early twentieth centuries, and it took on very different forms. Many farms were typical of those throughout most of the northern states—small, family enterprises, as much a way of life as a business. But a few, especially those that kept intact large land grants of the Spanish and Mexican era, became large-scale enterprises employing seasonal migratory

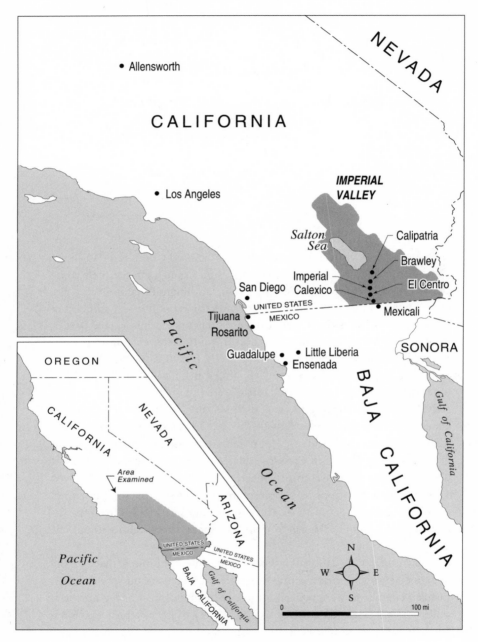

MAP 2. Allensworth, the Imperial Valley, and Baja California

labor. Many people also entered farming as a speculative venture in real estate as well as for the profit of growing crops.[2] African Americans were employed in various agricultural enterprises throughout the state, yet they
never were a conspicuous or significant element. This limited presence contrasts with their greater visibility in the state's large cities.

The absence of African Americans from California's rural areas and the
state's agriculture was typical of their experiences in most parts of the
United States outside of the South. However, almost all other minority
groups in California before World War II were well represented in rural
areas and in agriculture. First, American Indians, then Chinese, and later
Mexicans, Japanese, Filipinos, other Asians and Pacific Islanders, and some
European immigrant groups became substantial members of the farm labor
force, some becoming entrepreneurs in certain crops.[3] From the collapse of
Reconstruction to the 1920s, southern blacks made numerous efforts to establish racial agricultural colonies in the Midwest and Southwest, but only
a few were attempted in California.

Allensworth and Macbeth tried to mobilize large numbers of African
Americans to engage in agriculture and rural living, but their colonization
schemes illustrate the difficulties blacks encountered in agriculture in California at a time when it was increasingly becoming an industrial enterprise,
requiring substantial capital and a hired labor force. Both ventures, but particularly Macbeth's, also show that boosters promoted exaggerated visions
of their projects. When these enterprises failed to live up to their promises,
the result was a residue of distrust that would extend to race enterprises in
general. To Allensworth's and Macbeth's surprise, most African Americans
were unwilling to take up farming or rural life in California. Studying these
two ventures gives valuable insight into the demography, economy, and
views of the state's African Americans at that time.

Efforts to settle African Americans outside the South on farms were observed in the North before the Civil War. Abolitionists made several attempts to lure free blacks from northern cities into farming communities
with promises of free land. Most of these efforts failed, partly for economic
reasons, but largely because African Americans resisted moving to rural
areas. As Frederick Douglass lamented in 1853, "From some cause or other,
colored people will congregate in the large towns and cities; and they will
endure any amount of hardship and privation, rather than separate, and go
into the country."[4] Another clue to the limited rural presence of African
Americans was the widespread fear among whites of blacks coming to

northern or western states in large numbers. This was a major factor in attempts to pass exclusion laws in several states, including California. That state inserted into its Homestead Laws of 1851 and 1860 a stipulation that "free white persons" were eligible for homesteads, leaving the impression that blacks were not welcome to obtain land. The net result was noted by a San Francisco editor in 1869, who observed that a few African Americans had settled in rural towns around Sacramento and San Jose, but that generally he found few in business, including agriculture.[5]

African Americans did appeal to some early white farmers as a possible source of cheap labor, usually for working with cotton. As early as 1854, California farm journals were predicting that the state would become a center for growing the crop, and the earliest plans to develop that idea envisioned importing a black slave labor force from the South. When antislavery feeling proved insurmountable, cotton proponents briefly considered employing white Americans. After 1870, thousands of Chinese workers released from building the transcontinental railroad became available as farm labor. Utilizing blacks for rural labor was rarely mentioned until the late 1880s, when the Chinese Exclusion Act of 1882 began thinning the ranks of Chinese immigrants. In 1888, some growers' organizations arranged with railroad companies to import several hundred African Americans from the South and built cabins for them. About that same time, grape growers in Fresno also brought in several hundred blacks. Neither effort was successful, as many blacks quickly found that they could obtain better wages elsewhere and often left before they had worked off their railroad fare.[6] Soon after, a depression and then Japanese immigration gave growers other sources of cheap labor, and African Americans effectively disappeared from large-scale California agriculture.

But blacks were not completely absent from farming and ranching. In 1890, 1,098 African Americans in California, one-fourth of all employed black males in the state, worked in agriculture, fishing, and mining, most of them in agriculture. Many appear to have been family farmers, and in some cases, they amassed considerable acreage. Wiley Hinds came to Visalia in 1858 and, after working as a hired hand for ten years, began buying land. By the turn of the century he owned more than 2,200 acres, mostly near Farmersville, and employed black ranch workers.[7] By that time, African Americans were present in several other Central Valley rural communities. A colony of black farmers was established in Fowler in 1890 and had grown to thirty or forty families by 1904. Bowles and Fresno also had black ranch owners, though their spreads often comprised no more than ten acres. In Bakersfield, several African American merchants combined city homes with livestock ranches outside town, a pattern also noted in Paso Robles, near the coast. In Madera, one black farmer who arrived in 1882 owned 1,750 acres by 1902.[8]

The new century brought several new efforts to attract African Americans to California as farmworkers. Following Washington's trip to the state in 1903, a San Joaquin Valley white farmer offered to hire Tuskegee graduates as laborers and provide each with a ten-acre plot. While local black leaders ridiculed this plan, the *Pacific Coast Appeal* supported its "back to the soil" spirit: "In the states and territories of the southwest there is room for millions of settlers. . . . There is work for every one who wants it. The crying need of California is faithful workers in the fields and orchards." A year later, the paper proclaimed that "colored families are flocking to the San Joaquin Valley from all parts of the country" and lauded that region as offering "golden opportunities to the sober and industrious members of the race who are willing to go there and labor."[9]

There is little evidence, however, that any substantial number of African Americans responded to such invitations. Following the 1880s, farm meetings and journals suggested utilizing a wide range of labor, from white tramps to American Indians, but blacks were never mentioned. Possibly because of the successive arrival of other minority groups, or because many farmers continued to hope that the immigration of Chinese laborers would again become legal, or possibly because African Americans were aware that growers associated agricultural laborers with "slaves," "mud sills," and other derogatory stereotypes, the black presence in California's fields remained minor.[10] But by 1907, one prominent member of the race felt that locating a black farm colony there would be both feasible and noble.

Colonel Allen Allensworth was born a slave but escaped bondage and joined the Union Army's Civilian Hospital Corps during the Civil War. After his discharge, Allensworth secured an appointment as a teacher in the Freedman's Bureau. Later he attended Roger Williams University in Nashville, where he studied theology. Ordained as a Baptist minister, Allensworth became a pastor in Kentucky and Ohio, and then chaplain in the African American Twenty-fourth Infantry. His army service included both the Spanish-American War and the Philippine-American War. Upon his retirement in 1906, Allensworth held the highest rank of any black officer in the army at that time: lieutenant colonel. In 1907, along with other African

American investors, he purchased farmland in the San Joaquin Valley, where he established the all-black townsite of Allensworth. He organized the California Colony and Home Promoting Association, which incorporated in 1908 to establish the township north of Bakersfield. He and his associates envisioned a self-governed community for African Americans free from discriminatory laws and practices.[11] Allensworth created a news release in the *Daily Tulare Register* that asserted that "the town . . . is to enable colored people to live on an equity with whites and encourages industry and thrift in the race." Handbills depicting the countryside surrounding Allensworth "emphasized the possibility of gaining wealth while living in the San Joaquin Valley's Jim Crow-free society."[12]

Allensworth was a California version of all-black colonies that had been created in parts of the South, then in Kansas during the great "Exodus" of 1878–79, and later in Oklahoma. Motivation for those African American migrations rested largely on the search for a refuge from lynch law and the dependency of sharecropping in the South. Incorporation of all-black townsites and colonies required recruitment of people willing to migrate and invest in them. Colonel Allensworth followed patterns set by the exodusters when he established an association to promote migration and investment in the community.[13] The California Colony and Home Promoting Association was the organization that acquired a site for the colony. Starting with only ten dollars, and thus being unable to purchase land,

> [The] Association entered into a promotion agreement with three white-owned real estate companies that owned large blocks of land in the San Joaquin Valley. The three companies platted an eighty-acre townsite in Tulare County in the center of the valley, forty-five miles north of Bakersfield and sixty miles south of Fresno. . . . Evidence suggests that the black consortium contracted with the companies for some unrecorded amount of money to secure African-American settlers for the townsite and got the companies' agreement to reserve the surrounding lands for black farmers.

The association advertised for home buyers nationwide and in three years sold more than four hundred parcels of land, valued at $112,000. This promotion also appeared in some Los Angeles black newspapers, such as the *New Age*, which by 1914 was running a regular "Allensworth Notes" column, and in its own community paper, the *Sentiment Maker*, which began in 1912.[14]

Much of this promotion focused on themes that gave the colony a philosophical mission. One was the "agrarian ideal," a notion going back to Thomas Jefferson that crossed racial and ethnic lines, which held that moving to rural areas could transform the unproductive urban poor into proud, hard-working landholders and thus change a corrupt world by instilling a model of a better life.[15] This view was summarized by the Reverend Kinchen, a black pastor, when he visited Allensworth in 1917:

> Yes, it would be better if more of us had ourselves and children away from the kind of civilization with which we are surrounded and like the citizens of Allensworth, make for ourselves a civilization with an atmosphere of freedom and high moral ideals—a civilization that gives the womanhood of the race an opportunity to stay at home and help God build men and women of our boys and girls, and not leave them at the mercy of every evil influence.

Promotional brochures for the colony linked such lofty goals to its rural setting by portraying Allensworth as a community with "corn billowing in the wind, artesian water flowing several feet over its well casing, paved streets, and pretty houses by beds of flowers."[16]

Allensworth was also based on the ideal, widely promulgated by Booker T. Washington, that in a California setting African Americans could cultivate and reap the rewards of such virtues as industry and thrift. According to this philosophy, it was important that Allensworth was an all-black enterprise. As its founder wrote in 1912, the colony was "a unique school of citizenship" that would "show that we have a racial consciousness, racial homogeneity, and the faculty of racial initiative."[17] These goals culminated in an effort in 1914 by the leaders of the colony to have the state establish a State Industrial School at Allensworth. Endorsed by blacks in several other farming communities in the San Joaquin Valley, this school was to follow Washingtonian principles of industrial education. While this proposal, put forth in a bill by the local assemblyman, did not specify that the school was only for African Americans, Los Angeles black leaders quickly feared it would be "the entering wedge for segregated schools in the state." Their vocal opposition was one reason the state legislature rejected the proposal in 1915.[18]

During its early years, there was reason to believe that the Allensworth colony might live up to its lofty goals. Its location on a Santa Fe railroad stop promised ready access to markets. White-owned land firms, especially the Pacific Farming Company, helped install an artesian water system, and in a few years the site had grown to a complete town. Its base of small farms was supplemented by several black businesses, including a hotel and a post office. In 1910, the county set up a public school that four years later was rebuilt, with the original structure becoming a library. That year also saw the town become a judicial district, electing colony leader Oscar Overr as the first African American justice west of the Rocky Mountains. Its civic ideals were implemented by the Allensworth Progressive Association, which functioned as a multidepartment local government and offered its residents training in municipal affairs.[19]

Yet only a small number of settlers were attracted to the colony. Eleanor Ramsey's study of Allensworth found that it supported from 120 to 200 people between 1908 and 1920. By 1930, Allensworth's black population had declined to 44 residents. However, Tulare County's African American population had increased from 190 people in 1910 to 819 by 1930, suggesting that the colony might have attracted settlers into neighboring communities.[20]

In the years following Colonel Allensworth's death in 1914, the town continued to prosper, but its promotion shifted to a nationwide appeal to those African Americans who wished to migrate for "a medley of reasons such as health, politics, family, and military experiences." Joshua Singleton, an Allensworth settler who suffered from lung disease contracted while working in a Kansas stone quarry, was typical of many residents who chose to migrate to the township. Joshua's father, Benjamin "Pap" Singleton, had promoted an earlier migration of African Americans from Tennessee to Kansas in the late 1870s. In Joshua Singleton, one can see a convergence of the various leading race philosophies of African Americans in the twentieth century. His racial attitudes incorporated Booker T. Washington's belief that blacks would find liberation through a strong economic foundation based upon their own labor, skills, and landownership in separate communities. However, Joshua Singleton also embraced much of the philosophy of W. E. B. Du Bois, who believed that advancement for African Americans necessarily included social and political reform. Considering himself an "out-spoken Race man," Joshua, "according to his son Henry, had long been a Du Bois supporter, one who stood for anything intended for the good of the Race," and believed that both white and black people should be entitled to the same rights.[21] This philosophy was manifested in the establishment of a branch of the National Association for the Advancement of Colored

People (NAACP) in Allensworth in 1921. Allensworth residents later embraced a third ideology, one especially laden with potential for proponents of race colonies: Garveyism. By the mid-1920s they had established an Allensworth chapter of the United Negro Improvement Association (UNIA). This organization, based upon the principles of Marcus Garvey, encouraged both economic self-sufficiency and worldwide struggle against racial discrimination.[22]

But philosophical richness could not solve a problem that plagued Allensworth from the early 1920s: lack of irrigation water. This threat appeared as early as 1913, when the Pacific Farming Company took over the water supply to Allensworth and tried to stop sales of land to blacks. Allensworth citizens successfully fought this in court, and by 1914, the colony had grown to about 200 people. In 1919, another company renewed the colony's wells, but observers noted that some residents were jeopardizing their water rights through delinquency in payments. The early 1920s brought drought, and by 1924, Allensworth had less than 100 residents, had closed its NAACP branch, and was struggling to survive.[23] The California black press occasionally repeated pleas for African Americans to invest their lives and money in Allensworth, but as jobs dwindled, more residents moved out. In 1929, the Santa Fe railroad stopped service to Allensworth, and most of its residents had to go outside the town for work, often as farm laborers. In subsequent years, growing soil alkalinity and arsenic contamination of the water supply turned the agricultural colony into a virtual ghost town.[24]

While Allensworth was still a thriving rural community, a second scheme for an all-black colony was being formed, this one to be located in Baja California and dubbed "Little Liberia" by the *Los Angeles Times*. This project was less a whole community of African Americans formed for industrial and civic education as well as farming and more a speculative land investment. But the two shared many characteristics, including each being the brainchild of one California African American—in Little Liberia's case, Hugh Macbeth. Born in South Carolina in 1884, he received his education at the Avery Institute in Charleston and graduated from Fisk University in Nashville in 1905. Macbeth earned a law degree from Harvard in 1908. Moving to Los Angeles in 1913, he quickly joined the Los Angeles Forum, a group of African Americans determined to introduce newcomers to the community and to recognize promising entrepreneurs.

The debates held by Forum members proved crucial to African Americans in Los Angeles, as they were not concentrated in black residential areas during the first decades of the twentieth century. Introductions to newcomers and African American entrepreneurs often took place at the Forum rather than in the neighborhood. According to Dr. J. Alexander Somerville, a Jamaican emigrant who arrived in Los Angeles in 1903, "there were no so-called Negro Districts. Colored people lived in scattered neighborhoods all over the city, some in the West Temple district, some in Boyle Heights, some on West 10th and 11th streets. . . . Negroes owned valuable property in the heart of the business district."25 Much of the business block on Spring Street was owned by Robert C. Owens, an African American entrepreneur whose fortune derived from his real estate investments in the city. Willis Oliver Tyler, Hugh Macbeth's law partner, served as director of the R. C. Owens Investment Company, thereby keeping in close touch with many of the black community's entrepreneurial activities.26

By 1914, Los Angeles's African Americans sought opportunities for land investment beyond their city. That year a group of black settlers established an agricultural colony in the Victor Valley, near the emerging town of Victorville. Such was its growth that by the end of the decade it had a short-lived NAACP chapter, and by 1922 it claimed a branch of UNIA as well.27 In 1914, several leading black Angelenos, including some who had founded the city's NAACP chapter the previous year, formed the Los Angeles People's Realty Company. This real estate company sought to establish for African Americans a colony in Baja California, where, the *California Eagle* assured its readers, "no door of social or industrial preferment would be closed to them, and where they would be free to work out a civilization and a national life of their own."28 While there is no evidence that this company actually set up such a colony, its chosen location soon caught the eye of Hugh Macbeth.

From his earliest years in Los Angeles, Macbeth was a community booster and race advocate. In 1914, Owens, Macbeth, and Tyler appealed to Booker T. Washington to support their efforts to establish a column in the *Los Angeles Times* devoted to African American achievements. Washington introduced their idea in his letter to General Harrison Gray Otis, publisher of the *Times*, in 1914, but he received a skeptical reply. Undaunted, Macbeth pursued this effort to portray "the substantial facts of the worth-while [*sic*] achievements as they may occur among our people," though he never was able to gain entry into the *Times*.29 In 1915, he turned his attention to establishing an agricultural colony of African Americans in Baja California.

Macbeth's selection of Mexico for an African American colony had historical precedents beyond the 1914 land proposal. From its early abolition of slavery in 1829, Mexico had been regarded by blacks as a potential haven, and Mexicans were seen as a people who would treat them with greater equality. Prior to the Civil War, many runaways from Texas had made their way across the border into northern Mexico. In 1850 a group of displaced Seminole Indians and maroons, lured by Mexican schemes to establish military colonies on its frontiers, moved from the Indian Territory to Coahuila, where the Indians and blacks established separate colonies. This was the beginning of a substantial black community at Nacimiento, near Múzquiz, Coahuila, which has survived to the present day. Later, in the 1880s and 1890s, the same "emigration fever" that took many African Americans from the South to Oklahoma attracted others to Mexico.[30]

A potentially more troublesome precedent for Macbeth's plans was the interest the United States government and white entrepreneurs had long taken in Baja California. Partly conquered and nearly annexed during the U.S.-Mexican War, this remote part of Mexico attracted several colonization projects from the early 1860s to the early 1900s. Prophetically, all failed due to lack of colonists. The growth of cotton farming in the Imperial Valley revived interest in comparable farms across the border, however, and by 1916 nearly a thousand Chinese and Japanese workers had been imported to Baja to work on cotton farms.[31] In Macbeth's own city, the managers of the *Los Angeles Times* became interested in the area as a land investment, especially in light of the possibility that Baja's governor might declare it independent of Mexico and partly out of fear of Japanese and German immigration to the area. The latter was a fear shared by the United States government; there was talk of annexation into the early 1920s. When Governor Esteban Cantú opened land to settlers in 1917, the *Times* saw prospects for U.S. citizens to establish colonies there.[32] Thus, Hugh Macbeth brought blacks into an area with a rich heritage of American meddling.

Macbeth's dream of agricultural enterprises seemed to materialize as America entered World War I and increased agricultural production became necessary to sustain U.S. troops and allied military efforts abroad. The war in Europe became a focal point for Hugh Macbeth's address to the second conclave in 1917 of the All-American League. This Los Angeles group straddled the divergent philosophies of Washington and Du Bois while presenting itself as "the connecting link between two great schools, *viz.* Industrialism and Philosophical Education." Under Macbeth's leadership, the League proved more than a link between the two philosophies, for it also promoted interracial cooperation. Warning that the absence of cooperation among Europe's nationalities should be a lesson to all Americans, Macbeth urged an end to racial intolerance and lynch law in the United States.[33]

In his speeches for the All-American League, Macbeth portrayed an America besieged by spies and claimed that the United States "finds itself in the grip of a system of foreign espionage whose agents exist in numbers to the extent of over a hundred thousand." Ironically, this black patriot himself became a target of agents within the U.S. Department of Justice's Bureau of Investigation. The bureau after 1917 began investigating alleged draft evasions by conducting "slacker" raids, especially among California's African American and Latino populations. In early 1918, bureau agent Fred C. Boden contacted Macbeth to inquire about the Baja colonization project, fearing that it offered a way for young African American males to leave the country and thereby evade the draft.[34] Although Macbeth denied these charges, the bureau continued to monitor his travels between Mexico and Southern California throughout the war.

This did not discourage Macbeth from promoting the Baja colony all through the war, however. The local black press echoed his appeals, especially the idea that rural landownership was the solution to the problems of African Americans. Based on the supposition that "back to the Soil [is] the foundation from which all good things come," the *California Eagle* in 1919 proclaimed,

> There is only one solution of the Negro problem in America:
> First: The Negro must become self-supporting;
> Second: He must own enough soil to support himself and his family;
> Third: He must be in a country where his color is not against him. . . .
> Come join us in this colony and lead in the only sure way to freedom. Let us bid our boot-black jobs, our janitor jobs, our porter jobs, and all our scavenger jobs one fond goodbye and become landlords or owners of the soil.[35]

Macbeth added his own unusual twist to this time-honored middle-class view that the poor could be rejuvenated by being relocated in rural areas when he suggested to W. E. B. Du Bois in the midst of the 1919 race riots, "You quietly refer to us for deportation to Lower California, such rioting Negroes as may be causing the government trouble."[36]

For Macbeth personally, Little Liberia represented a means for achieving entrepreneurial success. He never indicated any interest in moving to the colony himself, although he promoted its salubrious climate and agricultural potential. Land and mineral wealth in Baja provided urban African American investors an opportunity for economic success. Edward J. Sullivan, another African American entrepreneur in Los Angeles, suggested the possibilities in 1921:

> Lower California is a garden only waiting to be tilled by American genius to yield a harvest of gold. . . . Lower California is a vast empire pregnant with great possibilities. It is a very inviting field for Los Angeles merchants and manufacturers. It is on the threshold of great prosperity. The mineral wealth of that peninsula is boundless. While I was there I met a number of Americans who are looking after that territory with a view to developing its mineral resources. I also met several representatives of the British government, who, I understand, have obtained valuable concessions for the development of oil. Geological surveys made by the Mexican government show that in Lower California there exist the most important oil deposits yet discovered.37

The mention of mining concessions in Baja, along with the agricultural promise of the promoters, is typical of the booster mentality that so many African Americans in California exhibited. The *California Eagle* ran articles suggesting the potential for lucrative mineral investments if African Americans invested in Baja's real estate. It proclaimed "that some day the Santa Clara mining district of Lower California would become notable as one of the greatest gold-producing camps in Mexico, reason enough to induce a number of well-organized companies, headed by expert mining men of ample means, into planning to properly develop some of the best known properties in the district."38

Under Governor Cantú, African American entrepreneurs found employment in Baja California and increased their ability to participate in real estate development in Mexico. Edward Sullivan welcomed the opportunity: "There are many things we can learn from our friends to the south of us. It is our duty to cultivate their friendship. They want to trade with us and it is our duty to meet them halfway." Cantú appointed James N. Littlejohn, an African American highway and sewer contractor from Los Angeles, to begin road construction from Ensenada to Calexico in 1917. The Mexican government chose as primary contractor for the Baja highway Heraclio Ochoa, who in turn employed Hugh Macbeth as his company's attorney. The *California*

Eagle endorsed the highway project as a way "to get in on the ground floor in the development of this rich country."[39]

Soon African American entrepreneurs in Los Angeles began to recognize the potential for land development in Baja, and in early 1918 Macbeth applied for incorporation of the Lower California Mexican Land and Development Company (hereafter Lower California Company). This company considered purchasing six different parcels of land in Baja California, including 21,000 acres of ranches in the Rincon and Santa Clara Valleys roughly thirty-seven miles northeast of Ensenada. The company secured approval of its project from U.S. Secretary of State Robert Lansing.[40] The officers of the board of directors included several African American entrepreneurs from Los Angeles, with Theodore M. Troy as president and Macbeth as secretary. The Lower California Company established a branch agency in New York to handle eastern applications for company land tracts. In 1918, the Lower California Company offered minimum tracts of five acres at $20 per acre to men and women seeking to be "sovereigns of [their] own labor, who want to be really free!" Macbeth's association with Ochoa proved profitable for the Lower California Company when Ochoa, the proprietor of a new flour mill in Ensenada, negotiated with the Lower California Company to ‑purchase its entire wheat crop from Santa Clara for $100,000 annually.[41]

The feasibility of establishing a colony in Baja had already been determined by Russian immigrants who had founded an agricultural community in 1905, eighteen miles south of the Lower California Company's properties. Although Guadalupe's principal crop became wheat, the soil of both Guadalupe and the Lower California Company also was good for growing oranges and vegetables. Water, located in wells on the property of the Lower California Company, offered the possibility of irrigation running from the property's northeast corner through Sulphur Canyon and its Sulphur Springs. Although the lands were too close to the coast for good cotton culture, the investors decided to try growing walnuts, citrus fruits, alfalfa, potatoes, and melons.[42]

Meanwhile, Manuel Aguirre Berlanga, the Mexican Minister of the Interior, issued an official statement on 21 June 1919 that encouraged colonization of Mexico by foreigners. Macbeth, acting as attorney for the Lower California Company, was bolstered by Berlanga's pronouncement:

> The prospects for those who would go into Mexico to become part and parcel of that great, though struggling Republic, are indeed bright. As is

indicated in the statement of [the] Minister of Interior, Manuel Aguirre Berlanga, Mexico desires immigrants who respect her country sufficiently to help build it up and live in the country. The Lower California movement has for its object the fulfillment in the peninsula of Lower California of the high purposes expressed by the Minister of Interior for the Republic of Mexico generally.[43]

Such friendly exchanges between Macbeth and the Mexican authorities led the Lower California Company to advertise that its colonists would be received by a welcoming population. For its part, the Mexican government appeared to welcome minorities and advertised this in its statements. While African American investors in Baja had little difficulty at first with the Mexican revolutionary governments, Anglo American investors found that many of their properties were threatened by Mexican nationalization after 1914. This fact was not lost upon either Macbeth or the African American investors in Lower California. Macbeth, with typical exaggeration, observed in 1921, "It has been demonstrated that the colored man is the only American who mixes harmoniously with the natives of Mexico." He apparently saw no contradiction in going on to predict that "it is not beyond the range of possibility that a negro state may be established in Lower California. It might be possible to create a state with [a population of] 20,000 . . . in the course of a decade or so."[44]

Some African Americans believed that they received more favorable consideration from revolutionary leaders in Mexico because Mexicans allegedly compared their experience of American intervention to the historic oppression of blacks within the United States. In 1919, the *California Eagle* proclaimed, "Mexico is the country in which the white man is the same as a Negro in Mississippi and where a Colored man is regarded as the equal of all men." John Prowd, an African American stockholder in Little Liberia, believed Mexico to be "the land of freedom and opportunity—where a man breathes the atmosphere of tolerance, where his ambitions and dreams be within himself for realization and not within his COLOR."[45]

The African American press often highlighted speeches given by visiting Mexican dignitaries who encouraged migration to their country. When Licentiate Juan B. Uribe arrived in Los Angeles to conclude the transfer of the Santa Clara Ranch to the Lower California Company in September 1919, the *California Eagle* ran an article proclaiming Uribe's vision of interracial harmony:

Although Macbeth exaggerated the amount of stock sales for the larger audience of the *Los Angeles Times* article, he believed the colonization efforts
of the Lower California Company would promote investment opportunities
for talented and ambitious African Americans.

With an ironic twist, the *Los Angeles Times* reported that Macbeth
thought the Lower California Company would

> serve as an entering wedge for the white man in Mexico. He [held] the
> opinion that as the Negro gains a foothold there and proves his value as a
> citizen, the Mexican will be more friendly to American capital. "If Los An-
> geles continues to grow it will soon be the Chicago of the West, and Lower
> California will eventually be the bread basket of Los Angeles," declared Mr.
> Macbeth. "That's why I am giving my best efforts to this colonization plan.
> It appeals to me as being a wonderful opportunity for colored people."53

Macbeth's middle-class proclivities became apparent when he emphasized
that "it is not our purpose to establish this colony as a retreat for poverty-
stricken Negroes. The country is raw and undeveloped, and it will take
cracker-jack farmers to bring out the best that is in it, but there are wonderful possibilities hidden there for the man who has a little livestock and a
little machinery and a great deal of determination."54

The 1920s brought another potential party into the land development
and colonization schemes of Los Angeles blacks: Garveyites. From its origins in New York, Marcus Garvey's UNIA established branches across the
country, including ones in San Francisco and San Diego in 1920. In January
1921, a group of black Angelenos who had admired Booker T. Washington's
ideas of self-help and black business formation established a Los Angeles
chapter. On 4 March 1921, Hugh Macbeth requested that the UNIA help
promote the Lower California Company. His letter received the attention of
J. D. Gordon, assistant president general of the UNIA in New York, who
replied that there appeared to be "a harmony" between the racial uplift objectives of his organization and the Lower California colony project. Gordon stated that "these Negroes going to Lower California will thereby keep
themselves in touch with the great body of Negroes of the world, having
freedom there, more than they could enjoy in America, and they would play
a most telling part."55

The stormy internal politics of the Los Angeles UNIA chapter, and its
quick division into two rival groups, should not obscure its work. Through-

out the 1920s, UNIA cooperated with some of the community's leading black residents and engaged in a variety of enterprises, including at least one proposal for a black colony in Arizona. While this ultimately failed to materialize—in part because of misgivings Los Angeles Garveyites had about the white minister-speculator who pushed the plan—it illustrates both the continued dream of black colonization as a path for "redeeming" the race and the ties some of those plans had to black nationalistic movements.56

The early 1920s promised an expansion of potential clients for the Lower California Company. In addition to Macbeth's speeches, the *Los Angeles Examiner* inadvertently helped by publishing in October 1921 a story of the automobile trip of "Cactus Kate II" to Baja, which featured her visit to the properties of the Lower California Company. Other African American boosters also showed interest in the colony. In November 1921, T. F. Neal and his wife traveled to Lower California from Oklahoma in their seven-passenger Packard, the "Katy Flyer." Emory and Edna Bowdoin of Los Angeles made the trip along with the Neals and became ardent promoters for the Baja investments. Edna Bowdoin claimed to have received "the most wonderful inspiration" on her trip:

> And so impressed is she with what she has seen that she has announced her intention to visit every colored women's organization in California, religious or fraternal, social or otherwise, big or little, and tell the story of the Lower California movement to every loyal colored woman in the state so that every colored child in California may have the advantage of sharing in this wonderful enterprise and enjoying its rich profits of the future.57

These boosters were successful in encouraging others to invest in the Lower California Company lands.

The following year saw more wealthy tourists from Oklahoma, led by a J. B. Key, make the trip to Little Liberia. Shocked by the deaths and property destruction caused during the Tulsa race riots of 1921, these individuals sought new regions for investment. The pressures of racism, which became blatant after Oklahoma achieved statehood in 1907, also served as a catalyst for migration. Oklahoma's black townships had offered political autonomy in the nineteenth century, but by the time of statehood, these towns were beginning to experience, as James R. Grossman has noted, "disappointment, disillusion, and hardship."58 It is not surprising then that the Key delegation drove to Lower California to meet with Governor Lugo in Ensenada and then with other Mexican officials in Mexico City to discuss investment opportunities. President Alvaro Obregón of Mexico met with the Key delegation on 16 June at Chapultepec, where he told them that "the laws of Mexico are very liberal and do not recognize the doctrine of Race supremacy, and because of this fact it was judged that there would be no serious obstacles in the way of permitting the colonization of colored people."[59]

Clarence Brooks, an actor from the African American-owned Lincoln Motion Picture Company in Los Angeles, and Hugh Macbeth were among the Californians accompanying the Oklahoma delegation to Mexico City. While Brooks filmed the journey, Macbeth introduced the delegation to President Obregón:

> We are here before you at the present moment representing the great majority of Colored American citizens who wish to become a part and parcel of this great and rich country. We do not mean to come here and acquire or exploit whatever part of the wealth of Mexico we can and then ship it to some other country for its benefit. On the other hand we want to become a part of this incomparable country and we want to become citizens of this Republic and bring to it all our wealth, our ability and efforts in order to help develop it and make it among the very greatest of nations.[60]

In addition to Obregón's affirmation that Mexico would never create a color line, the delegation obtained support for the Lower California Company's commercial endeavors. These discussions arranged for the establishment of a bank at Ensenada financed partly by Mexican investors as well as African Americans. The Mexican government also negotiated with the Lower California Company on the establishment of a sugar plantation and factory at Cuernavaca.[61]

As a result of the Oklahoma delegation's actions, the Lower California Company reorganized in 1922 and elected J. B. Key its president with Dr. A. O. Williams as treasurer. The company created twenty-four special boards of management to deal with immigration, interracial harmony, commerce, and transportation issues. While in Los Angeles, the Key delegation received recognition from the Chamber of Commerce, the first time an African American delegation had received such courtesies. In return for the Mexican hospitality, Macbeth promoted a petition campaign in November 1922 seeking recognition of the Obregón government by President Harding and the U.S. Congress.[62]

Such triumphs proved short-lived. Nineteen twenty-three saw the beginning of a series of setbacks that eventually put an end to the colony. Early that year, the U.S. Department of the Interior circulated to border offices an order from Obregón to prevent African Americans from entering Mexico. While professing no color bias, Obregón based his action upon concern that blacks would aggravate "the ethnic problem" Mexico already was experiencing with its Indian population. He was also influenced by "talk for weeks past of extensive colored immigration to Mexico." While no news stories linked this order with the Baja colony, Macbeth's pompous oratory may well have been one reason for it. Obregón's order was carried out in select instances at first. Later that year, for example, the Mexican government refused to allow an African American who had settled there in 1909 to return, after he had fled during the revolution. An American official observed that "the Mexican Government has no objection to settlers entering the country, with the exception of colored people." In 1926, Mexico issued a new order requiring all African Americans entering Mexico to obtain special passports.[63]

As this latest order was announced, African American author Arna Bontemps deplored the fact that few blacks had taken advantage of the colony. He attributed their hesitation to the fact that the Baja colony "was new and meant venture. It meant setting out where no paths had been worn and no white man had led." Years later, a black pastor attributed the unpopularity of the colony to its rural nature—"as country as country can be." Blacks saw little difference between such a settlement and the rural South and doubted they would benefit financially from moving there. The southern analogy was reinforced in 1926, when the San Diego branch of the NAACP complained that shops in Tijuana were posting signs stating "colored not wanted."[64]

With its twin hopes that Mexico was a land free of discrimination and that blacks would welcome the opportunity to "return to the soil" shattered, the Baja colony received another blow in 1927 when three stockholders in the Lower California Company, James N. Littlejohn, Claudius Troy, and Junius Stevens, called for the first audit of the company's books since its organization. They also tried to reduce Macbeth's control over the company by passing a motion to increase the number of directors from the seven originally designated in 1918 to nine. Macbeth and some other stockholders attempted to derail the motion to audit the company books at a public meeting in March 1927. He requested two armed policeman stand guard at the meeting to keep order. Although Claudius Troy publicly

accused him of being "nothing but a yellow Negro crook," Macbeth controlled the meeting's agenda by entertaining a motion from stockholders to
adopt the auditor's report and add it to the company's files without having
it read on the floor.[65] These actions, however, convinced many who followed the proceedings that Macbeth's interests in Little Liberia served only
his own self-promotion and financial well-being.

Claiming that the Lower California Company did not own clear title
under Mexican law to the Santa Clara ranch, throughout the spring of 1927
Junius Stevens criticized Macbeth's actions as company attorney. In a move
designed to discredit Macbeth, Stevens filed charges against him with the
Los Angeles Bar Association in April for misusing company monies. Arnold
Shankman, a historian writing of the image of Mexico in the black press,
viewed the negative publicity of these charges as one of the reasons why
Mexican colonization schemes began to wane among African Americans
during the late 1920s. Citing a series of articles appearing in the *California
Eagle* during 1927, Shankman noted:

> The Lower California, Mexican Land and Development Company went
> bankrupt in 1927. Several of its promoters and its legal counsel were
> swindlers, and within five years their mismanagement of the company's as-
> sets had been responsible for the accumulation of debts totaling $78,000.
> The ranch at Ensenada had been used not for farming but rather for lavish
> "drinking and poker" parties. Hundreds of investors discovered that their
> stock was worthless, and they were not likely again to view Mexico as a land
> of milk and honey.[66]

Despite allegations against him, Macbeth continued to promote real estate
ventures for African Americans in Lower California. A Los Angeles Bar Association hearing in May 1927 found no censure for Macbeth's legal counsel
to the Lower California Company. When Willis Petroleum Company began
to explore Baja properties in 1928, it offered to buy lands from the Lower California Company, which still existed under a new board of directors. Willis
Petroleum's board of directors passed a resolution refuting charges that Macbeth, "while an officer and Director in the Lower California Mexican Land
and Development Company, misused the public's funds." Although Willis
Petroleum did not buy the property, this report helped Macbeth repudiate
the charges against him. His reputation remained favorable among leading
Los Angeles investors within both the black and white communities.[67]

TABLE 1. African American Rural and Farm Populations
in California, 1900–1930

	Rural Population	Percentage of Black Population	Farm Population		Black Percentage of All	
			Operators	Laborers	Operators	Laborers
1900	2,970	26.9	135	267	0.2	N/A*
1910	3,246	15.0	159	365	0.2	N/A
1920	4,875	12.6	290	728	0.2	N/A
1930	10,529	13.0	424	2,304	0.3	N/A

*not available

James N. Littlejohn's account of the demise of Little Liberia suggests that the demands of the Mexican government for repatriation of its land after 1928 had as much to do with the colony's failure as did financial misman-agement. Littlejohn remained an investor in the Santa Clara ranch. In 1928, he became a Mexican citizen under President Calles, who tried hard to prevent any new American capital investment in Mexico. When the other shareholders of the Lower California Company did not become Mexican citizens, the Calles government disbanded it, leaving Littlejohn, the only Mexican citizen, "in full possession" of the former company's lands.[68]

The demise of Little Liberia and the decline of Allensworth by the end of the twenties also mark the end of Washington's dream that "Back to the Soil" movements would answer the needs of California's African Americans. Blacks continued to be involved in the state's agriculture—in fact their numbers grew more during the 1920s than in any previous decade. But agricultural pursuits and rural residence continued to involve only a small fraction of the African American population, and blacks constituted only a minuscule part of California's farm industry, as can be seen in table 1.[69]

While California's small African American rural and farm populations did grow during the 1920s, the results were hardly what Colonel Allensworth, Hugh Macbeth, or newspapers like the *Eagle* had envisioned. Most of the growth came in farm labor, especially on recently formed cotton farms in the Imperial Valley. This essentially amounted to African Americans returning to the low-pay, dead-end occupations they had sought to escape when they had left the South. The modest increase in farms operated was offset by a sharp decline in actual ownership and a rise in the percentage of tenants to nearly half of all black farmers by 1930. Decades of trumpeting the need to own land had brought African Americans only 1.2 of every 1,000 acres of California farmland by 1930, a lower percentage than twenty years earlier when colonization was starting.[70]

The African American ventures in Allensworth and Baja California provide interesting examples of black booster mentality and enterprise in California during the early twentieth century. Little Liberia's investors especially exemplify the entrepreneurial attitudes associated with Booker T. Washington that from the early 1900s through the 1920s were widely believed to be the key to uplifting the race. African Americans in that colony understood boosterism to mean promotion of racial self-sufficiency and thereby the realization of independence from white domination. Those ideals also underpinned the Allensworth project, but the more prominent hope in that case was that blacks could find in rural settings a healthier environment in which to build families and fortunes.

Both sets of ideals ran counter to the realities of California's agricultural economy and society. From the initial Spanish land grants, much of California's farmland had been controlled by a small number of landowners who owned large tracts of land, which put small farms at a competitive disadvantage. Even when many of these large holdings broke up, as happened to the bonanza wheat farms in the late nineteenth century, their smaller successors were usually specialized, commercial activities, requiring considerable capital and expertise. As one historian has stated, "Modern capitalism, not a pastoral idyll, reigned on western farms." The agrarian ideal worked no better for farm laborers, who found it increasingly hard to work their way into management or ownership and usually became part of an exploited body of workers that changed in ethnicity but rarely in status.[71] Many African Americans undoubtedly were aware of these realities, which helps explain their unwillingness to go "back to the soil."

The failure of Allensworth and Little Liberia also illuminates facets of African American business endeavors at that time. The project boosters were part of a broader movement to encourage blacks to patronize their own businesses and thus establish economic control over their own communities. This effort was pushed by several African American newspapers, initially as part of Washington's effort at building an ethic of individual enterprise among blacks. By the time of the Baja colony, that view had been modified by Garvey and the UNIA into a "philosophy that the only meaningful advancement for blacks was group advancement." As a prominent member of the Los Angeles chapter of the UNIA, Macbeth could envision

Little Liberia, as some had seen Allensworth, as a community in which blacks controlled all businesses and services.⁷²

But this ideal conflicted with a different set of realities. The same newspapers that urged blacks to "support their own" frequently noted the prevalence of contrary attitudes. An Oakland paper in the early 1920s observed that "petty spite, envy and jealousy have played an important part in destroying our Race enterprises; the anti-everything people have rendered yeoman service in the cause of retrogression in business." After several more years of advocating black businesses, one of that paper's writers bemoaned that "there exists a time honored prejudice that so many colored people have against doing business with their own people."⁷³ These attitudes help explain the limited financial support given to either colony and the wide net that promoters had to cast among their race to secure investors. Ironically, by ending in charges of misuse of funds and having all but one investor lose his land, Little Liberia may have reinforced blacks' doubts about their race businesses and contributed to discouraging further ventures.

The fate of these colonies may have inadvertently supported another African American skepticism about entrepreneurial activities: that outside forces would undo them. Allensworth settlers first had to resist the Pacific Farming Company's efforts to bar colonists and take over their water, then watch the colony decline as they realized they had been sold an area in which the water resources were inadequate and the soil too alkaline to support long-term farming. Blacks who invested time and money in the Baja colony, meanwhile, could only watch helplessly as the Mexican government ruled their deeds invalid and expropriated their land.

The last decades of the nineteenth and the first decades of the twentieth century mark a period in which some of California's black population tried to make a living and a place for themselves in the state through farming. Their presence in agricultural towns and their efforts at all-black colonies constitute a colorful and little-studied chapter of African American history. But their most grandiose ventures ended in failure; the Great Depression would substantially reduce the number of their farms, and by the 1940s, little more was heard of returning to the land. Two ambitious projects had promised harvests of gold, but they produced crops of disillusionment. The colonies' most lasting impact was to reinforce the trend of California's African Americans to congregate in major cities and urban occupations for the remainder of the twentieth century.

NOTES

1. Douglas Flamming, in his essay "African-Americans and the Politics of Race in Progressive Era Los Angeles," suggests that "studies of black Los Angeles have ignored the politics of progressivism." The essay appears in William Deverell and Tom Sitton, eds., *California Progressivism Revisited* (Berkeley: University of California Press, 1994), 203–4. For the importance of Washington's visits to Los Angeles in 1903 and 1914, see Rudolph M. Lapp, *Afro-Americans in California*, 2d ed. (San Francisco: Boyd and Fraser Publishing Company, 1987), 36–39; Louis R. Harlan and Raymond W. Smock, eds., *The Booker T. Washington Papers*, 14 vols. (Urbana: University of Illinois Press, 1972–1989), vol. 7, 20–25; and Louis R. Harlan, "The Secret Life of Booker T. Washington," *Journal of Southern History* 37 (1971): 394–95.

2. Cletus E. Daniel, *Bitter Harvest: A History of California Farmworkers, 1870–1941* (Ithaca, NY: Cornell University Press, 1981), 17–19.

3. On the succession of ethnic and racial groups in California's farm labor force, see Varden Fuller, "The Supply of Agricultural Labor as a Factor in the Evolution of Farm Organization in California," reprinted in Senate Subcommittee of the Committee on Education and Labor [La Follette Subcommittee], *Hearings on S. Res. 266, Violations of Free Speech and Rights of Labor,* 74th Cong., 2d sess., part 54; California State Relief Administration, *Migratory Labor in California* (San Francisco: California State Relief Administration, 1936); Mark Reiser, *By the Sweat of Their Brow: Mexican Immigrant Labor in the United States* (Westport, CT: Greenwood Press, 1976); Sucheng Chan, *This Bittersweet Soil* (Berkeley: University of California Press, 1986).

4. Leon Litwack, *North of Slavery: The Negro in the Free States, 1790–1860* (Chicago: University of Chicago Press, 1961), 176–77.

5. Ibid., 161; Delilah L. Beasley, *Negro Trail-Blazers of California* (1919; reprint, New York: Negro Universities Press, 1969), 60; *San Francisco Elevator,* 19 February 1869.

6. Daniel, *Bitter Harvest,* 24; Bryan T. Johns, "Field Workers in California Cotton" (Master's thesis, University of California, Berkeley, 1948), 5–16; Fuller, "Supply of Agricultural Labor," 17313–14; Robert Glass Cleland and Osgood Hardy, *The March of Industry* (Los Angeles: Powell Publishing, 1929), 122–23; Davis McEntire, *Population of California* (San Francisco: Parker Printing Company, 1946), 45.

7. Henry J. Gannett, "Occupations of Negroes," in U. S. Bureau of the Census, *Report on the Population of the United States at the Eleventh Census, 1890,* part

2 (Washington, DC: Government Printing Office [G P O], 1897), 1389; *A Memorial and Biographical History of the Counties of Fresno, Tulare, and Kern, California* (Chicago: Lewis Publishing Company, 1892), 288; Beasley, *Negro Trail-Blazers*, 131; *Pacific Coast Appeal*, 14 May 1904, 2.

    8. *Pacific Coast Appeal*, 16 August 1902, 4; 4 October 1902, 1; 18 July 1903, 1; 14 May 1904, 2; *California Eagle*, 20 July 1918, 5.

    9. *Pacific Coast Appeal*, 14 March 1903, 4; 23 April 1904, 4.

    10. Daniel, *Bitter Harvest*, 27–28; Alvin H. Thompson, "Aspects of the Social History of California Agriculture, 1885–1902" (Master's thesis, University of California, Berkeley, 1953), 276–79; Paul S. Taylor, "Foundations of California Rural Society," *California Historical Society Quarterly* 24 (1945): 223–26.

    11. *The Story of the Negro in Los Angeles County*, Octavia B. Vivian, comp. Federal Writers' Project of the Works Progress Administration (Washington, DC: 1936; reprint, San Francisco: R and E Research Associates, 1970). On Allensworth's military career, see John Phillip Langellier, "Chaplain Allen Allensworth and the 24th Infantry, 1886–1906," *Smoke Signal* 40 (1980): 190–208.

    12. Kenneth Marvin Hamilton, *Black Towns and Profit: Promotion and Development in the Trans-Appalachian West, 1877–1915* (Urbana: University of Illinois Press, 1991), 140.

    13. Land speculation ventures among African Americans in the nineteenth century were sporadic but resulted in over 100 black towns. During the period from 1890 to 1910, blacks found encouragement for westward settlement from such men as Edwin P. McCabe, founder of Langston, the first all-black town in Oklahoma. McCabe promoted Langston "as a new El Dorado where the black man was to prosper and rule supreme in his own community." Homer C. Hawkins, "Trends in Black Migration from 1863 to 1960," *Phylon* 34 (1973): 140–52.

    14. Eleanor Mason Ramsey, "Allensworth: A Study in Social Change" (Ph.D. diss., University of California, Berkeley, 1977), 57, 77.

    15. Daniel, *Bitter Harvest*, 15–17; Richard White, *"It's Your Misfortune and None of My Own": A New History of the American West* (Norman: University of Oklahoma Press, 1991), 433.

    16. E.W. Kinchen, "Observations from Allensworth," *California Eagle*, 16 July 1917, 8; Ramsey, "Allensworth," 77.

    17. *New York Age*, quoted in Hamilton, *Black Towns and Profit*, 142.

    18. *California Eagle*, 26 December 1914, 4; 9 January 1915, 4; 30 January 1915, 1.

    19. Beasley, *Negro Trail-Blazers*, 154–55; *California Eagle,* 29 August 1914, 3; *Sentiment Maker*, 15 May 1912, 1, 5.

    20. Ramsey, "Allensworth," 101; U.S. Bureau of the Census, *Fourteenth Census*

of the U.S. Taken in the Year 1920, Population (Washington, DC: G P O, 1921–22), vol. 1, table 53, vol. 3, table 9. U.S. Bureau of the Census, *Thirteenth Census of the United States Taken in the Year 1910, Population* (Washington, DC: G P O, 1913), vol. 2, table 1. U.S. Bureau of the Census, *Fifteenth Census of the U.S., 1930, Population* (Washington, DC: G P O, 1932), vol. 3, part 1, table 13, and table 21.

21. Nell Irvin Painter describes the motivations of Pap Singleton, including his millenarian vision for a black community, in *Exodusters: Black Migration to Kansas after Reconstruction* (New York: Knopf, 1977), especially 206. See also Ramsey, "Allensworth," 85.

22. Abraham Stockett to Robert W. Bagnall, 24 January 1924, Papers of the N A A C P, Branch Files, Box G–14, "Allensworth" file, Manuscript Division, Library of Congress [hereafter cited as N A A C P Papers]. Emory J. Tolbert, *The U N I A and Black Los Angeles: Ideology and Community in the American Garvey Movement* (Los Angeles: U C L A Center for Afro-American Studies, 1980), 58, 92–93.

23. *California Eagle*, 3 October 1914, 1; 16 April 1919, 1; Stockett to Bagnall, 24 January 1924, 18 March 1925, N A A C P Papers; Shirley G. Streshinsky, "The Town in the Old Man's Head," *Los Angeles Times, West Magazine*, 1 August 1971, 12.

24. Interview of Charlotta Bass by Lawrence de Graaf, 15 September 1966; *Los Angeles Times*, 1 June 1970, sec. 4; *Orange County Register*, 28 February 1993, E10. For an example of later appeals to settle in Allensworth, see *San Francisco Western Appeal*, 3 February 1926. In one respect, Allensworth beat the odds, as it lasted far longer than most colonization ventures. The all-black township survived sixty-eight years, until it was designated a historic state park in 1976.

25. Patricia Adler, "Paradise West: A Study of Negro Attitudes toward the City of Los Angeles" (paper presented for History 680, University of California, Los Angeles, 22 May 1969), 7, located in the Elizabeth and James Abajian Collection of Afro-American Bibliographical Correspondence, Bancroft Library, University of California, Berkeley.

26. Ibid.

27. Tolbert, *U N I A and Black Los Angeles*, 58.

28. *California Eagle*, May 1914, 1.

29. Harlan and Smock, eds., *Washington Papers*, vol. 7, 107.

30. Kevin Mulroy, *Freedom on the Border: The Seminole Maroons in Florida, the Indian Territory, Coahuila, and Texas* (Lubbock: Texas Tech University Press, 1993), chaps. 2, 3, and passim. On schemes promoting emigration to Mexico, see Karl Jacoby, "From Plantation to Hacienda," *Alabama Heritage* (Winter 1995): 36; and Rosalie Schwartz, *Across the Rio to Freedom: U.S. Negroes in Mexico* (El Paso: Texas Western Press, 1975).

31. Ruth E. Kearney, "American Colonization Ventures in Lower California, 1862–1917" (Master's thesis, University of California, Berkeley, 1944), passim; Paul S. Taylor, *Mexican Labor in the United States: Imperial Valley* (Berkeley: University of California Press, 1928), 13–15.

32. *Los Angeles Times*, 17 June 1913; 9 December 1917; 19 January 1918.

33. "The Economic Status of the Negro in California," *California Eagle*, 29 April 1916, 1; "The Second Conclave of the All-American League," ibid., 24 February 1917, 1.

34. Fred C. Boden, "Case file OG132476, Report on Colored Colony in Lower California, Mexico," in *Federal Surveillance of Afro-Americans, 1917–1925: The First World War, the Red Scare, and the Garvey Movement*, Theodore Kornweibel, ed., 25 microfilm reels (Frederick, MD: University Publications of America, 1986), reel 10, frame 135.

35. *California Eagle*, 5 July 1919, 1; 9 August 1919, 4.

36. W. E. B. Du Bois, *The Papers of W. E. B. Du Bois*, 89 microfilm reels (Amherst: University of Massachusetts, 1980), reel 7, Macbeth to Du Bois, 6 August 1919. For another example of the booster concept, see White, "*It's Your Misfortune*," 434–35.

37. "Edward J. Sullivan Paints Glowing Picture," *California Eagle*, 15 October 1921, 1.

38. "Lower California Is a Field for Investment," ibid., 23 January 1923.

39. Ibid., and 12 and 19 May 1917.

40. Ibid., 9 February 1918. The Santa Clara properties comprised 8,762 acres while the Vallecitos ranch in the Rincon Valley comprised 13,031 acres. Ibid., 1 October 1921; 8 February 1919.

41. Ibid., 30 March 1918; 14 June 1919.

42. Ibid., 5 July 1919. "Plan Little Liberia in Mexico," *Los Angeles Times*, 16 October 1921, sec. 2, 10.

43. *California Eagle*, 19 July 1919.

44. *Los Angeles Times*, 16 October 1921, sec. 2, 10.

45. *California Eagle*, 19 July 1919; Arnold Shankman, "The Image of Mexico and the Mexican-American in the Black Press, 1890–1935," *Journal of Ethnic Studies* 3 (1975): 45.

46. *California Eagle*, 13 September 1919.

47. Ibid., 27 April 1918; 25 May 1918. The C-M Ranch, owned by the Harry Chandler-Otto Brand syndicate, had extensive agricultural and ranch lands in both the Imperial Valley and Mexico.

48. Ibid., 29 November 1919; 14 February 1920.

49. Ibid., 6 December 1919.

50. Ibid., 21 December 1919; 17 January 1920.

51. Ibid., 27 December 1919. Properties south of Santa Clara on the Gulf of California islands Catalina and Carmen had reported petroleum deposits. The Mexican government appointed a special commission to investigate not only the deposits on these islands but also *chapopote*, a high grade of oil–bearing sand, near Ensenada.

52. *Los Angeles Times*, 16 October 1921, sec. 2, 10.

53. Ibid.

54. "Plan Little Liberia in Old Mexico," *California Eagle*, 22 October 1921.

55. Robert A. Hill, ed., *The Marcus Garvey and Universal Negro Improvement Association Papers*, 9 vols. (Berkeley: University of California Press, 1983–95), vol. 3, letter from J. D. Gordon to Hugh Macbeth, 14 March 1921, 321–22.

56. Tolbert, UNIA *and Black Los Angeles*, 53–54, 60–61, 66–67.

57. *California Eagle*, 29 October 1921; 5 November 1921.

58. Jimmie Lewis Franklin, *The Blacks in Oklahoma* (Norman: University of Oklahoma Press, 1980), 12, 26–27, 29–30; National Register of Historic Places, *African American Historic Places* (Washington, DC: Preservation Press, 1994), 402–3; James R. Grossman, *Land of Hope: Chicago, Black Southerners, and the Great Migration* (Chicago: University of Chicago Press, 1989), 25. See William Elmer Bittle, *The Longest Way Home: Chief Alfred C. Sam's Back-to-Africa Movement* (Detroit: Wayne State University Press, 1964) for an account of Oklahomans who tried to emigrate to the Gold Coast in 1914–15.

59. *California Eagle*, 1 July 1922.

60. Ibid.; information on Clarence Brooks's filming of the journey can be found in the *California Eagle*, 27 May 1922. The George P. Johnson Film Collection at UCLA's University Research Library Special Collections unfortunately does not contain footage of the journey.

61. *California Eagle*, 1 July 1922.

62. Ibid., 27 May 1922; "Recognition of Mexico, Pleas of Negro Voters," *Los Angeles Times*, 22 November 1922, part 1, 11. During the early Obregón administration, Harry Chandler of the *Los Angeles Times*, a developer of land in Mexico, encouraged friendship between the U.S. and Mexico. Anglo-American rapprochement with Mexico seemed possible. See Ed Ainsworth, *Memories in the City of Dreams* (Los Angeles?: n.p., 1959).

63. *Los Angeles Times*, 8 February 1923, sec. 1, 7; 8 November 1926, sec. 1, 10; *California Eagle*, 3 March 1923, 2; American Counsel, Bristow, OK, to William Vann, 26 June 1923, "Migration" files, NAACP Papers.

64. Arna Bontemps quote in *California Eagle*, 31 March 1923, 8; the Reverend L. F. Catley, interviewed by Lawrence de Graaf, 24 August 1966; *Western Appeal*, 1 October 1926, 1. Bontemps in 1923 was a student at Pacific Union College, Saint Helena, California; the Reverend Catley was a pastor in Los Angeles.

65. *California Eagle*, 4 March 1927; State of California, "Certificate of Change of Number of Directors of the Lower California Mexican Land and Development Company," 21 April 1927, originally indexed 85878, California State Archives, Sacramento.

66. *California Eagle*, 13 May 1927; Shankman, "Image of Mexico in the Black Press," 46.

67. *California Eagle*, 12 October 1928. Macbeth's continued legal advocacy of African Americans through his various appointments as counsel for the Los Angeles N A A C P and president of the African American lawyers' organization known as the Blackstone Club as well as his membership in the Republican Central Committee placed him near the center of most political activities in Los Angeles during the 1920s. In 1931, Macbeth became a cofounder of the Los Angeles Lawyers Club, which included prominent white attorneys such as Marshall Stimson. In 1936, Macbeth served as Consul for the Republic of Liberia in Los Angeles. Throughout this period, he maintained his interests in liberal leaderships in the Mexican government. See *Who's Who in California*, vol. 1 (Los Angeles: Who's Who Publications Company, 1942/43), 568.

68. "Mexican Rancher: Ensenada's Lone Negro Male is Hamlet's Leading Citizen," *Ebony*, October 1952, 84, 86.

69. Table 1 is drawn from U. S. Bureau of the Census, *Negro Population in the United States, 1790–1915* (Washington, DC: G P O, 1918), 92, 528, 607; U.S. Bureau of the Census, *Negroes in the United States, 1920–32* (Washington, DC: G P O, 1935), 593, 596; U.S. Bureau of the Census, *Fourteenth Census of the United States, 1920*, vol. 4, *Population, Occupations* (Washington, DC: G P O, 1922), 882; U.S. Bureau of the Census, *Fifteenth Census of the United States, 1930*, vol. 4, *Occupation Statistics: California* (Washington, DC: G P O, 1932), 27.

70. *Negroes in the United States, 1920–32*, 593–94, 596–97; *Negro Population, 1790–1915*, 589. M. Eva Thacker, "California's Dixie Land," *California History Nugget* (March 1938): 178–79.

71. White, *"It's Your Misfortune,"* 435 (quote); Daniel, *Bitter Harvest*, 18–19; Carey McWilliams, *Factories in the Field: The Story of Migratory Farm Labor in California* (Boston: Little, Brown and Company, 1939), 7.

72. Tolbert, *U N I A and Black Los Angeles*, 38–39, 66, 92–93 (quote).

73. *Oakland California Voice*, 7 January 1922, 2; 6 August 1926, 2. For a

summary of explanations of the relatively small number of African American businesses compared to other minority groups, see Ivan H. Light, *Ethnic Enterprise in America: Business and Welfare among Chinese, Japanese, and Blacks* (Berkeley: University of California Press, 1972).

In Search of the Promised Land

African American Migration to San Francisco, 1900–1945

ALBERT S. BROUSSARD

Since 1848, California has attracted African American migrants from all over the United States. Most of these, however, came to California after 1900 and originated from the South. Examining what caused them to migrate to the Golden State, when and from where they came, and what kind of people made this journey is essential to understanding black experiences in California. Did California, indeed, represent a land of unlimited opportunity for African Americans, or did, in fact, segregation restrict access to housing, employment, schools, and public accommodations, as happened in the South and in some northern and midwestern states?

The experience of blacks who migrated to San Francisco was unique. San Francisco is one of the most cosmopolitan and racially tolerant cities in the United States. Throughout its history, the Golden Gate city has welcomed immigrants from virtually every region of the world. These sojourners have come to San Francisco with the hope of creating a better life for themselves and their families. African Americans, who were among the earliest pioneers in San Francisco and participated in the famed California Gold Rush, also shared this recurrent dream: that San Francisco possessed an almost mythical ability to help them succeed and recast their lives.

This essay will explore the strategies African Americans used in migrating to San Francisco between 1900 and 1945, the adjustments that they had to make in their new locale, and the employment and housing opportunities available to them. This was a time of tremendous growth and sweeping change in San Francisco as well as throughout the West Coast states. A major economic and demographic shift toward the Pacific Coast from the

South Atlantic and Gulf states transpired during the 1940s. The American mobilization for World War II profoundly affected the growth of San Francisco's African American community and other black settlements in the far western states.

Studying migration to a western city like San Francisco provides a more complete picture of African American urban life and permits meaningful comparisons between black migrants in West Coast cities and migrants of all races and nationalities in other regions of the nation. Unlike many northern and southern cities during the late nineteenth and early twentieth centuries, San Francisco had never attracted a sizable black population. Less than 500 African Americans were reported in that city in the 1852 California census, though that represented approximately one-half of California's total black population. By 1860 the number of African Americans in San Francisco had increased to 1,176, while the state's black populace had swollen to 4,000, both significant increases in the space of eight years. Throughout the remaining decades of the nineteenth century, the city's black population continued to grow slowly, never reaching 2,000 inhabitants. San Francisco contained the largest black population in the state until 1900, when it was surpassed by Los Angeles's 2,131 African American residents.[1]

San Francisco's earliest black settlers were principally natives of the Northeast and New England and of states along the North-South border, such as Maryland, but approximately one-third were southern born. These migrants from the East and South journeyed to San Francisco using many means of transportation. Some, like Anne Fuller, who worked as a stewardess on a ship, came by steamer from the Isthmus of Panama or around Cape Horn. Others traveled by covered wagon, horse, or burro. A few slaves, such as Rheubin Murrell and Alvin Aaron Coffey, accompanied their masters to California in search of gold. Since travel from the East was expensive, it was also common to find blacks working as cooks, laborers, and stewards on ships. Afterwards some of these individuals stayed on in San Francisco or other Pacific Coast communities.[2]

Although African Americans migrated to San Francisco for many reasons, the majority, like their white and Asian counterparts, wished to improve their economic condition. The prevalence of blacks in the state's mining districts illustrates this point. One observer reported that their presence was noted by the "original naming of at least thirty-odd geographical features either Negro or Nigger."[3] Thus African Americans, though admittedly

arrived with only $30 in his pocket, Daly started a housecleaning business, saved his money, and purchased the Oakland, California, *Voice*, an established black newspaper, in 1927. By the early 1930s, his business acumen and ingenuity had enabled him to purchase three additional black weekly newspapers, giving Daly a monopoly of African American journalism in the Bay Area.[12]

Not all African American migrants came directly from the southern states. Some had worked in the East, Midwest, or Pacific Northwest before relocating to San Francisco. Such sequential migrations were not uncommon with black southerners, who often migrated first to northern industrial cities and worked at a variety of unskilled jobs to save enough money to take their families west. Yet we know far less about the pattern that black migrants followed once they arrived in the West, particularly those who settled in Bay Area cities. Evidence, drawn largely from oral interviews and biographical accounts, suggests that some western migrants, generally members of the middle class, settled in San Francisco after working in several other cities. The black attorney McCants Stewart, for example, relocated from Portland, Oregon, to San Francisco in 1918. Yet Stewart, who was raised in Brooklyn, New York, and educated at the Tuskegee Institute and the University of Minnesota Law School, had practiced law in Minneapolis and Portland before his arrival in San Francisco. His reasons for moving there were strictly economic, for he hoped to take advantage of the Bay Area's larger black community to support his struggling law practice.[13] F. L. Ritchardson, a Denison, Texas, native, migrated to San Francisco in 1917 from Parsons, Kansas, where he had resided with his parents. Ritchardson, however, was not attracted to San Francisco because of the lure of a better job; instead, he hoped to escape military service by moving west. Although he worked a number of unskilled jobs, Ritchardson ultimately obtained employment at the United States Post Office, where he became one of the highest-ranking black postal officials in the Bay Area by the time of his retirement.[14] These middle-class African Americans were attracted to San Francisco not because of factory jobs, but because they believed the city represented a hospitable, albeit competitive, environment where blacks could excel in white-collar jobs.

Revels Cayton, the brother of the noted writer Horace Cayton, also migrated from the Pacific Northwest to San Francisco in 1922. Although Cayton's family had resided in Seattle for three decades, he found the city economically restrictive for African Americans. Cayton worked as a seaman, an occupation that had attracted a small number of West Coast blacks since the nineteenth century. Cayton's migration and the relocation of McCants Stewart to San Francisco reveal that blacks in some Pacific Coast communities were more optimistic about their employment prospects in that city than in either Seattle or Portland. Cayton's optimism was well founded, as he became a leader within the Marine Cooks and Stewards Union and the Minorities Committee of the Congress of Industrial Organizations (CIO) during the 1930s and 1940s. McCants Stewart, however, became disillusioned with employment conditions in San Francisco and committed suicide in 1919.[15]

African American women migrated far less frequently than men during World War I, but some believed that San Francisco would be more hospitable for employment and educational advancement. Many had heard about San Francisco through friends or relatives or from soldiers who had visited, an indication that a small communication network was indeed in place by World War I. Still others followed their parents or husbands to the Golden Gate city, and a handful braved the trip alone. Such was the case with Larena Frances Herndon, who left St. Louis in 1913. Stating that she had grown tired of the cold weather in St. Louis and also was encouraged to migrate by a black soldier who had already settled in San Francisco, Herndon made the four-day journey by railroad alone. Shortly after her arrival, Herndon was joined by her sister, and the two women remained in San Francisco for the remainder of their lives.[16]

Herndon represents one of the few examples of black women who journeyed to San Francisco alone during the World War I era. Societal standards governing the behavior of women probably discouraged this type of travel. Moreover, African American women who traveled alone, as Darlene Clark Hine has noted, were at much greater risk of sexual exploitation and physical violence than black men. This must have discouraged many from considering this option. Others had the responsibility of raising small children, which gave them less freedom than men to migrate long distances.[17]

African American women also moved to San Francisco and other Bay Area cities to further their education or to provide better opportunities for their children than those offered by the limited Jim Crow schools in the South and some areas of the Southwest. Vivian Osborne Marsh, for example, migrated from Houston, Texas, to the Bay Area with her parents in 1913. Marsh cited the superior Bay Area schools as one of the principal reasons for her parents' decision to move there. Three years after arriving, she attended the University of California, Berkeley, where she earned a bachelor's degree in 1920 and a master's degree in anthropology in 1922. Marsh was later appointed head of the National Youth Administration's Division of Negro Affairs for California and also served as national president of Delta Sigma Theta Sorority between 1935 and 1939. The experiences of Herndon, Marsh, and other migrant black women are significant. The ways gender affected black migration have frequently been overlooked. We cannot automatically assume that African American women migrated for the same reasons as their male counterparts or that their expectations or experiences were identical.[18]

African American migration to San Francisco slowed during the 1930s, largely in response to the effects of the Great Depression. Between 1930 and 1940, San Francisco's black population grew by approximately 1,000 (from 3,803 to 4,806), an increase of 26.3 percent. By 1930, San Francisco's African American community was approximately one-tenth the size of that of Los Angeles and half that of Oakland. On the eve of World War II, just 4,806 blacks out of a population of 634,536 lived in San Francisco, less than 1 percent of the city's total.[19] Clearly the city was not as attractive to those choosing to migrate west in the 1930s.

Yet black migration to other parts of the state continued briskly throughout the decade, particularly to Southern California. Los Angeles, for example, increased its black population to 63,774 in 1940 from 38,894 a decade earlier. Moreover, poor white farmers migrated to California in large numbers during the 1930s to escape oppressive economic conditions in Oklahoma, Arkansas, Texas, and Missouri, although few chose the Bay Area as their destination. "Okie" and "Arkie" migrants also included many African Americans who originated from the states affected by those economic misfortunes. Although some of the 800,000 Dust Bowl migrants who came west during the 1930s and 1940s settled in urban areas, approximately one-half moved into the San Joaquin Valley, California's agricultural heartland. Job opportunities, however low paying, were key in the migrants' selection of an area in which to relocate.[20]

World War II was a watershed for African Americans throughout the nation and particularly in the West. No other place illustrates this as dramatically as San Francisco. The war stimulated a massive migration of African Americans to the Bay Area for the first time in California's history. Although San Francisco's black population growth had been relatively static between 1850 and 1900 and modest between 1910 and 1940, it swelled by more than

600 percent between 1940 and 1945. In 1945 a special census reported that 32,001 African Americans lived in the city. Five years later San Francisco's black community had grown to 43,460, almost a nine-fold increase from the 1940 census. Only a handful of western or northern urban communities had experienced such rapid growth during a comparable period.[21]

When the United States entered World War II, the nation's economy was transformed, and throughout the Bay Area the black population suddenly increased significantly. One factor above all made the Bay Area an especially attractive destination for blacks: the immediate availability of lucrative jobs, particularly in defense industries and in the shipyards. By 1943, the Bay Area had become the "largest shipbuilding center in the world," noted the San Francisco Chamber of Commerce. African American migrants, who were as pragmatic as their World War I counterparts when it came to recognizing employment opportunities, concluded that their economic status could only improve under these circumstances.[22]

The World War II African American migration to San Francisco also formed part of a general demographic shift to the city. The local Chamber of Commerce reported that between 1940 and 1943, 94,000 people moved to San Francisco, "the majority in less than one [year]." Although it is always difficult to estimate population changes between census years, the San Francisco Air Raid Warden Service conducted a 1942 count to "determine the quantities of rationed foods and other commodities which will be made available to the people of San Francisco." Chief Eugene Broderick reported that 728,236 people resided in San Francisco as of 1 December 1942. This figure represented a 15 percent increase from the city's 1940 population.[23]

African Americans migrated to the San Francisco Bay Area in greater proportion than whites. "Negroes are rapidly becoming the most significant minority group in California and if the six Bay Counties are taken together, it is seen that the largest growth of population, both absolutely and proportionately, occurred in this section of the state," wrote Davis McEntire, a professor at the School of Social Work of the University of California, Berkeley. He estimated that the six Bay Area counties reported an increase of 324,000 African Americans in 1943 above their 1940 figures. McEntire added that "the end of wartime migration to California is by no means in sight."[24]

McEntire based his population projections on two factors. Many industrialists had difficulty hiring the number of workers stipulated in their wartime defense contracts. Thus men like Henry Kaiser by 1942 were recruiting workers of all races to migrate to California to work in the shipyards.[25] Additionally, federal agencies, such as the United States War Manpower Commission, attempted to recruit 100,000 workers for Bay Area industries during 1943 alone. The United States Civil Service Commission also worked closely with large Bay Area employers, such as Marinship, Moore Dry Dock, and Kaiser shipyards, to recruit prospective workers. These factors, coupled with the zeal of African Americans to migrate to the West Coast to pursue unprecedented economic opportunities and to shape their own destiny after twelve years of economic depression, assured a constant westward flow of migrants. The vast majority of African Americans had little to lose and a great deal to gain by moving to Bay Area cities during World War II.[26]

African American migrants came to San Francisco by the thousands each month, crowding into established settlements and creating new ones. Sue Bailey Thurman, who later organized the San Francisco Chapter of the National Council of Negro Women, recalled that a small number of blacks (about 5,000) were "scattered all over the city" in 1942 when she visited for the first time. When she returned two years later she stated that "upwards to 40,000 blacks" were living in the city. "It had changed in just that time," she exclaimed.[27] The census bureau confirmed Thurman's observation when it conducted a special census of San Francisco's population by age, color, and sex in 1945. By that time San Francisco's total population had grown to 827,400, an increase of 30.4 percent in five years. Although the city's white population grew at a rate of 28.1 percent during this period, the black population increased by 665.8 percent.[28]

This dramatic increase realigned the percentage of African Americans relative to other minority groups within San Francisco. Blacks had constituted only 15.2 percent of the total nonwhite population in 1940, but by 1945 the African American population totaled 53.1 percent of the city's nonwhite population. The wartime Japanese relocation accounted for part of this startling turnabout, as the number of nonwhites other than blacks declined by almost 4,000 (14.6 percent) during this period. However, 27,155 black migrants moved to San Francisco during the same five-year period. The wartime migration pushed the city's black population far ahead of the Chinese, Japanese, and other nonwhite groups in absolute numbers. The Asian percentage of the population continued to shrink relative to the African American for several decades. The rapid growth of the Latino population occurred principally in Southern California, and African Americans continued to be the largest minority group in the Bay Area for about

also was evident in other western states and territories.[37] Although Johnson argued that the black migrant population possessed a "slight predominance" of females over males, his figures conflict with the special census of 1945, a far more comprehensive source than his limited sample. That census listed the black population as 54 percent male and 46 percent female, the opposite of Johnson's findings. Indeed, the census confirmed that the gender composition of the black wartime migration, which included a larger percentage of African American males, was consistent with that of most migrant populations.[38]

According to one historian of urban history, World War II brought to northern cities such as Chicago a black migrant who differed in many respects from the one who came during the Great Migration. These new settlers were less educated, less sophisticated and urbane, and thus were more likely to become involved in racial disturbances. Because of these characteristics, they were also less likely to find employment during the postwar era and had far greater difficulty escaping the ghetto. One unfortunate consequence was the creation of a "second ghetto" maintained by white developers, local officials, and the decentralizing policies of the United States Housing Authority, which led to segregation in low-income housing. The type of African American migrant who came to San Francisco, as well as to other California cities during World War II, does not seem to fit this theory, although the letters of some "old residents" appear to confirm the image. Rather, San Francisco's World War II black migrants, irrespective of gender, were almost as well educated as its established African American residents.[39]

African Americans used many of the same strategies in migrating to San Francisco during World War II that they had adopted successfully during the first Great Migration. Although government recruitment played an important role in their decision, as did the more vigorous recruiting campaigns of large industrialists like Henry Kaiser, black migrants likely were more influenced by the letters and stories of immediate family members, relatives, and friends. African American migrants in many instances made the westward trek to San Francisco and to other Bay Area communities after hearing informally that jobs were plentiful.[40] Blacks congregated on street corners, in beauty salons and barber shops, in pool halls and recreation centers, and in churches to spread the word that San Francisco offered high wages and economic opportunity to those who were willing to work. The "grapevine," an informal network of communication that had endured from the antebellum era, played a particularly important role. The 1941

Tolan Congressional Committee, which conducted an extensive investigation into "National Defense Migration," noted: "Almost every defense migrant who testified before the committee explained that he had heard from relatives, or from neighbors or friends, about the job openings." The committee concluded that "this information put these workers on the road."[41]

One of the African Americans who heard that high-paying defense industry jobs were available in California was Sarah Lane Hastings. Hastings's example is particularly intriguing because she was a widow raising two young adopted children in Kansas City, where she had settled after her husband died in World War I. Hastings represented the majority of gainfully employed African American women in the nation prior to World War II, for she had worked as a domestic her entire adult life and her meager earnings, approximately $10 a week, were reduced even further during the Great Depression.[42] She was employed by the Works Progress Administration in Kansas City in 1942 when she decided to take a night class on welding that she saw advertised in her neighborhood. After completing the course, which certified her to work as a welder in the shipyards, Hastings temporarily left her older daughter with relatives, packed up her eleven-year-old son and boarded a train to California.[43]

Sarah Hastings arrived in Los Angeles in June 1942. The presence of an established African American community there meant that a network of service and community organizations was already in place when migrants arrived. However, the new arrivals placed an enormous strain on housing, transportation, social services, and recreation facilities. A greatly increased African American community confined to little more than its prewar area also meant that segregation, particularly in housing, became an established feature; the emergence of the black ghetto in Los Angeles predated the World War II migration.[44] After working in Los Angeles for a year, Hastings and her children moved to San Francisco, where she was employed as a welder in the shipyards until 1945. Following the conclusion of World War II, Hastings resumed domestic work until she retired in the 1960s. Although she returned to Kansas City and Oklahoma periodically to visit relatives and friends, she remained in San Francisco until her death in 1977.

Black migrants like Hastings traveled to San Francisco in different ways, but the majority journeyed by train or bus. Rail transportation had been the preferred mode of transportation among southern blacks during World War I, and after twelve years of economic depression, it was unlikely that the majority could have purchased automobiles. But not all African American migrants were poor or destitute. Some owned cars as well as land and homesteads, and black as well as white migrants followed Route 66 to California. Willie Stokes, a black farm laborer from rural Arkansas, migrated to the Bay Area to work in the shipyards in 1943 and sent for his wife and children within six months. The entire family made the journey by bus. Indeed, southern rural blacks had been traveling in this manner for decades. As Peter Gottlieb concluded in his study of black migration to Pittsburgh between 1916 and 1930, African Americans "combined migration patterns from their rural environment with new ways of traveling."[45] Blacks and whites alike, motivated by the promise of economic opportunity and a better life, migrated to the West Coast along similar routes and by common modes of transportation.[46]

The World War II migration also significantly expanded San Francisco's black leadership class, as hundreds of skilled, white-collar African Americans came to work. Many eventually occupied important leadership positions in the coming decades, while others worked in interracial organizations to advance the cause of equality. They included Howard Thurman, one of the most distinguished black theologians in the nation, who migrated to San Francisco to establish Fellowship Church, which he described as the first "fully integrated" congregation in America. Seaton W. Manning, who formed the first Urban League chapter in the city, William McKinley Thomas, a physician and the first black selected to the San Francisco Housing Authority commission, and James Stratten, the first African American to serve on the city's board of education, also migrated during the war. The emergence of such leaders illustrates the importance of the wartime migration for the black community of San Francisco as a whole.[47]

The dramatic increase in San Francisco's black population between 1940 and 1945 had significant consequences, and one of the most important was intense competition for housing. Although African American residents and civil rights organizations such as the National Association for the Advancement of Colored People (NAACP) had occasionally charged that housing discrimination was present in the city, black San Franciscans had faced a relatively open housing market before 1940. Unlike their counterparts in many other cities, black San Franciscans were restricted by neither statute nor covenants from virtually any residential area. San Francisco did not have a black ghetto prior to World War II, and African Americans were dispersed throughout the city in relatively integrated neighborhoods. Indeed, many other western cities did not designate segregated neighborhood boundaries for African Americans during their formative decades, but adopted more restrictive housing practices as the black population increased during the course of the twentieth century. A marked increase in housing discrimination as well as in black ghettos became a conspicuous feature of San Francisco and other Bay Area cities such as Oakland and Richmond during the post–World War II era.[48]

By 1945, after approximately 27,000 black migrants had crowded into San Francisco, the majority during the pivotal years 1942 to 1945, housing was in short supply, and evidence of discrimination surfaced in almost every corner of the city. While San Francisco avoided the widespread racial violence associated with housing in such northern cities as Chicago and Detroit during the 1940s, competition between black and white San Franciscans heightened racial tensions and prompted a stiffer pattern of residential segregation than had been evident before the war. "[Housing] segregation is practiced almost rigidly with the use [of] occupancy clauses in deed and leases restricting colored races to certain well defined areas of the city," reported the *Christian Science Monitor* in 1943.[49] By 1960 Tarea Hall Pittman, acting director of the NAACP's West Coast Regional Office, testified before the United States Commission on Civil Rights that "residential segregation based on race is the general rule in the towns and cities in the West," a charge that no African American leader had made prior to the large migration to West Coast cities during World War II.[50]

Instead of serving as a catalyst to improve housing opportunities, World War II stimulated white hostility toward housing integration in San Francisco and intensified black residential concentration within the African American community. This process ultimately led to the development of San Francisco's first black ghetto in the postwar period. In large measure the ghetto resulted from restricted housing opportunities and the growing antipathy toward African Americans that developed during the World War II era.

The World War II migration accelerated the formation of a working class within San Francisco's African American community by significantly expanding the number of industrial jobs. It also gave rise to white-collar employment for black workers. Black San Franciscans had made only limited breakthroughs in skilled and semiskilled job sectors between 1910 and 1940 and had made even less progress in white-collar professions. On the eve of World War II, despite the efforts of the San Francisco branch of the NAACP to eliminate racial barriers in both public and private employment, African

Americans were conspicuous by their absence in numerous occupations in the city. Not a single black public school teacher, policeman, fireman, bank teller, bus driver, cab driver, or streetcar conductor could be found in San Francisco before 1940. African American men and women informed the NAACP between 1915 and 1939 that they regularly were denied positions as department store clerks, secretaries, and accountants because of de facto racial restrictions. Black physicians and nurses also encountered discrimination. Despite their qualifications, African Americans had trouble gaining admittance to nursing programs. The majority of hospitals in San Francisco also prohibited employing black physicians, a policy that some retained until 1950.[51]

Similarly, the majority of public and private employers in San Francisco had little contact with African American workers—save an occasional doorman, waiter, or janitor—before 1940. When the California CIO conducted a survey of fifty-six large San Francisco plants in 1940, they found only fifty-six blacks employed out of a total workforce of more than 38,000. The Pacific Gas and Electric Company, one of the largest employers in San Francisco, employed only four African Americans in its workforce of 1,400, all of whom were assigned to service or janitorial work.[52] The San Francisco Municipal Railway System had excluded African Americans from employment until Audley Cole successfully challenged the discriminatory practices of the local Carmen's Union in 1942. By 1945, Cole had opened the door for hundreds of black workers, both male and female.[53] African American workers expected employment in the traditional menial occupations open to nonwhites, but they also pushed for employment in the skilled and semi-skilled sectors. The African American workers' expanded involvement in the labor market during World War II, supported by a presidential executive order, a federal wartime commission, and the prodding of black and progressive white leaders, restructured employment patterns throughout the entire Bay Area during the 1940s and the postwar era.[54]

By 1944, African American workers were employed in numerous wartime industries.[55] The Bay Area shipyards, in particular, hired blacks in large numbers. As shipyards attempted to meet their hiring schedules and honor their defense contracts, workers of all races were in demand. African Americans, ironically, had been excluded from the shipyards in California and in many southern ports because of entrenched racial barriers within the International Brotherhood of Boilermakers, the parent union, which refused to admit either blacks or women. Union clearance was a prerequisite for em-

17–21. For information on Anne Fuller, consult Elizabeth Veneable to the Standard Oil Company, 3 September 1930, John Landeway Biography Collection, California Historical Society.

3. *Frederick Douglass' Paper* (newspaper), 30 October, 11 December 1851; Hardy Frye, "Negroes in California from 1841–1875," *African-American Historical and Cultural Society Monograph*, vol. 3 (San Francisco, April 1968), 1.

4. Mifflin W. Gibbs, *Shadow and Light: An Autobiography* (1902; reprint, New York: Arno Press, 1968), 44; Peter R. Decker, *Fortunes and Failures: White-Collar Mobility in Nineteenth Century San Francisco* (Cambridge: Harvard University Press, 1978), 118–20, 258; James A. Fisher, "The California Negro, 1860: An Analysis of State Census Returns," *African-American Historical and Cultural Society Monograph* (San Francisco, n.d.), 5–7.

5. Douglas H. Daniels, *Pioneer Urbanites: A Social and Cultural History of Black San Francisco* (Philadelphia: Temple University Press, 1980), 59–68.

6. On the importance of kinship ties to migration in a northern industrial city, see John Bodnar, Roger Simon, and Michael P. Weber, *Lives of Their Own: Blacks, Italians, and Poles in Pittsburgh, 1900–1960* (Urbana: University of Illinois Press, 1982), 5, 58–59, 92, 141. James R. Grossman examines the role of migration clubs in *Land of Hope: Chicago, Black Southerners, and the Great Migration* (Chicago: University of Chicago Press, 1989), 64, 66, 96–98.

7. *Population of the United States at the Eleventh Census: 1890*, part 1 (Washington, DC: G P O, 1895), 404; U.S. Bureau of the Census, *Twelfth Census of the United States, 1900*, vol. 1, part 1, *Population* (Washington, DC: G P O, 1901), 531; U.S. Bureau of the Census, *Thirteenth Census of the United States 1910, Population*, vol. 1 (Washington, DC: G P O, 1913), 116–17, 127, 304; U.S. Bureau of the Census, *Fifteenth Census of the United States, 1930, Population*, vol. 3, part 1, *Reports by States* (Washington, DC: G P O, 1933), 61, 69, 285–87; U.S. Bureau of the Census, *Sixteenth Census of the United States, 1940*, vol. 2, part 1, *Characteristics of the Population, Reports by States* (Washington, DC: G P O, 1943), 621, 657, 660.

8. See Allan H. Spear, *Black Chicago: The Making of a Negro Ghetto, 1890–1920* (Chicago: University of Chicago Press, 1967), 129–46; Kenneth L. Kusmer, *A Ghetto Takes Shape: Black Cleveland, 1870–1930* (Urbana: University of Illinois Press, 1976), 10, 157–73; Peter Gottlieb, *Making Their Own Way: Southern Blacks' Migration to Pittsburgh, 1916–1930* (Urbana: University of Illinois Press, 1987), 63–66.

9. Spear, *Black Chicago*, 122–23, 134–36; Florette Henri, *Black Migration: Movement North, 1900–1920* (Garden City, NY: Anchor Press, 1975), 66; Grossman, *Land of Hope*, 98–119.

10. Albert S. Broussard, *Black San Francisco: The Struggle for Racial Equality in the West, 1900–1954* (Lawrence: University Press of Kansas, 1993), 40, 48; Fred Stripp, "The Relationship of the San Francisco Bay Area Negro Worker with the Labor Unions Affiliated with the American Federation of Labor and the Congress of Industrial Organizations" (Ph.D. diss., Pacific School of Religion, 1948), 284–98. The discriminatory policies of organized labor also curtailed the growth of the black population in Seattle prior to World War II. See Quintard Taylor, *The Forging of a Black Community: Seattle's Central District from 1870 through the Civil Rights Era* (Seattle: University of Washington Press, 1994), 25–27, 64–68.

11. C. L. Dellums, International President of the Brotherhood of Sleeping Car Porters and Civil Rights Leader, interview conducted by the Bancroft Regional Oral History Office, University of California, Berkeley, 1973, 3, 139.

12. E. A. Daly, interview with Broussard, Oakland, California, 3 November 1976.

13. Katherine Stewart Flippin, interview with Broussard, San Francisco, 17 February 1976. Mrs. Flippin is the surviving daughter of McCants Stewart. See also Albert S. Broussard, "McCants Stewart: The Struggles of a Black Attorney in the Urban West," *Oregon Historical Quarterly* 89 (1988), 157–79, and Albert S. Broussard, *African-American Odyssey: The Stewarts, 1853–1963* (Lawrence: University of Kansas Press, 1998).

14. F. L. Ritchardson, interview with Broussard, San Francisco, 13 September 1976.

15. Revels Cayton, interview with Broussard, San Francisco, 21 October 1976. On the Cayton family, see Horace R. Cayton, *Long Old Road, An Autobiography* (Seattle: University of Washington Press, 1963), 1–17. Broussard, "McCants Stewart," 171–73.

16. Larena Frances Herndon, interview with Broussard, San Francisco, 7 June 1976.

17. Darlene Clark Hine, "Black Migration to the Urban Midwest: The Gender Dimension, 1915–1945," in Joe William Trotter Jr., ed., *The Great Migration in Historical Perspective: New Dimensions of Race and Class in Industrial America* (Bloomington: Indiana University Press, 1991), 127–46.

18. Vivian Osborne Marsh, interview with Broussard, Berkeley, California, 8 June 1976; Hine, "Black Migration to the Urban Midwest," passim; Paula Giddings, *In Search of Sisterhood: Delta Sigma Theta and the Challenge of the Black Sorority Movement* (New York: William Morrow and Company, 1988), 179–88, 227.

19. U.S. Bureau of the Census, *Sixteenth Census of the United States, 1940,* vol. 2, part 1, *Characteristics of the Population, Reports by States,* 621, 660.

20. Donald E. Worster, *Dust Bowl: The Southern Plains in the 1930s* (New York: Oxford University Press, 1988), 44–63; Walter J. Stein, *California and the Dust Bowl Migration* (Westport, CT: Greenwood Press, 1973), passim. See also James Noble Gregory, *American Exodus: The Dust Bowl Migration and Okie Culture in California* (New York: Oxford University Press, 1989).

21. U.S. Bureau of the Census, *Special Census of San Francisco, California, Population by Age, Color, and Sex, by Census Tracts*, August 1, 1945 (Washington, DC: G P O, 1945); U.S. Bureau of the Census, *Census of Population, 1950*, vol. 2, part 5, *Characteristics* (Washington, DC: G P O, 1952), 5–207. On the growth of the East Bay during World War II, see Marilynn S. Johnson, *The Second Gold Rush: Oakland and the East Bay in World War II* (Berkeley: University of California Press, 1993).

22. "1942 Annual Survey of Business Conditions in San Francisco," San Francisco Chamber of Commerce, 29 January 1943; and "1943 Economic Survey," Research Department, San Francisco Chamber of Commerce, n.d., 15, United Church Board for Homeland Ministries Archives, Amistad Research Center (hereinafter cited as Homeland Ministries Archives).

23. "Population of San Francisco as of December 1, 1942," San Francisco Chamber of Commerce, Industrial Department, n.d.; Eugene T. Broderick, chief, Air Raid Warden Service, "Instructions to Block Wardens," n.d.; L. Deming Tilton to R. W. Hawksley, 12 January 1943, and Harold J. Boyd, controller, to R. W. Hawksley, 12 January 1943, Homeland Ministries Archives. For an excellent discussion of World War II's impact on California, consult Roger W. Lotchin, *Fortress California, 1910–1961: From Warfare to Welfare* (New York: Oxford University Press, 1992).

24. Davis McEntire to Ruth Kaiser, 5 May 1949, California Federation for Civic Unity Papers, Bancroft Library, University of California, Berkeley; Davis McEntire, "California Population Problems, A Progress Report," 30 September 1943; Commonwealth Club of California and Davis McEntire, "Supplement II–The Negro Population in California," Commonwealth Club of California, Homeland Ministries Archives. See also Davis McEntire, *The Labor Force in California: A Study of Characteristics and Trends in Labor Force, Employment, and Occupations in California, 1900–1950* (Berkeley: University of California Press, 1952); and idem, *The Population of California: A Report of the Research Study Made by the Authorization of the Board of Governors of the Commonwealth Club of California* (San Francisco: Parker Printing Company, 1946).

25. See Johnson, *Second Gold Rush*, 69–82.

26. McEntire, "California Population Problems." Homeland Ministries Archives; Johnson, *Second Gold Rush*, 60–82; Raymond Wolters, *Negroes and the*

Great Depression: The Problem of National Recovery (Westport, CT: Greenwood Press, 1970), passim; Lawrence B. de Graaf, "Negro Migration to Los Angeles, 1930–1950" (Ph.D. diss., University of California, Los Angeles, 1962), 131–36.

27. Sue Bailey Thurman, interviews with Broussard, San Francisco, 9 June and 26 July 1982.

28. U.S. Bureau of the Census, *Special Census of San Francisco, California*, August 1, 1945.

29. Ibid.; Lawrence P. Crouchett, *William Byron Rumford: The Life and Public Service of a California Legislator* (El Cerrito, CA: Downey Place Publishing House, 1984), 39–71; James Richardson, *Willie Brown, A Biography* (Berkeley: University of California Press, 1996), 47–49.

30. McEntire, "California Population Problems"; U.S. Bureau of the Census, *Special Census of Richmond, California, Population by Age, Race, and Sex, by Census Tracts*, September 23, 1947 (Washington, DC: GPO, 1948); U.S. Bureau of the Census, *Special Census of Oakland, California*: October 9, 1945 (Washington, DC: GPO, 1946); U.S. Bureau of the Census, *Special Census of Los Angeles, California, Population by Age, Race and Sex*, February 28, 1946 (Washington, DC: GPO, 1946); U.S. Bureau of the Census, *Special Census of Berkeley, California*, April 12, 1944 (Washington, DC: GPO, 1944); de Graaf, "Negro Migration to Los Angeles," 242. On black migration to Richmond, see Shirley Ann Wilson Moore, *To Place Our Deeds: The African American Community in Richmond, California, 1910–1963* (Berkeley: University of California Press, 2000).

31. Charles S. Johnson, *The Negro War Worker in San Francisco* (San Francisco: n.p., 1944), 4–5, 13–15.

32. Ibid., 12, 79. The 1950 census material is taken from de Graaf, "Negro Migration to Los Angeles," 132, 134–35, 185; Wilson Record, "Willie Stokes at the Golden Gate," *Crisis* 56 (1949): 176.

33. Johnson, *Negro War Worker*, 7, 80. See Herbert G. Gutman, *The Black Family in Slavery and Freedom, 1750–1925* (New York: Random House, 1976); Grossman, *Land of Hope*; and Gottlieb, *Making Their Own Way*.

34. Johnson, *Negro War Worker*, 5–6, 9–10, 12.

35. Grossman, *Land of Hope*, 106.

36. Ibid., 12–13; Herbert Gutman found a high incidence of relatives residing among black migrant families in New York City following the First World War migration. See Gutman, *Black Family in Slavery and Freedom*, 454–56, 515–17.

37. Lawrence B. de Graaf, "Race, Sex, and Region: Black Women in the American West, 1850–1920," *Pacific Historical Review* 49 (1980): 286–88.

secretarial positions. In 1920, Los Angeles had only two telephone operators, twenty-nine store clerks, and eleven saleswomen who were African American out of more than 8,500 women in those positions. The few new occupations they entered usually came only with struggle. Black women had been almost totally excluded from the growing field of nursing, in part due to the refusal of hospital training schools to admit them. During World War I, the Los Angeles branch of the NAACP, in conjunction with several black women's organizations, secured from the county board of supervisors a resolution ordering the county hospital to cease racial discrimination in its training program. White nurses went on strike in protest but ended their action because of the dire needs created by a flu epidemic as well as assurances that the four African American women in line for admission "were far down the list . . . and would not be called for some time."26

Women were also becoming extensively employed as teachers, but here, too, African Americans in California made only token gains, mostly by exceptional women and often in districts where enrollment was already predominantly black. In 1926, Ida Louise Jackson, a University of California graduate, became the first black teacher employed by the Oakland public school system. Jackson remained the only African American teacher in that city until 1934, when the district hired Beth Pierre Wilson to teach Spanish. After a five-year campaign by the East Bay Women's Welfare Club, led by Albrier, Ruth Acty was hired in 1943 to teach elementary school in Berkeley. In Southern California, Bessie Bruington, who had graduated seventh in her high school class in the first decade of the century, encountered racial and gender prejudice in her attempts to obtain a teaching certificate in the Los Angeles city school system. Determination on the part of her mother and her sister, Ethyl Bruington, plus a scholarship from the Los Angeles Forum, an African American debating and political organization established in 1903, helped her accomplish her goal. Ethyl Bruington recalled that her sister had to overcome considerable skepticism from Forum men who "didn't think she was serious." Bessie's mother informed the Forum that "my daughter is going to the State Normal School and she is going to teach in Los Angeles." The Forum "got serious and respectful" when it saw that Bessie "meant business," and it held dinners and contacted school and state officials on her behalf. As a result, in 1922 Bessie Bruington "became the first teacher of her race" in the Los Angeles city school system.27

Ruth J. Temple overcame similar obstacles when in 1913 she was invited to speak at the Forum and so impressed the members that they "became deeply interested in my potential" for a career in medicine. The organization "did the unprecedented thing" of sponsoring Temple with a five-year scholarship for medical school. She graduated from the University of Southern California (USC) in 1919, becoming the "first colored woman physician in the state" and the first African American doctor on the Pacific Coast. Temple set up her practice and resided in Los Angeles. Vada Watson-Somerville, founding member of the Los Angeles branch of the NAACP, graduated from the Dental College of USC in 1918. She became the "first colored woman west of the Mississippi River to master the science of dentistry" and practiced in Los Angeles for several decades.[28]

Miriam Matthews's family brought her to Los Angeles in 1907 when she was two years old. Living and working in California, Matthews began a professional and community service career that spanned several decades. She received her A.B. degree from the University of California, Berkeley, in 1926 and obtained a certificate in librarianship from the school a year later. That same year, Matthews was appointed to the Los Angeles Public Library, becoming the first black professional librarian hired in the system. A lifelong interest in the history and contributions of African Americans in California has made her one of the leading authorities on the state's black bibliography. She also has amassed an impressive personal collection of books, documents, photographs, and art related to African Americans that has proven invaluable to researchers. Matthews has held office in numerous civic, cultural, and political organizations. As a member of the Los Angeles Bicentennial Committee, she conceived of and oversaw the construction of a monument commemorating the city's multiracial founders. In 1981, the city of Los Angeles dedicated a plaque to Matthews as the project's originator.[29]

African American women's concerns turned to the economy in the 1930s, as the Great Depression caused massive unemployment among California's blacks, even as more continued to enter the state. While women tried to alleviate their distress through church and social organizations, the extent of the Depression overwhelmed such private efforts and brought home the realization that the fate of many African Americans lay in the hands of government agencies. Among the most important were the State Relief Administration (SRA) and several New Deal agencies, especially the Civil Works Administration (CWA), the Works Progress Administration (WPA), both of which provided work relief, and the National Youth Administration (NYA), which trained and tried to find work for young people. Gender and racial discrimination plagued early relief efforts, as women were largely placed in such obviously female activities as the s r a Sewing Project, and the c w a segregated blacks into separate "Negro projects." However, these programs proved a lifeline for both unskilled, often elderly black women, who constituted a large portion of the sewing project, and blacks seeking to enter the labor force, who composed as much as 20 percent of the state n y a rolls in some female-oriented areas, such as clerical training.[30] Perhaps most importantly, participation in these projects gave women an awareness of the potential of government programs to break long-standing barriers to employment, and they reacted angrily to the closing of the sewing and other projects between 1938 and 1941. As Eleanor Brooks wrote to the national w p a office: "The Works Progress Administration has been the most forceful and vital sponsor in this field of much-needed Adult Education, and it is indeed regrettable that we who have pioneered[,] promoted and sacrificed to bring this to the workers should have our efforts frustrated and made useless by orders [closing such projects]."

Brooks emphasized the growing sense among blacks of their dependence on government programs: "I have been told that jobs for women were very scarce and hard to secure at W.P.A., and if this is so . . . what can a woman hope for in so-called Private Industry?"[31] Both this perception and the accompanying willingness to protest directly to federal agencies would become more pronounced among black women in the decades after the 1930s.

Though African American women have excelled in a variety of areas from the early days of the state, World War II was the catalyst that ushered in the most profound and widespread changes in their lives. As they began moving away from domestic service and into the shipyards, aircraft factories, and other defense industries that proliferated in California, black women accelerated their quest for full equality. One noted that "Hitler was the one that got us out of the white folks' kitchen." When industrial hiring abated after the war, African American women were laid off before black men and white women, but manufacturing soon revived. "By 1950, half of the black working women were in domestic service, but the other half were back in the skilled industrial, white collar, or professional positions that they had occupied during the war." This stood in contrast with the experiences of white women, the majority of whom remained at home. [32]

Black women now found that they had an alternative to domestic employment, but the Double V Campaign launched by the n a a c p during the war, calling for victory over fascism abroad and racism at home, took on additional importance for working-class African American women who encountered the duality of racial and sexual discrimination on the home-front. The "Manpower Utilization" division of California's War Manpower Commission advised the President's Fair Employment Practices Commission (FEPC) that "there is considerably more discrimination against Negro women than men." During the war and postwar years, working-class black women stood with their middle-class sisters at the forefront of activities that attempted to strike down both barriers. In 1942, for example, the Negro Victory Committee of Los Angeles was successful in placing black female workers in Southern California's aircraft industries after threatening to organize a march on the United States Employment Service. In Northern California, Flora M. Hilliard and Elmira Ake, like thousands of other African American women around the state, had to enlist the aid of the War Manpower Commission to obtain union clearance to work in the shipyards of Richmond and Oakland. Ake was denied membership in the American Federation of Labor and complained that "they did not take negro women in the Boiler makers union." Hilliard successfully fought for admission to the union to work as a shipfitter's helper in the Richmond shipyards. She demanded to know "why I can't have a [good-paying] Job as other american citison [sic]." Longtime community activist Albrier broke the color and gender barriers at Richmond's Kaiser shipyards when, after having passed the welder's test "with flying colors," she applied for a shipyard welder's position and was eventually accepted into the union.[33]

In the huge wartime influx of African Americans into the state, women also played a crucial role in building communities and institutions, especially in Bay Area cities. There, shouldering the responsibilities of mother-hood and housework proved a daunting task in the face of a desperate shortage of housing, intensified by segregation. Procuring permanent housing could take from one to twelve months, and in the interim women struggled to make homes, with limited resources and few proper facilities. Migrants came to rely on a network of reciprocal relationships that mirrored the social supports they had established back home. Though they often held jobs in shipyards or other defense plants, black women also frequently led their communities in obtaining schooling and housing and arranging for family and friends to migrate. They were instrumental in establishing churches and other community institutions and, in general, orienting this unprecedented number of immigrant southern and southwestern blacks to the society and life of western cities.[34]

African Americans poured into Southern California as well during the

echoed parents in Berkeley by demanding immediate integration. While the ultimate results of busing would often be disappointing, and many programs were repealed, the fact that so many were tried is a testament to the growing activity of black women in civil rights movements.[44]

Issues involving gender shaped the swirl of political activity that grew out of the postwar civil rights movement and evolved into Black Power. However, the feminist movement of the 1970s, initially dominated by the white middle class, seemed alien to the majority of African American women in California and around the country. They perceived gains in education and the workplace by groups like the National Organization for Women (NOW) and other feminist groups as primarily benefiting white women. The election of an all-white slate of officers at the 1979 national convention of NOW in Los Angeles only underscored a growing rift between white and black feminists. Diane Watson, state senator and member of NOW, declared, "If they don't really go after a mixed group of women, we should not support such an organization and we should dramatize our non-support."[45]

As a result, most African American women remained apathetic or ambivalent toward the leading organization in the feminist movement. Instead, the political and community activism of black women reflected their main concerns. As the 1960s and 1970s progressed, child care, equal pay, health care, and homelessness became more critical. The California Commission on the Status of Women, established in 1965, revealed a growing number of female-headed, minority households with incomes hovering at or below the poverty line, even as women moved into the workforce in growing numbers. The "feminization of poverty" hit African Americans disproportionately hard. In 1970, more than 27 percent of African American families in California had only a female parent, and this proportion steadily increased to 40 percent by 1990. More than a third of these families had incomes below the poverty line, giving the black population overall a poverty rate ranging from 19 to 21 percent, roughly three times that of the white population. Throughout the 1970s, 1980s, and 1990s, issues vital to race and gender were given increased priority among African American women within and outside the political arena.[46]

In the 1980s and 1990s, African American women in California attempted to develop a movement that would transcend the fragmentation that had plagued the earlier feminist movement and instead recognize the significance of race and class in the lives of women of color. Black feminism became an explicitly articulated ideology in the late 1980s, but it was rooted in an older tradition of African American female activism that valued service and persistently refused to acquiesce to racial and gender stereotypes. For example, the Oakland-based Women's Economic Agenda, founded by Ethyl Long Scott in 1983, sought to empower and develop leadership among low-income African American and other women in the Bay Area. The organization focused on issues of welfare rights, child care, homelessness, and social and economic justice. This program became a model for other grassroots women's organizations around the state. The Berkeley-based Women of Color Resource Center, founded by Linda Burnham, is a similar organization, as are the programs undertaken by attorney Eva Jefferson Patterson, executive director of the Lawyers' Committee for Civil Rights. These organizations reflect the philosophy implied in the term "womanist," coined by California writer Alice Walker in the 1980s. Walker attempted to replace the exclusionary connotations implicit in the term "feminist" by recognizing the legacy of African American female activism and the inseparability of gender and race in that legacy.[47]

Just as class and race bias marred the early feminist movement, sexism permeated the Black Power movement and compelled African American women to carve out paths of political activism and community service that would not limit their commitment to racial and gender equity.[48] For example, the Black Panther Party (BPP), the premier Black Power organization in the country, was established in Oakland in 1966 and became dominated by machismo in its male leadership. However, women in the party implemented and sustained its numerous programs, including community schools, breakfast programs, and senior services, which attracted a great deal of support from a wide spectrum of the black and white communities. When Elaine Brown took over the leadership of the BPP in 1974, she attempted to equalize the treatment of women in the organization by appointing them to leadership positions. Brown noted that the "agenda of the Black Panther Party and our revolution to free black people from oppression specifically included black women."[49]

The decision of California educator and political activist Angela Davis to join the Communist Party (CP) in 1968 also grew out of a desire to move beyond the limitations of race and gender. She followed in the footsteps of other African American intellectuals such as W. E. B. Du Bois and Richard Wright who "found promise in the CP of a political movement capable of changing race relations in the United States" and recognized women's capacity for intellectual leadership. The Alabama-born Davis came to California to complete her doctoral studies at the University of California, San Diego, in 1967, and became active in the Los Angeles chapter of the Student Non-Violent Coordinating Committee (SNCC) and the black nationalist organization United Slaves (US). She also took a teaching position in the philosophy department at UCLA in 1968. However, she encountered men who condemned leadership roles for women: "The constant harangue by the US men was that I needed to redirect my energies and use them to give my man strength and inspiration so that he might more effectively contribute his talents to the struggle for Black liberation." Davis joined an all-black Communist collective seeking support for her leadership and a more structured political movement that could change gender as well as race relations.[50]

The civil rights, Black Power, and Black Arts movements of the 1960s and 1970s stimulated sweeping changes in the nation and widened creative as well as political opportunities for black women in California and around the country. Throughout the twentieth century, black women have played a critical role in the preservation and dissemination of African American arts. This role is continued, for example, in the works of longtime San Francisco Bay Area resident Alice Walker, which are infused with her experiences of growing up in poverty in Georgia and her encounters with racism and sexism as a civil rights activist in the South during the 1960s. Her Pulitzer Prize-winning 1982 novel *The Color Purple* won acclaim for its examination of the duality of black female oppression in the United States and in Africa. Her works celebrate the healing and restorative powers of the rich heritage of black female ancestors and "black sister warriors."[51] Similarly, the works of Bakersfield-born literary critic, novelist, and poet Sherley Anne Williams utilize the folk traditions of African American culture and examine the struggles of working-class black women. University of California, Berkeley, graduate Terry McMillan continues to examine the gender dimension in the black experience in her writings, which deal with the lives of middle-class African Americans. She has won critical and popular acclaim with her novels *Disappearing Acts* (1989), the best-selling *Waiting to Exhale* (1992), made into a film in 1996, and *How Stella Got Her Groove Back* (1996), released as a film in 1998.

In other artistic fields, African American women in California have been in the forefront of pushing beyond the crude racial and sexual depictions that had limited black female performers in an earlier era. Longtime California resident Maya Angelou memorably portrayed an African tribal elder in the 1977 television production of Alex Haley's *Roots*, garnering her an Emmy nomination. Her bestselling autobiography *I Know Why the Caged Bird Sings* (1970), an instant classic, detailed how she left rural Arkansas during World War II for the opportunities the Golden State afforded. Angelou has also distinguished herself in the areas of poetry, music, and film.

In the realm of music, Cora Martin-Moore, celebrated gospel singer, choir director, composer, and publisher, became California's leading proponent of black sacred music after World War II. She began her musical career in Chicago, where she was adopted by gospel music legend Sallie Martin. Martin-Moore moved to Los Angeles in 1947. She has maintained a long-standing affiliation with the Saint Paul Baptist Church, one of the first churches on the Pacific Coast to popularize and record gospel music in response to the demand that grew with the influx of African Americans into the state. Martin-Moore received her formal music training from several educational institutions in the Los Angeles area, including UCLA and California State University, Dominguez Hills, and served as an instructor at Crenshaw-Dorsey Community Adult School.

Composer, arranger, and publisher Margaret Pleasant Douroux benefited from Martin-Moore's efforts at popularizing gospel music on the West Coast and from the advent of the civil rights movement in the 1960s. Born in 1941 in Los Angeles to gospel legend Earl Amos Pleasant and Olga Williams Pleasant, Douroux became actively involved in the civil rights movement as a student at Southern University in Baton Rouge, Louisiana, served as the West Coast music director for Jessie Jackson's Operation PUSH, and has composed nearly 200 gospel and other religious songs. In 1981, Douroux founded the Heritage Music Foundation, dedicated to the establishment of a gospel music hall of fame to nurture and preserve this African American art form.

Black women in California also made their mark in the realm of dance. For example, Janet Collins, who moved to Los Angeles as a child from New Orleans, in 1951 became the first black prima ballerina in America and danced in productions with the Metropolitan Opera. California choreographers and dancers Ruth Beckford and Carmen DeLavallade worked in numerous screen and stage productions, infusing their performances with the complexities and creativity of African-based forms as well as classical ballet and modern dance.

As the civil rights era gave way to the call for Black Power in the late 1960s and early 1970s, the images of African American women underwent a woman of color, Diane Watson. By 1996, Burke had apparently united the black community and her district, for she ran unopposed.

43. California Advisory Commission on the Status of Women, *California Women*, special issue: "The Feminization of Poverty," November/December 1982, 3–8; Elaine Brown, *A Taste of Power: A Black Woman's Story* (New York: Anchor Books, 1992), 321–26; Dr. Huey P. Newton Foundation, *The Legacy of the Panthers: A Photographic Exhibition*, Joe Louis Moore, Project Director (Berkeley: Dr. Huey P. Newton Foundation, n.d.), 16–20.

44. Neal V. Sullivan with Evelyn S. Stewart, *Now Is the Time: Integration in the Berkeley Schools* (Bloomington: Indiana University Press, 1969), 90; John Caughey, *To Kill a Child's Spirit: The Tragedy of School Integration in Los Angeles* (Itasca, IL: F. E. Peacock, 1973), 21.

45. Hine et al., *Black Women in America*, vol. 1, 418–22; "Feminization of Poverty," 3–8; Giddings, *When and Where I Enter*, 346–47 (last quote).

46. Jensen and Lothrop, *California Women*, 130; California Advisory Commission on the Status of Women, *California Women* (Sacramento, 1967), 30; "The Feminization of Poverty," 3–8; U.S. Bureau of the Census, *Census of Population, 1970*, vol. 1, *Characteristics of the Population*, sec. C, *General Social and Economic Characteristics*, part 6, *California* (Washington, DC: G P O, 1973), 385; U.S. Bureau of the Census, *Census of Population, 1980*, vol. 1, *Characteristics of the Population*, chap. C, *General Social and Economic Characteristics*, part 6, *California* (Washington, DC: G P O, 1983), 115, 734; U.S. Bureau of the Census, *Census of Population, 1990*, *Social and Economic Characteristics: California* (Washington, DC: G P O, 1993), 232–33.

47. Shirley Ann Moore, "African American Women," in Peter N. Stearns, ed., *Encyclopedia of Social History* (New York: Garland Publishing, 1994), 9–12.

48. Giddings, *When and Where I Enter*, 277–324; Jensen and Lothrop, *California Women*, 136–42.

49. Brown, *A Taste of Power*, 367–70.

50. Davis quoted in Jensen and Lothrop, *California Women*, 137.

51. This and the following brief biographies of African American women writers, performers, musicians, and dancers are drawn mostly from the encyclopedia by Hine et al., *Black Women in America*, op. cit.

52. Cripps, *Slow Fade to Black*, 40–69, 292–93; Hine et al., *Black Women in America*, vol. 1, 301–2.

53. Samella Lewis, *Art: African American* (Los Angeles: Hancraft Studios, 1990), 252.

54. Goode, *California's Black Pioneers*, 127–28; Samella S. Lewis and Ruth G.

Waddy, *Black Artists on Art* (Los Angeles: Contemporary Crafts Publishers, 1969), 127–28, 131; Romare Bearden and Harry Henderson, *A History of African American Artists: From 1792 to the Present* (New York: Pantheon, 1993), 145, 167, 313, 403; Samella Lewis and Mary Jane Hewitt, "Political Imagery from the Black Arts Movement of the 1960s and 1970s," in Joe Louis Moore, *Black Power, Black Art . . . and the Struggle Continues,* brochure of art exhibition and symposium held at San Francisco State University Art Department Gallery, 19 September–21 October 1994 (last quote); Lewis, *Art: African American,* 252.

55. Michael D. Davis, *Black American Women in Olympic Track and Field* (Jefferson, NC: McFarland and Company, 1992), 9–15, 23–37, 63–72; *New York Times,* 21 March 1999, 33 (quote).

56. U.S. Bureau of the Census, *Census of Population, 1960,* vol. 1, *Characteristics of the Population,* part 6, *California* (Washington, DC: GPO, 1963), 696–98; U.S. Bureau of the Census, *Census of Population, 1970,* vol. 1, part 6, 397; U.S. Bureau of the Census, *Census of Population, 1980,* vol. 1, part 6, 126; U.S. Bureau of the Census, *Census of Population, 1990, Social and Economic Characteristics, California,* 184; California Journal, *Roster: 1995 Pocket Edition* (Sacramento: California Journal Press, 1995), passim; David M. Grant, Melvin L. Oliver, and Angela D. James, "African Americans: Social and Economic Bifurcation," in Roger Waldinger and Mehdi Bozorgmehr, eds., *Ethnic Los Angeles* (New York: Russell Sage Foundation, 1996), 394–98.

57. U.S. Bureau of the Census, *Census of Population, 1970,* vol. 1, part 6, 397; U.S. Bureau of the Census, *Census of Population, 1980,* vol. 1, part 6, 126; U.S. Bureau of the Census, *Census of Population, 1990, Social and Economic Characteristics, California,* 184.

58. Roderick Conrad, "African-Americans Suffer Disproportionately from AIDS," New Visions Commentary paper (Washington, DC: National Center for Public Policy Research [NCPPR], May 1997); NCPPR World Wide Web site, www.nationalcenter.org/nvAIDsConrad597.html (April 1999), 1; *Los Angeles Times,* 6 November 1998.

59. *Los Angeles Times,* 20 August, 16 November, 28 November, 1998.

60. Ibid., 18 May 1998.

61. Ibid.

62. Ibid., 18 September 1998.

source of their dreams for a successful future. Those dreams often centered on the vibrant music and active club life on the street. Yet ironically, while Central Avenue served as the center of an increasingly segregated populace, its clubs and music attracted a substantial white audience, making the avenue "the only integrated setting in Los Angeles." This attractiveness made it a place that many blacks regarded with pride into the early 1950s. It was where "glamour and color was." In short, the story of black music in Los Angeles until the mid 1950s is in many ways the story of Central Avenue.[6]

Like all other urban areas, Los Angeles reflects types of black music that developed after emancipation, particularly in city settings. Two of the earliest forms were minstrel shows and various sorts of religious music. Spirituals, sung without accompaniment, evolved out of slave songs and chants and became widely associated with African American religious expression as more distinctly black churches were created, especially after the Civil War. Also antedating emancipation but most fully developed later were minstrel shows. These consisted both of black actors traveling around the country and, more familiarly, white actors in blackface performing parodies of aspects of African American life. Latter-day derision of such "coon shows" has obscured their significance both as training grounds for blacks in professional performance and as the earliest medium of disseminating African American music on a wide scale throughout the United States. In the early twentieth century, gospel songs, often written by well-known urban composers with various rhythmic accompaniment, became popular. The modern day counterpart of spirituals, they were sung with religious devotion but often with hand clapping and rhythmic excitement.[7]

By the late nineteenth century, African American music had developed new forms that were even more widely disseminated. The long, deep tradition of blues was transformed from folk music to performance by singers like Ma Rainey and Mamie Smith. Pianists, most notably Scott Joplin, meanwhile mixed midwestern and southern music and black banjo forms to create ragtime. African Americans also were becoming acquainted with European band instruments, especially in New Orleans, where both the elite Creoles and the "uptown" blacks established brass bands. When southern segregation laws ended the exclusive cultural privileges of Creoles and led them to join black musical groups, modern jazz emerged.[8] Also developing by the turn of the century was an African American community in Los Angeles that soon showcased most of these urban musical forms.

The history of black musicians in Los Angeles dates back to the 1890s when migrants, primarily from the South, brought their musical and religious traditions to the city. Although some African Americans resided throughout the city and would continue to do so into the 1910s, most of this early population was located near downtown, along the north end of Central Avenue. The two earliest cultural influences in the Los Angeles black community were its several African American churches and the distinctly middle-class aspirations of its population, though most held laborer or service jobs. Such aspirations, typical of many northern communities at this time, are seen in the most important early community organization, the Forum. Founded in 1903 by black clergymen and professionals, it strove to promote education and to open professional occupations to black Angelenos. The Forum later indirectly facilitated black musical development by helping to obtain teaching positions for several gifted instructors, including Samuel Rodney Browne.[9]

The earliest black music reflected both of these cultural influences. The first known musicians of color in Los Angeles were Colonel James Alec Beck, his wife, Loo, and their daughter Pearl. The Becks were singing evangelists and toured the country as well as offering annual concerts in downtown Los Angeles (ironically, but quite typical of the day, only to white audiences). They were probably the first African American musicians to perform on stage in Los Angeles.[10] Other prominent local musicians concentrated on religious music, including Sadie Chandler Cole, who came to the city in 1902 after performing with the original Fisk Jubilee Singers. Cole was a pioneer in training local choruses to sing jubilee songs and in promoting such programs.[11] Until the 1920s, churches remained the main, and often the only, outlet many African Americans had for musical performance in Los Angeles. Many later musicians either came from families connected with churches or obtained their musical appreciation and early training there.

The formal, European-style musical tradition among black Angelenos is especially evident in the prominent role played by African American music teachers. Early in the twentieth century, these instructors began to settle in Los Angeles. There were 22 in 1910, growing to 73 by 1920, 226 in 1930, and 260 in 1940, which then constituted nearly 20 percent of the city's black professional class. Musicians overall were the largest group in the small professional class.[12] Many Los Angeles parents sacrificed financially to provide music lessons for their children, hoping their efforts would guarantee their offspring successful careers. Between 1910 and 1920, piano teaching was the most popular form of music instruction. Unlike black "ear musicians" of the time, piano teachers could read music and thus were highly respected.[13]

One of the leading early teachers was William Wilkins, who founded Wilkins' Piano Academy on Central Avenue in 1912. At one point, his academy held more than 250 students at the main school, with seven piano teachers assisting Wilkins. The kindergarten class had forty children. Samuel Browne, a later music teacher who was trained by Wilkins, described him as the most charismatic of the early instructors, a spectacular showman as well as a respected teacher. Browne portrayed Wilkins as

> an imposing figure with long hair, in his cowboy hat, long coat, big bow tie, gloves, walking stick with golden knob and glasses with a long ribbon attached . . . . Flamboyant and dramatic, he was a tremendous source of inspiration to his students . . . . Passengers on the Central Avenue streetcar heard his amazing results as they passed Wilkins' majestic home where he had six pianos.

Browne also noted that, although Wilkins personally faced many obstacles, his academy was open to all races, and he trained white and Japanese students. Several of his teachers or students became prominent in the Los Angeles black music world, and his annual recitals did much to increase interest in music in the community.[14]

Other African American men also became prominent early music teachers. John Gray was educated at the University of Southern California and at the University of California, Los Angeles, where he studied piano and pipe organ as well as composition. After receiving his teaching diploma from L'École Normale de Musique in Paris in the early 1920s, he returned to Los Angeles, where he founded the Gray Conservatory of Music. Gray also became a prominent classical performer and founded the first West Coast organization of African American musicians, the Musicians Association. In 1928 this would become the Los Angeles branch of the National Association of Negro Musicians. Elmer Bartlett, a choir director at the First African Methodist Episcopal Church (AME), also had a private studio. In addition to teaching piano and organ, Bartlett developed some of the finest African American choirs in Los Angeles, which performed in both white and black churches and at the Hollywood Bowl. In 1930, these early teachers were joined by Willis Young, a professor of music from Louisiana. Setting up a studio next to the Musicians Union building, Young taught children on

Central Avenue for $.50 a lesson, organized bands, and, like other teachers, imparted a sense of discipline and appreciation to his students.[15]

Although these men became the most prominent African American instructors of their day, most black music teachers in Los Angeles prior to 1920 were women. Some, like Genevieve Barnes Lewis, went from house to house giving piano lessons. The most outstanding black violinist and violin instructor was Bessie Williams (later Bessie Dones). A native of nearby Riverside, Dones taught in both the Wilkins school and the Gray Conservatory before opening her own private studio, which she maintained for half a century.[16]

Significant as sacred and formal music were in establishing a musical consciousness, however, it would be more uniquely African American genres, particularly jazz, that would make the Los Angeles black community famous nationwide. Several factors contributed to the renaissance of African American music along Central Avenue by the 1920s. One was the rise of ballroom dancing after the start of the century, epitomized by the appearance of dance halls. Southern California soon became known for such establishments, and the first "dance marathon" was hosted by Sid Grauman, of Grauman's Chinese Theatre. The coming of the motion picture industry to Hollywood at that time further associated Los Angeles with new trends in popular entertainment. Ballroom dancing called for danceable music, and ragtime and jazz became standards. Los Angeles also had a growing African American population that increasingly was becoming attuned to emerging black music. The number of blacks grew rapidly after 1900, reaching 7,559 in 1910 and more than doubling to 15,579 by 1920. Much of this growth came from an influx of southern migrants, and their cultural impact can be seen in such trends as the "Azusa Street Movement" of 1906, a Pentecostal revival that Tom Reed contends gave birth to "some of Los Angeles' most spirited churches and choirs."[17]

In response to this attractive atmosphere, black musicians began to visit or move to the city, many of them from New Orleans. The earliest of these was Bill Johnson, who came in 1908 or 1909 and by 1914 had organized a Creole band in Los Angeles. Paul Howard, whose background was New Orleans music, became one of the first black saxophonists in Los Angeles in 1910. Also from New Orleans in 1914 came Freddie Keppard and his Original Creole Band. Perhaps the most famous New Orleans visitor was the pioneer jazz pianist Ferdinand "Jelly Roll" Morton, who arrived in Los Angeles in 1915 and was partly responsible for a transition from ragtime to jazz.

Another prominent New Orleans Creole, Kid Ory, began a six-year stay in Los Angeles and Oakland with his band in 1919. He would have a long career in Los Angeles, coming out of retirement during World War II to play with several Dixieland bands.[18] By 1921, these had been joined by more New Orleans groups, including Satchel McVea's Angel City Brass Band and the Wilson Orchestra, giving Los Angeles some of the most innovative jazz bands of the time. Most of these were "territory bands" that toured the West Coast and sometimes beyond. Their venues were often white music halls and clubs, from which black patrons were commonly excluded. However, as early as 1916, the Angelus movie house opened on 9th and Central, claiming to be "the only Show House owned by Colored Men in the entire West." That same year the Black and Tan Band played at a dance on 19th and Central, and Morton was soon appearing at the Cadillac Cafe on Central Avenue. All these were harbingers of an avenue ultimately filled with black-owned musical locales.[19]

The Los Angeles music scene was strengthened by the arrival of the Spikes brothers from Oklahoma. In 1912, John and Benjamin "Reb" Spikes came to the West Coast with a minstrel show. In 1919, they opened the first African American musical record store in the city at 1203 South Central. Selling musical instruments as well as recordings, the store soon became a highly profitable venture and served as a gathering and rehearsal place for Central Avenue musicians into the early 1920s. Jazz musicians themselves, the Spikes brothers organized their own band in 1921 and the following year made their first recording. In 1921, they became the first black band to play on local radio, and the following year they became the first African American band to make a Vitaphone record for a movie studio. These multiple roles made the Spikes brothers' store the first hub of what would become a thriving African American entertainment business in Los Angeles.[20]

The development of a distinct African American musical community ironically was enhanced by widespread discrimination and increasing residential segregation in Los Angeles by 1920. Race-restrictive covenants, the enforcement of which received approval from the California Supreme Court in 1919, closed off much of the city to African American residence. By 1920, at least 40 percent of the city's blacks were concentrated near Central Avenue. Exclusion from public accommodations, some stores, and many places of entertainment had grown throughout the 1910s. Employment discrimination also was common, and since most entertainment establishments were owned by whites, black musicians were often denied employment if the

In the early 1920s, New Orleans musicians such as Morton and Joe "King" Oliver, whose band came to Los Angeles and San Francisco in 1921 and 1922, continued to predominate. By mid-decade, more came from other areas or had received training in Los Angeles schools. They found work in the growing number of nightclubs along Central Avenue and in Watts. One of the most famous was the Apex, better known by its later name, Club Alabam. It featured singers, dancers, and showgirls, including Carolynne Snowden, Mildred Washington, Ivie Anderson (who later opened her own restaurant on the avenue), and the early film star Nina Mae McKinney, as well as jazz musicians.

Musicians and clubs also needed organizers to bring the various elements of an entertainment environment together. This need was met in part by the two music companies on the avenue. In the early 1920s the Spikes brothers' shop continued to serve as the hub of musical activity, serving as a referral service for musicians. But it was joined by another run by Curtis Mosby, who in 1928 set up the Apex. Musician, leader of a band, and eventually owner or manager of several clubs, Mosby was known as the "mayor of Central Avenue" well into the 1940s.[27] The largest venue on Central Avenue was the Lincoln Theatre, the "West Coast Apollo," which opened in 1926. The Lincoln showed motion pictures, but it also presented live stage performances, talent shows, and vaudeville. By featuring weekly musical entertainment as well as dramatic presentations, the Lincoln provided a stage for many of Los Angeles's black musicians. The avenue had several other theaters by the end of the decade, including the Rosebud, the Gaiety, the Florence Mills, and the Savoy. In each of these, movies were accompanied by organ music and supplemented by minstrel shows, live music, dancing, singing, and comedy. All of these outlets contributed to giving a new generation of African American Angelenos exposure to an evolving black music and recognition for performing it.[28]

Los Angeles's attraction to black musicians did not rest on Central Avenue alone. South of the city, the rural, multiracial community of Watts developed in the early 1900s. Located along the red car line and without the midnight curfew that the City of Los Angeles imposed at that time on dance clubs, Watts became a lively out-of-city nightspot by World War I. Such prominent black musicians as Morton and Oliver performed at its clubs. Annexation by Los Angeles in 1926 contributed to its being eclipsed by Central Avenue as a center of black music, but it remained the site of prominent clubs into the 1940s.[29] Some of the most celebrated African American musicians performed from the 1920s through the 1940s at Sebastian's Cotton Club, a white establishment miles away in Culver City. While the club provided employment for many, particularly the band of Les Hite, those Los Angeles black musicians played to white audiences only. Another source of work that began in the 1920s was the motion picture industry. As early as 1919, Curtis Mosby and his band began making soundtracks. But it was the coming of talkies in 1927, coupled with the widespread popularity of black music by then, that opened the door to African American actors and musicians in Hollywood. Two celebrated all-black musical films of that decade were *Hearts in Dixie* (1929), which featured jubilee, spirituals and stereotyped roles, and *Hallelujah* (1929), with more realistic characters, which used Mosby's band along with other African American musicians. The rage for black music was also evident in shorter movies, and William "Sonny" Clay, who came to Los Angeles in 1915, had his Sonny Clay's Plantation Orchestra play in sixty-five films starting in the late 1920s.[30]

The growth of Central Avenue in the 1920s culminated with the opening of the Dunbar Hotel in 1928. This three-story structure, with one hundred rooms, shops and banquet facilities, as well as a bandstand, was located next to the Apex Club, and four other clubs subsequently located within a block of it. The hotel hosted the first convention of the National Association for the Advancement of Colored People (NAACP) on the West Coast in its initial year. It became famous for the African American celebrities who stayed there, including W. E. B. Du Bois, Langston Hughes, and Thurgood Marshall. The Dunbar was also a haven for visiting black musicians, including Lena Horne, Billy Eckstine, Count Basie, Fats Waller, Sarah Vaughn, Lionel Hampton, Duke Ellington, Louis Armstrong, and Cab Calloway, who were denied service in most other Los Angeles hotels until well into the 1940s.[31]

Beneath the glitter of the avenue, the lives of Los Angeles's several hundred black musicians before World War II were in many ways a mirror of the condition and attitudes of the city's African American population. The influence of family and community was strong. Many leading jazz figures came from families who had performed or were professional musicians, and a network of professional teachers and informal contacts with fellow musicians nurtured their talents. While volunteer performing in churches especially attracted many women, a large majority of those seeking to be professionals up to the 1940s were male. They often launched their careers by their mid-teens, creating a conflict between education and performing that was often resolved by grueling schedules combining both. Afternoons of rehearsal were followed by evenings of performing and occasionally topped off by early morning "jam" sessions. For many, the monetary rewards were slim. Engagements paying $2.50 a night or $1.50 plus tips in the late 1930s "were considered good steady jobs." Some recall working "where they didn't give you nothing but beer." Below the big-name performers were many part-time musicians who could only make a living doing service jobs by day, performing at night for enjoyment. Some nightclub owners "forgot" to pay at all until pressured by the union, while others required kickbacks as a condition of work. Record companies also were known to refuse to pay royalties.[32]

Discrimination was as unavoidable for musicians as for other African Americans. The presence of two unions created a double standard in which the white local received most contracts to play for clubs, movies, and recording studios, and the black local got only the "leftovers" or sat in for whites who wanted a day off. This situation was made doubly frustrating by the sycophantic behavior of some black union officials toward whites in defending their members' contract rights.[33] Black musicians were excluded from most clubs outside of Central Avenue and Watts until the 1940s. In those where they were allowed to play, they often had to accept fellow black patrons being turned away with the simple explanation, "That's just the way it is."[34] Many jazz musicians expressed their independence in musical arrangement, choosing when they wished to take on a "gig," and their antics while performing, as the careers of Charlie Mingus and "Big Jay" McNeely illustrate. But those who went with bands that obtained steady work were often compelled to tailor their dress and behavior to white tastes. Lionel Hampton summed up the expected attitude by telling his players, "Look, I want you all to know, my band is three-fourths Tom and one-fourth play. Whoever don't like it can get out right now."[35]

The 1930s was a paradoxical decade for Los Angeles's black musicians, a period that began with the Great Depression and ended with both jazz and Central Avenue enjoying unprecedented popularity. In California and nationwide, African Americans suffered widespread unemployment, necessitating great frugality. One casualty was the purchase of phonograph records, so for nearly three years no records were issued by black performers. A further blow to Central Avenue came in 1933 with the repeal of Prohibition, for one attraction to white patrons especially was that clubs like the Apex had doubled as speakeasies. Diminished club patronage meant even lower incomes for jazz musicians.[36] Many of the small businesses on

Central Avenue also failed, although federal relief programs after 1935 brought some improvement in economic conditions. Central Avenue musicians especially flocked to the Federal Artists Program of the Works Progress Administration (w p a), which provided funds for the creation and performance of music as well as for other arts. One participant was Langston Hughes, who lived in Los Angeles in the 1930s and wrote scripts for movie studios. Singing groups qualified, and several church choir members joined w p a choruses; indeed, some whole church choirs simply became w p a choruses.37 But it was developments within the world of black music that made the period from the late '30s through the mid '40s the heyday of Central Avenue.

Black musicians enjoyed increasing roles in Hollywood films during that period. This was not easily noticed, as African American choral groups usually were not seen, and they often were omitted from the credits. Hollywood primarily hired these talented choral groups as well as African American songwriters and arrangers for all-black films. *Dixiana* (1930) and *Green Pastures* (1936) were two of the most prominent. Later films that made extensive use of black musicians included *Cabin in the Sky* (1943), *Stormy Weather* (1943), and *Carmen Jones* (1954). The two sons of Willis Young, Lee and Lester, made key contributions to the music of these films. Movies with southern themes also often used African American musical talent.38

Four "all-colored cast" Westerns, starring Herb Jeffries as a black singing cowboy, were made in the late 1930s. Shot on location at N. B. Murray's black dude ranch near Victorville, California, *Harlem on the Prairie, The Bronze Buckaroo, Harlem Rides the Range*, and *Two Gun Man from Harlem* featured songs by Jeffries and the Four Tones, his backing vocal group. The movies were produced primarily for small, segregated theaters in the South and West, but *Harlem on the Prairie* nevertheless ran as an opening attraction in prestigious movie houses in Los Angeles and New York. The music in these black Westerns differed dramatically from that of their white counterparts. The score of *Harlem on the Prairie*, for example, drew heavily upon African American folk songs, and the background vocals in all four features carried a distinct jazz or gospel flavor. Maceo B. Sheffield, who supervised *Harlem on the Prairie*, was a former Los Angeles policeman who had purchased several nightclubs along Central Avenue, and Connie Harris, who played Carolina Clayburn in the movie, worked as an entertainer along the same circuit. Herb Jeffries went on to become a vocalist with Edward "Duke" Ellington and became famous for his rendition of "Flamingo." He also opened his own after-hours club, the Black Flamingo, west of Central, on Avalon near Vernon.[39]

The 1930s also brought to Los Angeles two African Americans who would become world renowned in choral and classical music. Jester Hairston came to California with the Hall Johnson Choir in 1935 and stayed on as an arranger, conductor, composer, and lecturer on black folk music. He soon emerged as the most respected choir director of the period. Composer and conductor Dmitri Tiomkin was so impressed that he chose Hairston to conduct the choir for the movie *Lost Horizon* (1937). Forming the Jester Hairston Metropolitan Choir in 1943, Hairston was to work in Hollywood for four decades, writing and arranging more than a hundred songs. In 1963, his tune "Amen" was featured in the picture *Lilies of the Field*, with Hairston's voice backing Sidney Poitier's screen presence.[40]

African Americans in Los Angeles took particular pride in the achievements of William Grant Still, "the Dean of Afro-American Music," who was noted primarily as a composer and conductor of classical music. Still's career spanned four decades, from the 1920s to the 1950s. He is best known as a composer of symphonies, writing a total of twenty-five major works, including six operas and four ballets. His work *The Afro-American Symphony*, which premiered in 1931, was the first full symphony by an African American composer to be performed by a major orchestra.

After an early period in New York arranging and performing for such notable African American shows as the Noble Sissle/Eubie Blake musical *Shuffle Along*, Still came to Los Angeles in 1934. He was soon writing music for such films as *Pennies from Heaven* (1936). In 1937, he signed a six-month contract with Columbia Pictures, but a hostile music director ignored him "until at the very end he was asked to orchestrate some of Dmitri Tiomkin's music for *Lost Horizon*." The same hostility led Columbia not to renew his contract, and may explain why Still is not mentioned in the movie's credits.[41] During the 1950s, Still composed musical themes for *Gunsmoke* and *Perry Mason*. A Los Angeles resident until his death in 1978, William Grant Still was the most versatile and accomplished African American composer of his era.[42]

As in earlier decades, music teachers continued to play prominent roles in developing talent and promoting African American music. Typical of many women teachers was Alma Hightower, who directed the School for the Performing Arts from the 1930s to the 1960s. Her Hightower Youth Orchestra frequently performed in city parades, on street corners, and in churches.

In 1939 and 1940, her students performed by invitation at the California State Fair, where the orchestra won awards for the best youth group both years. Another celebrated teacher was Sam Browne, who in 1936 became the first African American music teacher in the Los Angeles city schools. A cum laude graduate of the University of Southern California's School of Music, Browne was a thoroughly trained musician, a performer of classical music, organist, pianist, and school bandleader as well. His classes at Jefferson High School, off Central Avenue, produced some of the world's outstanding jazz players, including Dexter Gordon, Chico Hamilton, Sonny Criss, and Paul Bryant, between 1936 and 1961. To this list of teachers must be added many performing musicians who tutored young beginners. Lloyd Reese was a private teacher to several prominent jazz performers and formed bands for young musicians. Such personal mentoring was so admired that some young blacks gave up opportunities to attend prominent music schools in favor of learning at "SWU—the sidewalk university."43

It was during the 1930s that jazz became the preeminent music form in many African American communities, including those of Los Angeles. It was also in this decade that several national trends combined to transform jazz from an individual, often improvised medium of expression, still largely composed and performed by African Americans for "big bands," to a less creative, less improvised, composed music called "swing." Performed in an effort to "cover" (or imitate) the style of "black jazz" for the concert platform, swing was increasingly performed by large white bands. The growing popularity of dance music, the entry of theatrical booking agencies into the band business, the decline of vaudeville, and the rise of radio and records all contributed to these changes. An early harbinger was Duke Ellington's hiring a white manager, Irving Mills, and soon afterward succeeding Fletcher Henderson as the leading black recording band. Soon Cab Calloway and other national groups were refining their music to fit popular markets. For a few years, black bands retained a monopoly on "hot" jazz, as white bands clung to slower, softer styles. But by 1935 white bandleaders like Benny Goodman were adopting the increasingly popular music of black bands, and the era of swing as an overall cultural movement had begun. A driving motive for many musicians in surrendering some of the artistic independence of jazz to the more formalized style of swing was the Great Depression. As one player put it, a musician "is going to starve if he doesn't get commercial somehow or another."44

The swing era brought an explosion of jazz along Central Avenue, reflected in the growing number of musical groups and the nightclubs where they performed. It also made Los Angeles one of the prime musical centers of America. Numerous black musicians became famous by performing in Central Avenue clubs in the 1930s. Alton Redd, a blues-singing drummer who frequented the avenue, led the Pards of Pepper band. In 1935, he became the first African American musician to sign a recording contract with Capitol Records. Other local bands shared the growing entertainment market, including George Brown and Sammy Franklin with the California Rhythm Rascals, Jack McVea and the Kings of Rhythm, and Roy Milton and His Solid Senders. By 1937, these and other Central Avenue bands had popularized a danceable music that they called "boogie-woogie." Aided by popular Los Angeles area radio programs such as "The Make-Believe Ballroom" with Al Jarvis and other disc jockeys such as Joe Adams, the first African American to host a show, boogie-woogie soon became the music of choice of thousands of young Angelenos of every race and color.[45]

The most conspicuous manifestation of this jazz explosion was the multiplying of nightclubs all around Los Angeles, but nowhere more notably than along Central Avenue. That avenue was the "'Big picture' musically. Big Band Swing, Rhythm and Blues, Bebop, dance and comedy were to be found in one nightclub or another. The 'Avenue' was a place to hang, be fashionable and style. To connect and score. It was the beginning of a culture, the only one of its kind on the West Coast."[46] As well as being the gathering place for the black bourgeoisie, Central Avenue's nightclubs had attracted a substantial number of whites, including many Hollywood celebrities and the Beverly Hills elite. Initially drawn to its speakeasies, after the repeal of Prohibition their main attraction became "slumming": breaking contemporary social mores by associating with African Americans, the experience often enhanced by exotic notions of blacks' cultural lack of inhibition. Increasing white patronage in the early '40s also resulted from an ironic source: Mayor Fletcher Bowron's imposition of a 2 a.m. curfew on serving liquor. Many black clubs along Central Avenue as well as some white clubs elsewhere that hired blacks flouted this regulation and so became favorite "after hours" haunts of whites seeking all-night entertainment.[47] By the early 1940s, the clubs numbered in the dozens and stretched from Little Tokyo downtown (taken over by African Americans during World War II following Japanese internment) south to Watts.

Club Alabam was one of the most sophisticated clubs, but many patrons also frequented the Downbeat Club, the Flame, and the Casablanca (all owned or managed by "Black Dot" McGhee); Jack's Basket Room, run by the former boxer, Jack Johnson; Shepp's Playhouse and Club Finale in Little Tokyo, both of which featured pioneering jazzmen in the '40s; and Joe Morris's Plantation Club in Watts. Some jazz musicians doubled as club managers, such as Ivie Anderson, who sang with Ellington's orchestra and ran Ivie's Chicken Shack. For those less interested in the quality of the music than the flesh of the entertainers, the avenue offered an array of exotic dancing and strip joints, including Little Harlem in Watts. Sebastian's Cotton Club continued to lead the white-owned, off-Central Avenue jazz clubs, but downtown theaters like the Orpheum, the Million Dollar, and the Mayan Theatre as well as dance halls like the Hollywood Palladium also featured African American entertainers. By the late 1940s, black bands like those of Walter "Dootsie" Williams and Floyd Ray began crossing the color line at previously all-white Hollywood clubs like the Trocadero and the Palomar Ballroom.[48]

World War II brought a significant change in the gender makeup of Central Avenue performers. While many young male jazz players were drafted (often into military bands), the demand for music did not abate. Therefore, women were often hired to fill positions and frequently formed trios, quartets, and ensembles, demonstrating great talent that had not been seen or heard before.[49] When violinist Ginger Smock was denied a place in the Los Angeles Symphony Orchestra, she started a new career as a jazz violinist. She formed Ginger and Her Magic Notes and performed on Central Avenue. In 1943, she joined Nina Russell, Mata Roy, and Camille Howard to form the Sepia Tones. Other female performers entertained during World War II at Central Avenue nightspots, including many nationally celebrated African American musicians. Lena Horne and Billie Holliday, for example, were regular performers at major Los Angeles nightclubs as well as on Central Avenue.[50] They joined an impressive list of nationally known male performers, including Louis Armstrong, who came as early as 1930, Hampton, Ellington, and Nat "King" Cole.

This growing parade of musical talent, coupled with a greater use of local African Americans in films, led the black newspaper, the *California Eagle*, to run a huge advertisement in July 1938: "Hollywood Meets Harlem." However, the very success of Central Avenue contained seeds of its eventual decline, for by the late 1940s such stars were being booked by downtown and Hollywood white clubs, such as Billy Berg's, the first to break the ban on black musicians. While this eventually opened wider employment opportunities to top African American musicians, it also eroded the unique attraction of the avenue and reduced job opportunities for lesser-known performers.[51]

In the early 1940s, some black performers were also being displaced by the jukebox. As it was much less expensive to buy a long lasting collection of records than to hire live players, many small clubs turned to jukeboxes for youth dance music. Since the first jukeboxes carried Bing Crosby, Paul Whiteman, and other white performers, both African American youths and musicians demanded recordings of locally popular black artists. Two New Orleans Creoles, Leon and Otis René, came to Los Angeles and in 1942 established the Exclusive Record Company to meet this demand, recording African American artists specifically for jukebox distribution. The brothers also recorded their own music, including such popular tunes as "When the Swallows Come Back to Capistrano" and "Sleepy Time Down South." Other entrepreneurs followed, and by 1944, the African American recording industry was well established in Los Angeles.[52]

While swing remained popular through World War II, several new forms began to appear that changed African American music and ultimately changed American music. One marked a rebellion among some black musicians against such commercialized music, a desire for something more exhilarating, which led to the development of bebop. New York's 52nd Street is usually considered its place of origin, but it was brought to Los Angeles when two of its pioneers, Charlie "Bird" Parker and John Birks "Dizzy" Gillespie, visited the city in 1945 and 1946. A few months earlier, Howard McGhee had arrived from Tulsa with similar innovative ideas. Through mid-1946, these musicians frequented the Club Finale, a black-run club in Little Tokyo, but they also played at such Central Avenue spots as the Bird in a Basket, Herb Jeffries's Black Flamingo, and Billie Berg's in Hollywood. Especially important were their jam sessions on Central Avenue, which helped attract followers. During the late 1940s and early 1950s, such leading bebop players as Dexter Gordon, Wardell Gray, Charlie Mingus, and Buddy Collette and popular bands like Billy Eckstine's brought new vitality to Los Angeles and Central Avenue within the circles of jazz aficionados.[53]

Pioneering in new forms of jazz did not necessarily bring economic success to many of Los Angeles's outstanding African American musicians of the '40s and '50s. Many listeners did not appreciate the innovative sounds of players like Charlie Parker, so their employment with large bands or recording companies was sporadic. Quite a few innovative players shunned groups that did not share their form of music, leading to fame among scholars of jazz but also poverty.54 Some also mixed unorthodox music with substance abuse, in some cases tragically shortening their careers. In the early 1930s, Louis Armstrong was chased out of Los Angeles for possession of marijuana. Parker battled multiple drug abuse problems throughout his life, being sent to Camarillo State Hospital for several months in 1946. Gray allegedly died of an overdose, and Hampton Hawes was imprisoned in the late 1950s on drug charges.55

Several African American bands were more popular and successful than the innovative jazz musicians. By 1953, these had modified bebop into a more danceable form that gained the name "cool jazz." A major figure in this music, and also one of the outstanding performers, composers, arrangers, and songwriters of the period, was Bennett "Benny" Carter. Along with Fletcher Henderson and Don Redman, Carter's early works established the basis for swing. He influenced later musicians in several varieties of jazz and become one of America's most honored black musicians. But the greatest economic rewards from cool jazz would fall to white bands in the West, such as that of Stan Kenton, who by the mid-1950s had further refined it into what was often called "West Coast jazz." In reaction to what seemed a dilution of "pure" jazz, some Los Angeles black musicians, most notably Eric Dolphy, experimented during the 1950s with "free jazz," laying the foundation for a revival of the form in the 1960s.56

The other major trend in African American music that arose in Los Angeles during and after World War II owed much of its popularity to the extensive migration of blacks from the South from 1942 well into the 1960s. They brought with them a love for gospel and blues, often in folk form. One result was the spread of gospel music; indeed, it became so popular that in 1945 the Los Angeles radio station KFWB began weekly broadcasts. Many African American churches established prominent gospel choirs, and the People's Independent Church of Christ became a center of musical performance in Los Angeles. Its pastor, the Reverend Clayton Russell, was the first African American minister in the city to have his own radio program. One of the outstanding choral directors to emerge from this movement was Albert McNeil, who also was a renowned music teacher in Los Angeles public schools in the early 1940s and afterward.57

Even more popular were the blues for which southern migrants clamored, especially when they became modified into "rhythm and blues" (R&B). This ensemble music featured a vocal unit, a rhythm unit, and a supplement (usually a saxophone) and mixed the traditions of blues and gospel. In Los Angeles, Joe Liggins and Louis Jordan experimented with orchestral predecessors of this music in the 1930s and early 1940s, and it soon became a leading type of recorded music among African American performers and consumers, spreading eventually to white Americans as well.[58] The René brothers formed several record companies that were among the first to put R&B on disc. They also became the first to record Nat "King" Cole and his "soft" ballad form. But it was the more earthy mixture of gospel and blues that emerged after the war that captured the greatest audiences. Artists such as guitarist "T-Bone" Walker, famous for "Stormy Monday Blues," Big Joe Turner, Ivory Joe Hunter, Wynonie Harris, and "Big Mama" Thornton led a growing trend of shouting and moaning blues singers, while emerging young singers such as Little Richard, Lloyd Price, Little Esther, and Etta James played at Central Avenue nightspots.[59]

Nevertheless, by the early 1950s, many of those nightspots were disappearing. Innovative young African American jazz musicians like Hawes still cut records or experimented with fellow musicians at the Club Alabam, Downbeat, the Haig, the Surf Club, and a few others at the start of the decade, but by then, the avenue was becoming a jazz ghost town. This decline is most often attributed to increasing police harassment of both blacks and white visitors in the late 1940s. While some of the frequent stopping and searching was associated with a crackdown on drugs and the reputation of some avenue clubs as drug havens, much of it is blamed on the growing numbers of southern whites in the Los Angeles Police Department and the hostile attitudes of many officers toward the interracial mingling that had become common during the war. White women were often asked what they were doing on Central Avenue and were advised to leave lest they risk being picked up on some charge, or were warned that "it was too dangerous to hang around black neighborhoods." By 1949, many former patrons became weary of such repeated hassling and sought entertainment elsewhere.[60]

The flight of white patrons ironically coincided with expanding employment opportunities for black musicians. A major factor increasing jobs was the amalgamation of American Federation of Musicians locals 767 and 47. This was the result of three years of work by a group of younger African American musicians led by Buddy Collette, Marl Young, William Douglass, and Charles Mingus. Spurred in part by a feeling that segregated unions were wrong in principle and partly by a desire to end their exclusion from better-paying jobs, younger black musicians battled older ones who feared losing the security and feeling of togetherness that the separate local represented.

Meanwhile, a group of white musicians carried on a parallel campaign within Local 47. In 1953, the campaign was successful, and Los Angeles gained one of the nation's earliest united musicians' unions, setting a trend that swept through much of the federation.[61] This integration was not without its negative consequences, however. A major casualty of the merger was Central Avenue. As more clubs hired blacks, new ones opened where the more affluent clientele was going—the Westside. This led many African American musicians to join the migration, with the result that clubs on Central Avenue found themselves deserted by big-name bands. An increasing number of black musicians remaining on the avenue fell into drug abuse, compounding the desire of others to leave. Some musicians blamed the resultant integration for a loss of cultural ties and the decline of some unique forms of African American music.[62]

Equally detrimental to Central Avenue was a changing clientele. The end of judicial enforcement of race-restrictive covenants, while doing little to open new, suburban housing to African Americans, did make available to black occupancy several square miles of older city housing west of Main Street. As late as 1950, most Los Angeles blacks had lived in the vicinity of Central Avenue, but by 1960 a majority lived in neighborhoods to the west. These migrants included most of the more affluent African Americans. Their move west coincided with the dispersal of musicians from Central Avenue, so many middle-class blacks ceased coming to the area. In their place came a growing clientele of wartime migrants and blue-collar workers who often visited clubs in their work clothes, thus damaging the aura of elegance and contributing to further abandonment of the avenue by affluent blacks. The end of the war and postwar unemployment also dried up some of the patronage that had kept the avenue booming in the early 1940s. A final factor lessening attendance may, ironically, have been an invention hailed by jazz musicians: the long-playing (LP) record. By extending the playing time on each side of a disk from three to twenty minutes, LPs allowed much longer and expressive recordings, but they also made the phonograph a convenient substitute for the club and dance hall.[63]

The swing era from 1937 to the late 1940s brought unprecedented fame to Central Avenue, made Los Angeles a center of African American music and turned what had once been a largely unique black form of expression into a national multicultural music. Since this coincided with efforts to improve interracial relations and was soon followed by the civil rights movement, many have wondered whether black music generally, and jazz in particular, brought some degree of racial equality, at least within the performance and entertainment communities. Others have debated the cultural and economic effects of these trends: did African Americans score a cultural triumph or witness the appropriation of much of their art by preferentially treated white performers? The answer to both questions is affirmative.[64]

The most notable advance during this era was the gradual decline of rigid segregation of white and black musicians. African Americans and whites had mixed in recording studios since the 1920s, and during the early 1930s, a few smaller bands around the country had held interracial contests or had experimented with mixing players. But the breaking of segregation in big bands is usually attributed to John Hammond, a white jazz aficionado and writer, who in 1936 persuaded Benny Goodman to take African American pianist Teddy Wilson into his quartet. The next year, in Los Angeles, Goodman added Lionel Hampton to his group, and from then on prominent black players were gradually added to several white big bands. Soon after, white bandleaders began hiring black musicians as arrangers. Tommy Dorsey was the first, hiring Sy Oliver between 1939 and 1943. By the early 1940s, the practice of excluding black musicians from prominent white clubs also began to break down. Both of these changes, however, remained token until well into the 1940s.[65] A similar tokenism attended recording and film outlets for African American musicians. The white musicians' union in Los Angeles pressured studios to hire whites to dub music onto soundtracks when blacks were playing. Each individual motion picture company had, if any, only one African American musician into the 1940s. With the amalgamation of the black and white unions in 1953, token integration became widespread, and the exclusion of African American musicians from many performance venues ended.[66]

If the swing era began to break down racial barriers among musicians, however, it had almost no effect on the areas in which they played. Residential segregation became especially rigid in the 1930s and during World War II, creating awkward situations for African American musicians who performed in white areas. Bandleader Roy Porter recalled that the police sometimes escorted black musicians from downtown clubs to areas south of Pico Boulevard, the only areas where African Americans lived. In exclusive areas such as Glendale, black musicians needed a permit to remain after 6 p.m.—later midnight—and they were promptly escorted away by police once their performances were over. Stardom brought no relief from housing discrimination, as Cole found when he tried to obtain a residence in the all-white

Roots: The Willis Young Family" (paper presented at the Black Route West conference, University of California, Davis, 30 September 1995), 4–12.

16. Bessie Dones interview by Cox, 23 March 1983; Cox, *Central Avenue*, 18.

17. Hobsbawm, *Jazz Scene*, 24–25; de Graaf, "City of Black Angels," 330; Tom Reed, *The Black Music History of Los Angeles—Its Roots* (Los Angeles: Black Accent on L.A. Press, 1992), 338.

18. Kelson interview, *Central Avenue Sounds*, 224–26.

19. Hobsbawm, *Jazz Scene*, 19; Peretti, *Creation of Jazz*, 41–42; Kelson interview, *Central Avenue Sounds*, 224–26; Ted Gioia, *West Coast Jazz: Modern Jazz in California, 1945–1960* (New York: Oxford University Press, 1992), 7–8; Thomas J. Hennessey, *From Jazz to Swing: African American Jazz Musicians and Their Music, 1890–1935* (Detroit: Wayne State University Press, 1994), 58–59; Lawrence Gushee, "How the Creole Band Came to Be," *Black Music Research Journal* 8 (1988): 83–100.

20. Haven Johnson interview by Cox, 23 March 1983; Reed, *Black Music History of L.A.*, 22, 44; Hennessey, *From Jazz to Swing*, 59.

21. Peretti, *Creation of Jazz*, 185; de Graaf, "City of Black Angels," 335–38, 341–42; Cox, *Central Avenue*, 23.

22. Peretti, *Creation of Jazz*, 63; Cox, *Central Avenue*, 24; William Douglass interview, *Central Avenue Sounds*, 238, 252.

23. Freita Shaw interview by Cox, 21 March 1983; Cox, *Central Avenue*, 25–29, 36; Reed, *Black Music History of L. A.*, 388–89.

24. Hobsbawm, *Jazz Scene*, 23; Jones, *Blues People*, 139–40; Hennessey, *From Jazz to Swing*, 32–34.

25. Marshall Royal interview by Cox, 9 January 1984; Peretti, *Creation of Jazz*, 72–73, chap. 6.

26. Lonnie G. Bunch III, *Black Angelenos: The Afro-American in Los Angeles, 1850–1950* (Los Angeles: California Afro-American Museum, 1988), 29–34.

27. Royal interview by Cox; Gioia, *West Coast Jazz*, 8–9; Bruce M. Tyler, *From Harlem to Hollywood: The Struggle for Racial and Cultural Democracy* (New York: Garland Publishing, 1992), 94–95.

28. Royal interview by Cox; Cox, *Central Avenue*, 30–32; Reed, *Black Music History of L.A.*, 20.

29. *Central Avenue Sounds*, 92–93; Cecil "Big Jay" McNeely interview, ibid., 180.

30. Tyler, *From Harlem to Hollywood*, 92–95; Donald Bogle, *Toms, Coons, Mulattoes, Mammies, and Bucks: An Interpretive History of Blacks in American Films* (New York: Bantam Books, 1974), 34–42.

31. Gerald Wilson interview, *Central Avenue Sounds*, 328. The Dunbar was

built and originally owned by a prominent Jamaican immigrant, J. Alexander Somerville. Hurt by the stock market crash, Somerville sold it to an African American, Louis Lomax, who renamed it after Paul Dunbar, the turn-of-the-century black poet. See *Who's Who in Colored Los Angeles, 1930–31* (Los Angeles: California Eagle, 1931).

32. McNeely, Clora Bryant, William "Brother" Woodman Jr., Kelson, Douglass, Fletcher Smith interviews, *Central Avenue Sounds*, 79, 191, 358, 108, 212–14, 234.

33. Lee Young interview, *Central Avenue Sounds*, 54, 57, 71–72.

34. "Brother" Woodman interview, ibid., 109–10.

35. "Brother" Woodman, McNeely, Britt Woodman interviews, ibid., 109–10, 123–24, 131 (quote), 188–89.

36. Jones, *Blues People*, 117; Peretti, *Creation of Jazz*, 164–65.

37. Browne interview by Cox. More celebrated than the choruses of Los Angeles was the Oakland w pa Chorus led by W. Elmer Keeton. See Michael Fried, "W. Elmer Keeton and His w pa Chorus: Oakland's Musical Civil Rights Pioneers of the New Deal Era," *California History* 75 (1996): 236–49.

38. Florence "Tiny" Brantley interview by Cox, 23 March 1983 and 2 January 1985; Bogle, *Toms, Coons*, chap. 3; Daniels, "Willis Young," 22–23.

39. Patricia King Hanson, exec. ĕd., *The American Film Institute Catalog of Motion Pictures Produced in the United States: Feature Films, 1931–1940*, 3 vols. (Berkeley: University of California Press, 1993), vol. 1, 247, 863–64, vol. 2, 2290; J. Marshall Anderson, "A Guide to Media Consultancy: Black Westerns as Case Study" (master's thesis, California State University, Fullerton, 1992), 76–79; Cox, *Central Avenue*, 66, 145, 231, 284–85.

40. Brantley interview by Cox; Reed, *Black Music History of L. A.*, 391.

41. Verna Arvey, *In Our Lifetime* (Fayetteville: University of Arkansas Press, 1984), 100.

42. Verna Arvey Still interview by Cox, 12 February 1983.

43. Cox, *Central Avenue*, 38–42, 48–52; Reed, *Black Music History of L.A.*, 36, 416; Buddy Collette, Douglass, Horace Tapscott interviews, *Central Avenue Sounds*, 142, 236, 293.

44. Peretti, *Creation of Jazz*, 169; Hennessey, *From Jazz to Swing*, 122–23, 133, 155–56; Hobsbawm, *Jazz Scene*, 42–43, 52–53.

45. Cox, *Central Avenue*, 59–61. The initial creation of boogie-woogie is credited to black migrant musicians in the early 1920s devising it as a piano music they could play at rent parties and juke joints in northern cities. See Jones, *Blues People*, 114–15.

46. Reed, *Black Music History of L.A.*, 45.

47. Bunch, "Past Not Necessarily Prologue," 113; Douglass and F. Smith interviews, *Central Avenue Sounds*, 239–41, 83.

48. Reed, *Black Music History of L.A.*, 60, 73–75, 156, 264, and passim; Cox, *Central Avenue*, 60.

49. *Central Avenue Sounds*, 202; David Bryant interview, ibid., 172.

50. Emma "Ginger" Smock interview by Cox, 24 February 1983; Reed, *Black Music History of L.A.*, 325–26; *Central Avenue Sounds*, 202; David Bryant interview, ibid., 172.

51. Reed, *Black Music History of L.A.*, 215–16; Hennessey, *From Jazz to Swing*, 133, 151; Tyler, *From Harlem to Hollywood*, 106.

52. Smock interview by Cox; Cox, *Central Avenue*, 67.

53. Robert Gordon, *Jazz West Coast: Los Angeles Jazz Scene of the 1950s* (London: Quartet Books, 1986), 24–41; Hobsbawm, *Jazz Scene*, 47, 54–55; Southern, *Music of Black Americans*, 474; Cox, *Central Avenue*, 65–66.

54. Gioia, *West Coast Jazz*, 20–21; Gordon, *Jazz West Coast*, 40–42.

55. Reed, *Black Music History of L.A.*, 207, 215–16; Gordon, *Jazz West Coast*, 49–50; Gioia, *West Coast Jazz*, 18–19, 23–36.

56. Cox, *Central Avenue*, 76–77; Reed, *Black Music History of L.A.*, 291; Gordon, *Jazz West Coast*, 184–94.

57. Cox, *Central Avenue*, 81–83; Southern, *Music of Black Americans*, 471–72.

58. By 1945, hundreds of thousands of white soldiers had heard R&B on the Armed Forces Radio and were captivated by this new music. By 1955, whites were "covering" this music in an attempt to reproduce it in the same manner that black musicians performed it, sometimes changing the sacred lyrics of gospel music for their commercial purposes. The ensuing music evolved into "rock and roll."

59. Cox, *Central Avenue*, 67, 70–71; Southern, *Music of Black Americans*, 499.

60. *Central Avenue Sounds*, 309; Britt Woodman, Collette, David Bryant, Art Farmer, Clora Bryant interviews, ibid., 132, 148, 177, 272, 365.

61. Douglass interview, ibid., 247–52; Marl Young interview, ibid., 386–98; Cox, *Central Avenue*, 85–88; William "Buddy" Collette interview by Cox, 26 November 1983.

62. *Central Avenue Sounds*, 310; Tapscott, Farmer interviews, ibid., 279, 296–97; Gordon, *Jazz West Coast*, 125; Reed, *Black Music History of L.A.*, 45, 157.

63. Cox, *Central Avenue*, 88; Lee Young interview, *Central Avenue Sounds*, 72–73; Sally Sandoval, "Ghetto Growing Pains: The Impact of Negro Migration on the City of Los Angeles, 1940–1960" (Master's thesis, California State University, Fullerton, 1973), 36–43. Some have noted that the decline of Central Avenue was a

harbinger of a decline in West Coast jazz music in general a decade later, for some of the same reasons. See Gioia, *West Coast Jazz*, chap. 17.

64. The first of these questions especially has been posed in Peretti, *The Creation of Jazz*, chap. 10. The second has been debated by several authors but is probably best set forth by LeRoi Jones in *Blues People*.

65. Peretti, *Creation of Jazz*, 191, 202–4; Cox, *Central Avenue*, 61, 67.

66. Peretti, *Creation of Jazz*, 185–86.

67. Tyler, *From Harlem to Hollywood*, 110; Gioia, *West Coast Jazz*, 17; Reed, *Black Music History of L.A.*, 268, 327–28.

68. George Lipsitz, "Creating Dangerously: The Blues Life of Johnny Otis," in Johnny Otis, *Upside Your Head! Rhythm and Blues on Central Avenue* (Hanover, NH: University Press of New England, 1993), xxv–xxvii.

69. Otis, *Upside Your Head!*, 1–2.

70. Southern, *Music of Black Americans*, 477; John "Dizzy" Gillespie, "Introduction," in Leonard Feather, *The Book of Jazz from Then Till Now* (New York: Horizon Press, 1965), vi.

71. Keil, *Urban Blues*, 43; Southern, *Music of Black Americans*, 554; Cox, *Central Avenue*, 301; Reed, *Black Music History of L.A.*, 225.

72. Kelson, Lee Young interviews, *Central Avenue Sounds*, 231–32, 72–73.

73. Bunch, "Past Not Necessarily Prologue," 124.

74. Jones, *Blues People*, especially chap. 9.

75. Clora Bryant interview, *Central Avenue Sounds*, 366–67.

Yvonne Burke of Los Angeles were elected in the early 1970s, signaling the increasing importance of California in national politics, especially in matters of race.[67]

As Hawkins was moving to Washington in 1963, Los Angeles experienced its own breakthrough in racial representation. Long denied access to the city council by racially gerrymandered districts, black Angelenos finally found success. By 1963, three African Americans, including future mayor Tom Bradley, were on the council, and a new liberal black and Jewish coalition was emerging to replace what was left of the old black and white labor alliance.[68]

Black Californians suddenly found themselves in their best political situation ever. They had witnessed major triumphs in Sacramento and unprecedented representation at the local level. In the nation's capital, Congress, spurred by the civil rights movement and by President Johnson, had finally put federal power to work for black civil rights. The Civil Rights Act of 1964 struck down Jim Crow by outlawing segregation in public places and prohibiting racial and gender discrimination in hiring, and the Voting Rights Act of 1965 outlawed southern disfranchisement. As a result, a two-party system emerged in the South, with millions of conservative white Democrats becoming Republicans and millions of black southerners joining the Democratic Party, thereby infusing the party of Roosevelt with huge numbers of racial liberals. In both California and America as a whole, then, the future of racial liberalism looked bright.

Then the light went out. With appalling suddenness, civil rights liberalism collapsed in the mid- to late-1960s. White attacks on black progress in California, such as the racist campaign against fair housing in the state, and black uprisings against the white establishment, such as the 1965 conflagration in Watts, soon made it difficult to recall or appreciate the legislative triumphs of 1959 and 1963. Equally problematic for civil rights leaders, the political tensions resulting from the United States' involvement in Vietnam soon tore California's Democrats apart.

But the collapse of the civil rights movement is another story—one addressed by other authors in this anthology—and it is one that has come to overshadow the longer history of civil rights activism in California. The accomplishments of the legislature in the late 1950s and early 1960s were impressive, and although they soon proved unequal to the challenge of race relations in modern California, they should be viewed in the light of the long-term struggle of Hawkins and others to secure basic rights for blacks in the state. By acknowledging the political gains African Americans made in the years immediately prior to the mid-1960s, we are confronted with a complex question: Why did the Watts uprising occur in the wake of such important civil rights breakthroughs? That question bears directly on how effective the relationship is between political democracy and social well-being in modern America. It is one we still need to confront.

NOTES

1. On southern disfranchisement, see J. Morgan Kousser, *The Shaping of Southern Politics: Suffrage Restriction and the Establishment of the One-Party South, 1880–1910* (New Haven: Yale University Press, 1974).

2. *California Eagle* (hereafter cited as *Eagle*), 10 June 1921, cited in James Adolphus Fisher, "A History of the Political and Social Development of the Black Community in California, 1850–1950" (Ph.D. diss., State University of New York at Stony Brook, 1971), 221.

3. Douglas Flamming, "African-Americans and the Politics of Race in Pro-gressive-Era Los Angeles," in William Deverell and Tom Sitton, eds., *California Progressivism Revisited* (Berkeley: University of California Press, 1994), 222.

4. California, secretary of state, *Statement of the Vote* (hereafter cited as *Statement of the Vote*), 1926 primary election. Generally, the statement of the vote was printed in Sacramento the year of the election.

5. *Eagle*, 24 August 1928. On Hubbard's 1922 campaign, see ibid., 19, 26 August 1922; he won only 193 votes in the 1922 Republican primary (see *Statement of the Vote*), so his talk of defection in 1928 was important not for the threat it posed to Roberts but for his symbolic support for Democratic liberalism.

6. George Beavers interview by Ranford B. Hopkins, 1982, UCLA Oral History Program, 193–96; Hopkins refers to a *Los Angeles Times* article in 1928, but gives no specific date.

7. Augustus F. Hawkins interview by Flamming, 1997 (hereafter cited as Hawkins interview by Flamming); Leonard J. Leader, *Los Angeles and the Great Depression* (New York: Garland, 1991), 6, 11, 14.

8. For the national trend, see John B. Kirby, *Black Americans in the Roosevelt Era: Liberalism and Race* (Knoxville: University of Tennessee Press, 1980); Harvard Sitkoff, *A New Deal for Blacks: The Emergence of Civil Rights as a National Issue: The Depression Decade* (New York: Oxford University Press, 1978); and Nancy J.

Weiss, *Farewell to the Party of Lincoln: Black Politics in the Age of* F D R (Princeton: Princeton University Press, 1983). For the realignment in the West, see Albert S. Broussard, *Black San Francisco: The Struggle for Racial Equality in the West, 1900–1954* (Lawrence: University Press of Kansas, 1993), chaps. 5–6; and Quintard Taylor, *The Forging of a Black Community: Seattle's Central District from the 1870s through the Civil Rights Era* (Seattle: University of Washington Press), chap. 3.

9. Winston W. Crouch et al., *State and Local Government in California* (Berkeley: University of California Press, 1952), 30.

10. The California Assembly was required by law to redraw assembly lines after each decennial census, but the legislature deadlocked in controversy following the 1920 census, and new assembly boundaries were not agreed upon until 1927. Lingering controversy delayed the implementation of those lines until the 1930 election. In 1931, the state assembly lines were once again redrawn, with Roberts successfully maintaining the boundaries of his Sixty-second District. For boundary lines, see *Statutes of California . . . Passed at the Extra Session of the Thirty-Ninth Legislature, 1911*, 163; *Statutes of California: 1927*, 1780; *Statutes of California: 1931*, 285. Roberts's obituary in the *Eagle*, 27 July 1952, credits him (without reference to the assembly district) with maintaining electoral lines that preserved racial representation; by default this would have meant drawing the lines for the Sixty-second District in 1927 and 1931.

11. When black leaders spoke of the "west side" of the Sixty-second District, it was code for "white side." (This west side should not be confused with the more conventional use of the term, which refers to the whiter and wealthier west side of Los Angeles proper.) Neighborhoods generally became whiter as one went west of Central, but the west-of-Avalon/San Pedro axis was truly white and resistant to black encroachment; it was also a solid source of Democratic strength from 1932 onward.

12. Black Democrats in Los Angeles gained more momentum after F D R was nominated, organizing a "Roosevelt Club," which met regularly. Four days before the state primary, the Roosevelt Club held a "mammoth" F D R-for-president banquet; see *Eagle*, 15 July, 26 August 1932. On F D R's nomination, put over by the all-white California delegation, see Arthur M. Schlesinger Jr., *The Crisis of the Old Order* (Boston: Houghton Mifflin, 1956), 308–10.

13. An elect-a-white-man campaign emerged on the West Side, which placed a single candidate, George Grimmer, on both the G O P and Democratic primary tickets for the primaries. He won the Democratic contest because two African American candidates split the black Democratic vote. Grimmer was registered a Republican, and, by law, could not run as the Democratic candidate because he

had lost his own party's nomination. The Democratic County Committee chose Ellsworth Courtney, a white political unknown, to run in Grimmer's place. *Eagle*, 22 July, 19, 26 August, 7 October, 4 November 1932; and *Statement of the Vote*, 1932 primary election.

14. Although in April 1934, the *Eagle* reported the heady rumor that Roberts would run for Congress, the paper's laconic note two months later—that there was no interest in the Republican primary in the Sixty-second and that "it looked for a moment that no one would file, including the incumbent"—was a more sober assessment of Roberts's political future. Roberts did file, and his only competition in the Republican primary was Thomas M. Myles, a young, well-respected civic activist in the African American community and a Republican party worker. Myles won some interesting endorsements, including that of the Los Angeles Japanese-American Citizens' League, but he had no realistic chance against Roberts in the GOP primary. *Eagle*, 29 June, 24 August 1934.

15. John J. Gold was the one white candidate in the field of six, but he was never in serious contention and all but dropped out before the election took place. In mid-August, the *Eagle* reported that Gold had "withdrawn" from the contest, but his name appeared on the ballot, and he finished in last place with 405 votes.

16. A genuinely giving soul (with a good eye for interest rates as well), Dones spent considerable time and money helping poor people in the Sixty-second. The language of the '30s was right up his alley. He claimed to be "the man of the working people and the unemployed people's candidate." He pledged to aid "the business man with his little problems, the man without work, and the woman without support, no one turned down whether they have money or not." Always the showman, Dones toured the district in a sixteen-cylinder Cadillac "just to show the boys the sort of speed he intends to put into the race." It was a curious dash of flash for the candidate of the unemployed, but, in any case, no one seriously expected Dones to win, in 1934 or any other year. *Eagle*, 6 April, 11 May, 8 June, 13 July 1934.

17. A native of Texas, Williams, who was blind, had arrived in Los Angeles in the early 1920s. He became publisher and editor of the *Pacific Defender*, a race paper, and soon gained respect in local Republican circles. In 1934, he was no token player in Los Angeles politics but a well-respected GOP manager who had served on his party's County Central Committee since 1926. The *Eagle* reported that Williams "was the sensation in the 62nd District on the last filing day," when he held a meeting at the post office to publicly change his registration to Democrat and file for the Democratic primary. The *Eagle* was astonished that this "staunch Republican and head man of the County Central Committee for the

district renounces his party, his position, and accepts the democratic faith within the twinkling of an eye, as it were." Williams expressed his reasoning implicitly, emphasizing his full intention to join the Roosevelt administration's efforts "to alleviate depression, distress, racial animosity, and class antagonisms, and to promote peace, happiness, prosperity, and opportunities for all individuals." Williams racked up an impressive list of endorsements. *Eagle*, 29 June 1934.

18. Somerville was a native of Jamaica who moved to California as a young man and became the first African American to graduate from the University of Southern California school of dentistry. The purpose of his visit to Washington remained a secret, but word had it that Somerville would meet first with a select group of high-profile black leaders and New Deal officials and then with FDR himself. He received a great deal of press in the Republican *Eagle*, where his campaign ads were accompanied by long lists of endorsements from local Democratic clubs and civic associations. Some later charged that he was a "fake" Democratic candidate, running at the behest of the Basses and Fred Roberts; that he, in effect, was to win the Democratic primary and then throw the election to Roberts. See *Eagle*, 15, 29 June, 10, 24 August 1934; and Hawkins interview by Flamming. On Somerville generally, see Alexander Somerville, *Man of Color: An Autobiography* (Los Angeles: L. L. Morrison, 1949).

19. On this national trend, see Sitkoff, *A New Deal for Blacks;* and Weiss, *Farewell to the Party of Lincoln.*

20. Baumann lost to Hawkins by only 232 ballots. *Statement of Vote*, 1934 primary election.

21. Hawkins interview by Flamming.

22. Augustus F. Hawkins interview by Carlos Vasquez, UCLA Oral History Program, 1988 (hereafter cited as Hawkins interview by Vasquez), 46–47, 50–51.

23. EPIC swept through the white working-class neighborhoods of east Los Angeles but did not fare as well in the Sixty-second. In fact, the Sixty-second was the only eastside district in the city that did not have an EPIC-endorsed candidate in the Democratic primary, and Hawkins himself never courted EPIC support. As the pro-labor candidate, he should have been EPIC's obvious choice, but when EPIC's central office circulated a questionnaire inquiring whether the candidate supported socialized medicine, Hawkins gave an uncertain response, thereby alienating EPIC leaders. Only after Hawkins won the primary did the EPIC *News* list Hawkins as an EPIC candidate, and then without fanfare. Hawkins interview by Vasquez, 48–49, 78. On the EPIC campaign and the absence of Hawkins in EPIC circles, see the issues of EPIC *News* throughout the 1934 campaign, Upton Sinclair Papers, Lilly Library, University of Indiana.

24. Macbeth was the only influential African American leader to strongly ally with EPIC, and he did serve a minor leadership role in the Los Angeles County EPIC group. In his role as an important Utopian leader, however, Macbeth was more successful in rallying black support for Hawkins's cause. For a discussion of Macbeth's career, see the essay by Delores McBroome in this anthology.

25. On the relationship of the Utopians to the black community and their support for Hawkins, see Luther Whiteman and Samuel L. Lewis, *Glory Roads: The Psychological State of California* (New York: Thomas Y. Crowell, 1936), chaps. 3–6, especially 23, 33–34, and 56–59; and Leader, *Los Angeles and the Great Depression*, 128–29.

26. Hawkins interview by Vasquez, 47–51.

27. Ibid.

28. *Eagle*, 5 October 1934.

29. Hawkins interview by Flamming.

30. Ibid.

31. *Eagle*, 2 November 1934.

32. *Statement of the Vote*, 1934 general election. Samuel W. Jones that year became the first Communist Party candidate to run in the district, but he received only 340 votes.

33. On the 1936 campaign, see the *Eagle* from mid-May through the general election in November, and the *New Age*, from late July through early November; *Statement of the Vote*, 1936 primary and general election. For the national black shift to Roosevelt that year, see Weiss, *Farewell to the Party of Lincoln*, 92–94, 200–204, 218.

34. *Statement of the Vote*, 1938 primary and general elections, and see also 1940, 1942, and 1944. After losing in 1936, Roberts refused to run again until 1944, when he entered the GOP primary, only to lose to a cross-filing Hawkins. Cross-filing arose in California with the adoption of primary elections in the Progressive Era and was especially widely used by Republicans to secure election during the spring primary vote rather than the fall general election. Once a candidate secured election this way, it was not uncommon to exploit the advantage of incumbency and continue to be elected by this device. Cross-filing lost some of its advantage in the early 1950s, when it became mandatory to identify the primary party a candidate was affiliated with on the ballot. The practice was completely abolished in 1959.

35. Hawkins was not completely unopposed in the general election of 1938. Dones had beaten Hawkins in the Progressive Party primary, 66 votes to 44. In

November, Dones tallied a surprising 4,410 ballots—nearly 20 percent of the vote. His tally as a "Progressive" probably represented the number of old-guard black Republicans who still could not bear to cast their votes for a Democrat, even an African American Democrat. As a practical matter, Dones's votes were meaningless, because Hawkins's reelection was never in doubt.

36. There would always be black Republicans in the Sixty-second, but they never again held power and they gradually thinned out. To cross-file as a Republican candidate every two years, Hawkins had to petition for a place on the GOP ballot; the petitioning process required that he obtain the signatures of some two dozen Republican Party members within his district. In 1938, he succeeded in finding a group of black Republicans who were willing to sign his petition, and after that he returned to those same Republicans each election year. In time, though, Hawkins found that those Republicans switched their registration to the Democratic Party. "It got to where I could hardly find enough Republicans in the district to fill my petition," he recalled. Hawkins interview by Flamming.

37. *Utopian News*, 15 November 1934.

38. Jackson K. Putnam, *Modern California Politics*, 2d ed. (San Francisco: Boyd and Fraser Publishing Company, 1984), 21–23.

39. Another administrative arm of New Deal money in California was the State Emergency Relief Administration (SERA), the function of which changed over time from briefly administering the CWA to providing direct relief funds to counties to serving as an assistance bureau for the WPA. The Sacramento-controlled SERA was not central to local relief in Los Angeles. On SERA's changing role, see Leader, *Los Angeles and the Great Depression*, chap. 11.

40. Ibid., 228, 244–45, 250–53 (quote 250).

41. See, for example, Frederick Roberts's discussion of the WPA's Federal Writers Project in Los Angeles. *New Age*, 2 April 1937. African American papers also printed news of local-level New Deal discrimination reported in other black papers from around the country; see, for example, ibid., 21 August, 3 September 1937. Civilian Conservation Corps camps were one of several programs in which blacks might have been integrated or segregated depending largely on the reaction of various communities to such camps and the administrator's willingness to bow to local pressures or to resist them. See John A. Salmond, "The Civilian Conservation Corps and the Negro," *Journal of American History* 52 (June 1965): 75–88.

42. The black-owned Golden State Mutual Life Insurance Company occasionally pointed out the social security exclusions in its newspaper advertisements, adding that this was a good reason to get a retirement pension contract

from Golden State. *New Age*, 15 January 1937. On New Deal racial discrimination generally, see Sitkoff, *A New Deal for Blacks*; and Kirby, *Black Americans in the Roosevelt Era*.

43. John Somerville served as technical advisor on Negro problems for the California S E R A, and Baxter Scruggs, an official with the black Y M C A, was an advisor for the Los Angeles district N Y A. "Historical Background of Negro Survey, for Los Angeles," 1935, unpublished ms., Index of American Design Collection, items B2–6, box 2, folder 1, Huntington Library, San Marino, CA.

44. Floyd C. Covington, "Where the Color Line Chokes," *Sociology and Social Research* (January/February 1936): 236–41, quote 236.

45. An extended discussion of the N Y A and the African American community in California will appear in the forthcoming book by Douglas Flamming, *A World to Gain: African Americans and the Making of Los Angeles, 1890–1940*.

46. Marilynn S. Johnson, *The Second Gold Rush: Oakland and the East Bay in World War II* (Berkeley: University of California Press, 1993), 53; Raphael J. Sonenshein, *Politics in Black and White: Race and Power in Los Angeles* (Princeton: Princeton University Press, 1993), 22; Paul R. Spickard, "Work and Hope: African American Women in Southern California during World War II," *Journal of the West* 32 (1993): 70–79; Lawrence B. de Graaf, "Significant Steps on an Arduous Path: The Impact of World War II on Discrimination against African Americans in the West," *Journal of the West* 35 (1996): 24–33.

47. Johnson, *Second Gold Rush*, chap. 7.

48. Fisher, "History of the Political and Social Development of the Black Community," 250–57.

49. Quote from Hawkins interview by Vasquez, 75; Hawkins interview by Flamming; Johnson, *Second Gold Rush*, 206.

50. For examples of this national trend, see Robert Zieger, *American Workers, American Unions, 1920–1985* (Baltimore: Johns Hopkins University Press, 1986), chaps. 4–5. See also Michael Honey, *Southern Labor and Black Civil Rights: Organizing Memphis Workers, 1929–55* (Urbana: University of Illinois Press, 1993), especially part 3.

51. Johnson, *Second Gold Rush*, 233, and chaps. 7 and 8 generally.

52. Race was always an explosive issue in the labor movement, and racial exclusion had often been a key to white union success. See Michael Kazin, *Barons of Labor: The San Francisco Building Trades and Union Power in the Progressive Era* (Urbana: University of Illinois Press, 1987); Henry M. McKiven, *Iron and Steel: Class, Race, and Community in Birmingham, Alabama, 1875–1920* (Chapel Hill: University of North Carolina Press, 1995); David R. Roediger, *The Wages of Whiteness:*

Race and the Making of the American Working Class (New York: W. W. Norton, 1991); Alexander Saxton, *The Indispensable Enemy: Labor and the Anti-Chinese Movement in California* (Berkeley: University of California Press, 1971). For tensions at the local level, see Becky M. Nicolaides, "Incubating the 'Silent Majority': Community and Political Life in a Working-Class Suburb of Los Angeles, 1945–1965," paper presented at the Organization of American Historians Conference, San Francisco, 18 April 1997.

53. On Warren, see Putnam, *Modern California Politics*, chap. 3. Warren and Hawkins also joined forces to push for prepaid health insurance, but Rumford, a pharmacist, opposed the measure, which was defeated by the outcry of "socialized medicine." This battle ultimately hurt Hawkins's career, for when he ran for speaker of the assembly in 1959, the powerful California Medical Association (CMA) had him defeated. Several liberal Democrats, including Rumford, allied with the CMA and voted against Hawkins, leaving him two votes shy of the chair. Hawkins interview by Vasquez, 78–79, 186–87.

54. Hawkins interview by Vasquez, 114–16, quotes on 115, 133.

55. Raphael J. Sonenshein, *Politics in Black and White: Race and Power in Los Angeles* (Princeton: Princeton University Press, 1993), 28–30; Rudolph M. Lapp, *Afro-Americans in California*, 2d ed. (San Francisco: Boyd and Fraser, 1987), 68.

56. On this process nationally and on the West Coast, see Arnold R. Hirsch, *Making the Second Ghetto: Race and Housing in Chicago, 1940–1960* (New York: Cambridge University Press, 1983); Nicholas Lemann, *Promised Land: The Great Black Migration and How It Changed America* (New York: Alfred A. Knopf, 1991); Johnson, *Second Gold Rush*; and Taylor, *The Forging of a Black Community*, especially chap. 6.

57. Hawkins interview by Vasquez, 109–12.

58. The change in cross-filing came when the Democrats placed a proposition on the ballot that called for its abolition. The GOP introduced its own proposition, hoping that confused voters would simply vote "no" to both (a common way to defeat a proposition). But while the Democratic measure failed, the Republican proposition actually passed. That proposition upheld cross-filing but mandated that candidates would now have to indicate their party affiliation on the ballot. That this change virtually wiped out the GOP advantage in the cross-filing process was clearly evident in Democratic gains in 1954 and 1956. See Putnam, *Modern California Politics*, chap. 4; and John Jacobs, *A Rage for Justice: The Passion and Politics of Phillip Burton* (Berkeley: University of California Press, 1995), chap. 4 and p. 63.

59. Jacobs, *Rage for Justice*, 64–65, and chap. 3 generally.

60. Recalling his meeting with Brown, Hawkins identified Leon Washington of the *Los Angeles Sentinel* and Oakland's C. L. Dellums as two who were with him; there were others he could not recall. Hawkins interview by Vasquez, 133–34.

61. Brown's point man in the assembly became the smart, power-hungry Unruh, who had managed Brown's campaign in Southern California. Unruh was rewarded with the chairmanship of the influential Ways and Means Committee and became a nearly dictatorial speaker in 1961. Unruh and Hawkins were at odds because Hawkins was too independent to be controlled by his fellow Angeleno and because he did not need Unruh's financial backers to be elected. Hawkins interview by Vasquez, 121, 160–64; Jacobs, *A Rage for Justice*, passim, offers an insightful portrait of Unruh.

62. The minimum fine increased from $100 (a fee set by Frederick Roberts back in 1919) to more than $200. Hawkins, who had long sponsored such legislation, bristled at Unruh's naming the law for himself, in part because Unruh got the bill through after making only a few technical changes to the bills Hawkins and Rumford had been introducing throughout the 1950s. The legislature also sent yet another antilynching resolution to the U.S. Congress. Jacobs, *Rage for Justice*, 75; Hawkins interview by Vasquez, 162–63.

63. Putnam, *Modern California Politics*, chap. 4; Royce Delmatier et al., *The Rumble of California Politics, 1848–1970* (New York: John Wiley, 1970), 424–25.

64. This was A. B. 801, "which banned discrimination in all private housing offered for sale, lease, or rental by any person except the owner of a single-unit residence occupied by him as a residence." Delmatier, *Rumble of California Politics*, 424.

65. A. B. 1240, "banned discrimination in the sale or rental of all publicly assisted housing and all privately financed housing other than dwellings with four or fewer units." Ibid.

66. Ibid., 349–51.

67. Lapp, *Afro-Americans in California*, 1st. ed., 1979, 84–85.

68. Sonenshein, *Politics in Black and White*, chap. 3; see also the essay by Sonenshein in this anthology.

"In the Interest of All Races"

African Americans and Interracial Cooperation

in Los Angeles during and after World War II

KEVIN ALLEN LEONARD

When Chester Himes left Cleveland for Los Angeles in 1941, he expected to escape the indignity of employment discrimination he had experienced in Ohio's largest city. Like many African Americans who had arrived in Los Angeles before him, Himes had been led to believe that the discrimination he would encounter in the Southern California metropolis would be less severe than the persecution blacks endured in other cities. His experiences in Los Angeles frustrated his expectations, however: he was denied access to jobs and to restaurants, theaters, and other businesses because of his "race."[1] Himes's experiences in Los Angeles between 1941 and 1944, when he left for New York, were not exceptional. Unlike most other blacks in Los Angeles, however, he published accounts of his experiences in two novels and a later autobiography.

Although he is best remembered for his fiction set in Harlem, Himes's first two published novels—*If He Hollers Let Him Go* and *Lonely Crusade*—were set in Los Angeles. In these books, Himes depicts African American men as isolated victims of racial discrimination. Bob Jones, the protagonist of *If He Hollers Let Him Go*, wakes up from nightmares each morning and then experiences nightmarish treatment during the day. Jones, who works as a "leaderman" in a shipyard, is called a "nigger" by a white woman; demoted for calling the woman a "cracker bitch"; decked by a white worker; upbraided by his girlfriend, whom he suspects of being a lesbian; accused of rape; savagely beaten; and forced into the army.

In the longer and more complex *Lonely Crusade*, protagonist Lee Gordon struggles to overcome his own weaknesses as well as a violently racist society.

Gordon, a graduate of the University of California at Los Angeles who worked only sporadically throughout the Depression, is hired by a union in 1943 to organize African American aircraft workers. Although Gordon is pleased to have a job, he still feels emasculated because his wife earns more than he does. To assert his masculinity, he rapes his wife the night before he begins working. Gordon's job brings him into contact with communists, and he has an affair with a white woman who is a party member. Troubled by his desire for and reliance upon a white woman, his wife's coldness and remoteness, and the labor leaders' willingness to cooperate with communists, Gordon betrays the union. At the nadir of his life, Gordon watches a black communist kill a white police officer. He tells his white paramour of his presence at the crime scene and is arrested and brutally beaten by the police. The novel ends ambiguously, with Gordon alive, out of jail, awaiting trial for the police officer's murder, and still an abject failure as a union organizer.

As this brief description of his novels suggests, Chester Himes had come to the conclusion that, in Southern California, there was no one an African American man could trust.[2] He could not trust white people, for no matter how earnest or "liberal" they appeared to be, they remained white—they could never understand the point of view of an African American, and they could never willingly give up the power that their whiteness gave them. An African American man could not trust other African Americans because black people had been so beaten and confused by white oppressors that they would betray their "brothers" for even a small price. And he could not trust any political party, especially the Communist Party. For Himes, then, the black man's struggle for respect and dignity was a lonely crusade.

Himes was struck not only by the racial discrimination that African Americans faced in Los Angeles but also by the multicultural character of the city.[3] Like most blacks who moved there before or during World War II, Himes came from biracial environments. He had grown up in the South and in Cleveland, where people generally divided themselves into two racial categories: "white" and "Negro."[4] Himes recognized that Los Angeles was not like Cleveland or southern cities. In *Lonely Crusade*, as Lee Gordon rides a streetcar to a union meeting, a phrase repeats itself in his mind:

> "Nigger, white man, gentile, Jew . . ."
> Mexicans, Europeans, Orientals, South Americans—and Filipinos, he added to the quartet. Southerners, Northerners, Easterners, Westerners—and Indians—this was manpower. . . . The bloated, hysterical, frantic

rushing city that was Los Angeles in the spring of 1943. And these were the people who made it go, Lee Gordon thought.[5]

Although this passage may seem overshadowed by the fact that Bob Jones and Lee Gordon rarely encounter people they cannot categorize as either black or white, it indicates that Himes saw that people of diverse African, Mexican, Asian, American Indian, Jewish, and European extraction coexisted in Los Angeles.

Because *If He Hollers Let Him Go* was widely read and critically acclaimed, Himes's pessimistic portrayal of wartime Los Angeles is better known than other interpretations. Unlike Himes, however, many African Americans in Southern California looked optimistically at the region's diversity. Wartime events led a number of black leaders to the conclusion that the experiences of African Americans in Los Angeles were similar to those of other racialized groups, especially Mexican Americans and Jewish Americans.[6] Some of these leaders decided that, in order to gain access to power, African Americans had to appreciate the similarities between their experiences and those of the city's other racial minorities and should work to establish a coalition of these groups. Ultimately, however, postwar redbaiting, the growth of the black and Mexican American communities, and divisions within those groups limited the effectiveness of this coalition.

Although Himes set his novels during the war, he did not portray World War II as a turning point for blacks in Los Angeles. But the war did have a dramatic, if temporary, impact on the lives of many African Americans in Southern California. Federal spending on airplanes, ships, other military hardware, and supplies dramatically increased the size of the region's manufacturing economy. Before the war, only about 1,000 workers were employed in Los Angeles's shipyards. At the peak of war production, the shipyards employed 90,000. The city's aircraft factories employed nearly 230,000 at the peak of production.[7] African Americans did not immediately benefit from the rapid growth of war manufacturing, however. Early in the war, most aircraft and ship manufacturers refused to hire blacks. The Fair Employment Practices Committee (FEPC), created by Franklin D. Roosevelt in late June 1941, held hearings in Los Angeles that October. Those hearings revealed widespread discrimination against African Americans: there were only ten black employees in Douglas Aircraft's workforce of 33,000, only two among Bethlehem Shipbuilding's nearly 3,000 Los Angeles employees, and only fifty-four among Lockheed Aircraft and Vega Airplane's 48,000 workers.[8]

Before mid-1942, African Americans often had to settle for the low-wage positions vacated by white workers who had moved into war production jobs. In the second half of 1942, however, aircraft and ship manufacturers could not find enough white workers to keep their plants running at full capacity, so many blacks found employment in the war industries. By February 1943, the War Manpower Commission reported that Douglas Aircraft had 2,200 black employees, North American had 2,500, and Lockheed-Vega, 1,700. Among shipbuilders, California Shipbuilding (Calship) reported 1,200 black employees; Western Pipe and Steel, 400; Bethlehem, 300; Consolidated, 300; Los Angeles Drydock, 200; and Haagson, 150. In March 1943, Charlotta Bass, since 1912 the publisher of the *California Eagle*, one of the West's oldest black newspapers, declared, "Where two years ago there were no Negroes employed in production at defense plants, there are now thirty thousand *or more* Negro workers in basic war industries of our city."[9] By the end of 1944, more than 7,000 African Americans were working for Calship alone. By early 1945, one observer estimated that "eighty-five percent of the Negroes here are doing work with their hands in war industries, principally aircraft and shipbuilding."[10] The war offered many blacks the opportunity to leave jobs as unskilled laborers for employment as skilled workers. In aircraft plants and shipyards, former janitors and domestic servants bucked rivets and welded seams.

The availability of jobs in war industries lured tens of thousands of African Americans to Southern California. Although no one knows for certain how many came to the Los Angeles area during the war, sources agree that the black population more than doubled between 1940 and 1946. According to the U.S. Bureau of the Census, just less than 64,000 African Americans (4.2 percent of the city's population of 1.5 million) lived in Los Angeles in 1940. Six years later, a special census reported that the number had risen to more than 133,000 (7.4 percent of the city's population of 1.8 million). A Red Cross estimate from 1945, however, placed the Los Angeles area's black population at 175,000.[11] Even if the lower estimate is more accurate, the African American population of Los Angeles grew at least four times more rapidly than the city's population as a whole during the war.

World War II attracted African Americans to Los Angeles and allowed both newcomers and long-term residents access to jobs from which they previously had been excluded. But it did not dramatically improve all aspects of life for blacks. Most African Americans continued to face discrimination in the workplace, even if they were making much more money than before. In most war-production plants, managers refused to promote African Americans into supervisory positions over white workers, and black shipyard workers found themselves restricted to a powerless auxiliary of the Boilermakers' Union.

Like employment prejudice, housing discrimination also persisted throughout the war. Restrictive covenants written into property deeds prevented blacks from living in most sections of the city. Most realtors and landlords refused to sell or rent to African Americans unless the property lay in areas where blacks already lived. Because the federal government allowed contractors to erect only a small number of housing units during the war, and most of these were built expressly for white war workers, crowding grew worse in most of the districts in which African Americans lived. According to a report published in the *Los Angeles Sentinel*, only 942 of 51,000 housing units constructed in Los Angeles between the bombing of Pearl Harbor and 1 January 1945 were open to blacks. "As a result," the newspaper reported, "hundreds of Negroes are living in alley shacks, abandoned garages and vacant stores, and any makeshift building available, wherever such places can be found."[12] In addition to employment and housing discrimination, African Americans continued to endure exclusion and segregation. Blacks were barred from many hotels, restaurants, theaters, and parks, and African American children often were forced to attend segregated schools.

If World War II did not alleviate many kinds of discrimination, it did offer African Americans a potentially more effective way to attack unfair treatment. The war presented blacks with the opportunity to use its rhetoric in their efforts to attack segregation and other forms of racial discrimination. Throughout the war, editorials in black newspapers insisted that racial discrimination in the United States damaged the morale of African Americans and threatened to sabotage the conduct of the war. These newspapers referred to racism in the United States as "Hitler's secret weapon" and to racists as "fifth columnists" and "disrupters whose Americanism bears so close a resemblance to the ideology of Hitler." Whether or not the use of this language had any effect on European Americans, it seems to have struck a responsive chord among blacks. In Los Angeles, the war effort inspired African Americans to form new organizations such as the Negro Victory Committee. Organized by the Reverend Clayton D. Russell, the energetic pastor of the People's Independent Church of Christ, in April 1942, this group held mass meetings and marches in its efforts to eliminate employment and housing discrimination, especially in the low-rent public projects operated by the City Housing Authority.[13]

Some members of groups established earlier, such as the National Association for the Advancement of Colored People (NAACP), thought that the war provided new opportunities for their organizations and their community. George A. Beavers Jr., a leader of the Los Angeles branch of the NAACP, told members, "The attention of the people has been focused upon the program and the work of the N.A.A.C.P. as never before. The people of the community are in a receptive attitude and are looking to this organization for leadership in fighting our battles against racial discrimination." Beavers suggested that the NAACP could best take advantage of wartime opportunities by replacing ineffective officials in the organization, courting influential whites, and forming committees to work for greater black participation in the war effort.[14] The NAACP did not wholeheartedly embrace the changes that Beavers suggested. Nonetheless, the war revitalized the Los Angeles branch of the association; its membership grew rapidly from 2,000 before the war to 14,000 in 1946.

These and other organizations described the situation of African Americans in terms that would have been familiar to black residents of most U.S. cities. Glossing over significant divisions within the African American community, leaders discussed problems in black and white terms: white supremacists had conspired to limit the rights and privileges of African Americans, as they had done throughout the history of the United States. In many of their descriptions of discrimination in Los Angeles, African Americans implicitly connected incidents and patterns to those with which blacks in the South and urban North and Midwest were familiar. As this rhetoric suggests, members of the local African American community considered themselves part of a larger national group.

Many organizations reinforced a sense of black identity among African Americans in Los Angeles. Many, if not most, of the city's African American residents worshiped at all-black churches. The wealthy and the middle class belonged to all-black social groups. Middle-class men and women participated in the activities of predominantly black advocacy groups such as the NAACP and the National Urban League, and middle-class women belonged to women's clubs. Within these confines, it was easy for many African Americans to picture the world around them in black and white. With a strong sense of group identity, most acknowledged that they had more in common with blacks in other cities than with any other group in Los Angeles.

But in many ways, the experiences of Los Angeles's African American community in the 1940s differed significantly from those of blacks in predominantly biracial environments. In Los Angeles, many lived next to districts with large numbers of European Americans, Mexican Americans, and Asian Americans. The predominantly black community that stretched south from downtown along Central Avenue, for example, lay approximate to the largely Japanese American neighborhood known as Little Tokyo, which in turn bordered the mostly Mexican American community to the east. Some blacks lived next door to people of European, Mexican, or Asian descent.[15] In 1940, significant numbers of Mexican, European, and African Americans lived in Watts, and the West Jefferson district west of downtown was home to many middle-class blacks and Japanese.[16] During the war, one white journalist wrote that he lived "in a racially mixed neighborhood which is preponderantly Negro, with many Mexicans and a few Chinese and whites." As George Sánchez concluded from a careful study of residential patterns of Mexican immigrants and their descendants, "ethnic intermixing characterized most, but not all, central and east-side communities."[17]

From their experiences of living in mixed neighborhoods and interacting with people from other minority groups, some African Americans began to see that the multiracial character of Los Angeles affected their lives and those of other blacks. They recognized that Los Angeles was different from where they had lived before, and many sought some way to understand the complex racial order within the city. Even before World War II, some community leaders tried to comprehend Los Angeles by dwelling on the differences among the city's minorities.

In the 1930s, Charlotta Bass, one of the most influential women in the black community, attempted to explain the differences between Los Angeles's African American and Asian American communities. In a November 1939 radio broadcast, Bass contrasted "Oriental" and "Negro" communities. She argued that the remarkable success of Asian Americans in Southern California emerged from the fact that even after being transplanted to U.S. soil, they retained their connections to their centuries-old Asian civilizations. Most Asian Americans, she said, "are descendants of the ancient laboring classes, trained by ruthless overlords for centuries into a submissive acceptance of their duties." However, African cultures, she argued, had been destroyed by slave owners in North America. The "remarkable sameness of thought and action" that led to "the economic advancement of L.A.'s Orientals" was "at this time a rank impossibility for Negroes," Bass insisted. "Just now we are too occupied in a great psychological effort to adjust ourselves to the paradoxes of American life—the bewildering civilization that says we are free in one breath, and lynches us in the next. We are a people in search of a soul."[18] Bass's identification of differences between African Americans and Asian Americans does not seem insightful; her portrayal of members of both groups relied on well-established stereotypes. Nonetheless, by trying to explain why Asian Americans had found greater economic success than blacks, she acknowledged that many experiences of African Americans and Asian Americans were comparable.

Whereas Bass emphasized the differences between Asian Americans and African Americans, other community leaders recognized similarities among Los Angeles's racial minorities. The most visible of these was Floyd Covington. A Denver native, Covington had come to Los Angeles after he graduated from Washburn University in Topeka, Kansas. He began serving as executive director of the Los Angeles Urban League in 1928, holding that post for twenty-five years. In the late 1930s, Covington had developed a working relationship with leaders of the Mexican American community in Los Angeles. He was asked to chair a session at the first meeting of El Congreso de Pueblos de Habla Española (the Spanish-speaking people's congress) in April 1939.[19] In 1940, Covington concluded, "There is the possibility of working toward a tri-minority relationship, comprising Mexicans, Orientals, and Negroes. These groups are very largely shunted together in the twilight zone areas and the problems of each parallel, although they are not identical." Covington's annual reports to the National Urban League also indicate that he argued for industrial training and employment for African Americans, Mexican Americans, and Asian Americans before and after the United States entered the war.[20]

Before the bombing of Pearl Harbor, therefore, some black community leaders had begun to think about the ways in which the multicultural character of Los Angeles affected the lives of African Americans. As Bass's radio speech suggests, however, most had not come to believe that the experiences of blacks were similar to the experiences of other groups. But U.S. entry into the war led more community leaders to connect the experiences of African Americans to those of others. Two months after Pearl Harbor, Roosevelt issued Executive Order 9066, empowering military authorities to embark on a policy of rounding up and incarcerating the 120,000 Japanese Americans who lived near the Pacific Coast. This action must have shocked those blacks who, like Bass, believed that Japanese Americans had achieved greater success than African Americans. Bass's response to the internment seems to reflect her negative perception of Asian cultures. She did not express sympathy for Japanese Americans or concern for the precedent set by the evacuation and incarceration of U.S. residents. Several *Eagle* editorials instead encouraged African Americans to take over lands previously farmed by Japanese Americans. "It is well known that the Japanese people have become masters of the soil throughout our great state," Bass wrote in February 1942, shortly before Roosevelt issued the executive order. "With unflagging industry and determination, these people have built here an a[gra]rian empire that is tremendous. If it must be lost to them, why shouldn't it fall into our hands?" In retrospect, Charlotta Bass's response to the Japanese American internment may seem callous. It is worth pointing out, however, that unlike other U.S. newspapers, Bass's did not publish editorials or cartoons that perpetuated stereotypes of Japanese people as subhuman or bloodthirsty.[21]

The frightening precedent set by the internment did not escape the attention of African Americans, even those far away from the Pacific Coast. An editorial in the NAACP's newspaper, the *Crisis*, asked, "If native-born Americans, of Asiatic descent, can be denied all civil rights and civil liberties, what about Americans of African descent?"[22] Although Chester Himes had only recently arrived in Los Angeles, he seems to have been affected by the Japanese American internment. It receives no mention in *Lonely Crusade* but serves as an important part of the backdrop for *If He Hollers Let Him Go*. As the novel opens, Bob Jones lies in bed, contemplating the debilitating fear that has gripped him. Jones thinks that his fear may have surfaced when the federal government rounded up all the Japanese Americans on the Pacific Coast and sent them to concentration camps. Jones recalled an image: "Little Riki Oyana singing 'God Bless America' and going to Santa Anita with his parents next day." The internment, Jones thought, "was taking a man up by the roots and locking him up without a chance. Without a trial. Without a charge. Without even giving him a chance to say one word. It was thinking about if they ever did that to me, Robert Jones, Mrs. Jones's dark son, that started me to getting scared."[23]

A year after the army rounded up Japanese Americans, Himes wrote an article about the internment for the *War Worker*, a Los Angeles magazine. The article contained four pages from the diary of an incarcerated Japanese American. Himes concluded the article with heavy-handed irony: if, he said, "all of us are still consumed with our relentless hate for them [Japanese Americans], let's not quibble, investigate, and vituperate; let's take them out and shoot them." Himes, like many of the African Americans who moved into Little Tokyo during the war, may have been reminded of the internment every time he returned to his home. He and his wife Jean lived for much of the war in the home previously occupied by Japanese American writer Mary Oyama and her husband, Fred Mittwer.[24] Although Charlotta Bass apparently did not shed any tears for imprisoned Japanese Americans, other blacks clearly weighed the implications of the incarceration for African Americans.

The character of the war as well as the Japanese American internment encouraged some blacks to perceive themselves as participants in a larger struggle for worldwide democracy. In describing this struggle, some black writers began to blur the distinctions between African Americans, Africans, Latin Americans, and Asians. In an editorial published in early February 1942, the *California Eagle* pointed out that most of the Latin American republics had "lined up behind the United Nations to wage war against Hitler and the Nazi way of life." U.S. officials who had pursued cooperation with those republics, the editorial reported, had begun to refer to the people who resided there as "our Latin American cousins." The editorialist warned, however, that "the U.S. conception of democracy as a white man's invention, to be ladled to darker races at some future period, will not set well with 'our Latin American cousins,'" one quarter of whom were "out and out Negro and the rest rather thoroughly mixed." The "snobbery and prejudice" displayed by U.S. officials in World War I, the essay concluded, "would certainly alienate not only the present-day American Negro but his 23,692,000 blood brothers in Latin America. The stupid jim crow which divides the nation's forces with a bitter, Nazi line even now must find ready condemnation in the hearts of the sun-tanned majority in the other Americas."[25] This editorial argued that bonds of race connected African Americans to many Latin Americans, and it suggested that the majority of Latin Americans detested discrimination against blacks in the United States. Other editorials diminished the distance between African Americans and Asians. One editor suggested in February 1942 that racism in the United States "is used [by America's enemies] throughout Africa and Asia to alienate millions of colored people whose cooperation at this very minute is essential to the Allied cause." Whether or not any Africans, Latin Americans, or Asians perceived themselves as "colored people," these editorials suggest that the war had encouraged some African Americans to argue that bonds of race connected them to many people around the globe who should be fighting against Hitler and his vision of "Aryan supremacy."[26]

In many U.S. cities, the suggestion that Latin Americans and Asians identified with blacks probably did not affect the political positions and actions of African Americans. Few U.S. cities, after all, had large Latin American or Asian American communities whose members could provide evidence for or against such assertions. The suggestion, however, had wide-ranging implications for local politics in Los Angeles. If, as the *Eagle* suggested, discrimination against African Americans concerned Latin Americans and Asians, blacks might assume that Mexican and Asian Americans in Los Angeles also would be affected. Similarly, African Americans might acknowledge that they should be worried about discrimination against Mexican Americans and Asian Americans.

The war does seem to have convinced some black leaders that they should be concerned about discrimination against other minorities. In May 1942, the *Eagle* published an editorial that contained a large excerpt from the California Congress of Industrial Organizations (c I o) organ, the *Labor Herald*. The *Herald* criticized employment discrimination by pointing out that "although eight of every 125 persons in Los Angeles are Negroes and 25 are Mexicans, only one Negro in 125 and only one Mexican in 550 are being trained for jobs in the vital war industries."[27] Although the *Eagle* editorial only reprinted a piece that merely mentioned discrimination against African Americans and Mexican Americans in the same sentence, it indicates that the editor was willing to accept the idea that discrimination against Mexican Americans was in some way equivalent to discrimination against blacks.

As the *Eagle*'s quotation of the *Labor Herald* suggests, people outside as well as within the African American community noticed similarities among the experiences of racial minority groups. Some of that impetus came from the left. c I o leaders Philip Connelly and Bert Corona and Communist Party member LaRue McCormick were among the most visible and vocal proponents of the idea that members of all racial minority groups shared similar experiences. The left-leaning attorney and author Carey McWilliams argued that, as a result of wartime events, "the various aspects of the race problem, seldom correlated in the past, have been drawn together so that all phases of the matter, involving Negroes, Mexicans, Orientals, Indians, Filipinos, etc., have come to be regarded as a single national problem."[28]

Not all of the people who noted similarities among minority groups, however, were associated with the left. Religious convictions seem to have motivated some supporters of interracial unity, such as the Reverend

Harold M. Kingsley, director of Pilgrim House, a settlement house that began serving African Americans in Los Angeles in 1943. Other supporters included Los Angeles county supervisor John Anson Ford, the Reverend Fred Fertig, and many Catholic priests, including bishops Thomas J. O'Dwyer and Joseph T. McGucken. Some business owners and managers seem to have believed that good relations among minority groups would help their enterprises. Some professionals, including doctors, lawyers, and social workers, supported interracial cooperation out of political pragmatism or social scientific observations. While many believed that minority groups had common experiences and should work together to eradicate racism and discrimination in U.S. society, others simply overlooked their political or philosophical differences during the war. For example, four ministers, E. C. Farnham, George Gleason, J. Raymond Henderson, and Clayton D. Russell; attorney Thomas L. Griffith Jr., the president of the Los Angeles branch of the NAACP; and two representatives of the CIO, Revels Cayton and Philip Connelly, served together on the board of directors of the Council for Civic Unity, which was founded after the so-called "Zoot-Suit Riots" of June 1943.[29]

Though many leaders within Los Angeles's black community came to see similarities between the experiences of African Americans and Mexican Americans during World War II, one of the most valuable sources of this viewpoint is the *California Eagle*, the only one of the three major black newspapers in the city whose wartime issues have survived. Because the *Eagle*'s editorial position during most of the 1940s ran parallel to the Communist "party line," this paper may have overstated the extent to which communists and others associated with the left participated in a movement for interracial unity. However, the *Eagle*'s columns also contained numerous articles by and about people who were not associated with the left.

After its initial editorial, the *Eagle* published a number of pieces that elaborated on the similarities among the experiences of African Americans and Mexican Americans. In August 1942, the *Eagle* praised the CIO for its efforts to eliminate discrimination against African American workers. The editorial described a mass meeting at the Embassy Auditorium at which Bert Corona, "a young Mexican union official," argued that "the coast's Negro and Mexican minorities [should] close ranks."[30] Although the *Eagle* did not describe his speech in detail, it did say that Corona's plea for unity was the "most significant" event of the evening.

By late 1942, the *Eagle* had begun to focus on the daily newspapers' reports of widespread crime and juvenile delinquency among Mexican Americans. In early August, the body of a young man named José Díaz was found near a swimming hole on Los Angeles's east side. Although evidence did not prove conclusively that Díaz had been murdered, law enforcement officials charged twenty-four young men, all but one of them Mexican Americans, with his murder. As the "Sleepy Lagoon" trial unfolded, and as concern about juvenile delinquency and gang activity among Mexican Americans increased, Charlotta Bass and other writers for the *California Eagle* began to explain why these events should interest blacks. In an editorial published in October 1942, the *Eagle* compared juvenile delinquency among Mexican Americans with the actions of a fictional African American, Bigger Thomas of Richard Wright's *Native Son*: "The revolt of urban Mexican youth against this environment here is a real outgrowth of oppression. It bears an unmistakable common identity with the tragedy that was Bigger Thomas' lot." The editorial further underscored the similarities between Mexican Americans and African Americans by arguing that "Mexican workers were brought into California as virtual slave labor for the agricultural imperialists of the state." Declaring that the oppression faced by Mexican Americans "far surpasses that endured here by Negroes" and was "comparable only to our condition in areas of the deep South," the editorial insisted that the elimination of discrimination against "the Mexican people as a whole" had "moulded on the agenda for too long."[31]

Although the *Eagle* had previously published several articles that told African Americans that they should be concerned about the treatment of Mexican Americans, this was the first to explain why blacks should care about their "Mexican neighbors": "So long as the principle of discrimination may be employed to cheat ANY group of justice, our achievements are not safe. Any division of the American people today is fraught with danger for us all. The fight for the rights of Mexican citizens is part of the struggle of Negro America. It is also part of WINNING THIS WAR!"[32]

Eagle editorials relating to Mexican Americans early in the war accepted as accurate the daily newspapers' reports of a rapid rise in juvenile delinquency among the group. In the fall of 1942, however, *Eagle* columns and editorials began to question the accuracy of these reports. At the same time, these articles continued to argue that African Americans had to defend Mexican Americans. In a front page article from 29 October 1942, Bass's nephew, John S. Kinloch, cited California CIO President Connelly, who had said that "it was 'damned queer' that crime among minority group kids in

New York (Negroes), Detroit and Los Angeles should suddenly find headline space in defeatist press." Kinloch concluded that "it ain't no accident," and the article's headline suggested that the Sleepy Lagoon trial was a "Nazi plot."33

A week later, Kinloch developed his ideas more completely in a front-page editorial that asserted, "There are [*sic*] a gang of pro-Fascists in this country who are scared sick at the prospect of victory for the United Nations." The gang ordered the newspaper editors in New York, Detroit, and Los Angeles to "whip up a phoney 'crime wave' among Negro kids in Harlem, Negro kids in Detroit and Mexican kids in Los Angeles." Kinloch explained that William Randolph Hearst and the *Los Angeles Times* did not find African Americans in Los Angeles an inviting target because they were organized and militant. Also, he said, "Most of our young men and women are finding proper employment in defense industries. THE DECREASE IN JUVENILE DELINQUENCY HAS BEEN ASTOUNDING!" In contrast, "Mexicans here boast nothing like the organization of Negroes," Kinloch reported. "There is a real cleft between the first and second generations; there is a church control of political activity; there is a very slight voting power." These divisions and weaknesses in the Mexican American community, he concluded, rendered Mexican Americans "nice and defenseless, you see. Fair prey for the vermin press."34 Many *Eagle* readers may have viewed Kinloch's conspiracy theory with skepticism, but Kinloch nonetheless was telling them again that the experiences of African Americans and Mexican Americans were comparable, if not similar.

Charlotta Bass did not simply write and publish editorials and columns that decried the treatment of Mexican Americans in Los Angeles, she also tried to assist the Sleepy Lagoon defendants and other group members. In November 1942, for example, she allowed the Mexican Youth Defense Committee, a group of young Mexican Americans who raised funds for the Sleepy Lagoon defendants, to meet in the assembly hall of the *California Eagle* building.35 In 1943, Bass became a member of the Citizens' Committee for the Defense of Mexican American Youth.36 This committee, established by Mexican American and European American activists in the autumn of 1942, worked to finance an appeal of the verdict in the Sleepy Lagoon case in 1943. It later changed its name to the Sleepy Lagoon Defense Committee. In 1944 Bass wrote a letter to the state parole board on behalf of the Sleepy Lagoon defendants. Several other African American community leaders and celebrities assisted the committee. Augustus Hawkins, the black member of the California State Assembly from Los Angeles, told the committee that it could use his name "in any way to support the Citizens' Committee."37 Motion picture stars Hattie McDaniel and Lena Horne also appeared at fund-raising events for the committee.38

In 1942, the *Eagle* had argued that discrimination against Mexican Americans was similar to, but worse than, discrimination against African Americans in Los Angeles. In 1943, the *Eagle* began to suggest that discrimination against Mexican Americans was indistinguishable from discrimination against blacks. Articles in the newspaper referred to "Negroes and Mexicans" as if the two groups were clearly and naturally related. In early June, Bass praised African Americans and Mexican Americans for their response to the murder of Lenza Smith. On 23 May, Smith, a 36-year-old African American defense worker, was shot four times by a police officer after his car sideswiped a police vehicle. According to Bass, Smith's slaying represented a "calculated effort of Los Angeles Big Business, spearheaded by the venal Hearst Press and the Los Angeles Times, to goad the Negro and Mexican communities of our city into rioting and bloodshed." Instead of provoking a riot, however, Smith's killing "wrought a miracle of unity among Negroes, Mexicans, trade unionists, and patriotic white citizens determined to draw the stiletto of police brutality out of the back of Los Angeles' all out war production."39

A week after Lenza Smith was shot, 1,500 people gathered at the Independent Church of Christ to protest the killing. At this meeting, Joe Marty, a representative of the Mexican Defense Committee, told the audience that "Mexican people are facing the same problem with which Negroes are confronted." Marty said that "the Santa Monica police department has trained high school boys to fight Mexican youth who visit the beach. Last week 55 Mexican boys were arrested at the beach, in different places, for 'inciting a riot.'" Police officers believed that "any Mexican is a good suspect," Marty reported. "We not only have enemies abroad, but we have them right here at home. And we had better beat them at home or else we won't win over there."40 By June 1943, therefore, the *Eagle* had effectively equated police brutality against blacks with police brutality against Mexican Americans.

The Zoot-Suit Riots reinforced that tendency. Ironically, the rioting began the same day that the *Eagle* published the editorial that praised African Americans' and Mexican Americans' peaceful response to police brutality. In these riots, mobs comprised of hundreds of sailors and soldiers—joined later by civilians—descended upon downtown and east Los

Angeles for a week-long period in early June 1943. These mobs roamed the streets in search of "zoot-suiters" and people who appeared to be Mexican American or African American. When they encountered any, they beat them brutally. The mobs also stripped the clothing from people who wore zoot suits. The violence ended only after military authorities declared downtown "off limits" to enlisted personnel.

A chorus of black community leaders responded to the riots with outrage. Thomas L. Griffith, the president of the local branch of the NAACP, sent telegrams to Roosevelt and Governor Earl Warren, asking them to take action to stop the rioting and to investigate the violence. Griffith also sent a telegram to Walter White, the national executive secretary of the NAACP. He suggested that the organization's national officials "urge immediate federal action to put an end to the persecution of citizens, particularly citizens of the Mexican race." An advertisement for the Victory Market, a cooperative on Central Avenue closely associated with Reverend Clayton D. Russell, stated that "our neighbors, the Mexican people, have been shamefully attacked by the metropolitan press of this city" and that "the police force has conducted a long terror campaign against the Mexican minority in Los Angeles . . . . Because we in [t]he Negro community are more unified and have greater political power," the ad concluded, "we must lead in the demand for FULL POLICE PROTECTION OF THE MEXICAN COMMUNITY IN LOS ANGELES."[41]

Like John Kinloch's earlier articles, some of the statements issued after the Zoot-Suit Riots indicate that a number of black leaders adopted a patronizing tone in their references to Mexican Americans. They argued that Mexican Americans were less unified, less organized and more thoroughly exploited and victimized than African Americans. The tone of many articles and statements, however, seems to have changed by late 1943 and early 1944, when African American and Mexican American leaders began meeting with each other in several interracial committees. Although minutes of most of these meetings do not survive, it seems plausible to assume that from these contacts some African Americans began to appreciate the extent to which Mexican Americans were organized and unified.

Initially, the riots had a powerful impact upon Chester Himes, although he seems to have remained skeptical of interracial unity. Anticipating that some African Americans might not consider the riots to have been racially motivated, Himes wrote an article for the *Crisis* that insisted that the "Zoot-Suit Riots Are Race Riots!" "What could make the white people more happy than to see their uniformed sons sapping up some dark-skinned people?" he asked rhetorically. "It proved beyond all doubt the bravery of white service-men, their gallantry. Los Angeles was at last being made safe for white peo-ple—to do as they damned well pleased." Although Himes was outraged by the riots, the passions that they aroused in him seem to have faded by the time he finished his Los Angeles novels. Himes did not mention the riots in *If He Hollers Let Him Go*, and he referred to the rioting only twice in *Lonely Crusade*.42

Many Los Angeles residents, following the lead of Bass and Kinloch, be-lieved that newspapers were responsible for the rioting. Elizabeth Cum-mings, a European American, said that the coverage of race relations by "metropolitan newspapers" distressed her and her husband William, an African American. These papers "either tended to ignore the problem of race relations, or . . . tended to add to existing tensions by giving space pri-marily to the negative aspects of the problem—the incidents of friction and so on." The "minority group publications" also failed to satisfy Mr. and Mrs. Cummings. "We felt that an important morale-building, educational service could and should be performed through a publication directed toward all groups and which placed primary emphasis upon the positive aspects of the problem, at the same time giving wholly constructive, educational treat-ment to the negative aspects." In July 1943 Elizabeth and William Cummings began publishing the *War Worker* every other week, in October 1944 chang-ing the name of their publication to *NOW*. According to Elizabeth Cum-mings, the *War Worker* was "based on a very simple but new tenet: the enemy says it can't happen—that we of different races and colors and creeds can work together in harmony; we say not only that it can happen, but that it is happening—and we prove it through picture and feature material." Cummings said that she and her husband published their newspaper "in the interest of all races, that all may join in closer unity for the good and ad-vancement of mankind."43 She considered the newspaper a model for U.S. society; in mid-1944, she wrote, "Our staff is comprised of people of varied races, and our readers are approximately 50% of the white group, 50% Negro and Mexican." She stated that 10,000 copies of each issue were printed and estimated that five people read each copy.44 More than any other publication, the *War Worker/NOW* reflected its publishers' belief that African Americans, Mexican Americans, Asian Americans, and European Americans had to work together to preserve and advance democracy in the United States.

The riots of 1943 led to the establishment of several organizations that crossed racial boundaries as well as to public condemnations of racism and discrimination. The Mexican Youth Defense Committee and the Junior Council of the NAACP, for example, sponsored a meeting "to form plans for youth mobilization against spreading race prejudice in the city." Jeanette Salvis of the Mexican Youth Defense Committee said that "all Los Angeles youth, in the face of last week's racial outbreaks, must assume its responsibility in striking at every form of race discrimination."45 Concerned adults in Los Angeles also joined the Council for Civic Unity, one of many such organizations formed in various cities during the war, and the American Unity Committee, an "emergency body" formed during the riots. This committee, according to the *Eagle*, was "supported by the CIO, California Eagle, Eastside Journal, Carey McWilliams, former state director of immigration, Ted LeBerthon, Daily News writer, the Los Angeles Urban League, Negro Victory Committee, Mexican organizations, along with scores of religious and civic bodies."46 As these actions suggest, some African Americans' acceptance of the notion that their experiences were comparable to those of Mexican Americans laid a foundation for cooperative action.

Not only African American and Mexican American community leaders responded with concern to the Zoot-Suit Riots. The violence convinced many public officials and some of their appointees that there was a clear need for a public committee to investigate and try to alleviate problems that might lead to additional race riots. In January 1944, Los Angeles Mayor Fletcher Bowron answered demands for action by expanding a previous ad hoc committee into the Committee on Home Front Unity. Its composition suggests the mayor believed that the problems faced by African Americans were more pressing than those encountered by other minority groups. Bowron appointed six African Americans, two Jewish leaders, one Mexican, a representative of business interests, a Protestant minister, and a Catholic bishop to the committee.47

Shortly after the Zoot-Suit Riots in July 1943, members of the Los Angeles County Committee for Church and Community Cooperation took action to create a countywide committee to deal with interracial problems. They called together an organizational conference and invited members of the county board of supervisors, the mayor of Los Angeles, the president of the Chamber of Commerce, the superintendents of the city and county schools, the president of the University of Southern California, and representatives of a number of civic organizations and agencies, such as the

Citizens Committee for Latin American Youth, the Interdenominational Ministerial Alliance (which the County Committee referred to as the "Negro Ministerial Alliance"), and the N A A C P.[48] Although the members of the Committee for Church and Community Cooperation "decided not to organize a large overall interracial committee," some county officials continued to think that such a group would serve a useful purpose. In January 1944 the county board of supervisors established the County Committee for Interracial Progress.[49] The committee had the following objectives: "To seek out the causes of racial tension and to eliminate these causes. To devise all possible means for the prevention of racial conflict. To cooperate with any group or agency having similar interests."[50]

These interracial groupings—the Council for Civic Unity, the County Committee for Interracial Progress, and the mayor's Committee on Home Front Unity—tended to be ineffective in addressing the problems faced by most of Los Angeles's African American, Mexican American, and Asian American residents.[51] They simply did not have the power to eliminate discrimination. Despite their ineffectiveness, however, these committees did create social spaces in which leaders from African American, Mexican American, Jewish, and other communities could meet and discuss the similarities or differences of their experiences. The encounters in the conference rooms in which these committees met laid a foundation for cooperation outside the meetings.

As representatives from different communities and interest groups met to discuss racial tensions in Los Angeles in 1943 and 1944, they began to prepare for the return of Japanese Americans to the city. As early as November 1943, the *Eagle* published an editorial that declared, "Persecution of the Japanese-American minority has been one of the disgraceful aspects of the nation's conduct of this People's War." The editor apologized for "past omissions" and printed information gathered by the Pacific Coast Committee on American Principles and Fair Play, a group that advocated "fair play" for Japanese Americans.[52] By early 1945, some *Eagle* articles drew direct comparisons between the experiences of African Americans and those of Japanese Americans. In his column "The Pulpit Voice," the Reverend Hamilton T. Boswell, the minister of Bowen Memorial Methodist Church, compared the South to California: "What the South has meant to colored people by way of outrageous injustice and flagrant brutality, our State of California is increasingly becoming to mean the same to Japanese-Americans. . . . Similar instances of mobocracy, betrayal by elected officials, and the same bugaboos about the necessity of keeping the minority in its place, are much in evidence in both." Boswell chastised African Americans for not doing more to defend Japanese Americans from terrorism. "The tragedy is that we who have come to the West Coast to escape the night riders of Texas and the Governor Johnsons of South Carolina, are turning a blind eye in the face of this western form of racism." Because African Americans were "acquainted with the enemy," Boswell said, "we must defeat them before waiting to be marked the scrapegoat [*sic*] ourselves. Careless law enforcement and fascist politicians are threats to the security of the country, and who among us knows this better than we?"[53] By 1945, some black leaders had concluded that the experiences of Japanese Americans and Mexican Americans were comparable to the experiences of African Americans. These leaders helped to lay the foundation for interracial cooperation in Los Angeles.

By the end of the war, leaders from all segments of the black community had come to embrace cooperative action and mutual support among all minority groups in Los Angeles. In a November 1945 speech before the Los Angeles Jewish Community Council, NAACP president Thomas L. Griffith Jr. emphasized "the importance of close cooperation between Negroes, Jews, and other racial and religious minorities in achieving a real democracy."[54] By itself, each minority group "is ineffective in attaining to full citizenship alongside the dominant attackers who have all the forces of government to back them up," said a 1946 article in the *Los Angeles Sentinel*. "Once consolidated in interests and objectives, however, and any two or more of these same suppressed and oppr[e]ssed groups could by entirely peaceful and legal means obtain not only justice and full citizenship for themselves, but power to dispense justice to the rest of the community, including the destructively-minded, power-mad dominant bloc, who are trying so desperately to keep the world under their thumbs by deliberately inciting enmity between the minorities."[55] The *Spotlight*, a weekly newspaper with offices in Watts and Bronzeville, declared that "racial and religious hatreds among the minorities must go. . . . The problem of the Jew, Mexican, Fillipino [*sic*], Chinese, Negroes are the same. Make friends with these people. They are Americans and traveling the same road as you. If you share the ride, it will be cheaper and give you more strength." And Bass's *Eagle* told its readers, "We, the minorities—Negroes, Mexicans, and Jews—must gather together as a group and fight back the Fascist wave that threatens to destroy the things we fought to win—freedom of speech and religion, and freedom from want and from fear."[56]

Both during and after the war, interracial cooperation did occur in Los Angeles. When parents of Mexican American children in Westminster, Orange County, filed suit to end segregation in the schools, their action was supported by lawyers representing Jewish organizations, the NAACP, and the Japanese American Citizens League. Throughout the late 1940s and into the 1950s, African Americans, Mexican Americans, Jewish Americans, and Japanese Americans worked together to try to convince state and local officials to pass fair employment practices legislation.[57]

Although most of this cooperation across racial boundaries occurred among attorneys, social-service providers, and other professionals, many minority group leaders believed that working-class members of their communities could be united in a coalition that could exercise electoral power. In her campaign for the Los Angeles City Council in 1945, Bass emphasized her ability to serve "all minorities," not simply the African American community.[58] In early 1946, the *California Eagle* reported that Carey McWilliams had expressed the opinion that "the half million Mexicans and Negroes in Los Angeles County are the balance of power in politics and can play a key role in the city." Later that year, the *Eagle* urged all minorities to support Clayton Russell's bid for the county board of supervisors.[59]

Bass was not elected to the city council in 1945, nor was Russell to the board of supervisors in 1946. Nonetheless, some African American leaders continued to try to forge a political coalition among Los Angeles's minority groups. They achieved their greatest victory in 1949, when Edward Roybal won a seat on the Los Angeles City Council. Roybal was the first Mexican American to serve on the council since 1881. He was elected from a district in which Mexican Americans were a minority of the voters. Crucial support for his election appears to have come from African Americans in his district.[60]

Roybal's election led to exultation for many community leaders such as Bass. The Independent Progressive Party that had worked for Roybal's election predicted that Los Angeles would soon elect an African American representative to Congress. Roybal's election did not, however, open the doors for the election of more members from Los Angeles's minority groups. No African American was elected to Congress from Los Angeles until 1962, when redistricting allowed both Augustus Hawkins, a twenty-eight-year veteran of the state assembly, and Roybal to win seats in the federal legislature. No African American served on the Los Angeles City Council until the council and Mayor Sam Yorty appointed Gilbert Lindsay to fill Roybal's vacant seat in January 1963.

There are various reasons why African American and Mexican American candidates did not win many elections between World War II and the early 1960s. Until redistricting, officials had drawn city council district boundaries so that black neighborhoods in Los Angeles were divided among several different districts. In each of these districts, white voters outnumbered African American voters. Such racial gerrymandering contributed to limiting minority representation in Sacramento until the 1960s.[61] Also important, though, were divisions within the black community and between African Americans and Mexican Americans. These were often strained when the two groups found themselves competing for limited housing, as Lloyd Fisher observed in Watts in 1946:

> The tension between the incoming Negroes and the Mexicans occurs principally in the older, more settled sections of Watts. It is in these sections that returning veterans, resentful over the striking changes which have occurred during their absence, have in some cases threatened to band together to expel the Negro invaders from the community. . . . Both Hollenbeck and Watts in recent months have been the scene of protracted violence.[62]

Nor did all African American spokespersons agree with the emphasis on interracial cooperation, especially its strong identification with positions taken by labor and leftist groups. Almena Davis, the editor of the *Los Angeles Tribune*, expressed concern during the war about many black leaders' enthusiasm for the CIO, including that of her archrival, Bass. Throughout the war and into the postwar period, the *Tribune* published a number of editorials that criticized Bass and other leaders for allowing themselves to be manipulated by forces outside the black community, whether those forces represented the CIO or the Democratic Party.[63]

Throughout the postwar years, this ambivalence toward interracial cooperation persisted among some African Americans. It was exacerbated by internal discord within a number of black organizations that had promoted racial unity during the war. By the late 1940s, factional disputes began to damage the Los Angeles branch of the NAACP. One group argued that Thomas L. Griffith Jr., who had served as the branch president since 1934, should step down and allow a new leader to take his place. Members of this faction accused Griffith of damaging the NAACP by refusing to delegate any real authority to the branch's executive secretary and by cooperating too closely with Los Angeles's mayor and other white politicians.[64] Another group defended Griffith's record and claimed that their opponents had been paid to disrupt the NAACP. Bass, Griffith's most outspoken supporter, even compared his detractors to Nazis. In January 1947, Griffith's opponents supported attorney Loren Miller's attempt to unseat him, but that attempt failed.[65]

In late 1948, the anti-Griffith faction began arguing that Griffith had struck a deal with Communist Party members and had worked to increase the number of communists in the branch in order to maintain his power.[66] National officers of the NAACP orchestrated efforts to remove him from power and prevent communists from winning election to office within the branch.[67] In the 1949 election, Griffith, a proponent of interracial cooperation, faced off against Pilgrim House director Harold M. Kingsley, apparently with the support of Communist Party members, who had supported cooperation between the races during the war. Kingsley, too, strongly advocated interracial cooperation. Griffith received 280 votes, Kingsley, only 145. Most of the branch's members did not attend the election. The vitriolic campaign almost certainly damaged the prestige of the NAACP and thus may have weakened organized support for interracial cooperation. Moreover, the discord that surfaced within the branch in late 1948 and early 1949 may have been only symptomatic of a more serious problem. The branch's membership had fallen from 14,000 in 1946 to 6,000 in 1948. This decline may indicate that some African Americans felt that both Griffith and Kingsley were out of touch with the needs and desires of many members of the black community.[68]

Such internal discord did not account entirely for the failure of most African American and Mexican American candidates for office. These candidates had to rely on support from outside their racial and ethnic groups to overcome gerrymandering and win elective office. Demographic changes during and after the war may have made this interracial support more difficult to obtain: the rapid growth of Los Angeles's black population after the war may have limited many African Americans' contact with Mexican Americans and Asian Americans. By 1950, the number of blacks in Los Angeles easily dwarfed the number of Asian Americans in the city. Although Mexican Americans and African Americans may have continued to live in the same neighborhoods near downtown, increasingly the physical locations of these communities moved in different directions. The black residential district expanded south and west from downtown, and the Mexican

American district expanded east into unincorporated areas of Los Angeles County. Also, as Jews and other European Americans moved from downtown and the east side to the sprawling west side of Los Angeles and to the San Fernando Valley, previously mixed neighborhoods became more thoroughly segregated. Many, if not most, of the African Americans who came to Los Angeles after World War II and before the massive migrations from Latin America and Asia of the 1970s may have seen their new home as a "black and white" city rather than as a multicultural metropolis.

It has long been recognized that World War II dramatically affected the African American community in Los Angeles. It stimulated massive expansion of manufacturing in Southern California, and high-wage jobs in aircraft plants and shipyards attracted tens of thousands of blacks. The war also seems to have changed how many African Americans saw themselves and their community. Charlotta Bass, Floyd Covington, Clayton Russell, William Cummings, and other black community leaders, influenced by the wartime rhetorical emphasis on unity, began to perceive Los Angeles as a multicultural city and to notice similarities between their community and those of other racial minority groups. These leaders argued that African Americans had to see their experiences differently from how they had viewed their lives in the South or the East. All emphasized that the black struggle for equality was closely related to the struggles of "other minorities," such as Jews, Mexican Americans, and Asian Americans.

Ultimately, these leaders encouraged blacks to see themselves not simply as African American but as part of a larger minority and to form coalitions for common goals. This outlook was in many ways similar to that which encouraged blacks to form coalitions during and after World War II with predominantly white labor and liberal groups in several California cities.[69] Both strategies would prove short-lived in the postwar period, yet they are suggestive of the future course of events. Some writers have suggested that the failure of coalitions of blacks and liberal whites forecast the physical separation of the races and the consequent problems of an increasingly black inner city that would explode in the 1960s. Gerald Horne, in his essay in this anthology, suggests that the failure of interracial cooperation, in particular a coalition of blacks, labor, and the left, laid the groundwork for the 1960s uprisings by leaving no viable avenue to power for young African Americans.

But the idea of mutual needs and experiences did not die. It would be revived in the 1960s by "Third World Nationalist" movements, often led by blacks, and in the 1970s and 1980s by state and national efforts at "rainbow coalitions," led again by such African Americans as Mervin Dymally and Jesse Jackson. Mayor Tom Bradley, meanwhile, would head a coalition uniting blacks and liberal Jews that would dominate Los Angeles politics from 1973 to 1993.[70] The cooperation across racial boundaries that occurred both during and after World War II is thus a fascinating dimension of the African American experience in California that should attract increasing study.

NOTES

1. See Chester Himes, *The Quality of Hurt: The Autobiography of Chester Himes* (Garden City, NY: Doubleday, 1972), 73–76.

2. I have used the term "man" to emphasize the point that Himes was writing as an African American man. The protagonists of *If He Hollers Let Him Go* (Garden City, NY: Doubleday, Doran, 1945) and *Lonely Crusade* (New York: Alfred A. Knopf, 1947) both express anger at white oppression's emasculation of African American men. Although Himes may have believed that African American women also faced "lonely crusades," his novels do not emphasize the thoughts and actions of females.

3. I use the term "multicultural" somewhat reluctantly, as it has been the focus of considerable political debate from the 1980s to the present. According to the *Oxford English Dictionary*, the term was first used in 1941. Los Angeles residents in the 1940s did not often use this word to indicate that they understood that many different ethnic and racial groups inhabited their city. Nonetheless, the term had emerged by that time, and it is useful to denote a setting characterized by the coexistence of a multiplicity of ethnic and/or racial (or "cultural") groups.

4. I am not suggesting that African Americans and European Americans did not recognize differences of ethnicity, color, and class within their groups. However, the "racial" distinction between "white" and "Negro," to use the terms that prevailed in printed discourse, was the most salient division among groups of people in most U.S. cities in which significant numbers of African Americans lived.

5. Himes, *Lonely Crusade*, 60–61.

6. The term "racialized" conveys that society has labeled a group as a particular "race" even though that label has no basis in human physiology. It is especially appropriate for groups like Mexicans and Jews, in which physical differences from other Europeans are often nil. In a broader historical sense of the emergence

of the whole concept of race in early modern Europe, Michael Omi and Howard Winart have written, "We employ the term *racialization* to signify the extension of racial meaning to a previously racially unclassified relationship, social practice, or group." *Racial Formation in the United States: From the 1960s to the 1980s* (New York: Routledge and Kegan Paul, 1986), 64.

7. For a good, brief discussion of the growth of manufacturing in wartime Los Angeles, see Arthur C. Verge, *Paradise Transformed: Los Angeles during the Second World War* (Dubuque, IA: Kendall/Hunt Publishing Company, 1993), 85–102.

8. Floyd C. Covington, "Biennial Report of the Executive Director, March 1, 1941 to March 1, 1943," "Urban League of Los Angeles" folder, box 104, series 1, Records of the National Urban League, Library of Congress.

9. Ibid.; speech prepared for delivery at Philharmonic Auditorium, 14 March 1943. "Bass, C. A.—Speeches," 1940s folder, box 1, Bass Papers, Southern California Library for Social Studies and Research, Los Angeles.

10. Alonzo Nelson Smith, "Black Employment in the Los Angeles Area, 1938–1948," (Ph.D. diss., University of California, Los Angeles, 1978), 224; "Says Bias Deprives Nation of Minority Contribution," *NOW*, second half of February 1945, 6. The figure of 85 percent was mentioned in a speech by Dr. Buell Gallagher, a professor of social ethics at the Pacific School of Religion. Gallagher did not reveal the source of this figure, but it may have come from his close associate the Reverend Harold M. Kingsley, director of Pilgrim House, a settlement house located in Bronzeville (formerly Little Tokyo).

11. "L.A. Negro Population Has Doubled since 1940," *California Eagle*, 15 August 1946, 3; "Los Angeles' Negro Population Rises to 133,082 in Six Years," *Los Angeles Sentinel*, 15 August 1946, 1; "Negro Population on Coast Now Tripled," ibid., 5 December 1946, 2.

12. "Negroes to Get 942 of 51,012 Homes Now under Construction," *Los Angeles Sentinel*, 15 February 1945, 1.

13. See, for example, "LeBerthon, Clayton, Ornitz to Speak," *California Eagle*, 18 November 1943, 9; and "Democracy's Fight Begins At Home," ibid., 25 January 1945, 7. For a brief discussion of the tactics of the Negro Victory Committee, see Harlan Dale Unrau, "The Double V Movement in Los Angeles during the Second World War: A Study in Negro Protest" (Master's thesis, California State College, Fullerton, 1971), especially 86–87, 91–94, and 150–51.

14. George A. Beavers Jr., to the other members of the Los Angeles branch, memorandum, 3 September 1942, "Los Angeles, Calif. 1942–43" folder, box C14, group 2, Records of the National Association for the Advancement of Colored People (hereafter Records of the NAACP), Library of Congress.

15. "From Restriction to Integration . . . How It Works in One Neighborhood," *NOW*, first half of November 1944, 5. This article describes a previously all-white neighborhood south of downtown into which African American, Mexican American, and Japanese American families began moving after 1940, when most of the restrictions on the property expired.

16. Lloyd H. Fisher, *The Problem of Violence* (Los Angeles: American Council on Race Relations, 1945), 7; Robert C. Weaver, *The Negro Ghetto* (New York: Harcourt, Brace, 1948), 88; Elizabeth R. Frank, *Background for Planning* (Los Angeles: Research Department, Welfare Council of Metropolitan Los Angeles, 1949), 39–40, cited in Unrau, "The Double V Movement," 31–32.

17. Ted LeBerthon, "The Psychopathic South," *NOW*, first half of October 1944, 9; George J. Sánchez, *Becoming Mexican American: Ethnicity, Culture, and Identity in Chicano Los Angeles, 1900–1945* (New York: Oxford University Press, 1993), 77. Shortly after the war, one social worker described the neighborhood east of the Civic Center—Little Tokyo—as "a jumble of freight yards, warehouses, oil tanks, factories, hotels, rented rooms and flophouses, and here and there the small, unrepaired, overcrowded homes of Negro-, Japanese-, Mexican-, and Anglo-American families." Although this neighborhood would have housed more Japanese Americans before the war, it was also most likely a fairly mixed neighborhood. Duane Robinson, "Los Angeles Youth Project, A Report—And a Call to a Meeting," stamped 4 June 1947, "Law Enforcement–Juvenile Delinquency, 1940–1949" file, box 34, John Anson Ford Papers, Huntington Library. Robinson was the Area 3 Coordinator for the Los Angeles Youth Project.

18. Untitled script for radio broadcast, November 1939, "Bass, C. A.— Speeches, 1930s" folder, box 1, Bass Papers. Biographical information about Bass can be found in Darlene Clark Hine, ed., *Black Women in America: An Historical Encyclopedia*, 2 vols. (Brooklyn: Carlson Publishing 1993), vol. 1, 93; and Barbara Sicherman and Carol Hurd Green, eds., *Notable American Women, the Modern Period: A Biographical Dictionary* (Cambridge: Belknap Press of Harvard University Press, 1980), 61–63. See also Gerald R. Gill, "'Win or Lose—We Win': The 1952 Vice Presidential Campaign of Charlotta A. Bass," in Sharon Harley and Rosalyn Terborg-Penn, eds., *The Afro-American Woman: Struggles and Images* (Port Washington, N.Y.: National University Publications, 1978), 109–18.

19. Mario T. García, *Mexican Americans: Leadership, Ideology, and Identity, 1930–1960* (New Haven: Yale University Press, 1989), 151.

20. Floyd C. Covington, "Political Activity Schedule," 25 May 1940, Los Angeles Urban League Collection, Department of Special Collections, University Research Library, University of California, Los Angeles; Covington, "Biennial Report," 3.

21. "Back to the Farm?" *California Eagle*, 12 February 1942, 8A. For a discussion of representations of Japanese people in the U.S. media during the war, see John W. Dower, *War without Mercy: Race and Power in the Pacific War* (New York: Pantheon, 1986). Dower condensed his argument in "Race, Language, and War in Two Cultures: World War II in Asia," in *The War in American Culture: Society and Consciousness during World War II*, Lewis A. Erenberg and Susan E. Hirsch, eds. (Chicago: University of Chicago Press, 1996), 169–201.

22. Quoted in an editorial in *Christian Century*, 16 September 1942, reprinted in the *Pacific Citizen*, 24 September 1942, 4.

23. Himes, *If He Hollers Let Him Go*, 3.

24. Chester Himes, "The People We Know," the *War Worker*, second half of November 1943, 7. Quoted in Michel Fabre, Robert E. Skinner, and Lester Sullivan, comps., *Chester Himes: An Annotated Primary and Secondary Bibliography* (Westport, CT: Greenwood Press, 1992), 26; *Pacific Citizen*, 17 November 1945, 5.

25. "Uncle Sam in Latin America: Bull in the Parlor?" *California Eagle*, 5 February 1942, 8A.

26. "Walter White Has Something to Say," *California Eagle*, 26 February 1942, 8A. Some African Americans had minimized the differences between themselves and Africans long before World War II. The rhetoric employed by the *Eagle* and by some black community leaders, however, clearly draws connections between African Americans, Africans, Latin Americans, and Asians based on the common interest in a victory over Hitler. There is irony in the fact that the *Eagle*'s editorial draws a distinction between the "colored people" of Asia, who had aligned themselves with the Allies, and the Japanese.

27. "Freedom Is on the March," *California Eagle*, 21 May 1942, 8A.

28. Carey McWilliams, "What We Did about Racial Minorities," in Jack Goodman, ed., *While You Were Gone: A Report on Wartime Life in the United States* (New York: Simon and Schuster, 1946), 99. McWilliams developed his ideas about race in articles published in the *Nation* during the war and in his book, *Brothers under the Skin* (Boston: Little, Brown and Company, 1943).

29. The letterhead of the Council for Civic Unity identifies these individuals as members of the board of directors. See Council for Civic Unity to "Dear Friends," 30 June 1944, folder 4, "Office Memo File," box 3, Records of the Sleepy Lagoon Defense Committee (SLDC), Department of Special Collections, University Research Library, University of California, Los Angeles (hereafter cited as SLDC Records).

30. "A Great Ally Comes to the Fore," *California Eagle*, 27 August 1942, 8A.

31. "Our Mexican Neighbors," *California Eagle*, 15 October 1942, 8A.

32. Ibid.

33. "Mexican Kids' Trial—Nazi Plot?" *California Eagle*, 29 October 1942, 1.

34. John Kinloch, "Mexicans Face Police Terror Round-ups; Vile Press Slurs," *California Eagle*, 5 November 1942, 1A, 7B.

35. "Mexican Kids Fight Police Drive," *California Eagle*, 12 November 1942, 1A.

36. Press release from Public Relations, Citizens' Committee for the Defense of Mexican-American Youth, 2 March 1943, folder 1 ("News Releases, Memeographed [*sic*] copies"), box 1, SLDC Records, 4.

37. *Appeal News*, vol. 1, no. 2, 21 April 1943, folder 1 ("*Appeal News* v. 1 n. 1 to v. 2 n. 6"), box 2, SLDC Records.

38. Press release, no date, folder 1 ("News Releases, Memeographed [*sic*] copies"), box 1, SLDC records.

39. "Eye-Witness Refutes Policeman's Testimony," *California Eagle*, 3 June 1943, 1A; "Note to Disrupters: NO RIOT HERE!" *California Eagle*, 3 June 1943, 8A.

40. *California Eagle*, 3 June 1943, 1A; "Charge Attempt to Goad Riot," *California Eagle*, 3 June 1943, 4B.

41. Thomas L. Griffith to Walter White, 9 June 1943, "'Zoot Suit' Riots 1943–44" folder, box A676, group 2, Records of the NAACP; Advertisement for People's Victory Market, *California Eagle*, 10 June 1943, 8B.

42. Chester Himes, "Zoot Suit Riots Are Race Riots," *Crisis* 50 (July 1943): 200–201, 225. This essay was republished in Chester Himes, *Black on Black: Baby Sister and Selected Writings* (New York: Doubleday, 1973), 220–25. The first reference Himes makes to these riots in *Lonely Crusade* occurs when Lee Gordon is reading a newspaper as he rides the bus to Jackie Forks's apartment. As he read, "He learned of the growing racial tensions throughout the city. . . . A group of white sailors had stripped a Mexican lad of his zoot suit on Main Street before a host of male and female onlookers." Later, the lawyer who files the writ of *habeas corpus* for Gordon mentions the riots in his argument before the judge. Himes, *Lonely Crusade*, 207, 349.

43. Masthead of *NOW*, first half of October 1944, 2.

44. Elizabeth Cummings to Marshall Field, 11 June 1944, box 50 (B. Los Angeles County Government/3. Services/12. Publicity/a. Correspondence/bb. 1940–1944), folder 4 (1944), Ford Papers.

45. "Mexican, Negro, White Youth Meet," *California Eagle*, 17 June 1943, 1B.

46. "Form City-Wide Anti-Bias Body," *California Eagle*, 24 June 1943, 5B. For further information on other California Councils of Civic Unity and efforts at a

statewide organization, see Albert S. Broussard, *Black San Francisco: The Struggle for Racial Equality in the West, 1900–1954* (Lawrence: University Press of Kansas, 1993), chap. 11.

47. George Gleason, "Report of the Executive Secretary, November 25, 1943–January 24, 1944," "Los Angeles County Committee for Church and Community Cooperation" file, box 69, Ford Papers. Gleason was the executive secretary of the County Committee for Church and Community Cooperation.

48. George Gleason to the Honorable Board of Supervisors, 23 July 1943, and Gleason, "Report of the Executive Secretary, July 21 to August 24, 1943," folder 6 (1943), "Los Angeles County Committee for Church and Community Cooperation" file, box 69, Ford Papers.

49. George Gleason to John Anson Ford, 25 Oct 1943, folder 6 (1943), "Los Angeles County Committee for Church and Community Cooperation" file; George Gleason, "Report of the Executive Secretary, January 25, 1944–March 15, 1944," folder 7 (1944), "Los Angeles County Committee for Church and Community Cooperation" file; both from box 69, Ford Papers. This committee was soon renamed the Los Angeles County Committee on Human Relations and in 1955 became the Los Angeles County Commission on Human Relations. Unlike most other wartime interracial agencies, it continued as an active research and mediation organization for several decades after the war.

50. "Procedural Rules and Administrative Practices of the Los Angeles County Committee on Human Relations," May 1946, folder 1 (1946), "Los Angeles County Committee on Human Relations" file, box 72, Ford Papers.

51. See Unrau, "The Double V Movement," 168–69.

52. "A Point Well Taken, We Think," *California Eagle*, 11 November 1943, 8A.

53. Hamilton T. Boswell, "The Pulpit Voice: The West Coast, the Japanese's 'Southland,'" *California Eagle*, 1 February 1945, 12.

54. "Griffith Talks on Minorities," *California Eagle*, 1 November 1945, 3.

55. "Interracial Harmony," *Los Angeles Sentinel*, 25 July 1946, 9.

56. *Spotlight*, no date, clipping in folder 9 (1944), "Racial Relations—Negro" file, Ford Papers; "A Call to Arms," *California Eagle*, 1 August 1946, 6.

57. See "Jewish Congress, NAACP Join Mexicans in Legal Attack on Segregation," *California Eagle*, 5 December 1946, 1. For details, see "Fair Employment Practices Commission" file, box 31, Ford Papers.

58. See "Minorities Unite to Abolish Jimcrowism," *California Eagle*, 8 February 1945, 7; Charlotta A. Bass, "On the Sidewalk," *California Eagle*, 15 March 1945, 1; and 29 March 1945, 1.

59. "Sees L.A. Groups as Leader in Fight on Housing Restrictions," *California*

Eagle, 28 February 1946, 12; "L.A. Citizens of All Races Join in Backing Russell for Supervisor Position," *California Eagle*, 9 May 1946, 1.

60. In the primary, Roybal lost the heavily black Second Assembly District to his opponent by a narrow margin. Roybal's campaign focused on the district in the runoff election. See "IPP [Independent Progressive Party] Works For Election of Ed Roybal, City Council," *California Eagle*, 19 May 1949, 3; and "Demand for Negro Congressman Seen in Roybal Election Win," *California Eagle*, 2 June 1949, 2. Future city council member and mayor Tom Bradley worked on Roybal's campaign. See J. Gregory Payne and Scott C. Ratzan, *Tom Bradley: The Impossible Dream* (Santa Monica: Roundtable Publishing, 1986), 43–44.

61. See Raphael J. Sonenshein, *Politics in Black and White: Race and Power in Los Angeles* (Princeton: Princeton University Press, 1993), 34. Sonenshein cites an analysis of the drawing of city council district lines that appeared in the *California Eagle*, 10 November 1960. For a treatment of the long battle of Gus Hawkins and William Byron Rumford, the two African American assemblymen, to secure civil rights laws, see the essay by Douglas Flamming in this anthology.

62. Fisher, *Problem of Violence*, 10–11.

63. See Unrau, "The Double V Movement," 157–58.

64. See Mary Alton Cutler to Gloster Current, 11 November 1948, "Los Angeles Branch Controversy 1948" folder, box C379, group 2, Records of the NAACP. Cutler served as executive secretary of the Los Angeles branch until late December 1948. Current was the NAACP's director of branches. See also Loren Miller's letter to the editor, *California Eagle*, 16 December 1948, 7.

65. Charlotta Bass, "On the Sidewalk," *California Eagle*, 6 January 1949, 1; "NAACP Members Defeat Move to Oust Griffith," *California Eagle*, 16 January 1947, 1.

66. See Miller's letter to the editor, *California Eagle*, 16 December 1948, 7; Cutler to Roy Wilkins, 11 December 1948; and Norman O. Houston to Roy E. Wilkins, 20 December 1948, "Los Angeles Branch Controversy 1948" folder, box C379, group 2, Records of the NAACP. Houston, the president of the Golden State Mutual Life Insurance Company, was a member of the NAACP's national board of directors. Wilkins was the assistant executive secretary of the NAACP.

67. See Wilkins to Houston, 29 December 1948, and Gloster Current to Noah Griffin, 30 December 1948, "Los Angeles Branch Controversy 1948" folder, box C379, group 2, Records of the NAACP. Griffin was the NAACP's West Coast regional secretary.

68. Gloster Current to the Committee on Branches, 8 December 1948, "Los Angeles Branch Controversy 1948" folder, box C379, group 2, Records of the NAACP.

69. On wartime and postwar coalitions in the Bay Area, see Marilynn S. Johnson, *The Second Gold Rush: Oakland and the East Bay in World War II* (Berkeley: University of California Press, 1993).

70. See Raphael Sonenshein's essay in this anthology and that author's book, *Politics in Black and White*.

PART IV

THE DREAM DEFERRED

Deindustrialization, Urban Poverty, and African American Community Mobilization in Oakland, 1945 through the 1990s

GRETCHEN LEMKE-SANTANGELO

Since the early twentieth century, African Americans have been a migratory people, moving from one farm to another, from rural areas to southern towns and cities, and out of the South to northern and western metropolitan centers. These journeys, frequently seasoned with Old Testament references to Exodus or deliverance, became a central feature of family and communal folklore and nourished the hopes and dreams of each new generation. Faith McAllister, who left Louisiana for the West Coast as a young adult, eloquently described the historical context of her own migration: "Mother didn't stay in one place very long. She was always trying to better herself. The whole family was like that. They were all hard workers and always tried to better themselves. When opportunity knocked, we were always packed and ready to go. And I guess that's how we survived." Faith's own opportunity came in the early 1940s, as defense contractors like Henry Kaiser were transforming California into a virtual Canaan for skilled and unskilled workers. But her journey, like that of countless others, would be bittersweet, marked with both promise and disappointment.[1]

During World War II, thousands of African Americans moved from the South to Northern California's East Bay area in search of the economic opportunities generated by federal investment in shipbuilding and the region's reputation for greater racial tolerance. As a consequence of this Second Great Migration, the East Bay's African American population grew dramatically. In Richmond, for example, the number of blacks rose from 270 in 1940 to 10,000 by 1945. Oakland's African American population grew from 8,462 to more than 37,000 during the same period. Such growth was not

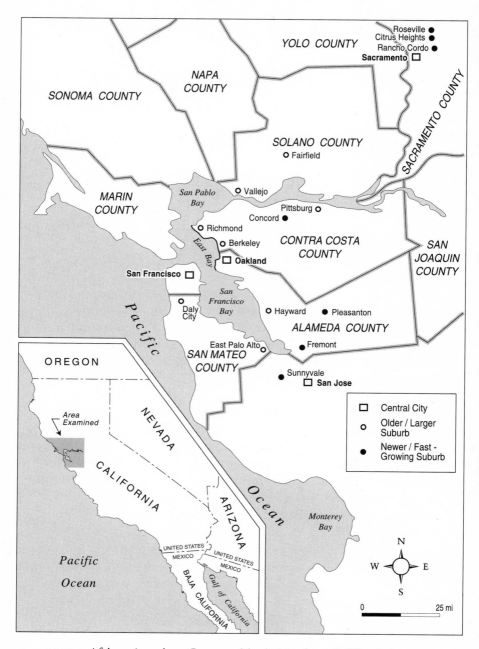

MAP 4. African American Communities in Northern California by 1990

limited to the East Bay, however. San Francisco, Los Angeles, Portland, and Seattle, as well as several midwestern and East Coast cities, were also affected by wartime migration.[2]

During the war years, the East Bay's defense-driven economy provided most migrants with a fleeting taste of the good life. Although they filled the lowest rungs of the occupational ladder and were the "last hired and first fired," migrants relished the fact that they were, in the words of one newcomer, "at least getting paid to put up with it. In the South it had been nothing but hard work and bad treatment. Here I made more in a day than I made back home in a month." Another migrant commented:

> [I] am a colored woman and I am forty-two years old. Now you know that colored women don't have a chance for any kind of job back there except in somebody's kitchen working for two or three dollars a week. I have an old mother and a crippled aunt to take care of, and I have to make as much as I can to take care of them. It costs so much to live these days. I went down to the government office in Marshall there and they said maybe I could find a war-job out here. I got my neighbors to look after my mother and aunt and came out here on the bus. I went to work for Kaiser and saved enough to bring my aunt and mother out here. I owed Mr. Baker four hundred dollars back home. I made enough to pay back all of it. He returned fifty dollars to me.[3]

But the war boom did not last. Unlike white workers, who benefited from what Gerald Nash has termed the "Great Transformation," black migrants faced increasing marginalization within the region's inner cities. Following the war, the economic vitality of East Bay migrant communities was severely undermined by poorly planned redevelopment and transportation projects, chronic capital flight, and persistent patterns of residential segregation and employment discrimination. In the East Bay and in other former defense centers across the nation, the postwar black ghetto began to take shape, characterized by overcrowded, substandard housing, declining employment opportunities, and a sharp rise in poverty among former migrants and their children.

As these problems deepened during the 1980s and 1990s, liberals and conservatives alike adopted a simplified version of the "culture of poverty" thesis to explain the continuing decline of inner cities. Contemporary proponents of this thesis have asserted that the poor adopted dysfunctional values and behaviors that operate independently of structural or economic forces to produce and perpetuate poverty: the lack of a work ethic, inability to defer gratification, deviant family structures, and casual attitudes toward sexuality, marriage, and illegitimacy. One study, for example, attributed the growth of Chicago's black "underclass" to pathological cultural values that supposedly came north with successive waves of black migrants. In ghettos like Chicago's, the author wrote, "It appears that the distinctive culture is now the greatest barrier to progress by the black underclass, rather than unemployment or welfare." In keeping with this logic, some policy makers now maintain that welfare programs are, at best, a waste of tax dollars and may even contribute to urban decline by undermining incentives to work, marry, and limit family size.4

But cultural explanations of poverty, particularly those that ignore the connection between behavior and economic opportunity, have been challenged by a substantial body of research tracing postwar urban decline to institutional discrimination and massive structural changes that have eroded the nation's industrial base and facilitated capital flight from inner cities. Indeed, deindustrialization, which captured the attention of the white public in the 1980s, has been a long-standing problem within black urban communities. In Oakland, Newark, Detroit, Los Angeles, San Francisco, and Portland, manufacturing jobs began to decline in the immediate postwar years as industry relocated to mostly white suburbs, removing a crucial source of upward mobility for minority residents. The more recent shift from an industrial to a service-based economy, characterized by capital flight overseas or to lower wage regions of the country, has merely added insult to much older injuries. In the East Bay, and most specifically within Oakland's African American community, the changing structure of the economy produced pockets of poverty during a period of general prosperity.5

The postwar economic decline of Oakland's black migrant community occurred in four overlapping phases: demobilization following World War II (1945–50), white flight and industrial relocation to the suburbs (1950–75), deindustrialization (1975–95), and, most recently, demilitarization and base closures (1991–97). Their combined impact, spanning five decades, all but erased the fragile economic gains of the 1940s and forced working-class migrants to fall back on their own institutional and familial resources to stabilize their neighborhoods in the hard economic times of the postwar era. Indeed, while a minority of Oakland's African American residents weathered these periods of decline and secured middle-class status, the largest segment of the city's black population did not fare so well.

Between 1940 and 1945, Oakland's black migrant community benefited from what economists have termed the "Great Compression": a marked decline in wage differentials between African American and white workers. The compression, a product of wartime labor shortages, black protest against employment discrimination, African American migration out of the low-wage South, and government intervention in the labor market, represented a sharp departure from the past. It was a moment when increased social and economic mobility at least partially offset persistent patterns of employment and housing discrimination. Although the last hired and first fired, and forced into the oldest, most dilapidated sections of the city, the majority of Oakland's black migrants still enjoyed a standard of living far higher than they had known in the past.[6]

By early 1945, however, these gains began to evaporate for many African American residents. Despite their relatively high levels of skill and education, roughly comparable to those of white migrants, black newcomers were among the first to lose their jobs as war industries closed altogether or retooled for peacetime production. By 1950, following five years of demobilization, unemployment among Oakland's nonwhite residents stood at 19.8 percent for men and 21.7 percent for women, more than double that of the city's white population.[7] There were, however, significant age differentials in the black unemployment rate, suggesting that adults who arrived in Oakland during the war years had the skills and seniority to make a stronger showing in the postwar job market than their children or younger siblings. In 1950, for example, the jobless rate for black men between the ages of twenty and twenty-four stood at 28.6 percent, or nearly double that for men between forty and forty-nine.[8]

By the mid-1950s, the unemployment rate among Oakland's migrant population began to decline as workers, particularly men and women over thirty, reestablished a stronger foothold in the city's industrial labor market. In some cases, these gains were a direct result of anti-discrimination campaigns against offending industries. By 1960, the blue-collar sector—including craftsmen, foremen, workers in related fields, operatives, and laborers—employed proportionately more African American men than any other group of workers. Men of the migrant generation were four times more likely to be concentrated in industrial occupations than all employed males. While many of them were forced to take jobs at lower pay and skill levels than during the war, blue-collar jobs, even in the unskilled and semiskilled categories, provided higher wages, greater job security, and better benefits than service-sector employment. Migrant women, whose postwar employment was central to the economic survival of working-class families, were less fortunate. Forced out of well-paying defense jobs at the end of the war, a majority took domestic work in private households or entered jobs in the institutional service sector as cooks, custodians, and nurse's aids. Nevertheless, a growing number of women did find manufacturing employment during the postwar years, particularly in the food-processing industry. Thus, for men and women alike, Oakland's industrial base in the 1950s provided a stable source of employment, holding the promise of upward mobility for migrants and their children.9

Postwar employment gains were particularly striking in a small cluster of industries: primary and fabricated metals production; transportation equipment manufacture; food processing; and assembly, packing, and longshore occupations. Yet even in the midst of this modest recovery, these jobs were already in decline. In the mid-1930s, the Oakland Chamber of Commerce established the Metropolitan Oakland Area Program (MOAP) "intended to encourage the development of industry in the county, outside of the city proper." Placed on hold during the war years, the program was fully implemented in the 1950s after the chamber concluded that "the old central city no longer offered the possibilities for economic exploitation now offered by the suburbs." The Bay Area Council, a nine-county regional planning organization established during the same period and joined by Oakland's business leaders, complemented the MOAP's efforts by focusing on region-wide economic development. Its goal, like MOAP's, was to transform open or "wasted" space into industrial parks and new residential developments outside of the city proper. But as city fathers were touting the benefits of decentralization, a few critics concluded that the "only agency looking out for Oakland's interests alone is the Port of Oakland." The survey went on to state that industrial relocation to the suburbs "causes a considerable amount of residential and commercial relocation," bleeding central cities of taxpayers as well as "retail and services establishments, including credit clothiers, home furnishers, appliance dealers, loan companies, attorneys specializing in compensation claims, etc."10

Ignoring such warnings, industry began to relocate to the suburbs as early as 1947, drawn there by lower taxes, cheaper land for plant expansion and employee parking, and the absence of environmental constraints associated with locating plants near residential areas. Indeed, by the mid-1950s, just as black residents were regaining their foothold in the industrial sector, capital flight was in full swing. Job loss to the suburbs, mostly to southern Alameda County, continued until 1975, with disastrous consequences for Oakland's black workers. Between 1960 and 1975, for example, Oakland lost one-third of its manufacturing jobs, with the sharpest declines in food processing (42 percent), primary and fabricated metals production (44 percent), and transportation equipment fabrication (92 percent). Not surprisingly, unemployment, particularly among the new generation of workers, rose sharply, from 28.6 percent in 1950 to 50 percent in 1970 for young African American men.[11]

Throughout the 1950s and 1960s, as plants like Ford, General Motors, Borden Chemical, Heil Equipment, and Trailmobile were relocating to southern Alameda County, the suburbs were also attracting thousands of new residents. New housing was highly affordable, built on low-cost land and subsidized by federal home loan programs. Simultaneously, newly constructed freeways and later the Bay Area Rapid Transit (BART) system, built with state and federal funds, were giving new suburban residents the choice of commuting to jobs on the urban fringe or retaining jobs in the central city. Moreover, work opportunities in the suburbs multiplied rapidly as service and retail establishments followed industry and the new suburbanites out of the inner city.[12]

Ease of commute, affordable housing, and plentiful jobs contributed to a spectacular level of growth in Oakland's suburbs during the postwar years. Between 1960 and 1970, Oakland's population declined 9.4 percent while the outlying suburbs of Hayward and Fremont grew by 28 percent and 131 percent respectively. Nearby Newark, San Leandro, and Union City experienced similar levels of growth during the same period. But nearly all of these new suburbanites were white. Between 1960 and 1970, Oakland's white population declined by 21 percent, while the city's black population increased by 41 percent. By 1966, the tri-city area of Fremont, Newark, and Union City had a total population of 122,000, only .02 percent of which was nonwhite.[13]

Capital flight to the suburbs would not have been as devastating for Oakland's migrant community if black workers had been able to relocate to outlying areas. However, discriminatory lending and real estate practices, coupled with local and federal government policies, confined black residents to the urban core. Even San Leandro, Oakland's nearest neighbor to the south, remained nearly 99.9 percent white as late as 1972, prompting one observer to comment:

Oakland's public finance burdens as well as its racial tensions are a consequence, in part, of San Leandro's discouragement of Negro immigration. San Leandro in recent years has wooed industry with promises of relatively low tax rates [recruiting] plants, which, if located in Oakland, would provide the tax base upon which Oakland needs to draw in order to serve the Negroes excluded by San Leandro.[14]

The "discouragement of Negro immigration" in San Leandro and in other new suburban communities took several forms. Throughout the 1950s and 1960s, the Southern Alameda County Real Estate Board steadfastly refused to share its property listings with Oakland's integrated board of realtors, effectively denying information about available properties to prospective minority buyers. Agents and brokers, if approached by black clients, would steer them away from white neighborhoods, show property at inconvenient times or in less desirable locations, or simply fail to keep appointments. Lenders, too, discriminated against black buyers, admitting that a "large factor" in loan eligibility is "the location of the property. Banks frequently will refuse to make loans on some houses in certain areas, forcing applicants to go elsewhere where lending rates are higher and more points are required." Local city officials, determined to do their part, refused to change zoning ordinances to promote the development of low- and moderate-income housing or revise building codes to accommodate less expensive construction. The federal government, as more than one study concluded, also bore major responsibility for the creation of all-white suburbs. Indeed, residential segregation throughout southern Alameda County "was determined in large measure by the Federal Housing Administration (FHA) and the Veterans Administration (VA) supported subdivisions built and marked on a discriminatory basis." Finally, state and federal funds financed the construction of new freeways and BART, transportation systems that facilitated suburban growth while simultaneously destroying affordable housing and black business districts in inner city neighborhoods.[15]

The link between jobs and housing was dramatically exposed in 1955 when Ford moved its plant from Richmond to Milpitas. The company's black workers, residing in Oakland and Richmond, retained seniority in the new location but faced a long commute because "under traditional real estate practice, they probably would not be admitted to new housing developments unless these were intended especially for Negro occupancy." In contrast, Ford's white workforce—a majority of whom were wartime or Depression-era migrants, had less than a high school education, and filled semiskilled jobs at the plant—moved into suburban housing tracts and quickly entered the ranks of the middle class.[16]

In a rare demonstration of compassion, the United Auto Workers (UAW) Local 560 and the American Friends Service Committee joined forces to develop an integrated housing tract on vacant land near the new Ford plant. Almost immediately, the developer of an adjacent white subdivision mounted a legal campaign against the project. To make matters worse, local mortgage companies, the FHA, and the VA were reluctant to finance the new housing. Although the tract, called Sunnyhills, was eventually built, many black Ford workers had already taken jobs elsewhere or resigned themselves to the long commute. By April 1960 only 15 percent, or ninety of the families in the development, were nonwhite. Thus, Sunnyhills, while paved with good intentions, only served to underscore how black workers were excluded from the suburban boom.[17]

As jobs left Oakland, city residents were forced to commute long distances to suburban industrial centers like Milpitas. One study, conducted in 1969, concluded that "an increasing number of the East Bay's relatively available, traditionally male blue-collar jobs are so far from West Oakland . . . that a car is required for both job hunting and commuting." Furthermore, "This is compounded by continued patterns of housing and employment discrimination which lead more Negroes than any other group to live in Oakland and commute to jobs elsewhere." To make matters worse, half of the high-paying industrial jobs that remained in Oakland continued to be monopolized by mostly white former city residents who had moved to the suburbs, despite the fact that a large percentage of black workers qualified for those positions. Regional apartheid, rather than a lack of job training and education, the report stressed, was the real culprit. Indeed, "Available data suggest that a good number of West Oakland residents already qualify for a large portion of the region's blue-collar jobs."[18]

While some Oakland residents initially made the commute, following their old jobs to the suburbs, their number gradually declined. Industry preferred to recruit more locally, replacing retiring workers with white suburban employees who "are more loyal, more cooperative, more productive workers than those in big cities."[19] In the meantime, the economic impact of capital and white flight was not lost on Oakland's black residents. Using a startlingly graphic metaphor, one observer noted,

> Here in Oakland all of the Negroes in Alameda County, save 1 or 2 percent, live in the central city, and we are ringed by a white noose of suburbia.... So we have the parasitical cities around Oakland that draw on all of the resources and at the same time do not put anything in the central city, and we have the problems of health and welfare and crime in the central city while we have the highest type of social irresponsibility by the inhabitants of San Leandro, Piedmont, Orinda, Lafayette.

Making matters even worse, some companies began to move out of the region altogether, foreshadowing a trend that would emerge more fully in the early 1980s. An unemployed worker keenly felt this added insult:

> Well you take Colorado Fuel and Iron a few years ago moved out of the city of Oakland into the Southern States, which put some 1,500 people unemployed at that time. Take Dole Pineapple, which is the cannery which employed some 2,000 people that looked forward for it each year as a part-time job. Some looked forward, for that was the only job that they had. Then, after they closed down Dole Pineapple and went back to Hawaii that put these people in the unemployment line also.[20]

The effects of capital flight would have been felt even more keenly had it not been for the safety net provided by government employment. The region's military installations, like the Alameda Naval Air Station, the Oakland Army Base, and Oak Knoll Naval Hospital, first employed black migrants during the war years and continued to be an important source of jobs through the early 1990s. Unlike private industry, the federal government strengthened its antidiscrimination policy in the postwar years and remained tied to its enormous infrastructure and strategic location near Oakland's port facilities. State, county, and city government also grew after the war, enlarging existing operations and developing new bureaucracies to administer federally funded housing and antipoverty programs. In all, government positions increased 29 percent between 1960 and 1975, employing 30 percent of the city's black civilian workforce by 1966. Women, locked out of retail and clerical jobs in the private sector, benefited substantially from this expansion, leaving a dwindling number of manufacturing jobs for clerical and custodial positions at the new postal complex in Oakland and for military bases and government offices in the downtown area.[21]

These gains, however, only softened the impact of chronic job loss in the industrial sector. By the early 1960s, the state, local, and federal officials who had created the infrastructure for postwar capital flight and suburbanization belatedly recognized that black Oakland was ready to "explode." Whether stemming from a rare moment of self-reflection or the cynical desire for a share of federal monies, this insight was parlayed into one of the largest antipoverty programs in urban America. Serious efforts began in 1961, when city officials convinced the Ford Foundation to fund a project "designed to blend minority groups into the city." Billed as a "Two Million Dollar Welcome for Newcomers," many of whom had lived in Oakland since the war years, the grant specifically targeted the "social problems of minority groups and the proper assimilation of new citizens into the community." The Ford grant, eventually supplemented with another $1.2 million, went largely to youth education for citizenship and juvenile delinquency prevention, ignoring, in the words of one critic, that "back in Oakland, there was no opportunity structure. Over the ten-year period of the last census, the city lost 9,000 jobs as big companies like General Electric and General Motors moved their plants to the suburbs where the taxes are lower and the whites live in even more abundant numbers."[22]

The Ford grant paved the way for additional outside funding after the research director of the Oakland project concluded that "local efforts have been too little too late" and "a federal program is needed to provide the necessary scale to deal with the Negro Problem." He went on to warn that "Negro-White conflict is likely to become sharper as time passes."[23] Thus, the image took shape of Oakland as a city ready to burn—an image that city leaders forged into a convincing rationale for federal investment in Oakland's declining infrastructure. But like the initial Ford grant, federal monies, including War on Poverty funds, did little to improve the city's opportunity structure. During the early 1960s, the redevelopment process was controlled by white city officials who invested federal funds in large capital improvement projects directed at attracting industry to Oakland. Such projects included port upgrades, freeway construction, rapid transit, and slum clearance. West Oakland, housing the majority of the city's black residents and situated adjacent to downtown, bore the brunt of this initiative. Between 1960 and 1966, as new freeways and transit lines obliterated its black business district and separated residents from vital city services, and as entire neighborhoods were demolished to make room for new moderate income housing, West Oakland's population declined by 25 percent. Labeled as "negro removal" by its critics, this process actually reduced affordable housing by 21 percent in a six-year period, forcing African American residents to relocate to East Oakland—a section of the city vacated by fleeing whites and divorced from the cultural amenities, businesses, and transportation networks of the downtown area.[24]

An unemployed Oakland resident, observing the connections between redevelopment, capital flight, and growth of the suburbs, commented that after factories closed and "put these people in the unemployment line," city officials pushed "through the Rapid Transit that is going through the black community and tearing out the factories, little places that were there, perhaps a lot of people that were employed there lost their jobs because these people will take this money and establish somewhere else." He went on to note that "in San Leandro out of 86,000 people we have only about 12 black people, and they hired one black police officer there and couldn't even find a place for him to live in San Leandro because of discrimination." Capital flight and white flight did indeed go together. In 1960, manufacturing occupied the premier position in Oakland's economy and employed more African American men than any other sector. But between 1960 and 1975, manufacturing employment decreased by 31 percent, with a net loss of about 12,700 jobs. As industry moved out of the inner city, white residents followed; more than 42,000 fled Oakland between 1960 and 1970 and more than 100,000 between 1950 and 1970. A federal employment official who visited Oakland after the Watts uprising of 1965 summed up the impact of these developments on the black community: "Racial tension does exist. . . . there is sufficient mistrust, disaffection, and frustration building up in the Negro community to make the situation potentially explosive." At the same time, a White House task force judged Oakland the most likely of fifteen cities to be the next Watts.[25]

In response to such dire predictions, the federal government decided to make Oakland the focal point of a new effort to deal with areas of high unemployment when it authorized the recently created Economic Development Administration (EDA) to fund a $23 million job creation program, which trained and hired unemployed workers to upgrade airport and port facilities. Although the EDA failed to generate permanent jobs, it temporarily eased tensions among residents and demonstrated growing federal concern over the plight of the urban poor. Simultaneously, the Office of Economic Opportunity (OEO) launched its Community Action Program (CAP), paying organizers to mobilize poor residents into citizen or neighborhood councils. These councils, bolstered with cash grants from OEO, then lobbied city government for job-training programs, recreation facilities, housing rehabilitation grants, improved police and fire protection, and citizen control over larger redevelopment projects. Of Oakland's War on Poverty programs, community-action efforts had the most lasting impact on poor and working-class residents. Nevertheless, such programs generated substantial controversy. In his retrospective critique of the War on Poverty, Daniel P. Moynihan argued that community-action projects precipitated conflict between local governments and poor residents, handed power to the uneducated and incompetent, and contributed to urban unrest by raising the hopes of the impoverished to unreasonable levels. Yet he also acknowledged that many community organizing efforts were successful: "Those most closely controlled by City Hall were disappointing, and the ones most antagonistic were destroyed. There was a large area in between, but it tended to receive little attention." Oakland's community-action beneficiaries, occupying this middle ground, did antagonize city officials by demanding a greater voice in how War on Poverty monies would be spent. Such conflict was productive, however, resulting in permanent change for poor residents.[26]

In 1966, the Johnson administration initiated the Model Cities Program as an alternative to community action—an alternative that CAP critics like Moynihan viewed as more firmly under the control of local political and business leaders. But by 1967, when Oakland's Model Cities proposal was accepted, black residents were already organized enough to demand and receive partial control over program staffing, administration, and funding. Many, in fact, became "new careerists," or paid model cities' community organizers. Under their direction, War on Poverty monies were successfully channeled into job-training programs, housing rehabilitation, child care and community health centers, and numerous other projects that cushioned the impact of capital flight. Moreover, Oakland's black residents, emboldened by their participation in antipoverty programs, obtained a greater role in city governance and ultimately became the dominant force shaping local politics.[27] But despite these gains, the structural basis of Oakland's problems remained intact. According to one observer, Oakland had merely fulfilled "a cynical prediction of the central cities of the future; that as blacks and other minorities gain political office and a voice in governmental affairs, whites exodus out to the suburbs, and most importantly, the major industries which carry a large load of the tax burden follow them. Nonwhites gain office to control, but they in effect control nothing because there are no industries and no money. The city becomes yet a larger ghetto, controlled and dependent upon forces from outside."[28]

By the late 1970s and into the 1990s, city redevelopment efforts, firmly in the hands of black elected officials, reverted to the 1950s model of attracting business through large capital improvements. These more recent efforts, however, were directed toward luring investors to the city proper and emphasized tourism, retail trade, and corporate administration rather than industrial development. The new Convention Center Complex, Jack London Square, City Center offices and retail space, and Victorian Row have created new jobs. Most are in the low end of the service sector, however, paying minimum wage and lacking the benefits and job security once afforded by industry. While some areas of Oakland are prospering, preliminary research indicates that the benefits of such expansion are not evenly distributed. The jobs and capital generated in the downtown Asian enclave, for example, primarily benefit a specific ethnic population. Moreover, its assets may be more strongly linked to the global, Pacific Rim economy than to those of Oakland and the East Bay as a whole.[29]

As Oakland continued to grapple with its chronic economic problems, more aggressive enforcement of fair-housing laws and pressure from local civil rights groups began to erode residential segregation in the suburbs. By the mid-1970s, Oakland's black residents, at least those with the resources to leave, finally had the option to move closer to industrial jobs in cities like Fremont, Newark, and Hayward. This positive development, however, occurred just as plants, which had relocated to the suburbs a decade earlier, began to leave the region completely. The two decades between 1975 and 1995 marked the end of the region's "smokestack era," leading one critic to conclude, "If Alameda County was a model of industrialization in the 1950s and 1960s, it is also a model for industrial closures in the '80s."[30]

Between 1979 and 1985 alone, more than 122 factories closed in the county, with a net loss of 24,000 jobs. Whether in the city proper or out in the suburbs, these jobs—provided by companies like U.S. Steel, Ford, General Motors, Bethlehem, Pacific States Steel, and Mack Western—were precisely those that had sustained older African American workers and held the promise of upward mobility for at least some members of the younger generation. During a particularly bitter battle to keep their jobs at East Oakland's Engine and Compressor Division of TransAmerica Delaval Inc., minority workers demonstrated a clear grasp of the problem:

Our community has lost more than 20,000 jobs in the last few years because of plant closures and lay-offs in all sectors of our economy. . . . Then there is the "ripple effect" that unemployed workers can no longer buy groceries or pay rent thereby hurting small businesses. And our local tax base also decreases just when unemployed workers and our families need more services and assistance. There are some new jobs being created, but most of them are part-time, temporary and pay minimum wage with no health care or other benefits.

Demanding that the city and county take immediate action to stem capital flight, Delaval workers went on to assert, "While the corporations amass huge profits and flee to cheap labor havens, our communities and families are being destroyed. We must fight now to stem the tide of corporate greed before they inflict more damage."[31]

In the end, Delaval workers lost their battle. Deindustrialization in the East Bay was part of a larger structural shift in the nation's economy, characterized by a decline in manufacturing jobs and growth in the information and service sectors. By the late 1970s, transnationals like Delaval's parent corporation, TransAmerica, had developed new production, management, and distribution systems that afforded greater mobility. Production and distribution sites could now be shifted within the United States and moved overseas in an ongoing search for docile nonunion labor, cheap raw materials, lucrative markets, and lax environmental standards.[32]

These transitions and redirections of industrial growth had a devastating impact on inner city residents in the industrial Northeast, the Midwest, and California. Black workers in the Great Lakes region were among the first to be affected, suffering a 50 percent decline in manufacturing employment between 1979 and 1984. Without training and education, these workers were forced to take low-paying service jobs that offered few opportunities for advancement or enter the ranks of the chronically unemployed. In California, black workers in Alameda and Los Angeles counties experienced the heaviest job losses. In some cases, plants moved overseas. Others, like Peterbilt, which left Alameda County in 1986, moved to nonunion and lower-wage states like Texas and Tennessee. As jobs in California's basic industry declined, newly unemployed workers were less likely than those in other sectors to find alternative employment. Between 1979 and 1984, nineteen basic industry jobs were lost for every ten created. The only growth sectors open to former blue-collar workers were in retail and service occupations, notorious for low wages, poor benefits, and lack of job security and union representation.[33]

During the 1970s, the East Bay saw considerable job expansion, but most of it was concentrated south of Oakland and well to the east along the 680 freeway corridor. By 1980, total employment on this suburban fringe exceeded that in Oakland, but the long commute and historic resistance to hiring black workers meant that little of this growth was shared by African Americans. In the 1980s, this area attracted virtually all of the employment growth in the East Bay, gaining nearly 148,000 jobs, while Oakland lost more than 10,000. African Americans composed only 3 percent of suburban residents as late as 1990, another example of the growing spatial gap between East Bay blacks and most of the region's economic growth.[34]

In Oakland, as a 1995 study revealed, this meant that older, displaced workers were competing with their children and grandchildren for minimum-wage service jobs paying an average of $8,840 per year, compared to a poverty-level income of $15,600 for a family of four. Older and younger workers alike were increasingly stuck in entry-level, nonadvancing positions, and the next generation seemed likely to be "unable to get its foot in the door at all." The researchers went on to state that they expected the problem to "get substantially worse. Government and the health-care industry, which have provided work for inner-city residents, are shedding workers and are likely to shed many more. At the same time, the welfare policy trend is to push as many recipients onto the job market as possible, whether there are jobs available for them or not."[35]

By the mid-1980s, the decline in blue-collar jobs nationwide had leveled off. But this was not the case in Oakland, where manufacturing employment continued to decrease through the mid-1990s. Making matters worse, the federal government, a major employer of Oakland's black residents since the early 1960s, began to initiate a series of base closures. In 1993, the Defense Base Closure and Realignment Commission voted to close Alameda Naval Air Station and Naval Aviation Depot and the Oak Knoll Naval Hospital at the cost of several thousand civilian jobs. Oakland's Naval Supply Center, employing hundreds of Oakland residents, would be phased out through an agreement between the Port of Oakland and the Navy. Finally, the Oakland Army Base, employing 2,100 civilian workers, was targeted in the 1995 round of military closures. The Oakland Chamber of Commerce, breaking five decades of silence on the problem of capital flight, commented, "They cut our heart out last time [1993] and left us with the extremities." Now it appeared that even the extremities might be lost.36

Numerous studies have documented the postwar difficulties of America's inner cities, attributing economic problems and accompanying social dislocation to external structural forces and policy decisions. Few, however, describe the black protest, activism, and institution building that have occurred in response to marginalization—an omission that inadvertently reinforces part of the culture of poverty thesis: that the poor are culturally programmed for passivity, dependence, and such antisocial responses to adversity as drug use, crime, welfare dependence, and family disintegration. Clearly, such problems exist within inner cities, but this popular preoccupation with the "pathology" of ghetto life obscures the fact that African American communities have considerable resources. In Oakland, and elsewhere, the majority of residents—poor and working class—have continually struggled to keep their families together, build and maintain community-sustaining institutions, and challenge racial stereotypes and restrictions. While these struggles have not kept jobs in inner cities—a task that defies local solution—they have helped temper the impact of capital flight on low-income communities.

By the end of World War II, 75 to 80 percent of Oakland's black residents were recent migrants, men and women who had actively sought a better life by transplanting their families from places like Texas, Louisiana, Mississippi, and Arkansas to the East Bay. This generation, with levels of skill and education comparable to those of white migrants who came during the same period, arrived with a common regard for economic autonomy, hard work, education, worship, family ties, cooperation, and independent, self-help organizations—the very values and institutions that enabled them to survive the hardships and humiliations of Jim Crow. Instead of transplanting an ethic of dependency, they came with the skills and determination to establish new communities and resist the prejudice and discrimination that greeted them.37

With few of the advantages that allowed white migrants to enter the middle class, black migrants nonetheless used their cultural and economic resources to help stabilize their communities in the hard economic times following the collapse of the wartime industrial boom. Their efforts included establishing new churches and swelling the membership of existing congregations, running church-based service programs, building the numerical strength of organizations like the National Association for the Advancement of Colored People (NAACP) and National Council of Negro Women, and contributing to campaigns to end housing and employment discrimination and elect black representatives to state and local office. As early as 1948, for example, migrant voters in Oakland and Berkeley, in coalition with white liberals and organized labor, elected the district's first black assembly member. William Byron Rumford then went on to facilitate the state's Fair Employment Practices Act and the Rumford Fair Housing Act. His legislative triumphs have been attributed to the "arrival in Oakland, Berkeley, and in California as a whole since 1940, of the hundreds of thousands of Blacks."[38]

Oakland's incoming migrants, unwilling to tolerate prewar racial boundaries, also became active participants in local civil rights organizations. In 1946, white activists, including some members of the Communist Party, launched the East Bay Civil Rights Congress (CRC) to address escalating police brutality, residential segregation, and employment discrimination in Oakland, Berkeley, and Richmond. By the end of the decade, however, the CRC had an African American executive director, Hursel Alexander, and a mostly black migrant membership. Jessica Mitford, who was active within the organization during this period, observed, "Under Hursel's guiding hand, the East Bay CRC was transformed from a small, sterile committee of aging, foreign-born whites into a dynamic, predominantly black organization with some five-hundred active dues-paying members—this at a time when the NAACP chapter in Oakland could muster no more than fifty." Indeed, the younger, more militant CRC became a vocal critic of the NAACP, accusing it of being a "do-nothing organization . . . dominated by the old inhabitants of the black community who had attained a degree of prosperity, and, having worked out a modus vivendi with whites, resented and looked down on the clamorous hordes of recent black migrants."[39]

Although many CRC members branded the NAACP as accommodationist, it was hardly a "do-nothing" organization. During the mid-to-late 1940s, for example, the Alameda County branch of the NAACP fought to integrate the Key System transportation line that ran buses and trains throughout the East Bay. During the same period, it also attacked restrictive housing covenants, police brutality, discriminatory admissions policies at the Heald and Armstrong business schools, and lack of minority access to low-cost housing. Spurred on by its more radical competitor, the Alameda County branch continued this spirit of activism into the 1950s, successfully pressing General Motors to open its Chevrolet plant to African American workers and the Oakland Fire Department to integrate its labor force. These and numerous other victories increased the NAACP's popularity among migrants just as the CRC was falling victim to Federal Bureau of Investigation (FBI) harassment and media red-baiting. Indeed, the Alameda County branch of the NAACP, frightened by charges that the neighboring Richmond branch was led by Communists, readily used antiradical propaganda to insulate itself from similar accusations and hasten the demise of the rival CRC. During a CRC sponsored demonstration against housing discrimination, for example, the NAACP issued flyers telling protesters, "Keep Your Eyes Wide Open. . . . They say they are working for your civil rights, but they work among us in the interest of the Communist Party or other subversive and UN-AMERICAN movements." By the mid-1950s, the CRC disbanded and local NAACP leaders created a separate Oakland branch to accommodate growth in membership. The new organization, perhaps reflecting some of the old CRC militancy, almost immediately launched a "Spend Your Money Where You Can Work" campaign and mobilized support for fair-housing and employment legislation.⁴⁰

Although men dominated the NAACP leadership, migrant women exerted considerable influence within their own organization, the National Council of Negro Women. Before the war, the council raised funds for separate African American institutions like the Linden Street YWCA, the Fannie Wall Children's Home, and the Home for Aged and Infirm Colored People. But as migrant membership increased, its new leadership joined forces with the NAACP to challenge housing and employment discrimination and to begin to address the needs and concerns of working women. Migrant women were also particularly active in Oakland's churches, forming the loyal and active core of most congregations. Enriched by women's fund-raising efforts and active participation on boards and committees, churches were able to broaden their commitment to community service, providing housing and job referrals, child care, after-school programs, free meals, emergency financial support, senior services, and scholarships. As institutions providing social services, churches like Allen Temple and Taylor Memorial softened the impact of capital flight and reflected migrants' desire for stability in their new communities.⁴¹

This early black activism and institution building emphasized integration and inclusion rather than separation and entrenchment. The very fact that fair-housing and employment battles took center stage reveals a liberal optimism about the postwar economy—hope that equitable distribution of resources could solve the economic and housing woes of Oakland's African

American community. By the early 1960s, however, capital and white flight to the suburbs had taken a noticeable toll, prompting city officials to implement antipoverty and urban redevelopment programs. Black activists, while continuing their attack on discrimination, shifted their focus to examining how urban resources, including antipoverty funds, were being allocated. The politics of inclusion thus gave way to bitter but productive contestations over who would control Oakland's jobs, housing, tax base, and share of outside funds.

During the community-action phase of the War on Poverty, Oakland's wartime migrant generation, now in middle age, took jobs as organizers and service providers within their neighborhoods. Identified by CAP administrators as trusted and influential community representatives because of their earlier activism and working-class backgrounds, they successfully organized poor residents to challenge the mayor's policy of hand-picking members of Oakland's Economic Development Council, the agency responsible for allocating the city's share of federal War on Poverty funds. By 1967, poor and working-class residents of designated poverty areas seized control of the council and began redirecting OEO monies to neighborhood-based antipoverty programs. Just as significantly, involvement in community-action programs led directly to heightened political activism among participants—activism that ultimately altered the city's political power structure.[42]

As community activists struggled for control over War on Poverty funds, they continued their long-standing attack on employment discrimination. In 1965, for example, representatives from CORE, the NAACP, the Council for Civic Unity, and the East Bay Ministerial Alliance accused BART officials of giving job preferences to white nonresidents. But unlike earlier battles, this one involved more than the allocation of jobs. The BART system, part of the transportation network that facilitated white and industrial flight to the suburbs, also cut through West Oakland's historic black neighborhoods. In the process, several blocks of affordable housing and the black business district along the southwest side of 7th Street were demolished. While activists did obtain more construction jobs for Oakland's African American workers and modest compensation for displaced residents, their efforts had little impact on the city's declining opportunity structure. BART jobs, like those created by the EDA, were temporary, serving only to mollify growing unrest and anger. And ironically, black workers were now helping to construct the very system that encouraged further decentralization.[43]

The sons and daughters of migrants—young men and women who most keenly felt the impact of capital flight from their communities—never harbored the liberal dreams of their elders. The Welfare Rights Organization and the Black Panther Party, both of which originated in Oakland, militantly asserted that efforts to stretch the opportunity structure to include more minorities were now futile because that very structure was disintegrating. Indeed, Panther founders Bobby Seale and Huey P. Newton had both worked for federally funded antipoverty programs just prior to launching the party. And they, like many other young people, began to conclude that War on Poverty "employment training programs have become an acknowledged hustle, since few jobs are available at the end of the training program." By late 1966, Seale and Newton were in the library piecing together a theoretical framework for a new organization—one that would emphasize black self-determination and community self-defense. But most significantly, the party's founding document directly addressed Oakland's economic problems, calling for "full employment for our people." It went on to state, "The federal government is responsible and obliged to give every man employment or a guaranteed income. We believe that if the white businessman will not give full employment, then the means of production should be taken away from the businessman and placed in the community so that the people of the community can organize and employ all of its people and give a high standard of living."44

Although better known for their revolutionary rhetoric, clinics, breakfast programs, crusade against police brutality, and the stormy political careers, arrests, and deaths of their leaders, the Black Panthers actively built coalitions with older activists. By 1967, for example, they joined the West Oakland Planning Council (WOPC), a grassroots coalition of neighborhood organizations, churches, and community groups that grew out of the Model Cities Program. By 1968, WOPC and other neighborhood planning councils enabled poor and working-class African American residents to take control of the city's Economic Development Council. Even more significantly, these neighborhood-based coalitions went on to organize Oakland's black electorate. The Black Caucus, for example, drawing its membership from the NAACP, Urban League, the WOPC, and other neighborhood councils, mobilized African American voters in support of Ronald Dellums's successful 1970 bid for the Seventh Congressional District seat.45

By 1972, the Black Panther Party also had shifted its focus to electoral politics, helping to register 30,000 new voters in Oakland's African American working-class communities by April 1973. Stunning the city's political establishment, Bobby Seale, the party's candidate for mayor, came in second, drawing 43,749 votes to the incumbent Republican's 77,634. Under the leadership of Elaine Brown, the Panthers continued to be a political force throughout the decade, contributing to sophisticated campaigns for John George, who became Alameda County's first black supervisor in 1976, and Lionel Wilson, who became Oakland's first black mayor in 1977. Soon after, however, the Black Panthers dissolved, torn apart by internal divisions, government surveillance and infiltration, and law enforcement harassment.[46]

The welfare rights movement began in Alameda County in 1962 when fire struck the house of a recipient of Aid to Families with Dependent Children (AFDC). The welfare office withheld the woman's monthly check because "she was living in unfit housing." With seven children in her care, the woman desperately turned to other recipients who then began to share common concerns and problems. Soon the movement spread:

> The grapevine in the low-income community is a very large one. It extends in many different directions. It wasn't long before welfare rights efforts began in Long Beach, California; in Los Angeles, California; in Monterey County; in Contra Costa County. In each community the issue which provided the greatest stimulus for organization was different. In some it was housing and jobs, in others lawlessness and disinterest on the part of the welfare department. In each instance, the result was the same . . . the beginning of a welfare rights group among recipients.[47]

The new Alameda County Welfare Rights Organization (WRO) soon confronted much larger problems. In early 1964, the state ended its Bracero Program, which had brought more than 5,000,000 Mexican workers into the United States, thereby producing a farm labor shortage in the county's strawberry fields. Shortly thereafter, the county sent letters to welfare recipients informing them that failure to take piecework field jobs would jeopardize their eligibility. But if recipients took such jobs, they would be identified as "gainfully employed" and still lose their benefits. Simultaneously, the county began withholding public assistance from new applicants, claiming that agricultural jobs were readily available. The WRO responded by stressing that recipients, many of whom were skilled and semiskilled workers displaced by capital flight to the suburbs, would not be able to find substitute jobs in manufacturing if forced to work in the fields. The WRO then staged a sit-in at the county welfare office and threatened to take similar action in front of the state welfare department in San Francisco. As a consequence, the state allowed those who took farm labor jobs to retain welfare benefits but still failed to address the more serious problem of forcing displaced workers into low-wage farm labor.

Emboldened by their partial victory, the w r o went on to lobby successfully for increases in general assistance, an end to waiting periods or residency requirements for benefits, and a complete ban on forced farm labor during all but the summer months.[48] Even more significantly, welfare recipients had begun to contest the authority of social service officials and challenge the mythology that poor people were responsible for their own condition. As one w r o activist so eloquently stated:

> I think that a welfare recipient knows more about running the welfare department than a professional does. They have to live on the welfare and they know more about welfare than the person that's sitting over there reading a book. . . . We are human beings just like everybody else. We have to eat like the rest of the people. . . . We don't get the taxpayers [*sic*] money free. We play the lowest games to get that money. You have to be harassed the whole month to get $200 from the welfare. . . . All you get is discouragement because you are told, if you go to look for a job, you can't have money for transportation. You're not getting enough money to eat so you'll have to have some type of money to go out and look for a job so you can take it out of your food money. You have to have somebody to take care of your kids, so you take that out of your food money. So you end up without being able to really look for a job. If they send you to vocational services to go to school, they re-train you for the same thing that you already know how to do. It's nonsense for a person to go to school all over again to be a nurse's aid when you've been a nurse's aid before. . . . The Welfare Rights Organization is part of the whole movement in the United States. It's one of the organizations giving people responsibilities and control of their own lives and knowing that they can go and demand things that they really want and need. . . . Another thing we need is to create jobs at a man's own level. If a man's going to clean out a canal ditch, if he's going to sweep floors, pay him a wage. Let him be a man.[49]

Did the Welfare Rights Organization and the Black Panther Party actually improve the lives of Oakland's black residents? Some writers contend that they may have had the opposite effect. In recent years, both organizations have been blamed for contributing to the collapse of the liberal consensus that shaped the Great Society. Critics like Moynihan, tracing the rise of these organizations to the "misguided" community participation mandate of the OEO, accused them of alienating sympathetic whites, fomenting social unrest, and promoting parasitism. Most of their participants, however, saw themselves as waging a battle for economic survival within a climate of not-so-benign neglect. By placing decent jobs at the top of their agendas, both organizations were highlighting grassroots dissatisfaction with federal and local spending priorities and rejecting the very parasitism they were accused of perpetuating. Community-action programs undoubtedly encouraged greater militancy among Oakland's poor, but chronic joblessness and its accompanying dislocations existed long before the Great Society came to Oakland. Indeed, it was fear over impending "Negro-White conflict" that led to the city's first War on Poverty efforts in the early 1960s.

By the 1970s, as the welfare rights and black power movements faded from the scene, Oakland's African American residents achieved one of the Panthers' goals—control over city politics. Lionel Wilson, elected in 1977, ushered in an era of black mayoral dominance that lasted until Jerry Brown took office in 1998. During much of this twenty-year period, African Americans also held a majority of council seats and an increasing number of high-level offices. In 1983, for example, Henry Gardner became Oakland's first black city manager. At the same time, the city's black middle class expanded, benefiting from affirmative hiring policies in the public and private sectors. Indeed, between 1970 and 1990, the percentage of black workers holding white-collar jobs increased from 17 to 60 percent. Journalist Robert Maynard typified this trend. In 1979, he became the *Oakland Tribune*'s first black editor and in 1983 assumed ownership of the paper. With a large, black-owned metropolitan newspaper, a growing African American middle class, and a black-controlled city government, Oakland was declared the most integrated city in the United States in 1983.

However, the gains of this growing black middle class stood in stark contrast to the economic problems faced by an even larger number of African American residents who were either unemployed or in low-wage occupations. A dwindling tax base caused by middle-class flight to the suburbs, Proposition 13, and severe reductions in state and federal aid during a decade of fiscally conservative Republican rule limited the ability of the public sector to ameliorate their condition. To make matters worse for this segment of Oakland's black population, deindustrialization and military base closures threatened significant sources of employment.

To address these concerns, Oakland's African American community moved from contestations over city resources to building broad-based coalitions that emphasized the common problems of blue-collar workers, including those of recent Latino and Asian immigrants. In the 1980s, as industry left the region altogether, multiethnic coalitions like the Peace and Justice Organization, the Oakland Plant Closures Project, and the Coalition for Economic Justice initiated local campaigns to register working-class voters, lobby for a higher minimum wage and an economic bill of rights, elect local officials who supported full-employment agendas, and press for state and federal legislation requiring industry to give advance notice of plant closures and provide funds to retrain displaced workers. The Coalition for Economic Justice, in particular, represented the new multiethnic organizational model, drawing members from groups as diverse as the N A A C P, Oakland Metropolitan Ministries, Women's Economic Agenda Project (W R O's successor), Filipino Immigrant Services, Asian Multi-Services, Center for Third World Organizing, Hispanic Caucus of the California Democratic Party, Gray Panthers, and the Homeless Organizing Project.[50]

By the early 1990s, community focus had shifted to the problem of base closures. Ron Dellums, still seated in the Seventh Congressional District, obtained $2 million for a defense conversion pilot, the East Bay Conversion and Reinvestment Commission, to explore nonmilitary uses of the Alameda Naval Air Station, Alameda Aviation Depot, and Oakland Naval Hospital. Similarly, Alameda County's African American state assembly member, Barbara Lee, chair of the Assembly Task Force on Defense Conversion, worked on a statewide strategic plan to coordinate regional conversion efforts.[51]

Finally, both Dellums and Lee mobilized their constituents in support of the National Campaign to Abolish Poverty (N C A P). Moving beyond the single issues of deindustrialization and base closures, N C A P issued a ten-point plan to end poverty that included guaranteed job opportunities, an increase in the minimum wage, comprehensive health and child care, and wage subsidies for the working poor. N C A P organizers also focused on building local support for HR 1050, "A Living Wage, Jobs for All Act," and a countrywide full-employment movement capable of influencing national elections. Thus, multiethnic coalitions across class lines, pioneered by organizations like the Coalition for Economic Justice a decade earlier, built a broader base, revealing a growing awareness among activists that structural economic problems could not be addressed on the local or even statewide level.[52]

Oakland's African American community has mounted a sustained and formidable struggle against five decades of economic marginalization—one that demonstrates an astonishing level of patience and flexibility as well as an ongoing, historically rooted commitment to economic independence. Some popular articles, however, continue to portray Oakland and other inner cities as focal points of urban pathology, as if crime, drugs, and despair are the main preoccupations of their residents.[53] Such an image ignores the long history of activism within these communities and the less visible struggles of poor and working-class citizens—many of them women—to maintain family and neighborhood stability.

Another body of literature on inner-city black communities suggests that the decline of manufacturing jobs has been at least partially offset by the rise of service and high technology sectors. Black residents, according to this research, have failed to take advantage of these new economic opportunities, unlike other ethnic groups who willingly accept low wages as a step toward more promising employment. While this may hold true for other inner cities, Oakland still stands as a classic study in "spatial mismatch," the distance between jobs and the residences of racial minorities.[54] Between the 1970s and the 1990s, most East Bay job growth—even in lower-paying sectors of the economy—occurred far from central Oakland. For poor residents, lacking access to transportation and the means to relocate to the suburbs, this presented a formidable barrier.

The 1980s and 1990s would bring mixed signals of hope and hopelessness to Oakland's black community. The global economic forces that led to capital flight out of the city created some new, although modest, economic opportunities for the city's black middle class. These gains, however, were not sufficient to offset the losses of a growing "underclass," particularly in light of state and federal cutbacks in social spending. African Americans also retained full control over Oakland's political power structure and press, but by the early 1990s this, too, would change. Robert Maynard, after a series of downsizing measures, was forced to sell the *Oakland Tribune*, and growing dissatisfaction with a lagging economy swept a white mayor into office in 1998.

In the midst of these changes, there was a single constant: the disillusionment of Oakland's black residents. The sequence of corporate flight, global restructuring, and government downsizing had left younger generations with fewer job opportunities than their elders and substantially increased the number of unemployed and working poor. Migrants and their older children at least stood a chance of obtaining industrial or government employment. But these jobs, which propelled the more fortunate into the middle class and allowed their children to complete college and enter the white-collar sector, were never plentiful or easily accessible. Today most are gone. The result has been a huge increase in the number of working poor, the permanently unemployed, and the profoundly disillusioned. Not surprisingly, many members of the first generation unable "to get its foot in the door at all" have adopted destructive survival strategies: alternative routes to status and prestige like drug trafficking, teen pregnancy, and gang membership, or self-anesthetization through drug and alcohol abuse.

To face these challenges, black residents continue to rely on their community institutions. East Oakland's Allen Temple Baptist Church, for example, runs youth tutorial and scholarship programs, drug and alcohol rehabilitation clinics, a credit union, a senior housing complex, a blood bank, and a seniors meal program. Continuing a long tradition of self-help, Allen Temple and other Oakland churches also offer a positive source of status and self-esteem to members. As one local pastor commented in 1985, "The Church is the only institution in the black community that an individual feels he owns, that he is a part of and controls. Where else in the black community can a person be diggin' a ditch all week, or scrubbin' floors, or cleaning bedpans, and then on Sunday morning dress up and be a deacon or deaconess, or lead a song, or teach a lesson, or be the president or superintendent? Where else?"[55]

From World War II to the end of the century, Oakland's African American residents have struggled to adapt to shifts in the region's economy. Many came during the war in search of economic opportunity and greater social freedom. But while the wartime boom extended into the 1950s and 1960s for white suburbanites, it ended abruptly for black migrants. For Oakland, and for other former defense centers, peace initiated a series of structural dislocations that created the social "pathologies" that many Americans have come to associate with the ghetto.

To address capital and white flight, Oakland's African American community chose a number of different strategies. The fact that several of them involved partnerships with the federal government led to the widespread view among white taxpayers that they were subsidizing black poor who had no claim to or need for such public largesse. But a careful study of Oakland casts doubt on that assumption. Not only have structural economic changes largely defied local solution, but many federal programs have actually encouraged such developments. Moreover, the Oakland case reveals a human dimension often ignored by culture of poverty theorists: the extensive grassroots efforts of the poor and working class to stabilize their communities in the absence of a national commitment to provide decent jobs for inner-city residents. The history of Oakland's African American community since World War II reveals a series of antithetical experiences: hope for a better life, the decline of jobs and exclusion from the more prosperous suburbs, the promise of federal intervention, and the growing disillusionment of the postmigrant generation. Oakland, then, is a microcosm of inner-city challenges. Are its current problems solely structural? If so, do they indeed defy local and national solutions? Or are improvements in the making; and is the greatest problem remaining the legacy of decades of frustration?

NOTES

1. Faith McAllister interview by Lemke-Santangelo, Emeryville, California, 2 May 1991.

2. Gerald Nash, *The American West Transformed* (Bloomington: Indiana University Press, 1985), 26, 66, 67; Robert O. Brown, "Impact of War Worker Migration on the Public School System of Richmond, California, 1940–1945" (Ph.D. diss., Stanford University, 1973), 109–10; U.S. Congress, House Committee on Naval Affairs, Subcommittee, *Investigation of Congested Areas*, 78th Cong., 1st sess., 1943, vol. 1, part 3, 855; Edward E. France, "Some Aspects of the Migration of the Negro to the San Francisco Bay Area since 1940" (Ph.D. diss., University of California, Berkeley, 1962), 24.

3. Wilson Record, *Characteristics of Some Unemployed Negro Shipyard Workers in Oakland, California* (Berkeley: Institute of Governmental Studies, 1947), 30.

4. Nicholas Lemann, "The Origins of the Underclass: Part 1," *Atlantic Monthly,* June 1986, 35; see also idem, *The Promised Land: The Great Black Migration and How It Changed America* (New York: Alfred A. Knopf, 1991); Daniel Patrick Moynihan, *Family and Nation* (San Diego: Harcourt Brace Jovanovich, 1986); Charles Murray, *Losing Ground: American Social Policy, 1950–1980* (New York: Basic Books, 1984); "Liberalism's Paradigm Lost," *Wall Street Journal,* 8 June 1995, A14.

5. See Barry Bluestone and Bennett Harrison, *The Deindustrialization of America* (New York: Basic Books, 1982); Richard Child Hill and Cynthia Negrey, "Deindustrialization and Racial Minorities in the Great Lakes Region, U.S.A.," in *The Reshaping of America: Social Consequences of the Changing Economy*, D. Stanley Eitzen and Maxine Baca Zin, eds. (Englewood Cliffs, NJ: Prentice Hall, 1989); John D. Kasarda, "Urban Change and Minority Opportunities," in *The New Urban Reality*, Paul E. Peterson, ed. (Washington, DC: Brookings Institution, 1985).

6. Robert A. Margo, "Explaining Black White Wage Convergence, 1940–1950," *Industrial and Labor Relations Review* 48 (1995): 470–81.

7. U.S. Department of Labor, Bureau of Labor Statistics, "Postwar Status of Negro Workers in the San Francisco Area," *Monthly Labor Review* (1950): 612–15; U.S. Department of Labor, Bureau of Labor Statistics, "The Labor Force in Durable Goods Manufactured in the San Francisco Bay Area, 1943," *Monthly Labor Review* (1945): 715, 718.

8. U.S. Bureau of the Census, *Census of Population, 1950*, vol. 2, *Characteristics of the Population*, part 5, *California* (Washington, DC: Government Printing Office [G P O], 1952), 262.

9. California Department of Employment, *The Economic Status of Negroes in the San Francisco-Oakland Bay Area* (May 1963), 6–7; City of Oakland, OEDP Committee, *Overall Economic Development Program* (1978), 36, 43–49; U.S. Bureau of the Census, *Census of Population, 1960 California*, vol. 1, *Characteristics of the Population*, part 6 (Washington, DC: G P O, 1961), table 78, 6–374; U.S. Bureau of the Census, *Census of the Population, 1970*, vol. 1, *General Population Characteristics*, part 6, *California*, vol. 1, part 6, sect. 1 (Washington, DC: G P O, 1973), table 93, 6–627.

10. Edward C. Hayes, *Power Structure and Urban Policy: Who Rules in Oakland?* (New York: McGraw, 1955), 66, 69, 70.

11. Industrial Survey Associates, *Oakland to 1980: A Population and Economic Analysis* [condensed report] (San Francisco: Industrial Survey Associates, 1955), 66–69; William L. Nichols II and Earl R. Babbie, *Oakland in Transition: A Summary of the 701 Household Survey* (Berkeley: University of California Survey Research Center, June 1969), 162–63; Oakland, *Overall Economic Development Program*, 31, 43–46; U.S. Bureau of the Census, *Census of Population, 1950*, table 66, 5–262.

12. Oakland, *Overall Economic Development Program*, 35, 39; Oakland, California, City Planning Department, *Oakland's Economy: Background and Projections. A Technical Supplement to the Economic Element* (1976), 13; Industrial Survey Associates, *Oakland to 1980*, 70.

13. Oakland, *Overall Economic Development Program*, 16, 24; U.S. Commission on Civil Rights, *Hearings Held in San Francisco, California, May 1–3, 1967, and in Oakland, California, May 4–6, 1967*, 587, 606; William M. Lunch, "Oakland Revisited: Stability and Change in an American City," 1970 (typescript, Bancroft Library, University of California, Berkeley), 59.

14. Wilson Record, *Minority Groups and Intergroup Relations in the San Francisco Bay Area* (Berkeley: Institute of Governmental Relations, 1963), 22–23.

15. State of California, Senate Select Committee on Housing and Urban Affairs, *Housing Problems in the San Francisco-Oakland Areas*, January 24, 1972, 27–31; Constance Curtis, *Home Free? New Vistas in Regional Housing* (Washington, DC: U.S. Department of Housing and Urban Development, 1974), 17–18; David E. Dowall, *Land Conversion and Regulation in the San Francisco Bay Area* (Berkeley: University of California Press, 1984), 17, 37.

16. Bennett M. Beyer, *Working-Class Suburb: A Study of Auto Workers in Suburbia* (Berkeley: University of California Press, 1968), ix, xi.

17. Eunice and George Grier, *Case Studies in Racially Mixed Housing: Sunnyhills, Milpitas, California* (Washington, DC: Center of Metropolitan Studies, 1962), 5–6, 21.

18. Oakland, City Planning Department, Transportation Division, *People, Jobs, and Transportation* (December 1969), 94–95; Oakland, *Overall Development Plan*, 35, 39.

19. U.S. Commission on Civil Rights, *Hearings*, 599, 600–601; Marilynn Johnson, *The Second Gold Rush: Oakland and the East Bay in World War II* (Berkeley: University of California Press, 1993), 211–12.

20. U.S. Commission on Civil Rights, *Hearings*, 443, 461–62.

21. Alan M. Ahart, "An Economic and Demographic Study of Oakland, California, 1960–1966 with Comparisons to Other Cities," 4 June 1970 (typescript, Institute for Governmental Studies, University of California, Berkeley), 26; Oakland, *Overall Economic Development Program*, 49.

22. *Oakland Tribune*, 28 December 1961; 16 February 1962; "Planning Swamps a City: $87 Million in Government Money Has Poured in and Oakland Still Has Slum Trouble," *Washington Post*, 7 August 1966.

23. *Oakland Tribune*, 15 May 1963.

24. Oakland, *People, Jobs, and Transportation*, 6; Judith V. May, "Politics of Growth versus the Politics of Redistribution: Negotiations over the Model Cities Program in Oakland," 24 March 1970 (typescript, Institute of Governmental Studies, University of California, Berkeley), 19.

25. U.S. Commission on Civil Rights, *Hearings*, 461–62; California Depart-

ment of Employment, *The Economic Status of Negroes*, H, J; Oakland, *Overall Economic Development Program*, 37, 42, 44; Lunch, "Oakland Revisited," 59; Jeffrey L. Pressman and Aaron Wildavsky, *Implementation: How Great Expectations in Washington Are Dashed in Oakland*, 3d ed. (Berkeley: University of California Press, 1984), 14.

26. Gene Bernardi, *Evaluation Analysis of the Council of Social Planning's Neighborhood Organization Program* (Oakland: City of Oakland Department of Human Resources, 1966), 1–7; Amory Bradford, *Oakland's Not for Burning* (New York: David McKay Company, 1968), 174–75, 204–5; Daniel P. Moynihan, *Maximum Feasible Misunderstanding: Community Action in the War on Poverty* (New York: Free Press, 1969), 128–66, quote on 131; Robert D. Plotnick and Felicia Skidmore, *Progress against Poverty: A Review of the 1964–1974 Decade* (New York: Academic Press, 1975), 25.

27. May, "Politics of Growth versus the Politics of Redistribution," 6–19.

28. Donald K. Tamaki, "Oakland Politics and Powerless Pressure Groups," 1969 (typescript, Institute for Governmental Studies, University of California, Berkeley), 141.

29. Oakland, *Overall Economic Development Program*, 35, 49–50, 100.

30. "Blue-Collar Blues: Hanging on to Alameda County's Heavy Industry," *East Bay Express*, 18 July 1980.

31. Laura J. Henze, Edward Kirshner, and Linda Lillow, *An Income and Capital Flow Study of East Oakland* (Charles Stuart Mott Foundation, 30 November 1979), 20; Philip Shapira, "The Crumbling of Smokestack California: A Case Study in Industrial Restructuring and the Reorganization of Work" (Berkeley: University of California Institute of Urban and Regional Development, Working Paper No. 437, November 1984), 20; idem, "Industrial Restructuring and Worker Transition in California Manufacturing" (Berkeley: University of California Institute of Urban and Regional Planning, Working Paper No. 425, January 1987), 33, 52, 56–57; Ahart, "An Economic and Demographic Study of Oakland," 25; Molders Local 164 and OPEU Local 29, flyer (n.d., in possession of author).

32. Shapira, "Crumbling of Smokestack California," 2.

33. Shapira, "Industrial Restructuring," 52. See also Bluestone and Harrison, *Deindustrialization of America*; Hill and Negrey, "Deindustrialization and Racial Minorities in the Great Lakes Region, U.S.A."; Kasarda, "Urban Change and Minority Opportunities."

34. Stephen Raphael, "Inter- and Intraethnic Comparisons of the Central City-Suburban Youth Employment Differential: Evidence from the Oakland Metropolitan Area," *Industrial and Labor Relations Review* 51 (1998): 508–9.

35. *Oakland Tribune,* 12 December 1995.

36. Maury B. Gittleman and David R. Howell, "Changes in the Structure and Quality of Jobs in the United States: Effects by Race and Gender, 1973–1990," *Industrial and Labor Relations Review* 48 (1995): 420–40; State of California, Employment Development, *California Labor Market Bulletin, Statistical Supplement* (January 1991, June 1993, September 1994); "Oakland Base on Hit List," *Oakland Tribune,* 25 February 1995; "Military Base Closings Leave Bay Area with Little to Lose," *Oakland Tribune,* 26 February 1995; "One Last Appeal to Base Closure Panel," *San Francisco Examiner,* 15 June 1995.

37. Gretchen Lemke-Santangelo, *Abiding Courage: African American Migrant Women and the East Bay Community* (Chapel Hill: University of North Carolina Press, 1995), 4–5, 33–47, 110–11.

38. Evelio Grillo, "D. G. Gibson: A Black Who Led the People and Built the Democratic Party in the East Bay," in *Experiment and Change in Berkeley: Essays on City Politics 1950–1975,* Harriet Nathan and Stanley Scott, eds. (Berkeley: Institute of Governmental Studies, University of California, 1978), 7.

39. Jessica Mitford, *A Fine Old Conflict* (New York: Alfred A. Knopf, 1977), 106, 133.

40. Lawrence P. Crouchett, Lonnie G. Bunch III, and Martha Kendall Winnacker, *Visions toward Tomorrow: The History of the East Bay Afro-American Community, 1852–1977* (Oakland: Northern California Center for Afro-American History and Life, 1989), 37, 39, 55; NAACP West Coast Region Records, 1946–1970, carton 25, monthly reports: 1946, 1951, 1955, annual reports: 1951, 1952, 1953, memorandum to Gloster Current, director of branches, from Franklin Williams, secretary of council, 23 May 1995, Bancroft Library, University of California, Berkeley; Delores Nason McBroome, *Parallel Communities: African Americans in California's East Bay, 1850–1963* (New York: Garland, 1993), 139–47, 151–52.

41. Lemke-Santangelo, *Abiding Courage,* 155–62.

42. May, "Politics of Growth versus the Politics of Redistribution," 15–16; Hayes, *Power Structure and Urban Policy,* 151–56.

43. "Mayor Asks for Fair Hiring by BART," *Oakland Tribune,* 6 June 1966; "BART to Pay Moving Costs," *Oakland Tribune,* 21 July 1966; "A Protest March on BART Jobs," *San Francisco Chronicle,* 6 June 1966.

44. Hugh Pearson, *The Shadow of the Panther: Huey Newton and the Price of Black Power in America* (Reading, MA: Addison-Wesley, 1994), 108–9; May, "Politics of Growth versus the Politics of Redistribution," 6.

45. City of Oakland, Department of Human Resources, *Evaluation and Analy-*

sis of the Council of Social Planning's Neighborhood Organizations Program (1966), 1–7; Hayes, *Power Structure and Urban Policy*, 123–25, 155.

46. Rod Bush, "Oakland: Grassroots Organizing against Reagan," in *The New Black Vote: Politics and Power in Four American Cities*, Rod Bush, ed. (San Francisco: Synthesis Publications, 1984), 323–25.

47. Anatole Shaffer, "Welfare Rights Organization: A Case in Point," in *Richmond Community Development Demonstration Project. The Welfare Rights Organization: A Case in Point* (Walnut Creek: Contra Costa Council of Community Services, 1967), 24–25.

48. Hayes, *Power Structure and Urban Policy*, 136–38.

49. Louise Morrison, "Why the Poor Need Welfare Rights," in *Richmond Community Development Demonstration Project,* 52–55.

50. Bush, "Oakland: Grassroots Organizing against Reagan," 323–25; Plant Closures Project and Coalition for Economic Justice File, miscellaneous flyers and memos (in possession of author).

51. Bruce Allen, "In the Driver's Seat: Assemblymember Barbara Lee on How to Convert California," *Positive Alternatives* 4 (1994): 8–9; idem, "The Good, the Bad, and the Ugly: A Look at Base Conversion Efforts since 1989," *Positive Alternatives* 4 (1994): 8–9; Bush, "Oakland: Grassroots Organizing against Reagan," 336–41.

52. *NCAP News*, December 1995.

53. See, for example, Paul Chavez, "Watts Still Mired in Poverty," *Associated Press*, 3 November 1999; Robert J. Samuelson, "The Culture of Poverty," *Washington Post*, 30 April 1997; William Bennett, "A Welfare Test," *Washington Post*, 18 August 1996; Charles Murray, *The Underclass Revisited*, AEI Studies in Social Welfare Policy, 1999.

54. See, for example, Harry J. Holzer, "The Spatial Mismatch Hypothesis: What Has the Evidence Shown?" *Urban Studies* 28 (1991): 105–22; John F. Kain, "The Spatial Mismatch Hypothesis: Three Decades Later," *Housing Policy Debates* 3 (1993): 371–460; Claudia Coulton, Julian Chow, Edward Wang, and Marilyn Su, "Geographic Concentration of Affluence and Poverty in 100 Metropolitan Areas, 1990" (Cleveland: Center for Urban Poverty and Social Change, Mandel School of Applied Social Sciences, Case Western Reserve University, 1990); Mark Hughes and Julie Sternberg, *The New Metropolitan Reality: Where the Rubber Meets the Road in Antipoverty Policy* (Washington, DC: Public Finance and Housing Center, the Urban Institute, December 1992); Matangulizi Sanyika and James Head, "Communities at Risk: Regional Transportation Issues in the Bay Area: The Concerns of

Communities of Color and Low-Income Neighborhoods," San Francisco National Economic Development and Law Center Issue Brief No. 6, August 1990; Martha Alt, "Does Access to Jobs Affect Employment Rates and Incomes of Inner-City Residents?" Earth Island Institute/Urban Habitat Program, December 1991.

55. *East Bay Express*, 11 October 1985, 18.

Black Fire

"Riot" and "Revolt" in Los Angeles, 1965 and 1992

GERALD HORNE

L os Angeles is notorious as the site of two of the most serious civil disturbances to rock the United States in the twentieth century. In 1965 and 1992, the city went up in flames in the wake of wrenching cases involving police brutality. Whether one regards these conflagrations as "riots" or "revolts," both episodes reveal much about California's largest city. They also help explain some of the most disturbing conditions associated with African American communities in California and nationwide—gangs, drugs, crime, and the growth of an "underclass." That these phenomena became widely publicized between 1965 and 1992 is not coincidental, for they and the uprisings become linked when the root causes of the two "riots" are examined.

The earlier uprising was a shock to most Californians, not only because it arose out of a background of progress on the part of African Americans but especially because of its duration and intensity. At least 34 people died during the civil unrest of August 1965, almost all of whom were African American; 1,000 more were injured, and 4,000 were arrested. The conflict lasted for almost an entire week. Property damage was estimated at $200 million in the 46.5-square-mile zone of conflict (an area larger than Manhattan or San Francisco), where approximately 35,000 adults "active as rioters" and 72,000 "close spectators" swarmed. On hand to oppose them were 16,000 National Guard troops, Los Angeles Police Department (L A P D) and California Highway Patrol (C H P) officers, and other law enforcers; fewer personnel were used by the U.S. government that same year to subdue Santo Domingo.[1]

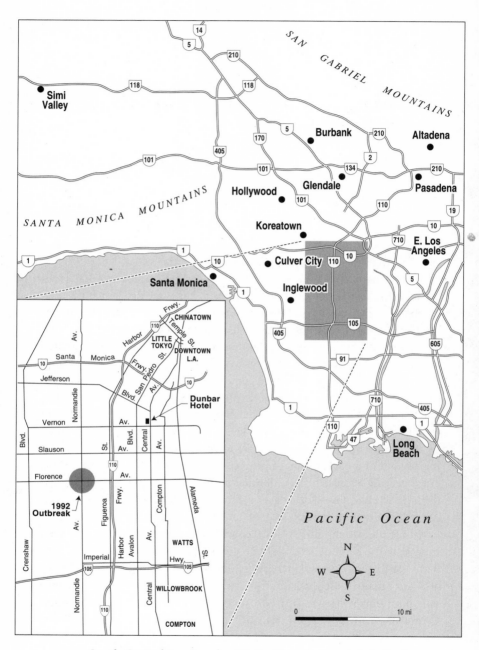

MAP 5. South Central Los Angeles, Watts, Compton, and their Environs

What was the immediate cause of this cataclysm? Early in the evening of 11 August 1965, Marquette Frye, an African American, and his brother were stopped by the CHP in south Los Angeles. Prior to being stopped, they had been drinking vodka and orange juice. It had been extremely hot in the city. The CHP was about to let them go when another patrol car arrived containing less forgiving officers. Impolite words were exchanged, attracting a crowd. The Fryes' mother, who lived nearby, arrived, upset with her sons and not too happy with the authorities who had detained them.

As the crowd grew, so did the panic of the authorities. They used force to place handcuffs on Mrs. Frye, and her screams did not calm the crowd. Marquette Frye apparently was hit in the head, and a shotgun was placed at his temple. The Fryes, mother and sons, were tossed into an officer's car. Further inflaming the crowd was the rumor that an African American woman, Joyce Gaines—who was believed to be pregnant (she was not; she simply had on a smock)—had been attacked by the police. Soon rocks, bottles, and sticks were tossed at the officers as they fled in their cars. From this spark grew a major conflagration that gripped the city for almost a week.

The violence escalated steadily for three nights. The first evening, Wednesday, it was confined to rock and bottle throwing at police and attacks on some white motorists in parts of Watts. Thursday brought the looting and burning of white-owned stores over a wider area. The selection of stores believed to be charging excessive prices or selling inferior goods gave rise to the misimpression that the uprising was a preplanned "conspiracy." The second night also produced fatalities, as snipers took occasional shots at law enforcement and fire personnel and police retaliated by shooting participants in the uprising. By Friday, the violence had spread to the edge of downtown Los Angeles. Only the deployment of several thousand National Guard troops, starting late Friday night, gradually lessened the violence and finally ended the uprising by the following Tuesday.[2]

What could have caused such anger to boil over? Police brutality was viewed as the immediate reason. For decades, the LAPD had built a well-deserved reputation for brutality, particularly against African Americans. But this was not the only factor. In fact, both in 1965 and 1992 the causes behind the eruptions were eerily similar: reduced hope and rising poverty generated by massive unemployment and the flight of jobs from the city and the decline of labor organizations that could have arrested this devolution. Indeed, the patterns that had been set when African Americans first began to migrate to Los Angeles in large numbers during World War II were still reverberating in the 1990s.

The events of 1965 have been characterized as a "riot of hope" and those of 1992 as a "riot of hopelessness," but that is too facile an interpretation. Those who charged into the streets on both occasions were prompted by the immediate prod of police misconduct; what compelled them to cross the line of legality was a sense of historic injustice. On both occasions, there was "hope" that their actions would jolt the authorities into reform, leavened by "hopelessness" that the "system" would not yield. It would be a mistake to view the distant events of 1965 with rose-colored glasses or assess more skeptically the more recent events of 1992. Sadly, the passage of time from 1965 to 1992 starkly demonstrated that little had changed for African Americans in South Central Los Angeles.

In 1992, three intense days of burning, looting, and violence resulted in 58 deaths, 2,500 injuries, 16,000 arrests, and nearly $1 billion in property damage and loss. This time it required approximately 20,000 LAPD and CHP officers, National Guard troops, and members of seven related military forces to confront those who were rioting and rebelling in the streets. Unlike 1965, this time a plurality, 37 percent, of those arrested was Latino (475 of whom were "illegal aliens" and subsequently deported), and only 30 percent were African American. Also, a much higher percentage of European Americans were arrested in 1992. The fire this time swept well beyond south Los Angeles into Hollywood, the West Side, the San Fernando Valley, and the edge of Beverly Hills.3

Police brutality was again the proximate cause of unrest. On 3 March 1991, motorist Rodney King was apprehended by LAPD and CHP officers after a high-speed chase. After forcing King to leave his car, the police fiercely beat the African American. Unfortunately for the officers involved, the beating was captured on videotape by George Holliday, who was trying out his new camera in a nearby apartment. When this tape was broadcast on television, locally and then nationally, yet another cause célèbre erupted. The officers on this occasion were tried in criminal court for their acts. A defense motion, however, forced removal of the trial from the city of Los Angeles to Simi Valley, a mostly white conservative suburb where a number of LAPD officers lived. Consequently, a jury with no blacks was selected. When the officers were acquitted in April 1992, Los Angeles exploded.4

As in 1965, whites were assaulted at random. The most celebrated case involved a truck driver, Reginald Denny, who was unfortunate enough to be driving through south Los Angeles at the wrong time. A group of black youths pounced on him at the intersection of Florence and Normandy, dragged him from the cab, and flailed away, symbolically and ritualistically avenging King's beating, as a helicopter with a camera broadcast the ugly scene live to a stunned national television audience. Latinos, Asian Americans, and others who did not resemble African Americans were also assaulted. Unlike 1965, lighter-skinned African Americans in south Los Angeles apparently were not targeted in 1992.5

Why has Los Angeles been the site for such calamity? Why have race relations there been racked with such tension? Part of the answer lies in the tangled history of that sprawling metropolis, for Los Angeles does not only contain the bipolar "black-white" conflict that characterizes much of the nation, it also has a more complicated racial and ethnic pattern that helps to give its race relations a distinctive coloration.

In 1910, there were an estimated 7,599 African Americans in Los Angeles; by 1940, this figure had risen to 63,774, and by 1944, to 118,888. In Watts, an area of south Los Angeles where many of these migrants decamped, the black population doubled in size between 1940 and 1946. During the 1940s, California received the largest decennial population increase of any state in the nation's history. Such sustained population growth inevitably induced a crisis of rapid change and disorientation; neighborhoods appeared overrun, local institutions seemed besieged. The venues where the races crossed paths became flashpoints. Even before 1965 and 1992, Los Angeles had been marred by tense confrontations between and among peoples of various races and ethnic groups.6

But this perception of being overrun also affected relations among blacks themselves. As the Los Angeles African American community expanded, it became increasingly divided. The report of the McCone Commission in 1965 noted that there were "two separate and distinct Negro populations: one east of the Harbor Freeway which is quite 'disadvantaged' and the other west of the Harbor Freeway" that was not. These areas became known as South Central and the West Side, respectively. The differences in socioeconomic condition were so heightened that South Central in general and Watts in particular had for years been the main "port of entry" of black migrants from the rural South into a large city environment.7

This last characteristic contributed to worsening conditions and attitudes in Watts in two ways. One was as a cause of the deterioration of that area. As two of its high school students reported a year before the uprising, migrants regarded Watts as "the bottom of the social and economic ladder" and a place to leave. Therefore, few took pride in or care of their community, and that became a root of many of its social problems. Association with deteriorating conditions also spawned negative stereotypes of its residents. Eldridge Cleaver, who grew up in Los Angeles in the 1950s, later recalled bitterly that the very term "Watts" had become an epithet "the same way as city boys used 'country' as a term of derision. To deride one as a 'lame' who did not know what was happening. . . . [T]he 'in-crowd' of the time from L.A. would bring a cat down by saying that he had just left Watts." This treadmill of poor self-respect and external derision did much to produce the angry mood of black youth in Watts in 1965.[8]

There were also color tensions among black Angelenos. A significant percentage of those migrating to Los Angeles hailed from Louisiana. The Pelican State had a long history of maintaining a kind of triracial polarity that featured a light-skinned group—*gens de couleur*, at times called "creoles of color"—that was a mixture of African and European and, sometimes, Indian ancestry. There was evidence to suggest that employers in Los Angeles—who were mostly white—favored those who were lighter skinned over those who were dark, which helped to stir resentments. In 1965, not only were whites randomly assaulted but so were some lighter-skinned blacks, reflecting tensions that existed from long before.[9]

African Americans brought with them to Los Angeles the collective memory of what had befallen them in the southern and southwestern states they had left behind. Louisiana was the site in 1811 of the nation's largest slave insurrection. After the Civil War, two of the most horrendous acts of racist violence during that era—the Colfax massacre of 1872 and the murder of dozens of striking sugar workers in Thibodaux in 1887—took place in the state. The Colfax massacre occurred on Easter Sunday 1873, when freedmen who had been entrenched in the town of Colfax resisted the reimposition of white rule and were overwhelmed and slaughtered by local whites. Two hundred eighty blacks died, the bloodiest single instance of racial carnage in the Reconstruction Era. Estimates also suggest that lynching claimed 355 black lives in Louisiana between 1882 and 1952, second only to Mississippi as a proportion of the total population.[10]

Blacks also migrated to Los Angeles from Texas, which had a similar pattern of violence—a pattern that continued well into the twentieth century. As Lorraine Adams and Dan Malone put it, "Texas police have been investi-

gated and prosecuted more frequently for beatings, torture, coerced confessions, rapes, and needless assaults than police in any other state." Some
African Americans also moved to Los Angeles with memories of profound
antiblack episodes in other places, such as the 1919 events at Elaine, Arkansas, where protesting sharecroppers were executed, and the 1921 Tulsa,
Oklahoma, riot, when the city's black community was bombed by airplanes.
Both of those episodes caused significant migration west.[11]

Yet the questions remain: Why has Los Angeles been the scene of such
bitter, racially marked unrest? And though their role in the troubles was not
exclusive in 1992, why have African Americans particularly been at the center of these events?

On the one hand, Los Angeles has been viewed as a racial paradise by
African Americans. Since World War II, it has been the center of one of the
nation's most vibrant economies; many of its black residents lived in detached, single-family homes that gave even poor neighborhoods an aura of
middle-class status. Historically, the presence of other targets of bigotry—
American Indians, Mexican and Asian Americans—meant that the hatred
that was directed almost exclusively at blacks in most parts of the nation
would be dispersed among others in Los Angeles. These groups were major
recipients of calcified bias in the pre-World War II era. When the Ku Klux
Klan arose in Southern California in the 1920s, for example, its major targets were those of Asian and Mexican ancestry. At that point, Japanese
Americans in Los Angeles were facing the sort of conflict that African Americans elsewhere felt was their sole province. Immigrants from Japan and
their American-born descendants faced housing discrimination and violence when they sought to move into previously all-white neighborhoods. A
Japanese American businessman was warned by local whites not to take up
residence in another area. When he moved there anyway, his neighbors
posted handbills proclaiming the area off-limits to those of Japanese ancestry and threw stones at the man's home until he moved. In one Los Angeles
suburb, a Japanese American who bought a home fled after local police refused to aid him when whites burned down the house. Local authorities in
Boyle Heights, Hollywood, Long Beach, Pasadena, and elsewhere also tolerated similar attacks against Japanese Americans.[12]

Later, during World War II, when persons of Japanese ancestry all along
the West Coast were expropriated and interned, anti-Japanese sentiment in
Los Angeles appeared to have a notably virulent character. According to

John Modell, "One out of three people in Southern California wished to see the Nisei placed in concentration camps, as compared with only one out of seven elsewhere on the Coast."[13]

There were even earlier precedents. The scholar Ralph Guzman, testifying before the panel investigating the events of August 1965, observed that by 1898 California had a higher incidence of unsolved homicides than all of the other states in the Union put together and that the Los Angeles area had a higher incidence than the rest of the state. A disproportionate percentage of those slayings involved victims who were American Indian, Asian American, and Mexican American. Guzman also suggested that between 1850 and 1870, the City of Angels was the "wildest, toughest, hell-for-leather town west of the Rockies." Los Angeles was a town full of "drifters, thieves, and con men, who, in addition to everything else, were for the most part racist and given to cruel outbursts of violence." This violence exploded in 1871 in what might have been the first "race riot" in Los Angeles's history, when whites attacked the city's Chinese.[14]

But this historical pattern had been greatly altered by 1965 as African Americans eclipsed the combined population of Asians and became much more conspicuous, if not more numerous, than the Mexican element. Another reality of prejudice in the United States became evident: it was coded by color, and those who were the darkest were furthest down the economic and social ladder. The anger of African Americans who had believed California was a promised land grew exponentially upon discovering that instead of a racial paradise, they were living in an area where the carriers of prejudice were not only those of European ancestry.

Thus, long before 1965, Los Angeles had a reputation as a city marked by violence perpetrated upon various racial and cultural groups. The period from 1965 to 1992 marks both a continuation of historical trends of violence and a divergence in that during those years African Americans had stepped forward to occupy center stage. This "diversified" racism was not necessarily a boon for blacks. There were now many potential targets for prejudice and many different carriers of bias. This combined with antiblack animus to create a uniquely virulent form that I have called "compounded racism."[15]

The antilabor bias of Los Angeles's political and economic elite also fostered conditions that led to the racial confrontations of 1965 and 1992. The repression of organized labor provided an opportunity for the refinement of police brutality methods, as evidenced in the city police's notorious "Red Squad." The undermining of the city's trade union movement from the beginning of the twentieth century to the 1950s also prevented working-class solidarity across racial lines, isolating African Americans from potential allies in the early 1960s.

Los Angeles has had a justifiable reputation as an antiunion bastion, particularly when compared to San Francisco and Seattle. The turning point for labor in Los Angeles came in 1910 during the McNamara case, when trade unionists were charged with bombing the headquarters of the *Los Angeles Times*, the historic voice of antiunionism in the city.[16] These antilabor trends accelerated after 1945 and the onset of the Red Scare, when unions with reputations for antiracism were branded "Communist." When working-class people of different races have been unable to unite in unions, often it has left them frozen in hostility, staring across a racial divide.[17]

As African American migration to Los Angeles accelerated during the 1940s in response to the needs of the defense industry, blacks found that those most willing to embrace them were themselves under attack. John Howard Lawson, for example, was a cofounder and the first president of the Screen Writers Guild and, in films like *Sahara* (1943), penned antiracist lines that resonate even today. Charlotta Bass, publisher of the *California Eagle*, the city's leading black newspaper, asked Lawson to join her board of directors as a testament to his antiracist credentials.[18] Shortly thereafter, however, Lawson and other progressive trade unionists in the film industry—some of whom were members of the Communist Party—were ousted from influence in the wake of searing labor conflict fomented by a jurisdictional dispute between the Conference of Studio Unions (CSU) and the gangster-ridden International Alliance of Theater Stage Employees (IATSE). Bass, who was also an activist, went on to play a leading role in the Progressive Party, which challenged the consensus on the Cold War, the Red Scare, and antiunionism. In 1950, she ran for Congress and lost. In 1952, she ran for vice president of the United States, again as a Progressive, and lost. Her electoral defeats, often seen as emblematic of the weakness of the Progressive Party, also reveal the decline of antiracist unions and the loss of influence of activists who stood firm against racism.

Certainly, before the onset of the Red Scare there was substantial evidence of cooperation across racial and ethnic lines. This took place most dramatically in the unions of autoworkers, packinghouse workers and furniture workers. The trend was not just evident in Los Angeles. After World War II, Oakland was hit with a general strike and then the seizure of city government by a labor-black coalition.[19] The fading presence of these unions, which in large part was the result of industry moving out of South Central Los Angeles to suburban locations, left the area without resources to combat the growing economic crisis. Thus, when deindustrialization accelerated and employment opportunities fell in south Los Angeles, this catastrophic development was not met with an effectively organized response. Indeed, deindustrialization was a factor in eroding the basis for unions themselves. This loss had particular impact in 1965 and 1992. The crushing of organized labor as race conflict unfolded was symptomatic of developments that transformed Los Angeles in the decades following 1965.

Black gangs in south Los Angeles played no small role in the civil unrest of 1965 and 1992. Observers of the 1965 uprising attributed the rapid spread of violence and the obvious choices of businesses to loot and burn to groups of youth networking in places like Will Rogers Park on 103rd Street in Watts.[20] More organized gangs soon followed, and they have filled a socioeconomic vacuum left by the decline of unions and a psychological and "caring" void left by the erosion of family structure. Why have gangs proliferated in Los Angeles? Why have the "Crips" and "Bloods"—products of Southern California—come to symbolize the black gang phenomenon and engender imitators across the nation?

Léon Bing has suggested that the gang phenomenon was sparked by Mexican American *pachuchos* who "initiated the emblematic tattoos, the signing with hands, the writing of legends on walls." The oldest street gang in Los Angeles, Bing argues, dates back to the 1930s and is Chicano. Others have maintained that gangs stemmed from the arrival of thousands of immigrants from Mexico, in the aftermath of problems gripping that country between 1910 and the end of World War I. These networks were a mechanism by which chaos and bigotry in an alien environment could be confronted. Black gangs, according to Bing, came later, "in the late fifties, early sixties, with the black social clubs—young guys who . . . banded together for camaraderie and, to a certain extent, for protection."[21]

As African Americans arrived in Los Angeles, they encountered a rigid residential segregation that made it dangerous to venture out of the neighborhoods to which they were assigned. Thus, the name of one of the early black gangs—the Slausons—symbolized African American resolve to cross this central artery of the city. Gangs in many ways are an organic response to the political economy.[22] By 1965, basic industries and unions were fleeing from south Los Angeles, signaling a similar major transformation in capitalistic activity, while hypersegregation restricted blacks to designated areas.

At this stage, some young African American males turned to organized criminal activity, which marked a refusal to conform to the established order.

Gangs and gangsters, with their heightened sense of masculinity and machismo, had a special appeal to many young African Americans. For some time, blacks had been referred to as the "female of the races," a people who allowed themselves to be enslaved and subordinated. The rise in black consciousness in the 1960s did not just involve an acceleration of racial awareness; it also reflected a change in gender consciousness as African American men redefined themselves in an assertive fashion. Moreover, the ascendancy of black nationalism, as seen in the growth of the Nation of Islam in South Central Los Angeles, took place alongside rising gangsterism and a declining working-class movement, influencing markedly this new iteration of masculinity.[23]

Though gangs were active in 1965 and 1992, by the latter date their environment had changed markedly. Deindustrialization—the flight of industry—which had been gathering steam by 1965 was now in full force. Los Angeles, which had been a leading auto, steel, and tire center, by 1992 no longer held this lofty position. As jobs left the city, along with them went the wherewithal necessary to support a family.[24] In 1965, gang members and those who emulated them had dealt with the despair flowing from unemployment and racism by drinking alcohol and smoking marijuana. By 1992, Los Angeles had been hit with an epidemic of crack cocaine abuse. Almost instantly addictive, this drug guaranteed a growing market of consumers, including those who had considered use a one-time experiment. Crack addicts, crack babies, devastated neighborhoods, and gangsters armed with automatic weapons were the direct result of this epidemic.[25]

If gangs helped to fill the vacuum left by the decline of unions, Black Power helped to fill that resulting from the decline in working-class ideology. When unions that united people across racial and ethnic lines could no longer fill their role effectively, inevitably the idea took root that African Americans could no longer rely on others but had to depend upon themselves. Thus arose Black Power, a movement promoting African American assertiveness in the social, political, and economic spheres. Between the decline of unions and hopes for a liberal/left-black coalition in the 1940s and the rise of black nationalism in the 1960s was an interlude when many African Americans thought political activism within the Democratic Party might fulfill their needs. But few of the civil rights acts passed in the early 1960s addressed the needs of the inner city. Confidence in liberals and the Democratic Party, and ultimately in whites in general, also was badly eroded by two events in mid-1964. One was the Democratic Party convention held in Atlantic City, New Jersey, which nominated Lyndon B. Johnson for president. African Americans, in particular, were bitterly disappointed when an all-white delegation representing the regular party in Mississippi was seated instead of the racially integrated Mississippi Freedom Democratic Party delegation. The national Democratic Party's action undermined the notion among many black activists that interracial cooperation was feasible.[26]

That same year, California endured a bruising battle over Proposition 14, which essentially ratified the idea that segregated housing should be allowed under the laws of the state. African Americans, who had been facing major difficulty in moving from south Los Angeles to other areas, viewed this measure as designed to insure that their choices in housing would be limited, amplifying the idea that interracial cooperation was not worthy of pursuit.[27]

Proposition 14 was supported by a large majority of California's white voters and was widely seen by African Americans as reflecting their hostile attitudes. Rather than blame all whites, however, many blacks attributed that measure to the growth of right-wing movements in the early 1960s, particularly in Southern California. Most noted was the John Birch Society, whose general suspicion of government power translated into blanket opposition to civil rights laws and a special hatred of the Warren Court. Some earlier movements in California characterized by racism and xenophobia had been counterbalanced by liberal or left-wing movements. The Red Scare of the late 1940s and early 1950s, however, had eroded the left and lessened the militancy of many liberals, giving rise to an array of "radical right" groups in the early 1960s, including the Christian Anti-Communist Crusade and the Minutemen, whose racially insensitive rhetoric continued to upset African Americans long after their power had declined.[28]

In this atmosphere, it was virtually inevitable that the idea of Black Power would sink roots in African American Los Angeles. The Nation of Islam had arrived in the city in the 1930s but, strikingly, did not achieve significant influence until the 1960s. The Black Panther Party, which unlike the Nation of Islam did not demonize whites, saw itself as pushing for African American self-determination, which was a constituent element of the Black Power movement. The Student Non-Violent Coordinating Committee (SNCC), which was headquartered in the South, had members and influence in Los Angeles. After the debacle in Atlantic City and the difficulties faced by anti-Jim Crow advocates in Selma, Alabama, in 1965, the Los Angeles arm of the organization became a harbinger of the Black Power movement that was enunciated formally by sNCC leader Stokely Carmichael in rural Mississippi in 1966. Cultural nationalism, in particular an emphasis on reverting to West African names, dress, and customs, was another manifestation of Black Power. Symbolized by the figure of Maulana Ron Karenga, the movement was born in Los Angeles immediately following the Watts revolt.[29]

The Watts uprising of 1965 can be seen as a watershed in the evolution of black America. It marked a shift toward nationalism and away from integration, toward racial conservatism and away from liberalism. Watts 1965 signaled the retreat of the passive nonviolent resister as a symbol of the movement for racial equality and the commencement of the image of the marauding "Negro" angrily confronting police. After the flames of August 1965 came the flames of Newark and Detroit in 1967 and eruptions in scores of cities in 1968 after the murder of Dr. Martin Luther King Jr. The 1960s have acquired a reputation as a decade of turbulence; this can be attributed directly to trends initiated in Los Angeles in 1965. Slogans calling for Black Power and cries for black nationalism were still being heard in South Central Los Angeles in 1992.

Though the most aggressive advocates of Black Power would not have claimed him as part of their legacy, the election of Tom Bradley, the first African American mayor of Los Angeles, could be viewed as an expression of this increased assertiveness. In 1965, this former police officer served on the city council and distinguished himself with his sharp assault on the excesses of the LAPD. Bradley first ran for mayor in 1969, won the office four years later and remained Los Angeles's chief executive until 1993.[30]

Ironically, the revolt of 1965 also boosted the political career of Ronald Reagan. He had served as president of the Screen Actors Guild from 1947 to 1952 and again during 1959 to 1960. Though he had been a liberal during World War II, he moved steadily to the right. By the time he was elected governor of California in 1966, Reagan had become a symbol of conservative forces in the state. His winning message that year promised that another black revolt would not occur during his tenure. Ronald Reagan's campaign and period in office came to symbolize a white backlash against black assertiveness. This backlash proved a powerful influence on electoral politics in the United States in the decades following 1965, simultaneously aiding an increasingly conservative Republican Party and undermining the Democratic Party, which had come to be identified closely with African Americans. These two forces—Black Power and white backlash—became part of the lasting legacy of the events of August 1965.[31]

Los Angeles was a city renowned for a police department that routinely administered brutal force. Gunnar Myrdal argued that brutality by police officers was an essential component of white supremacy. The system of race relations in the United States demanded that "even minor transgressions of caste etiquette should be punished," and with the decline of lynching and private violence generally as acceptable tools of social control, the public sector stepped forward to fill the breach in the form of police brutality.[32] The LAPD took to this task with a macabre relish; the social explosions that took place in Los Angeles in 1965 and 1992 came as a direct result of this brutality. As the most visible manifestation of state power and as a living symbol of the sorry state of race relations, it was inevitable that the police department would be at the center of the city's racial conflict. Likewise, it was virtually inevitable that as organizations that bridged the racial divide declined, black gangs, and those under their influence such as the Nation of Islam and the Black Panther Party, would arise to confront the LAPD.

Why has the LAPD earned such a reputation for brutality? Attorney Stephen Yagman has stated that brutality may have been worse in Los Angeles because officers were compensating for the fact that the city, so large and sprawling, had a comparatively low ratio of police to citizens. In the early 1990s, there were approximately 8,000 officers in the LAPD, compared to 27,000 in the New York Police Department, though the area covered in Los Angeles was much larger than that of New York City. Brutality in Los Angeles was a form of draconian deterrence, intended to make potential lawbreakers think twice before risking arrest.[33]

Police brutality in Los Angeles has been a complaint of minorities since before World War II, but African Americans bore the brunt of it from the time of the Watts uprising to the Rodney King events. During this period, the LAPD viewed itself as more akin to Marines than social workers. This paramilitary tendency was expressed most forcefully in poor black neighborhoods, where it was felt that there was less political clout to counter LAPD rampages. William Parker, police chief from 1950 to 1965, was a prototype of the LAPD leader. He earned his military spurs during World War II, boasted about helping to "plan the invasion of France," and bragged that he was "one of 1500 men in the theater that were privileged to read all of the invasion plans." Parker helped train police in post-Nazi Germany, and the hostility with which he approached this defeated nation was mirrored when he confronted south Los Angeles.34

The virulence of racism in Los Angeles, a crude mixture of the Wild West and the Old South, reached its zenith in the L A P D. Mike Rothmiller, a white former officer, has drawn an ugly portrait of antiblack animus in the department over the past few decades: "Racism was expected, part of the group persona. Shrink from it and you were an odd duck, perhaps a pink one . . . . [R]ace hatred was . . . a dominating force." Officers told lies in arrest reports on routine felony cases. Some officers randomly and arbitrarily beat and tortured black men, even those who were not suspected of anything: "Bending fingers back, twisting ears, tightening handcuffs into medieval torture devices, slamming the victim's head into the door while placing him in a vehicle" were some of their techniques. "Sometimes they dangled suspects by their ankles from the edge of buildings." Overwhelmingly, police illegalities were perpetrated against black men, not only because they were perceived to be least able to protest effectively but also because such misdeeds were part of the identity—the group persona—constructed by the mostly white L A P D.35

Consistent with its role as inheritor of the social control function of the lynch mob, the L A P D operated in south Los Angeles like an occupying army. From Parker to Chief Daryl Gates, the department pioneered in introducing quasimilitary tactics into the area, including whirring helicopters, Special Weapons And Tactics (SWAT) teams, and choke holds that at times killed as they restrained. From 1965 to 1992, the victims of such harsh tactics were disproportionately African American. Between 1975 and 1982, for example, sixteen Angelenos died as a result of L A P D officers' use of choke holds and other tactics of restraint; twelve of those were black. Chief Gates explained the disproportionate fatalities by surmising that African Americans were more susceptible to death from choke holds because they had a different physiology than that of "normal people." This statement, like the 1979 shooting of Eula Love for wielding a shovel, epitomized the racial attitudes within the L A P D.36

Both the McCone Commission, which examined the causes of the 1965 events, and the Christopher Commission, which investigated the circumstances surrounding the beating of Rodney King, focused on the L A P D. Warren Christopher, the attorney who eventually became the U.S. secretary of state in 1993, was the link between both efforts, having served as chief deputy on the McCone Commission in 1965. Sadly, the Christopher Commission was necessary in part because the McCone Commission had not been sufficiently vigorous in pushing for reform of the LAPD.

The Christopher Commission's report, released in 1991, made a number of recommendations, most notably a call for "community policing." If implemented, this model would do away with the old idea of treating south Los Angeles as a colony that needed to be subdued: the LAPD would act more like social workers and less like Marines. Instead, community policing would focus on crime prevention, with officers cooperating closely with residents and merchants in solving problems rather than just arresting criminals. The core of the project called for the establishment of a network of police advisory boards, panels that the department hoped eventually would draw hundreds of volunteers and form the focal point of police-community relations. However, two years after the events of 1992, the community policing model remained on the drafting board.37 Thus, a major cause of civil unrest in 1965 and 1992—a police department that aggressively used force—had yet to be addressed effectively. The potential for other outbreaks in the near future remains.

In the years between 1965 and 1992, high rates of unemployment and poverty continued to plague south Los Angeles. Though the city had produced numerous employment opportunities in government and in the defense, film, garment, and retail industries, African Americans still seemed unable to enjoy the fruits of that bounty. The continuing absence of an organized response to this basic problem kept tensions high and provided fuel for the 1992 unrest.

The deindustrialization that had begun in the 1960s was accelerated by the ending of the Cold War. Southern California had been a major recipient of Pentagon contracts throughout the Cold War era. The reduction of this source of capital and employment, coupled with the start of several years of closing military bases, triggered a recession by 1990 that hit California especially hard. Low-skilled African Americans in areas such as South Central Los Angeles had little to cushion them from this downturn. The celebrated restructuring of the Los Angeles economy during the Bradley years had largely attracted high technology and international finance, industries with little use for most residents of South Central. As one African American columnist bitterly noted after the 1992 upheaval, Bradley "rebuilt downtown, the westside, the valley, the whole city[,] while his own beginnings turned to blight and despair."38

The microeconomy of south Los Angeles was so bleak that rare post-1965 successes in attracting business and industry to the area only served to underscore the depth of the problem. Between 1965 and 1990, the number of supermarkets in south Los Angeles dropped from fifty-five to thirty, with the number of jobs disappearing commensurately. The area now has 25 percent fewer supermarkets per capita than other parts of the county. When the Alpha Beta supermarket chain pledged in April 1994 to build a store at Adams and Vermont on a plot of land that had been vacant for nine years, the decision captured headlines.[39] When the Denny's restaurant chain, under fire because of charges of racism, pledged that same year to open shop in the Watts-Willowbrook area, it was noted that this would be "the first full-service restaurant to open in the area since the Watts riots of 1965."[40] On the second anniversary of the unrest of 1992, one study found that half of the 607 properties severely damaged or destroyed then had not been rebuilt. The pace of rebuilding proceeded more rapidly north of the Santa Monica Freeway, where 63 percent of damaged or destroyed properties had been rebuilt or were under construction. South of the freeway, where racial minorities were more prevalent, only 44 percent had been rebuilt.[41] But north or south of the freeway, the fact remained that there were widespread complaints that African American workers were not being hired for the numerous construction and clean-up jobs that had emerged.

Of course, images of south Los Angeles as a ghost town bereft of employment were inaccurate. A study published in early 1996 noted that the area described as "South Central" Los Angeles ranked second in the number of jobs in the area behind the San Gabriel Valley and ahead of the Burbank/Glendale/Pasadena area.[42] Unfortunately, many of these were low wage jobs in the apparel and furniture industries. There is also evidence that some employers had a preference for hiring undocumented immigrants who could be deported if they protested, as opposed to African Americans who were citizens with a reputation for protest and pro-union sentiments. This development contributed to the creation of a black "underclass."[43] Certainly, the disappearance of jobs had a particularly harmful impact on African American men; not only did it hurt their economic well-being, but the lack of the discipline that work would provide also eroded their ability to function in society. Unemployment, moreover, reduced their marriage prospects and thereby undermined the black family.

A major effect of the civil rights movement, ironically, was a widening of the gap between the black middle class, centered heavily nearer the West

Side of Los Angeles, and south Los Angeles, the epicenter of unrest in 1965 and 1992. This fundamental cleavage among African Americans reduced the leverage of South Central, since it perpetuated the impression that the interests of the more articulate and organized members of the black middle class were identical to those of the more numerous working class and poor. They were not.44

South Central Los Angeles's black working class and poor faced another challenge: a rapidly growing Latino population within their midst. This change has come with conflict and tension, as reflected in the controversy at Martin Luther King Jr./Drew Medical Center, built in the wake of the 1965 unrest to serve south Los Angeles. Up until 1972, when this center was dedicated, there were no hospitals in Watts, Willowbrook, or any other communities in that vicinity. In 1992, Los Angeles County had agreed to increase the number of Latinos working in the health services department generally, but four years later the *Los Angeles Times* reported, "Latinos were underrepresented and African Americans were significantly overrepresented in the department's full-time workforce of nearly 21,000 employees." More specifically, King/Drew was charged with being laggard in reflecting the surrounding community, which had become increasingly Mexican and El Salvadorean.45 This development, African Americans being charged with insensitivity toward another underrepresented minority, was relatively new, but as the black population continues to lag behind the growing Latino and Asian American populations, it is possible that this trend will increase.

It had appeared for some time that regional elites had less difficulty in absorbing successful African Americans than they did Latinos. Black politicians had risen to the highest level at city halls in Los Angeles, Oakland, and San Francisco, and in the state assembly in Sacramento, before representatives were elected from the larger Latino population. Though Latinos represented 67 percent of students in the Los Angeles Unified School District, compared to an African American population of 14 percent, a representative from the black community had been selected to head the school system long before one was elected from the Latino community.46

Just as African Americans had charged Jewish Americans in New York City with blocking their path toward upward mobility in the schools and other sectors, in Los Angeles some Latinos were making similar allegations against blacks. Of course, these situations were not parallel. Though prominent black lawyers like Tom Bradley and Willie Brown benefited from the erosion of racial barriers, it was impossible to say that the African American community, reeling from high levels of unemployment, was the barrier to Latino progress. Deindustrialization and the dearth of unions that could bridge racial and ethnic divides were the major stumbling blocks for all.[47]

The weakness of labor and the mobility of capital meant that African Americans, a group that remained predominantly working class, were bound to be disadvantaged. The same held true for their Latino and Asian counterparts. Amidst the squabbles that often erupted between and among these groups, few took note of the insight offered by historian Adam Fairclough that the civil rights struggle for the vote and access to public accommodations was handicapped when it became detached from the "labor-left agenda" of economic redistribution. This was a result of the unfortunate coincidence that the civil rights movement had taken place concomitant with the ascendancy of anticommunism and the weakening of unions. In effect, the movement allowed blacks in the South to catch up with a south Los Angeles that was virtually standing still.[48]

Unfortunately, racial and ethnic conflict was not just manifested in competition for employment. In 1965, conflict between Jewish shopkeepers and African American customers led to stores being burned. In 1992, conflicts between black customers and Korean and Korean American owners again led to stores being torched. The shooting of a young black girl, LaTasha Harlins, in an altercation with a Korean American shopkeeper, another incident captured on videotape, inflamed passions between the two groups just before the unrest of 1992.

The entertainment industry was not a passive bystander in this process. As a columnist in the local *Korea Times* pointed out, a number of films released just prior to and after the unrest—*Menace II Society*, *Quick Change*, *Falling Down*, *Do the Right Thing*, and *Crossing Delancey*, for example—all featured Korean or other Asian American shopkeepers in conflict with other racial or ethnic groups. Korean Americans were on the receiving end of offensive jokes in a film, *Boomerang*, featuring Hollywood's biggest African American star, Eddie Murphy, and were a constant source of repulsive humor in the television show *Martin*, starring another popular black comedian, Martin Lawrence.[49] The images projected by such productions not only harmed interracial relations but also projected a caricature of Korean Americans that was broadcast not only nationally but also internationally.

Though receiving less publicity, there were other racial and ethnic conflicts tearing at the fabric of Los Angeles that gave April 1992 a different tenor from 1965. Latino immigrants, for example, in the Pico-Union section of Los Angeles, near Koreatown, clashed with Korean American merchants. Los Angeles featured a potpourri of conflict involving Anglo-Latino, black-Latino, Latino-Asian, and other forms of bias stretching far beyond the biracial polarity that characterized the rest of the nation.[50]

That diversity was small consolation to an African American population whose shrinking numbers also could portend shrinking political clout. This was no minor matter, since it was the public sector, presided over by powerful legislators and executives, many of whom were black, that had brought some of the most significant gains for African Americans in Los Angeles. After three decades of substantial growth, by 1990 the city's black population had dipped by 3 percent from its 1980 level. This census found 487,674 blacks in Los Angeles, about 14 percent of the city's 3.5 million residents. Similar declines occurred in some older suburbs adjacent to Los Angeles, particularly Compton and Lynwood. However, the number of African Americans grew rapidly in some suburbs during the 1980s. In Palmdale, the black population rose by an astounding 946 percent, by 275 percent in Burbank, and by 287 percent in Walnut. To the east, San Bernardino and Riverside counties picked up nearly 30,000 black residents, mostly from Los Angeles County, during that decade. No longer were all African Americans penned in south Los Angeles—those with the economic means could move.[51]

Ordinarily, one could celebrate the fact that obstacles to black residential mobility are, apparently, being removed. Yet the dilemma of African Americans in Southern California is reflected in the fact that even news that appears to be positive may carry a negative message. The areas that blacks are leaving are represented by elected officials like Maxine Waters, Julian Dixon, Mark Ridley-Thomas, and Rita Walters, all African American and fairly progressive. The areas to which African Americans are moving, on the other hand, often are represented by officials who are not as progressive and not as sensitive to racial issues. This diminished political clout could prove to be even more significant if race relations deteriorate further.[52]

Black Angelenos have trodden a rocky road since the founding of the city in 1781. Still, 1965 and 1992 stand out as pivotal years in this riveting odyssey. Nineteen ninety-two may be more of an indication of what the future holds than 1965. Los Angeles has passed the time when African Americans, virtually by themselves, could be the locomotive of major change in the city. This is not out of tune with changes in the city's population. As of 1990, black Angelenos were a racial minority that, after all, represented only 11 percent of the city's population.[53]

In more pessimistic moments, some black Angelenos conclude that their role in the political economy has been undermined by deindustrialization, capital flight, and the decline of unions. Prisons seem to be the only institutions that can utilize black labor. In 1996, the *Los Angeles Times* reported that California's controversial "three strikes and you're out" law has resulted in a "third strike" imprisonment rate for African Americans that is more than 13 times that of European Americans. That same year, though constituting only 7 percent of the state's total population, blacks accounted for 31 percent of its prison population.[54] Latinos, too, are overrepresented in prisons. Sadly, murderous conflicts involving fights between Chicano and black gangs have become a feature of California prison life.

Though these facts and statistics are dismal, the potential remains for these two groups to reverse the tide. Just as they founded Los Angeles more than 200 years ago, African Americans and Latinos, with the assistance of others of goodwill, have the potential to join forces to make the city a better place for all. Their joint effort to build unions in the Alameda Corridor industrial sector, for example, provides an indication of how this can be achieved. This will benefit everyone, for the flames of 1992 illuminated the sober reality that the fire next time in Los Angeles, if it comes, may leave none unscathed.

NOTES

1. Gerald Horne, *Fire This Time: The Watts Uprising and the 1960s* (Charlottesville: University Press of Virginia, 1995), 3; David O. Sears and John B. McConahay, *The Politics of Violence: The New Urban Blacks and the Watts Riot* (Boston: Houghton Mifflin, 1973), 13.

2. Governor's Commission on the Los Angeles Riots, *Violence in the City—An End or a Beginning?* (Los Angeles: n.p., 1965), December 2, 1965, 10–21; Jerry Cohen and William S. Murphy, *Burn, Baby, Burn! The Los Angeles Race Riot, August, 1965* (New York: E. P. Dutton, 1966), passim.

3. *Wall Street Journal*, 4 May 1992; *USA Today*, 5, 6 May 1992; *Los Angeles Times*, 8 May 1992.

4. See Mark Baldassare, ed., *The Los Angeles Riots: Lessons for the Urban Future* (Boulder: Westview Press, 1994); Joe Domanick, *To Protect and To Serve: The LAPD's Century of War in the City of Dreams* (New York: Pocket Books, 1994);

Robert Gooding-Williams, ed., *Reading Rodney King, Reading Urban Uprising* (New York: Routledge, 1993); James H. Johnson and Walter C. Farrell Jr., "The Fire This Time: The Genesis of the Los Angeles Rebellion of 1992," *North Carolina Law Review* 71 (1993): 1403–20; Tom Owens with Rod Browning, *Lying Eyes: The Truth behind the Corruption and Brutality of the LAPD and the Beating of Rodney King* (New York: Thunder's Mouth Press, 1994); Raphael J. Sonenshein, *Politics in Black and White: Race and Power in Los Angeles* (Princeton: Princeton University Press, 1993).

5. Horne, *Fire This Time*, 355.

6. Ibid., 31.

7. Ibid., 172. This dichotomy of the black community was noted by other writers in the late 1960s. See Paul Bullock, ed., *Watts: The New Aftermath* (New York: Grove Press, 1969), 18, 22.

8. Eldridge Cleaver, *Soul on Ice* (New York: McGraw-Hill, 1968), 26–27; William R. Armistead and Richard E. Townsend, "Watts: Its Problems and Possible Solutions, 1964," in U.S. Department of Commerce, Area Redevelopment Administration, *Hard-Core Unemployment and Poverty in Los Angeles* (Washington, DC: Government Printing Office [GPO], 1965), 3, 14.

9. Adam Fairclough, *Race and Democracy: The Civil Rights Struggle in Louisiana, 1915–1972* (Athens: University of Georgia Press, 1995), 16; see also Arthe Agnes Anthony, "The Creole Community in New Orleans, 1880–1920: An Oral History," (Ph.D. diss., University of California, Irvine, 1978); John Blassingame, *Black New Orleans, 1860–1880* (Chicago: University of Chicago Press, 1973); Virginia Dominguez, *White by Definition: Social Classification in Creole Louisiana* (New Brunswick, NJ: Rutgers University Press, 1986); Gwendolyn Midlo Hall, *Africans in Colonial Louisiana: The Development of Afro-Creole Culture in the Eighteenth Century* (Baton Rouge: Louisiana State University Press, 1992); Arnold Hirsch and Joseph Logsdon, eds., *Creole New Orleans: Race and Americanization* (Baton Rouge: Louisiana State University Press, 1992); Gary B. Mills, *The Forgotten People: Cane River's Creoles of Color* (Baton Rouge: Louisiana State University Press, 1977); Sister Frances Woods, *Marginality and Identity: A Colored Creole Family through Ten Generations* (Baton Rouge: Louisiana State University Press, 1972).

10. Eric Foner, *Reconstruction: America's Unfinished Revolution, 1863–1877* (New York: Harper and Row, 1988), 437; William Ivy Hair, *Bourbonism and Agrarian Protest: Louisiana Politics, 1877–1900* (Baton Rouge: Louisiana State University, 1969), 181–88; idem, *Carnival of Fury: Robert Charles and the New Orleans Riot of 1900* (Baton Rouge: Louisiana State University Press, 1976), 137–215.

11. Lorraine Adams and Dan Malone, "Abuse of Authority," *Southern Exposure* 20 (1992): 41–44; see also Don Carleton, *Red Scare! Right-Wing Hysteria, Fifties Fanaticism and Their Legacy in Texas* (Austin: Texas Monthly Press, 1985). On the Tulsa and Elaine riots, see John Hope Franklin and Alfred A. Moss Jr., *From Slavery to Freedom: A History of African-Americans* (New York: McGraw-Hill, 1994), 351–52.

12. See Christopher Cocolthchos, "The Invisible Government and the Viable Community: The Ku Klux Klan in Orange County, California, during the 1920s" (Ph.D. diss., University of California, Los Angeles, 1979); and Brian Masaru Hayashi, *For the Sake of Our Japanese Brethren: Assimilation, Nationalism, and Protestantism among the Japanese of Los Angeles, 1895–1942* (Stanford: Stanford University Press, 1995).

13. John Modell, *The Economics and Politics of Racial Accommodation: The Japanese of Los Angeles, 1900–1942* (Urbana: University of Illinois Press, 1977), 181. See also Bill Ong Hing, *Making and Remaking Asian America through Immigration Policy, 1850–1990* (Stanford: Stanford University Press, 1993); Kevin Allen Leonard, "The Impact of World War II on Race Relations in Los Angeles" (Ph.D. diss, University of California, Davis, 1992).

14. Testimony of Ralph Guzman, 27 October 1965, in Governor's Commission on the Los Angeles Riots, *Transcripts, Depositions, Consultants' Reports, and Selected Documents*, 18 vols. (Los Angeles: The Commission, 1965), vol. 7, 11, 18, 26, 41; Gordon DeMarco, *A Short History of Los Angeles* (San Francisco: Lexikos, 1988), 21, 32, 35.

15. Horne, *Fire This Time*, 25.

16. See Marshall Berges, *The Life and Times of Los Angeles: A Newspaper, a Family, and a City* (New York: Atheneum, 1984).

17. See E. Frederick Anderson, *The Development of Leadership and Organization Building in the Black Community of Los Angeles from 1900 through World War II* (Saratoga, CA: Century Twenty One Publishing, 1980); Sally Jane Sandoval, "Ghetto Growing Pains: The Impact of Negro Migration in the City of Los Angeles, 1940–1960" (Master's thesis, California State University, Fullerton, 1973); Alonzo Nelson Smith, "Black Employment in the Los Angeles Area, 1938–1948" (Ph.D. diss., University of California, Los Angeles, 1978).

18. Charlotta Bass to John Howard Lawson, 18 July 1946, John Howard Lawson Papers, box 12, folder 3, Southern Illinois University Archives, Carbondale, IL.

19. See Ann Fagan Ginger and David Christiano, eds., *The Cold War against Labor: An Anthology*, 2 vols. (Berkeley: Meiklejohn Civil Liberties Institute, 1987), vol. 1; see also Norman Dolnick, "Packinghouse Workers Face the Cold War: A

Memoir," *Labor History* 38 (1997): 492–507; Hilmar Ludvig, "The Rise of an African-American Left: John P. Davis and the National Negro Congress" (Ph.D. diss, Cornell University, 1997); Rick Moss, "Not Quite Paradise: The Development of the African-American Community in Los Angeles through 1950," *California History* 75 (1996): 222–35, 297–98; David Oberweiser, "The C I O: A Vanguard for Civil Rights in Southern California," in Sally M. Miller and Daniel A. Cornford, eds., *American Labor in the Era of World War II* (Westport: Praeger, 1995), 200–216. On Oakland, see Marilynn Johnson, *The Second Gold Rush: Oakland and the East Bay in World War II* (Berkeley: University of California Press, 1993).

20. Cohen and Murphy, *Burn, Baby, Burn!*, 89–90. Again, the social malaise left by deindustrialization was not a phenomenon peculiar to Los Angeles. A similar pattern can be detected in post–World War II Detroit, for example. The urban turbulence of the 1960s—and 1990s—was not the product of these periods alone but had deep and tangled roots dating back to the 1940s. See Thomas Sugrue, *The Origins of the Urban Crisis: Race and Inequality in Postwar Detroit* (Princeton: Princeton University Press, 1993).

21. Léon Bing, *Do or Die* (New York: HarperCollins Publishers, 1991), xiv, 148; see also Martín Sánchez Jankowski, *City Bound: Urban Life and Political Attitudes among Chicano Youth* (Albuquerque: University of New Mexico Press, 1986); idem, *Islands in the Street: Gangs and American Urban Society* (Berkeley: University of California Press, 1991); Kody Scott (aka Sanyika Shakur and Monster Kody Scott), *Monster: The Autobiography of an L.A. Gang Member* (New York: Atlantic Monthly Press, 1993).

22. See Maureen Cain and Alan Hunt, *Marx and Engels on Law* (New York: Academic Press, 1979); David Greenberg, ed., *Crime and Capitalism: Readings in Marxist Criminology* (Philadelphia: Temple University Press, 1993); Eric J. Hobsbawm, *Bandits* (Harmondsworth: Penguin, 1985); Douglas Massey and Nancy A. Denton, *American Apartheid: Segregation and the Making of the Underclass* (Cambridge: Harvard University Press, 1993); Tony Platt, "'Street Crime': A View from the Left," *Crime and Social Justice* 9 (1978): 26–34.

23. See Cynthia Enloe, *Bananas, Beaches and Bases: Making Feminist Sense of International Politics* (Berkeley: University of California Press, 1990); James William Gibson, *Warrior Dreams: Paramilitary Culture in Post-Vietnam America* (New York: Hill and Wang, 1994); Horne, *Fire This Time*, 185–86; Robert Park, *Race and Culture* (New York: Free Press, 1950); Junichi Saga, *Confessions of a Yakuza: A Life in Japan's Underworld* (Tokyo: Kodansha International, 1995); Claire Sterling, *Thieves' World: The Threat of the New Global Network of Organized Crime* (New York: Simon and Schuster, 1994).

24. Horne, *Fire This Time,* 146. See also the essay in this anthology by Gretchen Lemke-Santangelo on the deindustrialization process in Oakland; Los Angeles underwent similar developments.

25. William H. Webster and Herbert Williams, *The City in Crisis: A Report by the Special Advisor to the Board of Police Commissioners on the Civil Disorder in Los Angeles,* 21 October 1992, 42. It was charged that this 1980s epidemic was fueled in part in Los Angeles by the Central Intelligence Agency, which assisted the "contras"—fighting the then left-wing regime in Nicaragua—who were using the receipts from crack sales to subsidize their army. Though hotly disputed by the agency, this revelation stoked outrage in Los Angeles. Congresswoman Maxine Waters called for a thorough investigation. See the *San Jose Mercury News,* August 18–20, 1996; *Los Angeles Sentinel,* August 29–September 4, 1996: The Los Angeles City Council, which had been "plagued by factionalism," approved a resolution unanimously calling on the U.S. attorney general to investigate this matter.

26. See Stokely Carmichael and Charles Hamilton, *Black Power* (New York: Random House, 1967); John T. McCartney, *Black Power Ideologies: An Essay in African-American Political Thought* (Philadelphia: Temple University Press, 1992).

27. See Lawrence P. Crouchett, *William Byron Rumford: The Life and Public Services of a California Legislator* (El Cerrito, CA: Downey Place Publishing House, 1984); idem., "Byron Rumford: Symbol for an Era," *California History* 66 (1987): 13–23, 70–71.

28. See Tomás Almaguer, *Racial Fault Lines: The Historical Origins of White Supremacy in California* (Berkeley: University of California Press, 1994); Lester Cole, *Hollywood Red: The Autobiography of Lester Cole* (Palo Alto, CA: Ramparts Press, 1981); Arnold Forster and Benjamin R. Epstein, *Danger on the Right* (New York: Random House, 1964); M. J. Heale, "Red Scare Politics: California's Campaign against Un-American Activities, 1940–1970," *Journal of American Studies* 20 (1986): 5–32; Dorothy Healey and Maurice Isserman, *California Red: A Life in the Communist Party* (Urbana: University of Illinois Press, 1993); Horne, *Fire This Time,* 265–66; Greg Mitchell, *The Campaign of the Century: Upton Sinclair's Race for Governor of California and the Birth of Media Politics* (New York: Random House, 1992); Upton Sinclair, *My Lifetime in Letters* (Columbia: University of Missouri Press, 1960). For a decidedly negative appraisal of the impact of the Communist Party and left-wing forces generally, see Richard Gid Powers, *Not without Honor: The History of American Anticommunism* (New Haven: Yale University Press, 1998); Wilson Record, *The Negro and the Communist Party* (Chapel Hill: University of North Carolina Press, 1951); Arthur M. Schlesinger Jr., *The Vital Center: The Politics of Freedom* (Boston: Houghton Mifflin, 1949). Of course, it

would be a mistake to conflate the Communists, who specifically espoused the philosophy of Marxism-Leninism, and the left, whose members were not necessarily part of any party, though both groups pressed militantly on such issues as civil rights, union rights, and decolonization. For example, Charlotta Bass, the leading African American journalist and publisher in Los Angeles, was part of the left but not part of the Communist Party. Her uncompromising militancy against racism at a time when such a stance was far from the mainstream marked Bass as a radical. John Howard Lawson, on the other hand, was a member of the Communist Party. Bass and Lawson cooperated but did not share a full set of political ideologies.

29. See Clayborne Carson, *In Struggle: SNCC and the Black Awakening of the 1960s* (Cambridge: Harvard University Press, 1981); David Hilliard, *This Side of Glory: The Autobiography of David Hilliard and the Story of the Black Panther Party* (Boston: Little, Brown, 1993); Horne, *Fire This Time*; idem, "Myth and the Making of 'Malcolm X,'" *American Historical Review* 98 (1993): 440–50; C. Eric Lincoln, *The Black Muslims in America* (Boston: Beacon Press, 1963); Hugh Pearson, *The Shadow of a Panther: Huey Newton and the Price of Black Power in America* (Reading, MA: Addison-Wesley, 1994).

30. See J. Gregory Payne and Scott C. Ratzan, *Tom Bradley, the Impossible Dream: A Biography* (Santa Monica: Roundtable Publishing, 1986); Horne, *Fire This Time*, 135, 295.

31. See Thomas Byrne Edsall and Mary D. Edsall, *Chain Reaction: The Impact of Race, Rights, and Taxes on American Politics* (New York: W. W. Norton, 1991); Allen J. Matusow, *The Unraveling of America: A History of Liberalism in the 1960s* (New York: Harper and Row, 1984).

32. Gunnar Myrdal, *An American Dilemma: The Negro Problem and Modern Democracy*, 2 vols. (New York: Harper and Brothers, 1944), vol. 2, 535–36.

33. *National Law Journal*, 25 March 1991; see also John DeSantis, *The New Untouchables: How America Sanctions Police Violence* (Chicago: Noble Press, 1994).

34. Spencer Crump, *Black Riot in Los Angeles: The Story of the Watts Tragedy* (Los Angeles: Trans-Anglo Books, 1966), 27; Deposition of William H. Parker, 24 November 1965, volume 11, *Transcript of the Governor's Commission on the Los Angeles Riots*; see also James Gazell, "William Parker, Police Professionalization, and the Public: An Assessment," *Journal of Police Science and Administration* 4 (1976): 31–32; Dean Jennings, "Portrait of a Police Chief," *Saturday Evening Post* 232 (7 May 1960): 87, 89.

35. Mike Rothmiller and Ivan Goldman, *L.A. Secret Police: Inside the LAPD Elite Spy Network* (New York: Pocket Books, 1992), 29–46.

36. Johnson and Farrell, "Fire This Time," 1406; Webster and Williams, *City in Crisis,* 33–34; Jerry Watts, "Reflections on the Rodney King Verdict and the Paradoxes of the Black Response," in Gooding-Williams, *Reading Rodney King,* 240–41 (quote, 241); *Los Angeles Times,* 28 March 1988.

37. *Los Angeles Times,* 5, 17 April 1994. By way of contrast, the Mollen Commission, which investigated similar problems afflicting the New York City Police Department, recommended using polygraphs when questioning officers during corruption investigations, halting the "dumping" of officers with problems in poor neighborhoods, stripping pensions from officers convicted of crimes, giving stiffer penalties to officers who violated departmental regulations, punishing officers who failed to report corruption, disqualifying applicants with a history of domestic violence, and many other recommendations that the L A P D could well consider. *Newsday,* 21 April 1994.

38. Quote is from Sonenshein, *Politics in Black and White,* 172. See Roger Lotchin, *Fortress California, 1910–1961: From Warfare to Welfare* (New York: Oxford University Press, 1992); and Seymour Melman, *The Defense Economy: Conversion of Industries and Occupations to Civilian Needs* (New York: Praeger, 1970).

39. *Los Angeles Times,* 22 April 1994; see also ibid., 10 April 1996.

40. *New York Times,* 25 March 1994.

41. *Los Angeles Times,* 22 April 1994.

42. Ibid., 21 January 1996; *Los Angeles Sentinel,* 7 March 1996.

43. See Gerald Horne, *Reversing Discrimination: The Case for Affirmative Action* (New York: International Publishers, 1994).

44. For more discussion on this point, see the essay by Lawrence B. de Graaf in this anthology.

45. *Los Angeles Times,* 18 February 1996.

46. *Los Angeles Sentinel,* 22 February 1996.

47. See the essay by Raphael Sonenshein in this anthology for an analysis of low voting percentages and related electoral powerlessness among the Latino population of Los Angeles.

48. Adam Fairclough, *Race and Democracy,* 417. See also Gerald Horne, *Black and Red: W. E. B. Du Bois and the Afro-American Response to the Cold War, 1944–1963* (Albany: State University of New York Press, 1986); idem, *Black Liberation/Red Scare: Ben Davis and the Communist Party* (Newark: University of Delaware Press; London: Associated University Presses, 1994); idem, *Communist Front? The Civil Rights Congress, 1946–1956* (London: Associated University Presses, 1988).

49. *Korea Times,* 30 June 1993.

50. Armando Navarro, "The South Central Los Angeles Eruption: A Latino Perspective," *Amerasia Journal* 19 (1993): 69–85; Manuel Pastor, *Latinos and the Los Angeles Uprising: The Economic Context* (Claremont, CA: The Tomás Rivera Center, 1993), passim; *LA Weekly*, 1–7 April 1994.

51. *Los Angeles Times*, 24 October 1995. For more on the dispersal of African Americans in the 1980s, see the essay by Lawrence B. de Graaf in this anthology.

52. *Los Angeles Sentinel*, 25 April 1996; *Los Angeles Times*, 20 April 1996.

53. By 1990 African Americans made up 10.7 percent of Los Angeles County. Ali Modarres, *The Racial and Ethnic Structure of Los Angeles County: A Geographic Guide* (Los Angeles: Edmund G. "Pat" Brown Institute of Public Affairs, California State University, Los Angeles, 1994), 18.

54. *Los Angeles Times*, 5 March 1996.

African American Suburbanization
in California, 1960 through 1990

LAWRENCE B. DE GRAAF

For much of the twentieth century, the history of African Americans in California has focused on their populations in major cities. In the years since 1960, this emphasis has been perpetuated by the attention given to the Los Angeles uprisings, activist central city organizations like the Black Panthers, prominent urban political figures, and city-based sports and entertainment celebrities. But these years have also seen a growing movement of African Americans away from cities to suburban areas, resulting in desegregated residential patterns and a wider range of occupations. The factors that have enabled many blacks to move to suburbs, and the impact of these changes, are among the most important topics in the recent history of African Americans in California.

The word "suburb" has two definitions. The first refers to a physical area adjacent to central cities. Spatially, censuses since 1950 have designated large, contiguous urbanized areas as Metropolitan Statistical Areas and have distinguished between their central city and urban fringe populations, usually following political boundaries. Since 1945, the urban fringe has been the most dynamic metropolitan area. Between 1950 and 1970, 83 percent of the nation's population growth occurred in suburbs, and by 1990, for the first time in history more than half of all Americans living in urbanized areas resided in suburbs.[1]

For millions of Americans in the postwar era, however, "suburb" had a second, more subjective meaning: an area with pleasant living conditions and expanded economic opportunities. Suburban communities symbolized the middle-class American Dream of homeownership, a comfortable income,

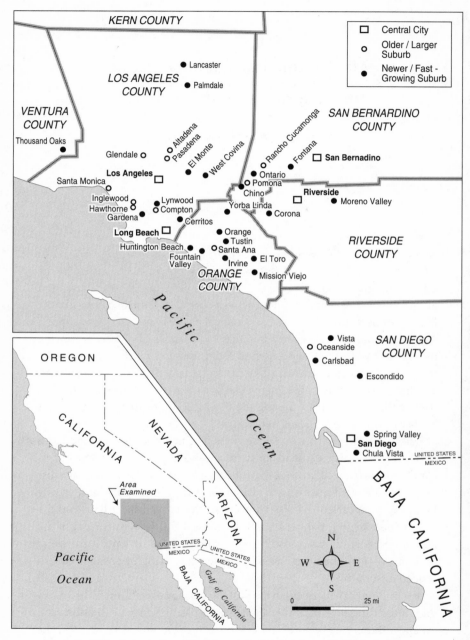

MAP 6. African American Communities in Southern California by 1990

and high occupational status. A growing tax base made suburban schools and civic amenities superior to those in central cities. In addition to offering affordable housing in the early years of development, many suburbs became centers of economic growth, as more than three-fourths of all new manufacturing and retail jobs between 1950 and 1970 located there. Landmarks associated with suburban development, such as shopping malls, industrial parks and housing tracts, have become so common that the postwar era has been called "the suburbanization of the United States."[2]

Few states reflect this trend better than California. Since World War II, its population has concentrated in its metropolitan areas. By 1960, the seven largest of these—Anaheim-Santa Ana, Los Angeles-Long Beach, San Diego, Sacramento, San Bernadino-Riverside, San Francisco-Oakland, and San Jose—contained nearly 70 percent of the state's population. This proportion rose to almost 80 percent during the 1960s and stabilized at more than 77 percent through the next two decades. Many of these Californians were suburbanites, constituting more than 40 percent of the population in 1960, rising to nearly half by 1980 and 57 percent by 1990.[3]

Not all of these communities reflected the ideal of suburbia. The "urban fringe" included decades-old cities with neighborhoods more similar to those in central cities than in suburbs built after the war. Berkeley in the north and Compton in the south were examples of such "ring suburbs." By the late 1960s, newer or outlying communities that had grown in the early postwar period shared the social problems and declining job opportunities of the inner city. Hayward and Pomona are cases in point.[4] To convey a sense of the exclusion or participation of African Americans in the promise of the Golden State, the areas classified as "suburb" need to be adjusted to reflect the changing opportunities in each decade.

Two indicators of increasing economic opportunities are the size and rate of growth of suburban populations. Economic opportunities tended to be greatest in smaller, often newly formed and rapidly growing communities. After World War II, these were almost invariably suburban cities. Conversely, suburbs that developed pockets of poverty and social problems were often already cities of substantial size by 1950.[5] This study will distinguish suburban cities that by 1960 had a large African American population, labeled as "large cities" and defined as having a population equal to .25 percent of the total black population in the state, from those that ranked among the twenty-five fastest-growing suburban cities during that decade, which will be defined as "fastest-growing cities." Additional cities have been added to the list of "large" or "fastest-growing" cities each ten years as they met either of these criteria. In a few cases, cities that were fastest-growing in the 1960s by the 1980s had attained a "large" black population and ceased to be among those with significantly expanding opportunities. Such cities are shifted to the other category. This technique, while not perfect in statistical rigor, should offer a valid measure of the extent to which African Americans were able to share in the opportunities offered by the most vibrant suburban communities between 1960 and 1990. The statistical data and analysis of the causes of black suburbanization will cover the whole state and focus on select suburban cities from the seven Metropolitan Statistical Areas noted, but most examples of personal experiences that suggest its impacts will be drawn from one area in particular, Orange County.

Through much of the twentieth century, California's African Americans have concentrated in central cities and have been conspicuously absent from suburbs. In 1960, 91 percent lived in metropolitan areas, nearly three-fourths in central cities, while barely one-fourth lived in urban fringe communities. A majority of the last group lived in areas adjacent to existing ghettos. Many of the fastest-growing suburban communities had no blacks at all or only a very small number. By 1960, these divergent patterns of settlement had divided California's black and white populations into what the Kerner Commission would call "two societies; one largely Negro and poor, located in the central cities, the other, predominantly white and affluent, located in the suburbs and outlying areas."[6]

Historically, that situation evolved from two sets of conditions. The first is the adverse consequences attributed to the concentration of African Americans in what were long called "ghettos." While that term has also been applied to neighborhoods of European immigrants, Latinos, and Asian Americans, recent studies contend that "no group in the history of the United States has ever experienced the sustained high level of residential segregation that has been imposed on blacks. . . . [For] urban blacks the ghetto has been the paradigmatic residential configuration for at least eighty years."[7] Inner-city neighborhoods were often environments characterized by high unemployment, poverty, inferior education, and social disorders, ranging from crime to single-parent families. The second is the housing discrimination that prevented blacks from moving to suburbs. Widespread residential segregation originated early in the twentieth century with the adoption of race-restrictive covenants to keep African Americans from moving into white neighborhoods. World War II brought a larger influx of African Americans to California, which reinforced earlier exclusionary boundaries and rendered major sections of central cities more heavily black. The federal government built racially exclusive housing as "temporary quarters" for war workers, and many of these projects defined postwar patterns of segregation. White residents' prejudice and fear of declining housing values were reinforced by realtors, lending institutions, and insurance companies. In many postwar tracts, developers made mutual agreements with realtors to exclude African Americans.[8]

Efforts to obtain older housing in suburban communities during the 1950s and 1960s were often frustrated by the prejudices of landlords and local residents. One black professional who managed to secure an apartment in Anaheim in 1960 was greeted with racial epithets, threatening phone calls, pressure from the mayor, and gunfire into his bedroom.[9] Such discrimination had the support of public agencies, especially the Federal Housing Administration (FHA), which refused to guarantee mortgages that would introduce "inharmonious groups," such as African Americans, into a neighborhood. While it modified its manuals after 1950, the agency remained reluctant to bring legal action against those practicing housing discrimination.[10]

These conditions were noted in all parts of California. In the early 1960s, Wilson Record observed that San Francisco Bay Area realtors and government officials channeled "new waves of Negro migrants into [older] neighborhoods. Rarely have Negroes in the Bay Area had an opportunity to purchase homes in the spreading suburban developments of the post-war period." In rapidly growing suburbs such as San Leandro, "where minimum requirements for residence seem almost invariably to include a pale skin," the black population actually decreased between 1950 and 1960 from twenty to seventeen.[11]

Similar practices were common in Southern California, which received the largest number of blacks in the 1950s. Los Angeles County's African American population grew by 243,665, but 163,707 settled in the city of Los Angeles. Many suburbs had few more blacks in 1960 than in 1950. Such exclusion was especially striking in Orange County, just south of Los Angeles, which became the epitome of California suburbanization. Historically an area in which few blacks settled, Orange County had only 889 African American residents in 1950. During the next decade, the county's overall population grew 350 percent to more than 700,000, but although the number of blacks increased by a similar percentage, the overall numbers remained low. Most of those blacks were located in Santa Ana and the Marine Corps Air Station. African Americans were also widely excluded from better-paying jobs. Aside from a few military contractors, virtually no companies hired blacks in white-collar positions. By 1960, only 14 percent of black males, compared to 44 percent of white males, had such jobs, and more than half of black women were employed as household workers.[12]

The most destructive feature of these problems was their interactive nature. African Americans who lost inner-city jobs were excluded from suburbs, in which most postwar employment developed. Residential segregation was paralleled by school segregation, which often consigned blacks to crowded or run-down facilities. In many other ways, "Racial segregation confines blacks to a circumscribed and disadvantaged niche in the urban spatial order [with] profound consequences for individual and family well-being."[13] If residential segregation and inner-city confinement were the main inhibitors of social and economic mobility for blacks, the opening of suburbs seemed their best hope for advancement. By the early 1960s, suburban areas were gaining industries from central cities and posting notably faster rates of economic growth and job creation. Epitomizing this trend was the shifting economic status of Los Angeles and Orange Counties. The latter's economy grew rapidly as it became a major center of the aerospace and electronics industries. Between 1950 and 1960, Orange County's manufacturing jobs grew more than 500 percent, a much faster rate than any other county in the state. Through the 1960s, its real estate and defense-based economy broadened into service, finance, and non-defense-based industries, and it led all Southern California counties in the rate of growth in each sector. Between 1960 and 1985, Orange County's share of jobs in the greater Los Angeles area grew from 6.4 to 18.4 percent, with the lowest unemployment rate of any California metropolitan area, while Los Angeles County's fell from 82.8 percent to 67.9 percent, with escalating welfare payments.[14] Similar booms occurred in the Silicon Valley (around San Jose and south Alameda County) and outside of San Diego.

Suburbanization also held for African Americans the promise of better schools, higher quality housing, greater employment opportunities, and escape from the social disorders of the ghetto. As one writer put it, "Black suburbanization [is] more than the mere act of securing a suburban residence. It is the process in which blacks gain position in distinct but interacting structures of opportunity." But at the start of the 1960s, few black Californians could share in this growth, as they were "denied an equal opportunity to choose where they will live. Much of the housing market is closed to them for reasons unrelated to their personal worth or ability to pay."[15] How African Americans broke this suburban exclusion and how much that triumph has changed their condition are key subjects in the recent history of California.

Nationally, the 1960s marked the last decade of continuing black exodus from the South to northern and western cities. This migration coincided with growing "white flight" to suburbs, dramatically increasing the proportion of African Americans in major cities. Between 1960 and 1970, the percentage of African Americans living in central cities rose from 53 to 58. In 1960, only Washington, D.C., had a black majority population. By 1970, that majority had grown to more than 70 percent, and the African American populations of seven other nonsouthern cities had risen to include between 30 and 54 percent.[16]

In contrast to the growth of central cities, the number of African Americans in suburbs increased slowly, from 15 to 16 percent of their total national population, between 1960 and 1970. Much of this growth came at the end of the decade, when a federal government study found a quarter of a million blacks per year were moving to suburbs nationwide, ten times the number at the start of the decade. While this move was often motivated by a desire to escape "crime, grime, bad schools, and a shortage of housing in the inner city," some hailed this migration pattern as an indicator that blacks could move to places where most new jobs were being created. However, other scholars were skeptical of the potential of such a limited movement to improve the condition of blacks. They noted that many of these suburbs were older, often with deteriorating housing and high unemployment rates, and were being abandoned by whites. Since many such suburbs bordered ghettos, the move appeared simply to expand the boundaries of existing black communities.[17]

California's African Americans, for the most part, followed a similar pattern of settlement. By 1960, the Los Angeles and San Francisco-Oakland areas housed two-thirds of the state's blacks. These two centers continued to attract a large majority of the state's African American population through the 1960s. Yet by the second half of the decade, signs of movement out of central cities appeared. The Los Angeles and San Francisco-Oakland metropolitan areas had out-migrations of more than 32,000 and 35,000, respectively, and the rate of increase in fringe areas suggests substantial increases in black suburban populations. Both patterns are illustrated in table 1.[18]

TABLE 1. Patterns of African American Residence, 1960–70

	1960		1970		Change, 1960–70	
	Number	Percent	Number	Percent	Number	Percent
California	883,861	100.0	1,400,143	100.0	516,282	58.4
Central city	591,830	67.0	922,394	65.9	330,564	55.9
Urban fringe	212,072	24.0	425,047	30.4	212,975	100.9

The limited potential of suburbanization in the 1960s to change African Americans' socioeconomic condition becomes more evident when individual communities are studied. Using data drawn from the two sets of suburban cities—older ones characterized by a large black population by 1970 and the fastest-growing suburbs of the 1960s—the residential patterns are shown in table 2.[19]

As table 2 shows, most of the increase in the African American population in California suburbs during the 1960s took place in large cities. Some held long-established black neighborhoods, such as those of Berkeley, Richmond, and Pasadena, or ones more recently vacated by whites. During this decade, African Americans also moved into affluent areas of West Los Angeles, such as Baldwin Hills, where they established what to this day are some of the most prestigious black communities in the state. The most spectacular growth, however, occurred in a few "ring" communities adjacent to large ghettos, especially Carson and Inglewood. African American populations there grew from 50 and 29 in 1960 to 8,752 and 10,066, respectively, in 1970. Within those areas, blacks often were concentrated in a few tracts in older housing. In Inglewood, for example, most black settlement was in blocks immediately adjacent to the ghetto, in a city whose population was rapidly becoming as Hispanic as it was Anglo.

One apparent exception to black suburban expansion being adjacent to ghettos was Pomona, where the Veterans Administration (VA) and FHA took over vacated houses and sold them without discrimination. Between 1961 and 1971, 17,000 African Americans settled there, many coming in the wake of the Watts uprising. But most of these houses were in three small enclaves, which by 1970 had become minighettos little different from the pattern of racial concentration in ring suburbs. Rapid transition from white to nearly all-black neighborhoods was often primarily due to "white flight" as soon as blacks entered an area. Efforts by city officials to discourage panic

TABLE 2. African American Populations and Population Change
in Large and Fastest-Growing Suburban Cities, 1960–70

African American Population in	Number of Cities	1960 Number	%(a)*	1970 Number	%(a)*	Change in African American Population, 1960–70
Large cities, 1960	8	95,872	17.9	164,243	28.4	53,856
Large cities, 1970	6	4,654	1.3	51,334	10.0	46,680
Total, large cities	14	100,526	11.3	215,577	19.7	101,755
Fastest-growing cities, 1960–70	10	299	0.1	6,669	1.0	6,370

*%(a) is the percentage of African Americans in the total population.

sales, such as Inglewood's 1967 ordinance limiting the size of "for sale" signs and attempts by voluntary associations to maintain racial balance, could not stem the transition. Thus, in their physical location and resulting white efforts to vacate racially changing neighborhoods, most moves by blacks into large suburban cities seemed like little more than "ghetto expansion."[20]

The comparatively tiny black population of the ten fastest-growing suburban cities suggests that African Americans continued to be excluded from the most vibrant communities. From Huntington Beach and Orange in Orange County to Concord and Sunnyvale in Northern California, the increase of blacks in many suburban cities was token, though significant gains were sometimes made in towns adjacent to military bases, such as Oceanside, near Camp Pendleton, and North Highlands, near McClellan Air Force Base. Orange County epitomizes the problems blacks experienced in trying to penetrate suburbs during the 1960s. Its African American population more than tripled, from 3,171 to 10,179, but mostly in Santa Ana, its only significant black community at the start of the decade. By 1970, that city contained two-thirds of the county's blacks, and officials feared it could become "another Watts." In more dynamic communities, African Americans managed gains of only 36 in Fountain Valley, 97 in Huntington Beach, and 204 in Orange.[21]

State and federal fair-housing laws enacted in the late 1950s and 1960s, however, created the promise of an eventual end to this exclusion of blacks from California suburbs. In 1959, the state legislature passed the Unruh and

Hawkins acts. Though the former was not expressly passed as a fair-housing act, several court decisions in the early '60s brought real estate brokers and home developers under its power.[22] The Hawkins Act, sponsored by Augustus F. Hawkins, the African American assemblyman from Los Angeles, declared discrimination in publicly assisted housing to be against public policy. Moreover, in 1962, President Kennedy issued Executive Order 11063, banning discrimination in federally aided housing. All three laws required that the aggrieved party file a civil suit in order to enforce these provisions. This limitation was rectified in 1963 when Assemblyman Byron Rumford, a black legislator from Berkeley, sponsored the California Fair Housing (Rumford) Act, which expanded the scope of the Hawkins Act and empowered the Fair Employment Practices Commission (FEPC) to receive and try to resolve all complaints.[23] Some localities joined the effort, as fair-housing organizations were formed in many counties in the early to mid-1960s, while Berkeley passed a local fair-housing ordinance.

These laws met widespread resistance from white residents. Efforts to break into suburban areas were usually individual and involved considerable effort and risk. The purchase of a single home by an African American in a 196-unit tract in Fountain Valley in 1965 led to mass meetings that left the tract "reeking with tension." Black celebrities and servicemen were not immune from discrimination. When the California Angels moved to Anaheim in 1966, José Cardenal and Rudy May were rejected in their quest for apartments there. Black Marines at the El Toro Air Station who sought housing in nearby Tustin had to invoke Hawkins Act suits to obtain it.[24]

Orange County was typical of most California suburban areas in the 1960s. In relatively liberal Berkeley, a 1961 survey found blacks were able to rent only 23 of 117 available residences. A 1963 Riverside survey reported that only 6 percent of that city's African Americans lived in predominantly Anglo neighborhoods, and most of those were restricted to Mexican areas. When Marin County closed its public wartime housing in the early '60s, nearly half of the dispossessed white families moved to other locations in the county. Only 30 of the 340 blacks, however, were able to relocate in that county, most others moving elsewhere into segregated public housing. In 1958, a Sacramento court found that African Americans were systematically excluded from all federally insured housing in that city.[25]

White antipathy to fair housing culminated in efforts to repeal state legislation. Home and apartment owners in Berkeley led the way in 1963 by securing voter repeal of that city's housing ordinance. That effort led to

Proposition 14 on the June 1964 ballot, which prohibited the state from denying any property owner the right to refuse to sell or rent to "such persons as he, in his absolute discretion, chooses." Enthusiastically backed by the California Real Estate Association, this measure was approved statewide by a nearly two-to-one margin. In Orange County and many white suburban communities, it carried by three to one.[26]

Such a sweeping invalidation of state fair-housing laws did not go uncontested, and ironically, the challenge came from Orange County. Lincoln Mulkey had filed an Unruh Act suit that was ruled invalid after Proposition 14 passed. Mulkey appealed to the state supreme court, which in May 1966 ruled that Proposition 14 violated the Fourteenth Amendment, a decision upheld by the U.S. Supreme Court in 1967.[27] This victory restored California's fair-housing laws. Simultaneously, the F H A made its insurance more accessible to African American home buyers and lower-income families, and Congress subsidized home purchases and renting by low- and moderate-income families under the sections 235 and 236 programs of the 1968 Housing Act. The culminating measure was Title VIII of the 1968 Civil Rights Act, which prohibited most forms of discrimination based on race, color, religion, or national origin in the sale, rental, or financing of housing.[28] On paper, at least, residential segregation seemed to be at an end.

These legal victories, along with efforts by individual blacks to secure suburban housing and the substantial growth of local fair-housing groups, bore tangible results by the end of the decade. Many builders dropped their policies of excluding minorities, and by 1970 a San Francisco study concluded that "minority prospects get much better treatment from tract builders with their own sales force than from realtors." Dealers in cities like Pomona opened refurbished F H A homes to blacks, and some real estate boards accepted African American members. The Southwest Branch of the Los Angeles Realty Board in 1966 opened up house listings throughout the Los Angeles area to black member brokers.[29]

The Watts uprising indirectly contributed to the movement of African Americans to suburbs in the late 1960s. This event more than any other made whites in many Southern California suburbs aware of black needs. Before the uprising, few whites or political leaders in Orange County were aware of the small African American population. The few complaints about discrimination were dismissed by denying that the area had racial problems, but the Los Angeles uprising quickly changed their attitudes. Local black leaders found themselves invited by police chiefs and corporate executives to answer such questions as, "What do blacks want?" For several years after this event, civil rights leaders made advances by challenging local authorities to make Orange County "a model to the nation" and not "a Chicago or Newark tomorrow."[30] Some officials began to acknowledge that one way to achieve that end was to change exclusionary housing policies. The uprising itself, the threats of renewed violence in Los Angeles that arose through late 1965 and early 1966, and subsequent national outbreaks convinced many African Americans that the inner city was unsafe. While between 1965 and 1970 nearly ten blacks moved into Los Angeles for every four that moved out, such a rate of out-migration was unprecedented, and it reflected a growing trend of poor, unskilled persons entering the ghetto while more affluent and educated ones left.[31]

By the end of the 1960s, an accelerated movement of blacks out of central cities had arisen side-by-side with the larger out-of-state influx to those cities. To some observers, this had made little impact on white suburbs. Many fair-housing groups echoed the evaluation of one in San Francisco that "although the community climate is more favorable to fair housing than it was five years ago," years of work had "failed to produce a perceptible improvement in housing market discrimination practices."[32] These conditions were especially entrenched in rentals, often the only housing African Americans could afford in suburbs. Continued confinement of most blacks to ghettos placed families of widely different occupation and income levels in the same neighborhoods and their children in the same schools. These discouraging conditions reinforced attitudes of race nationalism and the tendency of many African American organizations to concentrate their efforts on established black communities rather than on breaking down suburban exclusion.[33]

But the small numbers who had penetrated newer communities set a significant precedent of residential dispersal. By 1970, blacks had established a presence in more than 80 percent of Orange County's census tracts, in contrast to 1960, when they were absent from nearly two-thirds of them. The decade saw a doubling of the number of African Americans in the San Fernando Valley and their initial settlement in such previously closed communities as Northridge and Sylmar. Similar patterns can be seen in outlying Bay Area communities like Concord, where the small African American population was present in all but one of twenty tracts, and in Sunnyvale, where blacks were scattered among all of its substantially populated tracts. In other cities, patterns were developing of concentration in a few areas but presence throughout the city.[34] Perhaps most importantly, the 1960s brought unprecedented legal support for such expansion as well as increasing numbers of African Americans with the financial ability to move to suburbs. Thus, a decade that seemed to be filled with discouragement for California blacks can also be seen as the harbinger of better conditions.

The decades that followed the 1960s produced the most significant changes in black residency nationwide and within California. In the 1970s, the movement of African Americans out of the South dramatically declined; by the end of the decade, more blacks were moving from the West to the South than in the opposite direction. It was also a decade in which the black suburban population grew twice as quickly as in the 1960s. African Americans in California continued to be very mobile, with half of those in the state by 1980 having moved since 1975. But only a fifth of them came from other states. Nearly two-thirds moved within a county, and population figures indicate that most of them moved from central cities to suburbs. More than 73,000 blacks moved out of the Los Angeles metropolitan area between 1975 and 1980, more than 5,000 of them to suburban towns in the Inland Empire. Black populations in California's urban fringe communities increased at four times the rate of those in its central cities.[35]

Those trends accelerated in the 1980s, as more than half of all blacks in the state changed location between 1985 and 1990. Less than 16 percent came from other states, most of them settling in central cities. Those migrants thus perpetuated the "urban crisis" pattern of settlement within the black population first noted in the late 1960s. The much greater movement was the intrastate exodus from central cities into suburbs, which during the 1980s exceeded major cities in African American population growth. In Southern California, the Inland Empire remained a favorite destination, due largely to lower housing costs. The black populations of Riverside and San Bernadino counties more than doubled between 1980 and 1990, while the new city of Moreno Valley tripled its black population in just three years. These trends for the 1970s and 1980s are shown in table 3.[36]

Many observers in the 1970s interpreted these figures as showing that African Americans remained the most segregated minority group, disproportionately concentrated in inner cities, with much of their suburban growth coming in areas adjacent to ghettos.[37] While California's total population was more than 57 percent suburban by 1990, only 41 percent of blacks resided in suburbs. But much of the African American growth in central cities in the 1970s and 1980s came in smaller metropolitan areas, particularly

TABLE 3. Patterns of African American Residence, 1970–90

| Place | African American Population | | | | Population Increase | | | |
| | 1980 | | 1990 | | 1970–80 | | 1980–90 | |
	Number	Percent	Number	Percent	Number	Percent Change	Number	Percent Change
California	1,818,660	100.0	2,208,801	100.0	418,518	29.9	390,141	21.5
Central city	1,058,823	58.2	1,263,97	57.2	136,429	14.8	205,156	19.4
Urban fringe	676,684	37.2	915,239	41.4	251,637	59.2	238,555	35.3

San Jose during the 1970s and San Bernadino-Riverside during the 1980s and 1990s. The Los Angeles and San Francisco-Oakland areas grew much more slowly in the 1970s and hardly at all in the 1980s. The two largest African American communities, those in the cities of Los Angeles and San Francisco, lost black population in the latter decade and continued to do so in the 1990s.[38]

The declining black populations of California's largest cities reflected a growing "black flight" motivated by mounting problems and dangers within those cities. Street gangs became more numerous and violent, and drug trafficking increased proportionately. For many blacks, the key factor in deciding to move was having a gun pulled on them or being robbed multiple times. Others complained of the opposite side of the law: black public officials and distinguished professionals joined common citizens in complaining of being arbitrarily pulled over or treated violently by city police. Nearly all blacks in Los Angeles by the end of the 1970s complained about the city's public schools, and moving to the suburbs competed with misstating addresses or enrolling in magnet, parochial, or private black schools as a way of securing a better and safer education for their children. But newspaper accounts contain few examples of blacks moving in response to the favorite academic criticism of central cities: their declining supply of well-paying jobs for low-skilled workers. Instead, some blacks kept positions in Los Angeles and commuted up to four hours a day from as far as the Inland Empire to "avoid the problems 'of being a young black man in Los Angeles.'"[39]

Half of the African Americans leaving California's central cities in the 1970s and 1980s went to other, usually suburban, communities within the state. The most striking feature of this intrastate migration was its shift from older, larger suburbs to the newer, fastest-growing ones, as is shown in table 4.[40]

This shift developed gradually. During the 1970s, older communities closest to the inner city continued to contain a large majority of the African American suburban population. The six cities in this study that gained more than 5,000 blacks between 1970 and 1980 were all older communities around Los Angeles.[41] The modest increase of blacks in the fastest-growing suburbs reflects escalating housing costs and continuing discrimination. As fair-housing laws and activities lessened the latter problem, African Americans who could afford to turned toward newer suburbs. This shift became more evident in the 1980s. Seven older suburbs with large African American populations experienced absolute decline: Daly City and Berkeley in the Bay

TABLE 4. African American Populations and Increase in Large and Fastest-growing Suburban Cities, 1970–90

African American Population in	Number of Cities	1980		1990		Change in African American Population	
		Number	%(a)*	Number	%(a)*	1970–80	1980–90
Large cities, 1960	8	172,443	28.9	170,943	24.6	8,200	–1,509
Large cities, 1970	6	128,917	21.8	129,169	17.1	77,583	252
Large cities, 1980	6	57,506	12.5	76,418	12.8	45,83	18,912
Total large cities	20	358,866	21.8	37,652	18.4	131,620	17,655
Fastest-growing							
cities, 1960–70	10	23,172	3.9	38,222	3.7	16,503	15,050
cities, 1970–80	10	10,034	1.9	22,910	2.9	8,751	12,876
cities, 1980–90	10	12,768	3.6	58,682	7.4	10,206	45,914
Total, fastest-growing cities	30	45,974	2.4	119,814	4.6	35,460	73,840

*%(a) is percent of total population that was African American.

Area; Compton, Lynwood, Altadena, and Carson in the Los Angeles area; and Santa Ana in Orange County. In several other large suburbs, African Americans constituted a declining percentage of the population by 1990. This pattern is in sharp contrast to the substantial increase in the thirty fastest-growing cities.[42]

The dramatic increase of Mexican and Asian immigrants contributed to the black exodus from both central cities and older suburbs. This was especially evident in Southern California. By the second half of the 1980s, the Los Angeles region gained 488,000 Hispanic and 212,000 Asian immigrants. In Los Angeles County, Hispanics by 1990 accounted for nearly 38 percent of the population and Asians more than 10 percent; those percentages continued to grow into the 1990s. The tendency for Hispanics to move into predominantly black neighborhoods was especially noticed in South Central Los Angeles, which declined from being 80 percent black in 1970 to barely 50 percent by 1990; over the same period, the area's Latino population grew from 9 to 44 percent of its total population. Compton and several older cities around Los Angeles witnessed the same trend.[43] The willingness of many Mexican and Central American immigrants to work for minimal wages placed pressure on less-educated blacks, making them an unusually substantial part of the exodus from Los Angeles. African Americans tended to move to suburban communities with affordable housing, contributing to the dramatic growth of Rialto and Fontana west of San Bernadino, Lancaster and Palmdale in the Antelope Valley, and Moreno Valley east of Riverside.[44]

This penetration of suburbs did not mean the end of discrimination against the African Americans living in them. Students coming to Orange County's state college in the early 1970s found apartments closed to blacks, forcing many to commute from Los Angeles. The Orange County Fair Housing Council concluded in 1973, "Discrimination itself has not dropped significantly in Orange County [even] though it is now couched in more devious deceptions and manipulations."[45] Other suburbs offered similar conditions. A 1970 report on Bay Area suburban housing concluded that "every routine act, every bit of ritual in the sale or rental of a dwelling unit can be performed in a way calculated to make it either difficult or impossible to consumate [*sic*] a deal." A 1971 audit of apartments in Palo Alto found only fourteen of 1,133 units occupied by African Americans, and eleven of those were near the East Palo Alto ghetto.[46]

These discriminatory practices persisted into the early 1990s. A Department of Housing and Urban Development (HUD) audit in 1989 found that nearly half of all African Americans, and more than 40 percent of Hispanics, received "unfavorable treatment" from realtors, lenders, and landlords, and that blacks' mortgage applications were twice as likely to be rejected as those submitted by whites.47 The persistence of such practices led many African Americans to feel that integration was a failure, even as increasing numbers were renting or buying in predominantly white suburban neighborhoods.

Such pessimism proved unwarranted. Amid its catalog of continuing discrimination, a 1977 HUD audit noted that none of the areas it investigated presented the solid wall of exclusion that blacks had faced in suburbs during the 1950s and 1960s. Local fair-housing groups compensated for the weakness of state and federal enforcement by conducting a wave of audits from 1969 to 1976 that pressured government agencies to combat discrimination. Most active was the Mid-Peninsula Citizens for Fair Housing, whose 1971 findings led the Justice Department to file a "pattern and practice" suit against several apartment owners and subsequently led Palo Alto to expand its mixed-income housing projects. Also effective were the growing number of local human-relations commissions, such as that of Orange County, formed in 1971. Four years later, it pressured the city of Santa Ana to include more affordable housing in its community development plan. Developers also became wary of violating the law and ceased earlier agreements with realtors to exclude blacks from new tracts.48

These efforts gradually produced substantial change. The first affirmative action coordinator at California State University, Fullerton, noted that when he took the position in 1972, African American employees no longer had great difficulty obtaining housing if they could afford the area's prices. A black Marine who left the area in 1959 and returned in 1972 found many of the "more responsible" African Americans leaving the Santa Ana ghetto for other parts of Orange County and took this as a sign that "segregation was just about over" in the area.49 By the early 1980s, observers were commenting upon the presence of African Americans in all parts of the county.

Unlike earlier suburban moves that established a substantial black presence in only a few cities, African Americans in the 1970s and 1980s moved into numerous communities and established large clusters in only a few. Of the thirty fastest-growing suburbs selected for this study, all but five contained more than 1,000 African Americans by 1990; all but four were more than 1 percent black, yet only three were more than 10 percent black.

Census data for 1990 on seven fastest-growing suburbs with 110 tracts reveals only one case in which African Americans numbered fewer than ten and only four tracts in which they constituted fewer than 1 percent, yet it shows only twelve tracts where they totaled more than 10 percent and none where they constituted a majority.[50] The growth of African American populations in suburbs by 1990 clearly was not producing the "mini-ghettos" that had been observed and feared only twenty years earlier.

As racial discrimination declined as a barrier to African Americans entering suburbs, another problem grew more acute: runaway inflation in housing costs. Between 1970 and 1988, the median home price in California rose from $28,680, or more than twice the state median income, to $168,560, more than five times the median income. Southern California led this inflation. The median home price in Orange County rose from $34,000 in 1971 to $247,636 by the late 1980s. San Diego was close behind in the 1970s, and by the late 1980s, San Francisco, Orange, and Los Angeles Counties ranked second, third, and fourth in housing costs nationwide.[51] Such prices placed houses in suburban areas beyond the reach of most families. The situation was worsened by the demolition of older housing, rapidly rising apartment rents, and the conversion of apartments into condominiums. By 1978, the Orange County Human Relations Commission declared this "housing crisis" to be the county's "number one social problem."[52]

This development was paralleled in Northern California suburbs by consequences of the antigrowth movement. Many outlying communities elected local governments pledged to restrict population growth in the interests of environmental quality. These cities passed zoning ordinances that limited housing opportunities and escalated residential costs. Antigrowth initiatives spread throughout the state in the 1980s, being adopted by nearly 100 communities.[53] By the late 1980s, the impact of these policies fell hard on African Americans in light of the group's high incidence of poverty-level, female-headed, single-parent families.

The private market did little to meet California's escalating need for affordable housing. The main hope for African Americans lay in federal and state laws passed to encourage the production and dispersal of moderate-cost housing. Federal subsidies provided for the formation of local housing authorities, and by the early 1970s even conservative areas like Orange County had established such agencies. The state required all cities and counties to establish a general plan that included a housing element, and the Housing and Community Development Act of 1974 (HCDA) authorized

423

Section 8 grants to benefit low- or moderate-income families.[54] Especially effective was the provision of Section 8 for sponsorship of projects by non-profit groups. In Orange County, a Housing Coalition and a Human Relations Commission Housing Committee promoted and assisted affordable housing projects and pressed local government to approve them. By 1979, Orange County had adopted an inclusive housing program mandating that 25 percent of future units in unincorporated areas be "affordable." Anaheim and several other cities set up units eligible for Section 236 rent supplements. Unlike public housing projects of the 1930s to 1960s, most of these were dispersed in predominantly white areas.[55]

Several factors limited the impact of affordable housing acts on suburban opportunities for African Americans. Some programs required local approval, and either voter rejection or long delays stopped many projects, as white residents often equated low income with black home seekers. In Orange County, the city of Irvine resisted any affordable housing projects through most of the 1970s. When they were finally established, a study concluded that much of the projects' housing "remains beyond the reach of most low-income workers and their families." While many suburbs eventually sought HCDA Section 8 funds, the money often went toward eliminating blight or housing seniors rather than for dispersing low-income residents into suburbs. During the 1980s, the Reagan administration reduced HUD low-income program budgets by 82 percent.[56] The ideal of both racial and economic integration of California suburbs was realized only partially, and in many communities the increased black population was predominantly middle class.

African Americans who could afford to were often wary of moving into white suburbs for fear of becoming victims of hate crimes. Violence had been a common experience of early black suburbanites. These memories, plus the conservative orientation of many suburban communities, created images of such areas as "John Birch [Society] Country" and the "Mississippi of the West." The Ku Klux Klan gave occasional reality to these fears, painting its signs on houses in Contra Costa County from the late 1960s through the early 1980s and reorganizing chapters in other parts of the Bay Area, through the Central Valley, and in the Inland Empire. Racial incidents accompanied dramatic increases in the black population in Pomona in the late 1960s, in Fontana in the 1980s, and the San Gabriel Valley community of Azusa in the early 1990s. In two of those cases, violence against blacks was instigated by Mexican Americans, an unfortunate example of the increasingly multiracial and multiethnic character of California.[57]

Yet hate crimes also revealed significant changes from earlier decades. African Americans were not alone in being targeted. Gays and lesbians drew many attacks, Jews bore the brunt of religious violence, and Hispanics were the most common victims of school incidents. Officials and communities paid increasing attention to these problems by the 1980s. State Attorney General John Van de Kamp set up a Commission on Racial, Ethnic, Religious, and Minority Violence in 1984, and out of its work came the Bane Civil Rights Act of 1988, which provided penalties for hate crimes. Many suburbs in the late 1970s and 1980s set up commissions to report on such crimes and mobilize community opposition. Police departments in several cities also initiated special teams to deal with hate crimes.[58] Thus, while fear of violence remained in the minds of many African Americans seeking suburban housing, such behavior was less widely accepted by suburban whites.

Obtaining a residence in an outlying community and escaping the violence and declining opportunities of the inner city were only some of the reasons blacks moved to suburbs. People also sought the implicit promise long associated with suburbia: middle-class social and economic status and the comforts and security that accompanied it. As African Americans acquired an increasing percentage of California's new businesses between 1960 and 1990, suburbs seemed to promise them an avenue out of their low occupational status, small incomes, and high rates of unemployment and poverty.[59] In order to weigh the historic consequences of black suburbanization in a period after whites moved to suburbs, therefore, one must ask: Was the opening of suburbs accompanied by an improvement in the economic condition of African Americans?

This improvement was most nearly realized by blacks who attained higher occupational status. In the early 1960s, African Americans had almost as much difficulty gaining better employment in suburban communities as they had obtaining housing. The first blacks who broke into engineering jobs in Orange County needed the assistance of churches or were hired at lower positions despite their education. While African Americans had obtained teaching jobs in most larger cities by 1960, they remained almost entirely shut out of suburban schools well into that decade. In some cities, blacks had obtained public sector employment in numbers out of proportion to their population, but much of it was in low-skilled positions. In 1967, the city of

Riverside had sixty-seven African American employees, forty-four of whom worked as garbage collectors. Similarly, in Richmond most black city employees in 1966 were in the departments of public works or recreation and parks. Only in 1967 did Santa Ana hire its first African American police officer, while a 1963 investigation of San Diego concluded that "the racial pattern or distribution in City employment is similar to that of other government and business organizations; that is, there are numerous minorities working in menial, unskilled, and service jobs, whereas there are relatively few in managerial, professional, administrating, and public contact positions."[60]

Yet the 1960s also saw unprecedented legal efforts to break these barriers. In 1959, California passed a fair-employment practices law, establishing the FEPC to investigate and resolve complaints of job discrimination. The landmark Civil Rights Act of 1964 made discrimination in hiring, promotion, or retention a federal crime and established the Equal Employment Opportunities Commission (EEOC) to investigate complaints. Recognizing the great burden of historic patterns of exclusion, the following year President Johnson issued Executive Order 11246, establishing a program of affirmative action that encouraged the hiring of African Americans in a growing number of jobs during the next two decades.[61]

While fair-employment measures, like housing laws, suffered from limited staff and enforcement powers, they nevertheless provided an incentive for individual blacks to set up local programs to procure more and better jobs. In Orange County, the first African American engineer hired by the Autonetics Company persuaded employers to set up job fairs for minorities and, by the end of the decade, to start affirmative action programs. Another black engineer established a "Partners for Progress" program that placed African Americans for the first time in such companies as Bank of America.[62] Such grassroots efforts, coupled with gradually increasing enforcement of state and federal laws, were crucial to opening suburbs to African Americans. Since most new higher-paying jobs were emerging in suburbs, blacks moving there also lessened the conspicuous differences between their occupational profile and that of the total population, as can be seen in table 5.[63] California's blacks continued to improve their job status in the 1970s and 1980s. Growing acceptance of nondiscrimination and affirmative action goals, together with increased education among African Americans, led to substantial increases in higher-status jobs throughout the state. By 1990, blacks had attained an occupational profile not too different from that of the population overall, as is shown in table 5.

TABLE 5. Occupations of Total and African American Populations in California, 1960–90

| | | | | Percentage of Labor Force Employed as: | | | | |
	Managers	Professionals	Salespeople	Clerical workers	Craftsmen	Operatives	Service workers
1960							
Total	9.6	13.7	7.8	16.3	13.9	15.3	10.4
African American	1.9	5.7	1.8	10.3	8.4	35.2	29.4
1970							
Total	9.3	17.4	8.0	19.8	12.9	17.8	12.6
African American	3.2	11.1	3.4	20.5	9.6	25.9	25.3
1980							
Total	12.0	16.4	10.8	18.5	12.3	14.5	12.6
African American	7.9	13.5	7.0	24.8	9.3	17.1	19.3
1990							
Total	13.9	18.5	12.1	16.6	11.1	12.8	12.4
African American	11.2	16.7	9.1	24.2	8.1	13.3	16.6

The increasing movement of African Americans to suburbs was only one of several factors responsible for these occupational advances. All cities surveyed showed occupational gains, reflecting an increase in "white-collar" and a decline in "blue-collar" jobs throughout the U.S. economy. The most striking advances were in the smaller percentage of African Americans in low-status jobs, especially household work, and the penetration of several areas of the private sector, especially financial and personal services, while a large share of government jobs was maintained. But a sense of the relationship between suburban residence and higher occupational status can be gained by comparing the proportion of white-collar jobs (broadly defined as managerial, professional, clerical, and sales) in central cities with those in older and newer suburbs.[64]

The 1970s first demonstrated the association between African American occupational mobility and residence in newer suburbs. By 1980, more than 50 percent of the black labor force in Irvine held managerial or professional jobs, as did more than 35 percent in Huntington Beach and Sunnyvale. Only Riverside and San Jose among central cities had 25 percent of their African Americans in such positions, and each of these had less than 60 percent of the black labor force in all white-collar occupations. The pattern was similar among older suburbs, with only Carson, Hawthorne, and Inglewood of ten surveyed having more than 60 percent of their population in white-collar occupations. Among the twelve fastest-growing, newer suburbs surveyed, seven had more than 25 percent in managerial/professional and 60 percent in all white-collar jobs. Only when they moved to traditionally blue-collar cities like Rialto or concentrated in low-income enclaves, as in Palm Springs, did blacks moving to fastest-growing suburbs not reflect a higher occupational status than those who moved to other areas.[65]

By 1990, the percentage of the African American labor force in California holding white-collar jobs—61 percent—was identical to that of the total population. This was less than either non-Hispanic whites or Asians. But the largest gap in occupational status lay between African Americans and Hispanics, who had only 36 percent of their labor force in white-collar positions. Even more than in the 1970s, this upward occupational status was evident in newer suburban communities. No central city in 1990 had two-thirds of its blacks in white-collar positions. Only Hawthorne among ten older suburbs with large African American populations fell into that category. But nine of fourteen newer suburbs had two-thirds of employed blacks in white-collar jobs. Managerial and professional occupations were held by half the blacks residing in Huntington Beach and more than 40 percent of those in Sunnyvale and Irvine, while seven other fastest-growing suburbs had at least 30 percent in those positions. Only Carson, Berkeley, and Pasadena of the ten larger suburbs and only San Jose among eight central cities had a comparable portion of African Americans in such jobs.[66]

Educated blacks who sought the occupational opportunities of suburban residence came under criticism in the 1980s and 1990s from black community leaders. "Don't move, improve" became a widespread slogan of those who sought to keep talented blacks in the inner city. These pleas became especially strong in an effort to stem an escalating exodus after the 1992 Los Angeles uprising. Black scholar William Julius Wilson criticized these occupational advances in suburbs on the grounds that by taking more affluent and educated African Americans from their inner-city communities, they deprived those areas of leadership and role models and accentuated the growth of an underclass. Yet, given the shift in new jobs and the growing tendency of suburban industries to hire local residents, it is difficult to see how blacks could have secured occupational mobility by remaining in central cities. Some African Americans extolled the greater opportunities of suburbs. A businessman who came to Orange County in 1969 proclaimed that his move was "the best thing that could have ever happened to me, especially coming from Texas. The opportunity here is great." The city manager of Santa Ana agreed: "Orange County presents a unique opportunity for black professionals and others to become part of the American Dream in terms of living in a location which has tremendous economic growth."[67]

While African Americans living in suburban communities benefited from the fact that they led the state in job creation through the 1970s and 1980s, the nature of those employment opportunities had ominous implications. Many of the rapidly growing industries either were capital intensive, hiring few workers, or utilized a highly skilled workforce. Their growth was offset by a nationwide reduction in labor intensive industries and manufacturing jobs with decent pay but lower educational requirements. Los Angeles County was especially hard hit by the contraction of conventional manufacturing jobs in the 1970s and early 1980s, but the shutdown of the Kaiser Steel plant in Fontana in 1983 demonstrated that some suburbs shared this problem. Thus, while breaking employment discrimination had increased blacks' share of manufacturing jobs in the Los Angeles region from 3.3 percent in 1950 to 6 percent by 1970, that share fell to 4.8 percent by 1990, with the number of manufacturing jobs they held declining absolutely between 1980 and 1990. Similar declines occurred in the Bay Area. This transformation of metropolitan economies from manufacturing goods to service industries essentially deprived low-skilled African Americans of the historic avenue to upward mobility that had served them during World War II and European immigrants for decades earlier.[68]

This shift in the nature of work limited the impact of suburbanization upon the entire African American population and contributed to a major disappointment: gains in occupational status did not narrow the historic gap between blacks and whites in unemployment, poverty, or income. While blacks in suburbia were better off than those elsewhere, such differences seemed minimal compared to the continuing racial gap, as is shown in table 6.[69]

Opportunities within individual cities varied widely, yet black fortunes usually mirrored those of the general population. At the end of the 1960s, African Americans in Carson had a higher income and lower unemployment and poverty rates than that city's total population. By the 1980s, Inglewood was cited as having the highest income and lowest poverty rates of any predominantly black city in the United States. But in Pomona, the black poverty rate was more than that of the state. In 1980, black unemployment rates were as low as 4.6 and 4.7 percent respectively in Sunnyvale and Rancho Cucamonga, cities caught up in computer industry expansion and tract development, yet more than 17 percent in Rancho Cordova, indicative of particularly high unemployment in the Sacramento area. Likewise, in 1990 African American unemployment was below that of the total population in cities like Santa Ana and Anaheim, where much of the labor force was Hispanic, but nearly 16 percent in Lancaster and 13 percent in Spring Valley, cities hit by defense cutbacks. The differences are especially striking in the percentage of the black population in poverty, reflecting the relative affluence of those moving to suburbs. Overall, in most newer, fastest-growing suburbs, the economic condition of African Americans was better than the state average, but in half the older suburbs and most central cities, it was worse.[70]

The persistence of gaps between the economic condition of blacks and whites reflected national trends since the mid-1970s. A brief period of lessening racial differences in unemployment, poverty, and income ended, and in the 1980s these differences, especially in unemployment, grew greater. Substantial gains by whites meant that minorities had to make even greater gains to reduce the long-standing differences. African Americans who entered high-status occupations were often able to narrow this gap significantly, but

TABLE 6. Income, Unemployment, and Poverty, Total and for African American Populations, in State, Central Cities, and Select Suburbs, 1970–90

Year/Area	Median Income		Percent Unemployed				Percent in Poverty	
			Total		African American			
	Total	African American	Male	Female	Male	Female	Total	African American
1970								
California	$10,732	$7,484	6.0	7.0	10.6	10.0	8.4	20.9
Central cities	7,369	5,734	6.8	6.1	11.3	10.1	10.1	21.7
Select suburbs	9,499	7,492	5.6	6.8	8.1	10.4	6.5	14.5
1980								
California	$21,537	$14,887	6.5	11.1	8.7	20.6	9.8	21.7
Central cities	20,320	13,307	7.0	12.0	10.8	23.3	15.0	27.3
Large suburbs	19,485	17,758	7.6	10.2	12.8	17.2	15.4	20.4
Fastest-growing suburbs	23,250	21,710	6.1	9.6	5.7	11.2	7.9	10.5
1990								
California	$40,559	$29,453	6.6	11.9	9.3	19.0	9.3	19.0
Central cities	37,309	26,168	7.3	13.1	11.8	22.0	12.4	22.4
Large suburbs	38,968	34,876	7.6	10.3	13.1	15.5	13.1	15.5
Fastest-growing suburbs	47,807	37,669	5.4	8.4	7.7	10.8	7.7	10.8

their gains were statistically offset by the declining real income of the growing number of African Americans in low-skilled jobs and the shrinking percentage of black men in the labor force, due to immigrant competition for
low-skilled jobs, employer preference for immigrants, and the growing
number of black males in prison. Such was the impact of these factors that
by 1990, in California and nationwide, women constituted more than half of
all employed African Americans, a condition unique to that segment of the
population.[71]

Another result of these economic trends was a growing polarization within
the African American labor force. On one extreme there were highly skilled
and professional workers and at the other were low-skilled, minimum-wage
service and low-profit industry workers as well as the unemployed underclass. Migration to suburbs tended to contribute to this trend. As better-
educated blacks were moving into white-collar jobs, low-skilled African
Americans found that immigrant competition left them few of the construction jobs created by the real estate booms of the 1970s and 1980s. This
polarization, in turn, helps explain why the unprecedented breaking of
barriers to suburban residence and higher occupations since the 1960s has
received little celebration among African Americans. As Melvin Oliver
has noted, middle-class blacks "still feel a sense of failure, that in spite of
this great [civil rights] movement that achieved some very worthwhile
things . . . very little has changed for the mass of black people."[72]

Another source of complaint for blacks who have moved into suburban
cities has been the "loss of community." The dispersal of African Americans
often brought with it a sense of isolation, of being disconnected from their
past, their friends and families, and from any substantial numbers of other
blacks. This is particularly noticeable in an area like Orange County, where
in 1990 blacks constituted only 1.7 percent of the population and 5 percent
in only one of its thirty cities. An African American psychologist in Irvine,
Christine Hall, observed in the early 1980s, "Most blacks in Orange County
are hurting for social contact with other blacks . . . . Especially for women
and singles, it's lonely. You go day after day and you don't see anybody like
you."[73] Students at the county's universities complained of feeling lost "in a
sea of white faces." This was compounded by naive and stereotyped inter-
rogations and frequent haltings by campus police, who automatically
equated African Americans' color with "not belonging there."[74] Black professionals yearned for a chance to converse with their racial peers. Teenagers
agonized over obtaining an African American companion for dates. While a

Los Angeles Times survey in 1982 found that blacks who moved to suburbs welcomed the opportunity to live "in something that resembled an integrated community," they also worried about the impact on their children of growing up in a virtually all-white society. Two black parents from the San Fernando Valley recalled that their teenage son was reluctant to go to the Watts Summer Festival "because all of his life [in the Valley] he's heard about the bunch of negative things that go on there."75 Some saw deeper losses, including the decline of a "caring attitude" that they associated with a network of community organizations in more segregated neighborhoods. This left blacks looking out for themselves instead of for each other.76

This sense of isolation inspired efforts by suburban African Americans to unite and provide a continuing sense of identity and heritage. The range and impact of those efforts can be seen in Orange County. Until the mid-1960s, the county had only a National Association for the Advancement of Colored People (NAACP) chapter, a few black churches, and one lodge, all in Santa Ana. Great Society programs such as Head Start created service centers in Santa Ana to offer day care to low-income black and Hispanic working mothers. One African American woman expanded this Santa Ana service center to a private day care center in 1968. Another established the Southwest Community Service Center, which served Santa Ana's black homeless population through the '80s. In 1971, an African American psychologist opened the People's Clinic, which combined child guidance and cultural awareness. These efforts were augmented by human relations and civil rights organizations composed largely of whites that offered black activists a voice in the community. By the end of the decade, two African Americans had sought local political office, and a third had been named to the county grand jury and subsequently to several county government commissions.77

The late 1970s and the 1980s witnessed the formation of more community organizations in many suburban communities, which gave their scattered black families a feeling of being connected with each other and their children a sense of racial identity. Orange County blacks mirrored this trend, establishing an Urban League chapter; the Black Business Alliance; a chapter of Links, a black women's national service organization; and the Orange County Black Historical Commission, which from 1979 to 1991 sponsored the annual Black History Parade. During this period, the number of African American churches also increased to more than thirty. One weakness of most of these community-building efforts was their location in

Santa Ana, which after the early '70s lost many blacks to other cities. One example of the ability of African American institutions to follow this dispersal, however, was the Friendship Baptist Church, which located in the overwhelmingly white city of Yorba Linda and in 1985 drew more than 1,000 people a week. The proliferation of organizations led one black resident to comment in 1986 that Orange County African Americans had "a fairly tight social network. [Most] of the blacks in the county would know almost any other black personally by name."78

But community groups could not dispel the persistence of race as a negative factor in the lives of African Americans in late-twentieth-century America. There are numerous examples of such racial experiences among blacks living in Orange County and other Southland suburbs. Many travelers were stopped so many times by police that they came to accept it "like a traffic light." These negative experiences of African Americans with police were reflective of racial profiling occurring nationwide, but they were intensified by the allegedly accidental killing of a black Orange County sheriff's deputy by a fellow officer in 1994 and by police shootings of a young black girl in Riverside in late 1998 and a young male in Claremont in 1999. Many in the black community questioned the lack of indictments in the first incident, while the Riverside shooting led to protests by the city's African American community and a Federal Bureau of Investigation (FBI) probe into charges that the Riverside Police Department followed racist patterns.79 Quite a few with white-collar positions were in "race-related jobs," such as affirmative-action officers or community-relations specialists. While a number had established small businesses, few African Americans attained top executive positions in large corporations. This suggests that at a certain level, blacks in Orange County encountered not a glass ceiling but "one made of cement and steel."80 Some organizations were established expressly to create "comfort zones" for African Americans, especially students, who felt a lack of companionship. In sum, the experience of Orange County suggests that African American suburbanization may be the catalyst to a new set of concerns, as blacks find themselves with "greater affluence [integrated] but submerged in white-dominated areas."81

Yet, the opening of California suburban communities to African Americans had several positive effects. For many, escaping from economic stagnation, crime, violence, and the sense of being "imprisoned in one's own home" were the most important positive aspects of moving to suburban cities. Suburbanization also represented an unprecedented expansion of their geographical scope. Since the late nineteenth century, most blacks had lived in a few large cities and adjacent older communities, reinforcing the view that their absence from other areas was normal. This exclusion resulted in decades of social isolation, during which most white Californians had little or no contact with African Americans. One can see how this changed after 1960 by noting the number of cities that had a significant population of African Americans. Using a definition of "significant" as one-tenth of one percent of the state's total black population, only 26 California cities had that many (900) African Americans in 1960. By 1990, 118 had a comparably sized (2,200) population. This dispersal is especially notable in that many of those cities in 1960 had fewer than 100 African Americans and in several cases none at all.[82] Suburban expansion was lessening a century-long isolation of most black Californians from most whites.

Virtually all of these additional cities were suburban, and many were newer, fastest-growing areas in which African American residents were able to share in the growth of local economies and institutions. Blacks not only had greater access to higher-status occupations, but some also reported that living in suburbs "gave them stronger motivation to improve themselves and get jobs."[83] Others who moved to suburbs found that integrated housing led to greater contact with whites in the workplace, schools, and community organizations. This helped dispel racial stereotypes and improve relations between blacks and whites. Still others lost their fears of leaving home, fears that had governed their lives in cities.[84] In these and other ways, the movement of blacks to suburbs was a move toward a better life.

The entry of many African Americans into suburban communities also promised greater educational opportunities. Some blacks selected suburban neighborhoods on the basis of their schools' academic achievement test scores. Not only were elementary and secondary schools better funded and the overall environment more conducive to learning than in many central city neighborhoods, but suburbs were also the sites of most of California's higher education institutions. Again, Orange County may be taken as typical. Its rapid growth after 1950 led to the founding of a state college at Fullerton in 1959 and the establishment of a University of California campus at Irvine in 1965. In the late 1960s, both of these institutions began outreach programs to underrepresented communities and gained substantial black and other minority enrollments. They also established ethnic studies programs and special student services such as the Educational Opportunities Program. The county's transformation was capped by at least four African

Americans, three of them women, being named president of California State University, Fullerton, or local community colleges between 1977 and 1990.[85]

The history of African American suburbanization in California offers scholars an opportunity to move beyond the decades-old paradigm of black history outside the South being an inner city experience. Communities that as late as 1960 had only a handful of black Californians now are home to thousands of African American newcomers. Indeed, one could argue that the shifting of black populations from central cities such as Los Angeles to communities like Huntington Beach, Moreno Valley, and Sunnyvale constituted if not quite the latest "Great Migration," then at least the most significant demographic development in California's African American history.

The study of African American suburbanization also forces a reappraisal of fair-housing and employment laws, whose utility has been widely questioned. These laws, while not as effective as their proponents had envisioned, nonetheless opened residency and economic opportunities to a segment of the black community. Additionally, suburbanization demands that we view the process of racial integration as a spatial construct rather than a legal abstraction. Unlike dwellers in central cities, whose neighborhoods were often fixed by historic patterns of occupancy, inhabitants of newly opening suburban tracts could not claim "traditional residential patterns" to block integration. Efforts by local residents to block low-cost housing suggests their unwillingness to open suburbs to all races and classes. But the sharp contrast between the near universal exclusion of African Americans from suburbs in the 1950s and early 1960s and the widespread entry of blacks thereafter suggests that suburban residents had become more receptive to neighbors of diverse racial backgrounds.[86]

But with the end of widespread housing discrimination, African Americans who moved into suburbs were ambivalent about their new circumstances. Although they were the generation that came of age during the civil rights movement and experienced the idealism of that era, "an acute sense of pessimism is built into their lives." While they were aware that this was a move that few had been able to make for generations, they also realized that this opportunity was still marred by occasional incidents of discrimination. Moreover, most other groups had for some time been able to take such a move for granted. What from a historical perspective might seem a triumph, many African Americans regard as rights too long withheld. Thus, suburbanization should be viewed as a key arena for studying one of the most interesting aspects of African American culture at the beginning of the twenty-first century: the tendency of many middle-class blacks to cease to believe in the American Dream even as they are realizing many of its components.[87]

Suburban life for African Americans has hardly been ideal. Instead, the procession of advances and disappointments set forth in this study is reminiscent of the model of human progress as three steps forward, two steps back. The historic opening of new residential areas and job opportunities has been accompanied by an array of new issues such as social isolation, loss of a sense of community, and feelings of disconnectedness with other African Americans as well as by old problems such as police harassment and limitations on income and job opportunities. Both the old and new issues have generated a wide array of complaints and shifting attitudes. Since most California suburbs have become multicultural communities, of which African Americans often represent but a small portion, their study should increase the emphasis placed on multiethnic approaches and interracial activities. But all of these considerations make the study of blacks in suburbs a fresh, exciting new prism for reinterpreting the entire California African American experience.

NOTES

1. U.S. Bureau of the Census, *Census of Population, 1990, General Population Characteristics, United States Summary* (Washington, DC: Government Printing Office [G P O], 1992), table 1.

2. Ann Durkin Keating, "The Suburbs," in Mary Kupiec Cayton, Elliott J. Gorm, and Peter W. Williams, eds., *Encyclopedia of American Social History*, 3 vols. (New York: Charles Scribner's Sons, 1993), vol. 2, 1277.

3. U. S. Bureau of the Census, *Census of Population, 1960*, vol. 1, *Characteristics of the Population*, part 6, *California* (Washington, DC: G P O, 1963), 58; U. S. Bureau of the Census, *Census of Population, 1970*, vol. 1, *General Population Characteristics*, part 6, *California* (Washington, DC: G P O, 1973), 86; U. S. Bureau of the Census, *Census of Population, 1980*, vol. 1, *General Social and Economic Characteristics*, part 6, *California* (Washington, DC: G P O, 1983), 57; U. S. Bureau of the Census, *Census of Population, 1990*, *General Population Characteristics: California* (Washington, DC: G P O, 1993), 4.

4. Mike Davis, "The Suburban Nightmare," *Los Angeles Times*, 23 October 1994, M1, 6.

5. The "fastest-growing" suburbs have been selected from 1960 to 1990 by combining several rankings of California cities from publications of the Center for the Continuing Study of the California Economy: *California Economic Growth: Lessons of the 1980s, Outlook for the 1990s* (Palo Alto: 1989), 47–57; and *Top 25 California Cities since 1980* (Palo Alto: 1984), 3–4, 54–56, 98–101. These rankings and this study will be limited to demographic and economic conditions. They will not consider the argument that suburbia *per se* is an obsolete entity since many cities in the urban fringe by the 1980s had become "technoburbs" that were essentially a new version of the central city rather than realizations of the suburban ideal. This view is especially advanced by Robert Fishman, *Bourgeois Utopias: The Rise and Fall of Suburbia* (New York: Basic Books, 1987). A convenient survey of historical interpretations of the suburb is offered by Stuart M. Blumin, "The Center Cannot Hold: Historians and the Suburbs," *Journal of Policy History* 2 (1990): 118–28.

6. *Report of the National Advisory Commission on Civil Disorders,* 1 March 1968 (Washington, DC: G P O, 1968), 1.

7. Douglas S. Massey and Nancy A. Denton, *American Apartheid* (Cambridge: Harvard University Press, 1993), 2, 19.

8. Robert Wenkert et al., *An Historical Digest of Negro-White Relations in Richmond, California* (Berkeley: Survey Research Center, University of California, 1967), 18, 43–44; Loren Miller, "Residential Segregation and Civil Rights," speech given 12 May 1956, reprinted by Los Angeles County Human Relations Commission, 1960, 1, 5.

9. Interview of Josh White in Priscilla Oaks and Wacira Gethaiga, eds., *Harvest: A Compilation of Taped Interviews on the Minority Peoples of Orange County* (Fullerton: California State University, Fullerton, Oral History Program, 1974), 100–101.

10. Massey and Denton, *American Apartheid*, 54–55; Leonard S. Rubinowitz and Elizabeth Trosman, "Affirmative Action and the American Dream: Implementing Fair Housing Policies in Federal Homeownership Programs," *Northwestern University Law Review* 74 (1979): 518–19.

11. Wilson Record, *Minority Groups and Intergroup Relations in the San Francisco Bay Area* (Berkeley: Institute of Governmental Studies, University of California, 1963), 3 (San Leandro quote), 10–11, 22 (first quote).

12. U. S. Bureau of the Census, *Census of Population, 1950*, vol. 2, *Characteristics of the Population*, part 5, *California* (Washington, DC: G P O, 1952), 100, 163; U.S. Bureau of the Census, *Census of Population, 1960*, vol. 1, part 5, tables 21, 28;

Sue Hitchman, "Black and White and Orange," *Orange County Illustrated*, November 1965, 16; *Orange County Register*, 5 February 1985, E6.

13. James E. Rosenbaum and Susan J. Popkin, "Employment and Earnings of Low-Income Blacks Who Move to Middle-Class Suburbs," in Christopher Jencks and Paul E. Peterson, eds., *The Urban Underclass* (Washington, DC: Brookings Institution, 1991), 244; Massey and Denton, *American Apartheid*, 2, 149 (quote). For an earlier study that popularized the idea of the "pathology of the ghetto," see Kenneth Clark, *Dark Ghetto* (New York: Harper and Row, 1965).

14. Security First National Bank, *Growth and Economic Stature of Orange County, 1961* (Los Angeles: Security First National Bank, 1961), 10, 15–16; Southern California Association of Governments [SCAG], *SCAG Region Employment from 1960 to 1985 for the SCAG Region and the State and Nation* (Los Angeles: SCAG, August 1985), 6, 8; Edward Soja, Rebecca Morales, and Goetz Wolff, "Urban Restructuring: An Analysis of Social and Spatial Change in Los Angeles," *Economic Geography* 59 (1983): 208–10, 215; Security First National Bank, *The Growth and Economic Stature of Orange County* (Los Angeles: Economic Research Division, May 1967), 20; *Paradox of Need: Poverty in Orange County*, vol. 1, *Needs Assessment: A Report to the Community by the Orange County Development Council* (typescript, February 1980), 4–45.

15. Thomas A. Clark, *Blacks in Suburbs* (New Brunswick, NJ: Rutgers University Center for Urban Policy Research, 1979), 103; Massey and Denton, *American Apartheid*, 150; U.S. Civil Rights Commission, *1961 Report*, book 4, *Housing* (Washington, DC: G P O, 1961), 1.

16. Timothy J. Kenney, "Black Population Distribution and Racial Change in Major American Cities: A Modified Sector Model of Black Neighborhood Growth" (Ph.D. diss., Loyola University, Chicago, 1981), 51; U. S. Bureau of the Census, *Statistical Abstract of the United States: 1972* (Washington, DC: G P O, 1972), 26.

17. Harvey H. Marshall and John M. Stahura, "Determinants of Black Suburbanization: Regional and Suburban Size Categorization Patterns," *Sociological Quarterly* 20 (1979): 238–39, 251; "From Inner City to Suburbia: Negroes Join in Exodus," *U. S. News and World Report*, 29 December 1969, 17–18 (quote).

18. James H. Johnson Jr. and Curtis C. Roseman, "Increasing Black Outmigration from Los Angeles: The Role of Household Dynamics and Kinship Systems," *Annals of the Association of American Geographers* 80 (1990): 207. Data for this table was drawn from 1960 Census of Population, vol. 1, part 6, table 21; 1970 Census of Population, vol. 1, part 6, sec. 1, table 23. The combined increases for central city and urban fringe exceed the increase for the state because the number of nonurban blacks in California declined during the 1960s.

19. U.S. Bureau of the Census, *Census of Population, 1960*, vol. 1, part 6, tables 21, 22; U.S. Bureau of the Census, *Census of Population, 1970*, vol. 1, part 6, tables 25, 29. "Large cities" are suburban areas where the black population constituted .25 percent of the state's total black population. In 1960, these were Berkeley, East Palo Alto, Pittsburgh, Richmond, Vallejo (which by 1970 was outside the San Francisco-Oakland MSA but is being included due to its proximity), Pasadena, Santa Monica, and Compton. In 1970, these were joined by Daly City, Altadena, Carson, Inglewood, Pomona, and Santa Ana. The "fastest-growing" cities are the ten suburbs with a total population of 25,000 in 1970 that had the fastest rate of population growth, 1960–70. They were Concord, El Monte, Fairfield (like Vallejo, just outside the Bay Area MSA), Fremont, Fountain Valley, Huntington Beach, Orange, Rancho Cordova, Spring Valley, and Sunnyvale.

20. Harold X. Connolly, "Black Movement into the Suburbs," *Urban Affairs Quarterly* 9 (1973): 100; *Los Angeles Times*, 22 October 1967, C1, C5; 13 December 1967; 24 January 1971, B1, B3–4; 26 August 1986, sec. 2, 1; 16 June 1996, K1, K5. For a gloomy assessment of Los Angeles-area black residential patterns by 1970, see Maurice D. Van Arsdol Jr. and Leo A. Scheurman, "Redistribution and Assimilation of Ethnic Populations: The Los Angeles Case," *Demography* 8 (November 1971): 459–80.

21. U.S. Bureau of the Census, *Census of Population, 1960*, vol. 1, part 6, tables 21, 22; U.S. Bureau of the Census, *Census of Population, 1970*, vol. 1, part 6, tables 25, 29.

22. California Civil Code, secs. 51 and 52, Unruh Civil Rights Act of 1959; John H. Denton, *Apartheid American Style* (Berkeley: Diablo Press, 1967), 8. Those cases were *Burks v. Poppy Construction Co.* (1962), 57 Cal. 2d 463; *Lee v. O'Hara* (1962), 57 Cal. 2d 476; and *Vargas v. Hampson* (1962), 57 Cal. 2d 478.

23. Denton, *Apartheid American Style*, 9; California Health and Safety Code, secs. 35700–35744; American Association of University Women, Santa Ana Branch, "A Study of Fair-Housing Legislation in California and the Proposed Initiative Constitutional Amendment against Fair-Housing Legislation" (1964, mimeographed).

24. Interview of Josh White in Oaks and Gethaiga, *Harvest*, 100–101; *Orange County Register*, 4 February 1965, C1, C4; *Los Angeles Sentinel*, 17 March 1966; *Los Angeles Times*, 12 August 1966.

25. Thomas Casstevens, "The Defeat of the Berkeley Fair Housing Ordinance," in Thomas Casstevens and Lynn Eley, eds., *The Politics of Fair Housing Legislation* (San Francisco: Chandler Publishing, 1968), 201; California Fair Employment Practices Commission, *City of Riverside: Report on Employment Practices, 1967–68*

(n.p.: FEPC, 1969), 4; Stutsman, "Marin City Redevelopment," 2–3, in Marin County Human Relations Commission, "Report of the Task Force on Housing," (n.p., 3 December 1965); *Los Angeles Mirror News*, 24 June 1958, sec. 1, 1–6.

26. Casstevens, "The Defeat of the Berkeley Fair Housing Ordinance," 233–35; "Sales and Rentals of Residential Real Property. Initiative Constitutional Amendment" [Proposition 14], June 1964; California, *Statement of the Vote: General Election, November 3, 1964* (Sacramento: Office of State Printing, 1964), 25; Wenkert et. al., *Historical Digest*, 47.

27. *Lincoln W. Mulkey et al. v. Neil Reitman et al.* (1966), 50 Cal. Rptr. 881, 413 P2d 656.

28. Rubinowitz and Trossman, "Affirmative Action," 520–21, 498–501; Michael N. Danielson, *The Politics of Exclusion* (New York: Columbia University Press, 1976), 80–81, 96; Massey and Denton, *American Apartheid*, 195; National Committee against Discrimination in Housing (NCDH), *Citizens' Guide to the Federal Fair Housing Law of 1968* (New York: NCDH, 1968), 5–8.

29. John Denton, *Report of Consultant,* appendix J of summary report by NCDH, quoted in Donald Foley, "Institutional and Contextual Factors Affecting Housing Choices of Minority Residents," in A. Hawley and V. Rock, eds., *Segregation in Residential Areas* (Washington, DC: National Academy of Science, 1973), 101–2; James P. Allen and Eugene Turner, *The Ethnic Quilt: Population Diversity in Southern California* (Northridge, CA: Center for Geographical Studies, 1997), 84; *Los Angeles Times*, 14 February 1966, A3, 27.

30. *Los Angeles Times*, 13 November 1963, sec. 2, 8; *Anaheim Bulletin*, 28 February 1985, A1, 9; interview of Everett Winters by Lawrence de Graaf, 25 May 1982. The last two quoted phrases are from "A New Era in Housing," brochure of the Orange County Fair Housing Council, c. 1969, but there are numerous other examples of civil rights proponents in Orange County and elsewhere using the fear of urban riots in their locales to stimulate racial reform. The effect of the Watts uprising on the inner city is discussed in Gerald Horne's essay in this anthology.

31. Johnson and Roseman, "Black Outmigration," 207, 209; *Los Angeles Times,* 24 January 1971, B4; 22 September 1987, sec. 2, 1; 13 August 1992, A26; "From Inner City to Suburbia," 18.

32. Midpeninsula Citizens for Fair Housing, "Racial Discrimination in the Midpeninsula Housing Market" (Palo Alto: c. 1969), appendix B, quoted in Foley, "Institutional and Contextual Factors," 128.

33. Foley, "Institutional and Contextual Factors," 97–98; Alan B. Wilson, *The Consequences of Segregation: Academic Achievement in a Northern Community* (Berkeley: Glendessary Press, 1969), 7–9; Record, *Minority Groups*, 22.

34. *Los Angeles Times*, 25 August 1982, sec. 1, 3; U.S. Bureau of the Census, *Census of Population and Housing, 1970, Census Tracts*, Final Report PHC (1)–9, Anaheim–Santa Ana SMSA (1972), table P–1; Final Report PCH (1)–117, Los Angeles–Long Beach SMSA (1972), table P–1; Final Report PCH (1)–178, Sacramento (1972), table P–1; Final Report PHC (1)–190, San Jose (1972), table P–1.

35. U.S. Bureau of the Census, *Census of Population, 1970*, vol. 1, part 6, table 16; U.S. Bureau of the Census, *Census of Population, 1980*, vol. 1, part 6, tables 1, 27; *Los Angeles Times*, 22 September 1987, sec. 2, 1; Johnson and Roseman, "Black Out-migration," 207, 209.

36. U.S. Bureau of the Census, *Census of Population, 1980*, vol. 1, part 6, table 75; U.S. Bureau of the Census, *Census of Population, 1990, Social and Economic Characteristics, California*, tables 69, 182; *Los Angeles Times*, 13 August 1992, A26. Table 3 is drawn from U.S. Bureau of the Census, *Census of Population, 1970*, vol. 1, part. 6, table 23; U.S. Bureau of the Census, *Census of Population, 1980*, vol. 1, part. 6, table 56; U.S. Bureau of the Census, *Census of Population, 1990, General Population and Characteristics, Metropolitan Areas* (Washington, DC: G P O, 1993), table 1.

37. See, for example, Massey and Denton, *American Apartheid*, 74; Clark, *Blacks in Suburbs*, 22; Robert D. Bullard, Eugene Grigsby III, and Charles Lee, eds., *Residential Apartheid: The American Legacy* (Los Angeles: CAAS Publications, 1994), 24–25; George C. Galster, "Black Suburbanization: Has It Changed the Relative Location of Races?" *Urban Affairs Quarterly* 26 (1991): 622.

38. U.S. Bureau of the Census, *Census of Population, 1980*, vol. 1, part 6, tables 27, 34; U.S. Bureau of the Census, *Census of Population, 1990, General Population Characteristics, California*, tables 1, 4; *Los Angeles Times*, 4 December 1998, A1, 38.

39. *Los Angeles Times*, 27 August 1982, sec. 1, 3; 1 September 1982, sec. 1, 3; 9 September 1982, sec. 2, 6; 15 November 1987, sec. 1, 1; 13 August 1992, A26.

40. U.S. Bureau of the Census, *Census of Population, 1970*, vol. 1, part 6, tables 16, 23; U.S. Bureau of the Census, *Census of Population, 1980*, vol. 1, part. 6, tables 27, 34, 56–57; U.S. Bureau of the Census, *Census of Population, 1990, General Population Characteristics, California*, tables 1, 4, 6. "Large" cities continue to be defined as those with .25 percent of the state's total blacks, which would be a minimum of 3,500 in 1970, 4,500 in 1980. Those qualifying in 1960 and 1970 are listed in note 19. Cities attaining a large African American population in 1980 were Fairfield, Hayward, Gardena, Hawthorne, Lynwood, West Covina, and Oceanside. "Fastest-growing" cities were the ten cities with a population of 25,000 that had the highest rate of total population growth at the end of each decade. Those for 1960–70 also are listed in note 19. Those for 1970–80 were El Toro, Mission Viejo,

Yorba Linda, Cerritos, Chino, Rancho Cucamonga, Citrus Heights, Carlsbad, Escondido, and Thousand Oaks. Those for 1980–90 were Irvine, Pleasanton, Lancaster, Corona, Fontana, Moreno Valley, Rialto, Roseville, and Vista.

41. The six were Carson, Inglewood, and Lynwood, all of which gained over 10,000 blacks, and Hawthorne, Altadena, and Pasadena, which gained over 5,000 each.

42. U.S. Bureau of the Census, *Census of Population, 1980*, vol. 1, part. 6, tables 56–57; U.S. Bureau of the Census, *Census of Population, 1990, General Population Characteristics, California*, table 6. In the 1980s, Hawthorne would gain over 10,000 African Americans, the only older Los Angeles "ring suburb" to register a substantial increase. Richmond, Vallejo, Hayward, and Ontario would be the larger suburbs that gained over 5,000.

43. William A. V. Clark, "Residential Patterns, Avoidance, Assimilation, and Succession," in Roger Waldinger and Mehdi Bozorgmehr, eds., *Ethnic Los Angeles* (New York: Russell Sage Foundation, 1996), 115; Georges Sabagh and Mehdi Bozorgmehr, "Population Change: Immigration and Ethnic Transformation," ibid., 86; David M. Grant, Melvin L. Oliver, and Angela D. James, "African Americans: Social and Economic Bifurcation," ibid., 382.

44. James P. Allen and Eugene Turner, "Ethnic Diversity and Segregation in the New Los Angeles," in Curtis C. Roseman, Hans Dieter Laux, and Gunter Thieme, eds., *EthniCity: Geographic Perspectives on Ethnic Change in Modern Cities* (London: Rowman and Littlefield, 1996), 23–24; *Los Angeles Times*, 24 June 1996, A1, 14. Rialto and Moreno Valley would each gain over 10,000 African Americans. Lancaster and Fontana, along with Rancho Cucamonga, would gain over 5,000.

45. Professor Ronald Hughes, California State University, Fullerton, interview by de Graaf, 17 September 1990; Orange County Fair Housing *Newsletter* 3 (1973): 1–2; ibid. 2 (1972): 3.

46. The quote is from National Committee Against Discrimination in Housing, "Phase I Report" [1970], in Danielson, *Politics of Exclusion*, 12; Juliet Saltman, "Housing Discrimination: Policy Research, Methods, and Results," *Annals of the American Academy of Political and Social Science* 441 (1979): 189–90.

47. W. Dennis Keating, *The Suburban Racial Dilemma: Housing and Neighborhoods* (Philadelphia: Temple University Press, 1994), 14; Joe Feagin, "'A House Is Not a Home': White Racism and U.S. Housing Practices," in Bullard, Grigsby, and Lee, eds., *Residential Apartheid*, 35.

48. Massey and Denton, *American Apartheid*, 206; Saltman, "Housing Discrimination," 192, 194; Danielson, *Politics of Exclusion*, 110, 116–17; Stanley Buder,

"The Future of American Suburbs," in Philip C. Dolce, ed., *Suburbia: The American Dream and Dilemma* (Garden City: Anchor Books, 1976), 207–8; Rusty Kennedy, "Report on the Activities of the Orange County Human Relations Commission for the Fiscal Year 1988–89"; ibid., 1989–90; Orange County Human Relations Commission, "Complaint to HUD Re Santa Ana Housing and Community Development Act Grant," 5–6.

49. Winters interview by de Graaf; Jim Tippins interview by de Graaf, 30 April 1994, 27.

50. U. S. Bureau of the Census, *Census of Population and Housing, 1990, Population and Housing Characteristics for Census Tracts and Block Numbering Areas*, Oakland, CA, PMSA (Washington, DC: GPO, 1993), table 8; San Diego, CA, MSA (1993), table 8; Sacramento, CA, MSA (1993), table 8; Riverside-San Bernardino, CA, MSA (1993), table 8. The cities surveyed were Pleasanton and Concord in the Oakland PMSA, Moreno Valley, and Rancho Cucamonga in the Riverside-San Bernardino MSA, Citrus Heights in the Sacramento MSA, and El Cajon and Oceanside in the San Diego MSA. The last two were not on the list of thirty but are comparable to other San Diego communities that were.

51. California Senate Office of Research, "Grasping at the Dream: California Housing: Who Can Afford the Price?" (Sacramento: Joint Publications, 1990), 2; Cost of Housing Committee, "Study of the Cost of Housing in Orange County: A Survey" (March 1975), n.p.; Talmadge Wright and Corinne Reave, "The Decline of Orange County's Urban Oasis: Regional Problems in Employment, Housing, and Transportation"(Orange County Fair Housing Council, November 1986), 10–12; Rob Kling, Spencer Olin, and Mark Poster, "The Emergence of Postsuburbia," in Kling, Olin, and Poster, eds., *Postsuburban California: The Transformation of Orange County since World War II* (Berkeley: University of California Press, 1991), 27, n. 33.

52. "Study of the Cost of Housing," n.p.; *Paradox of Need*, 4–11, 4–12.

53. Danielson, *Politics of Exclusion*, 64–66; Carl F. Neuss, *California and San Diego County: Economies in Crisis, a Report to HUD*, California Interagency Council on Growth Management, and Council on California Competitiveness, March 1992, 150.

54. State of California, Government Code, sec. 65302(c); Chester McGuire, "The Urban Act of 1974: Community Development Funds and Black Economic Programs," *Black Law Journal* 5 (1976): 30.

55. Robert E. Mitchell and Richard A. Smith, "Race and Housing: A Review and Comments on the Content and Effects of Federal Policy," *Annals of the Amer-*

ican Academy of Political and Social Science 441 (January 1979): 179–80; Orange County Fair Housing Council, *Forum* (winter 1979): 37–38; *Orange County Apartment News* (November 1980).

56. NCDH, "Phase I Report," in Danielson, *Politics of Exclusion*, 86–87, 91, 99–100; Orange County Fair Housing Council *Newsletter* 10 (1971): 1; Martin J. Schiesl, "Designing the Model Community: The Irvine Company and Suburban Development, 1950–88," in Kling, Olin, and Poster, eds., *Postsuburban California*, 84. On the efforts of the Reagan administration to gut fair and affordable housing programs, see Massey and Denton, *American Apartheid*, chap. 7.

57. Massey and Denton, *American Apartheid*, 232; Jewell Plummer Cobb interview by Lawrence de Graaf, Oral History Transcript, California State University, Fullerton, 1991; Mae Ussery interview by de Graaf, 2 March 1996; California Fair Employment and Housing Commission, *Report and Recommendations: Public Hearings on Racial, Ethnic, and Religious Violence in Contra Costa County*, held October 5–7, 1981 (Richmond, CA, 1982), 4, 42–43; *Los Angeles Times*, 24 January 1971; 2 December 1984, sec. 1, 3; 29 November 1992, B1, 3.

58. California Attorney General's Commission on Racial, Ethnic, Religious, and Minority Violence, *Final Report, April 1990* (Sacramento: California Department of Justice), 16, 21–22, 35. As an example of the relative incidence of various hate crimes, Los Angeles County in the 1980s registered 95 racial hate crimes, 60 percent of which were against blacks; 731 religious crimes, 90 percent against Jews; and 2,265 school hate crimes, mostly against Hispanics.

59. *Los Angeles Times*, 22 August 1982, sec. 9, 1; 23 June 1997, A1, 14. The latter article summarized a June 1997 HUD report that 97 percent of all new businesses created in the 1990s were based in suburbs.

60. Jean Mahlberg, "The Negro Community in Santa Ana" (Master's thesis, California State University, Fullerton, 1967), 23–24, 26; interviews with Everett Winters and Josh White in Oaks and Gethaiga, *Harvest*, 99, 141–42; Wilson Record, "The Negro Teacher in California Public Schools" (unpublished collection of articles, 1964); California Fair Employment Practices Commission, *Employment Practices, City of San Diego* (San Francisco: FEPC, 1964), 2; FEPC, *City of Riverside*, 15–17; Wenkert et al., *Historical Digest*, 70.

61. Affirmative action was initially a vaguely stated mandate strictly applying to federal contractors. However, the rule-making of the EEOC and favorable Supreme Court decisions steadily broadened the scope of affirmative action through the 1970s and 1980s until it was embraced by a majority of employers. See especially Herman Belz, "Affirmative Action," in Kermit Hall, ed., *Oxford*

Companion to the Supreme Court of the United States (New York: Oxford University Press, 1992), 19; and Hugh Davis Graham, *Civil Rights and the Presidency, 1960–72* (New York: Oxford University Press, 1992), 38–39, 121.

62. FEPC, *City of Riverside*, 1–2; Winters interview in Oaks and Gethaiga, *Harvest*, 147–48; interview of Winters by de Graaf; interview of Wyatt Frieson by Danelle Moon, 4 May 1994, 34–37, 42. For a recent critique of the understaffing of fair-housing and employment agencies, see George Lipsitz, *The Possessive Investment in Whiteness: How White People Profit from Identity Politics* (Philadelphia: Temple University Press, 1998), chap. 2.

63. U.S. Bureau of the Census, *Census of Population, 1960*, vol. 1, part 6, table 122; U.S. Bureau of the Census, *Census of Population, 1970*, vol. 1, part 6, table 54; U.S. Bureau of the Census, *Census of Population, 1980*, vol. 1, part 6, tables 102, 135, 164; U.S. Bureau of the Census, *Census of Population, 1990, Social and Economic Characteristics, California*, tables 50, 185. This table represents some combining of categories: "operatives" covers a wide range of occupations below skilled craftsmen. In earlier decades, these workers were called "semiskilled." Most of them were in manufacturing, but operatives were also in transportation, food industries, and some service industries. In this case, I am combining their numbers with those of laborers. "Service Workers" includes private household workers. Farm managers and farm laborers are excluded, as are persons reporting no occupation.

64. Grant, Oliver, and James, "African Americans," 392; U.S. Bureau of the Census, *Census of Population, 1960*, vol. 1, part 6, table 122; U.S. Bureau of the Census, *Census of Population, 1970*, vol. 1, part 6, table 54; U.S. Bureau of the Census, *Census of Population, 1980*, vol. 1, part 6, tables 102, 135, 164; U.S. Bureau of the Census, *Census of Population, 1990, Social and Economic Characteristics, California*, tables 50, 185.

65. These observations are drawn from U.S. Bureau of the Census, *Census of Population, 1980*, vol. 1, part 6, tables 135, 164. The peculiar plight of blacks in Palm Springs is covered in the *Los Angeles Times*, 5 November 1984, sec. 5, 1, 4. Some authorities have declared the occupational framework used from 1940 through 1990 as archaic, and the stereotypes of white-collar and blue-collar are equally so. Nonetheless, these remain the most common ways of associating occupation with status and in that sense are being employed in this essay.

66. U.S. Bureau of the Census, *Census of Population, 1970*, vol. 1, part 6, table 54; U.S. Bureau of the Census, *Census of Population, 1990, Social and Economic Characteristics, California*, tables 50, 174, 185.

67. Quotes are from *Los Angeles Times*, 9 February 1986, sec. 2, 10–11; 15 November 1987, sec. 1, 13; 13 August 1992, A1; William Julius Wilson, *The Truly Disad-*

vantaged: The Inner City, the Underclass, and Public Policy (Chicago: University of Chicago Press, 1987), 56.

68. *Paradox of Need*, 4–47; Soja, Morales, and Wolff, "Urban Restructuring," 215; Grant, Oliver, and James, "African Americans," 388–89; Allen J. Scott, "The Manufacturing Economy: Ethnic and Gender Divisions of Labor," in *Ethnic Los Angeles*, 223. For an account of the collapse of Kaiser Steel in Southern California, see Mike Davis, *City of Quartz: Excavating the Future in Los Angeles* (New York: Vintage Books, 1992), chap. 7. On the decline of manufacturing jobs in the Bay Area, see Gretchen Lemke-Santangelo's essay in this anthology.

69. Table 6 is drawn from the U.S. Bureau of the Census, *Census of Population, 1970*, vol. 1, part 6, tables 53, 58, 85, 90, 92–93, 95; U.S. Bureau of the Census, *Census of Population, 1980*, vol. 1, part 6, tables 57, 78, 121, 135–36, 164; U.S. Bureau of the Census, *Census of Population, 1990, Social and Economic Characteristics, California*, tables 3, 9, 173, 177–78, 183, 186–87. The median income figures for central cities are for the seven used in this study, and they are simply the average of the total for each city, without weighting for population. The unemployment and poverty rates are the average of the sum of representative city rates, again without weighting for population.

70. *Los Angeles Times*, 29 March 1987, sec. 2, 1, 5.

71. Andrew Hacker, *Two Nations: Black and White, Separate, Hostile, Unequal* (New York: Ballantine Books, 1992), 100–115; Soja, Morales, and Wolff, "Urban Restructuring," 215; U.S. Bureau of the Census, *Census of Population, 1990, Social and Economic Characteristics, California*, table 50; Allen and Turner, *Ethnic Quilt*, 170–75, Grant, Oliver, and James, "African Americans," 392, 406.

72. *Los Angeles Times*, 23 August 1982, sec. 1, 1, 3; Grant, Oliver, and James, "African Americans," 385, 390, 407.

73. *Los Angeles Times*, 22 August 1982, sec. 9, 16.

74. James Tippins interview by Noah Kimbwala, 5 April 1994, 2; *Los Angeles Times*, 22 September 1990, A24.

75. *Los Angeles Times*, 25 August 1982, sec. 1, 1, 31–32.

76. James Tippins interview by Noah Kimbwala, 5 April 1994, 2; *Los Angeles Times*, 22 September 1990, A24; 13 August 1992, A25.

77. Jo Caines interview by de Graaf, 25 September 1990; Winters interview by de Graaf; Josh White interview in Oaks and Gethaiga, *Harvest*, 109–10; *Paradox of Need*, vol. 1, 4–24, 4–25; Sadie Reid Benham interview by Danelle Moon, 2 May 1994, 73–76, 79–84; Ruth Fox interview by de Graaf, 26 September 1990; James M. Pugh interview by Jody Wallach and Murphy Holmes, October 1974, in Oaks and Gethaiga, *Harvest*, 43–51.

78. *Tri-County Bulletin*, 25 May 1988, 3; *Los Angeles Times*, 16 January 1994, A1, 16; 9 February 1986, sec. 2, 10, 7 June 1998, B1, 8; *Anaheim Bulletin*, 28 February 1985.

79. Ellis Cose, *The Rage of a Privileged Class* (New York: Harper Collins, 1993), 28; *Los Angeles Times*, 11 May 1999, A7; 9 July 1999, A1, 20; 5 August 1999, A16; 2 September 1999, A1, 24; 11 March 1994, A1, 23.

80. Cose, *Rage*, 76, 80; *Los Angeles Times*, 9 February 1986, sec. 2, 11; 27 February 1994, A12 (quote). Not all successful African Americans in Orange County fit this pattern, however. By the mid-1980s, a black person was city manager of Santa Ana, while two others had become presidents of local colleges. In 1998, the election of an assessor marked the first time an African American had attained a countywide elective office. A systematic survey of African Americans in white-collar positions throughout California is needed to verify the extent to which Cose's model has correctly represented black occupational mobility.

81. *Los Angeles Times*, 9 February 1986, sec. 2, 11; *Orange County Register*, 17 January 1994, Metro, 2; Henry W. McGee Jr., "Power(lessness) and Dispersion: Comments on Chester McGuire's 'The Urban Development Act of 1974, Community Development and Black Economic Progress,'" *The Black Law Journal* 5 (1976): 39. The term "comfort zones" comes from Thomas A. Parham, *Psychological Storms: The African American Struggle for Identity*, rev. ed. (Chicago: African American Images, 1993). Fittingly, Parham is a psychologist and director of the counseling center at the University of California, Irvine.

82. *Los Angeles Times*, 13 August 1992, A26; U.S. Bureau of the Census, *Census of Population, 1960*, vol. 1, part 6, tables 21, 22; U.S. Bureau of the Census, *Census of Population, 1990, General Population Characteristics, California*, table 6. The 118 includes 17 "Census Designated Places" (CDP) that are not incorporated but are often referred to as distinct communities. The total number of places in California with more than 1,000 people in 1990 was 860, but nearly half of those did not have 2,200 people of any one racial group, hence African Americans constituted a significant element in one-fourth of California's substantial communities. In 1960, California had 542 cities with populations over 1,000 (three of which were CDPs). Nearly all of these had one group of more than 900, so blacks were a significant presence in only one-twentieth of the state's substantial communities in 1960.

83. Rosenbaum and Popkin, "Employment and Earnings," 352.

84. Ibid.; Keating, *Suburban Dilemma*, 4.

85. *Los Angeles Times*, 25 August 1982, sec. 1, 3; author's recollections as an active participant in multicultural programs at California State University, Fuller-

ton, 1968–79; *Los Angeles Times*, 9 February 1986, sec. 3, 10–12; 10 May 1990, N1, 6–7. As with most aspects of suburbanization, there have been setbacks in educational advances. African American college enrollments began to level off in the 1980s, and in 1996 the elimination of affirmative action enrollment programs by the University of California and Proposition 409 accentuated this decline.

86. The contention that whites in newer suburbs have been more receptive to African Americans might be challenged as contrary to theories of racial "tipping points" and "resegregation." Proponents of the first theory contend that whites are only tolerant of blacks in a neighborhood up to a small percent, often seen as 25. Beyond that "tipping point," few whites will move into an area, and many will leave. The result will be "resegregation," especially since African Americans are said to prefer neighborhoods in which they constitute about 50 percent of the residents. See Massey and Denton, *American Apartheid*, 95–96; William A.V. Clark, "Residential Mobility and Neighborhood Change: Some Implications for Racial Residential Segregation," *Urban Geography* 1 (1980): 95–117. A few sociologists have challenged the argument that the "tipping point" is an unavoidable phenomenon. See Marshall and Stahura, "Determinants of Black Suburbanization," 324–25. The strongest rebuttal of this gloomy scenario is the data on California suburbanization. Very few suburbs where the African American population has substantially increased since 1970 have experienced dramatic loss of white residents or transition from white to predominantly black neighborhoods. Most communities have combined an increase in their black population with that of other groups, often including whites, thus suggesting the greater willingness of suburban whites to live in mixed neighborhoods and of African Americans to integrate into predominantly nonblack areas.

87. *Los Angeles Times*, 23 August 1982, sec. 1, 13. This paradoxical attitude has been analyzed by Jennifer L. Hochschild, *Facing Up to the American Dream: Race, Class, and the Soul of the Nation* (Princeton: Princeton University Press, 1995).

Coalition Building in Los Angeles

The Bradley Years and Beyond

RAPHAEL J. SONENSHEIN

Something remarkable occurred in the political landscape of Los Angeles between 1960 and 1993. In the urban center of Southern California, a small black community won a major share of political power through membership in a biracial coalition with white liberals. Under the leadership of African American mayor Tom Bradley, this liberal coalition dominated city politics for two decades, between 1973 and 1993. But by the mid-1990s, the Los Angeles coalition was on its last legs, torn asunder by racial and class conflicts. After the videotaped beating of Rodney King in 1991 and the massive civil unrest of April 1992, the city seemed to be careening out of control. Bradley chose not to run for a sixth term in 1993 and was replaced by a white Republican businessman, Richard Riordan. The issue for the future was not the relationship between blacks and whites that had animated city politics for decades but the stresses among the city's many racial and ethnic groups.

Los Angeles had become the prototype of the new western city. The expansion that began in the 1880s continued well beyond World War II, as its population rank among cities rose from 135th in 1880 to 2d in 1982. Los Angeles grew another 10 percent in the 1980s. During the period of its greatest growth, the city was dominated and shaped by white Protestant migrants from the Midwest who hoped to create an urban model of the heartland lifestyle.[1] Their intention was to avoid becoming like the big eastern and midwestern cities, dominated by Catholic immigrants, labor unions, and minority groups. The political doctrines that came to dominate Los Angeles spelled a limited civic role for African Americans.

Midwestern values helped create and sustain a policy of nonpartisanship in California cities. In both formal structure and actual practice, Los Angeles has been a strongly nonpartisan city. As a result, party organizations have been virtually nonexistent. Despite a clear majority in party registration, Democrats failed for many years to take over city hall until the rise of the liberal coalition in the early 1970s.[2]

With the absence of partisan competition and the dominance of a system that rewarded elite networks, African Americans languished politically. The only black officeholders were Fred Roberts, a Republican member of the state assembly from 1918 to 1934, and Augustus Hawkins, a Democrat who defeated Roberts and held the seat for more than a generation before going on to Congress. For the first half of the twentieth century, blacks remained largely invisible in city politics to a much greater degree than in the East and Midwest, where party organizations sometimes provided partial incorporation. The first minority Los Angeles city council member, Edward Roybal, a Latino, was elected in 1949, and until 1962 no blacks sat on the council. In fact, not a single African American held public office of any sort in Los Angeles until that year.[3]

The homogeneous community ideal of the midwesterners' new city implicitly excluded minority groups such as blacks, Jews, Mexicans, and Japanese. However, the steady migration of minorities into Los Angeles during and after World War II eroded the predominance of conservative whites. The city's economy also dramatically changed as Greater Los Angeles became the most important aircraft production center in the nation and thousands of black workers migrated from the South in search of industrial jobs. The city's black population, already 63,744 in 1940, grew to 171,209 by 1950 and 334,916 by 1960. This growth eclipsed all resident Asian populations, exceeded the Mexican numbers, and made African Americans the preeminent minority group in city politics.[4]

It took several decades for these population and economic changes to generate political effects, but by the 1950s and early 1960s, the growing black community was actively organizing for electoral power. The rise of African American politics reflected the growth of a strong working-class community built around employment in manufacturing and ties to organized labor, a thriving middle class of professionals and public employees with their own set of political organizations, and the unifying influence of racially based institutions, especially churches. The two class-based constituencies were each so powerful that they generated factional political struggles within the African American community, beginning in the late 1950s. The working-class group underlay the power of Mervyn Dymally, an African American politician with close ties to "regular" Democratic leader Jesse Unruh. The middle-class group became the power base of Tom Bradley.5

Dymally built a political base in the South Central area of the city, which historically had been the center of the African American community but by 1960 had become the home of its working class. He collected a team of allies who helped him monopolize state senate and state assembly seats as the Democratic Party began to extend its reach in the mid-1950s and 1960s. Dymally supporters took pride in being practical deal makers, able to deliver concrete benefits to the community.

In the early 1960s, a second segment of the Los Angeles African American community, centered in upwardly mobile neighborhoods to the west, built an organizational base in association with the more liberal white members of the Democratic Party, particularly the California Democratic Club movement. This group supported the political ambitions of a black former police officer, Tom Bradley. The heart of the movement was a black-Jewish coalition of liberal forces that took over the city in 1973.6 This biracial coalition, which would become a powerful political force, gained its first major success with the election of Bradley to the city council in 1963. In 1962 and 1963, Los Angeles blacks organized with remarkable effectiveness to elect three members to the fifteen-seat council, a 20 percent proportion the group has held through the 1990s. In the process, Latinos lost their one seat to blacks, not to attain another until 1985. Bradley's victory was particularly impressive because his Tenth District was only one-third black. His African American and Jewish allies built a powerful biracial alliance that overwhelmed Joseph Hollingsworth, the conservative white appointee to a vacant council seat. As the central focus of these interracial efforts, Bradley became well known citywide.7

But the African American gains on the council were diluted by the hostility of the incumbent mayor, Sam Yorty. Elected in 1961 with strong minority support, Yorty became a relentless foe of minorities and progressives, backing Police Chief William Parker, who held notably racist attitudes toward the black community. Police mistreatment of African Americans became a major issue, and Bradley often challenged Parker and Yorty to rein in the department. But blacks continued to be on the outside until they built their historic citywide alliance with the Jewish community.8 The cataclysmic Watts uprising of 1965 reflected both the frustration of the African American in the face of relentless police brutality and the growing sense of optimism that things could be different. In fact, those arrested in the violence expressed the belief that the grievances of the African American community would lead to a positive response from those in power.[9]

During the same decades, the Jewish population had also grown substantially, moving from the downtown area through mid-city out to West Los Angeles; a large bloc also moved over the mountains into the San Fernando Valley. Jews responded to their exclusion from the business world of white Protestants by building their own economic power centers away from downtown.[10] The political and cultural exclusion of Jews from the mainstream community in the first half of this century suggests that despite their economic success, they experienced the feeling of being outsiders. This sense of being excluded combined with their liberalism and activism to establish the basis for a political coalition with blacks.[11]

The social provincialism of Los Angeles's Protestant economic leaders therefore helped divide and weaken their dominance of city life. Indeed, the election of the maverick Yorty as mayor in 1961, despite the near-total opposition of the business community, suggested that the downtown alliance of corporate leaders and the *Los Angeles Times* (which had backed his rival, incumbent Mayor Norris Poulson) was not an unbeatable monolith.[12] In the early 1960s, Jewish liberal reformers came together with blacks in mutual frustration over Yorty's conservative, pro-police policies. They formed a powerful, biracial reform coalition able to challenge the downtown establishment. Their initial effort came in 1969, when Bradley ran against Yorty for mayor. Bradley made a stunning showing in the nonpartisan primary, far outdistancing Yorty with 42 to 26 percent of the vote. But Yorty's blatantly racist appeals dominated the runoff campaign, as the mayor succeeded in portraying the moderate Bradley as the tool of black militants and white leftists. To the dismay of his followers, Bradley lost by 53 to 47 percent. He had, however, set a record for black candidates in major American cities, winning more than one-third of the white vote.[13]

Bradley again challenged Yorty in 1973, utilizing a highly effective campaign organization that had matured significantly since the 1969 crusade. Dominating the media with powerful television commercials and keeping Yorty on the defensive, the Bradley forces reversed the outcome of 1969 and solidly defeated the three-term mayor. Bradley gained 46 percent of the white vote along with 91 percent of black voters and a bare majority of Latinos. His allies also dominated the city council, providing a base for a progressive mayoralty. His victory marked the ascendancy of the black "reform" faction over Dymally's "regular" faction in local politics for the next two decades.[14]

With Bradley's election as mayor in 1973, African Americans and their liberal Jewish allies gained seats at the city hall head table. The mayor appointed allies to city commissions and boards, and the coalition's electoral fortunes were assured by the support of blacks and Jewish liberals. The biracial coalition was built on shared liberal ideology, common political interest, and strong, mutually trusting leaders. Some advocates of Black Power, such as Stokely Carmichael and Charles V. Hamilton, had argued forcefully that only economic self-interest could guide an interracial coalition; liberal ideology could not. Liberal ideology among whites, particularly Jews, was essential to Bradley's majority coalition, but emphasizing either self-interest or ideology alone cannot explain the full, human dimensions of the coalition's success, which ultimately depended upon strong leadership connections.[15]

Bradley's coalition was immeasurably strengthened by the close political and personal ties among the black and white liberals who had worked together since the early 1960s. Trust among leaders is an underrated element of coalition development. The Bradley coalition showed the value of trust in 1979 when the controversy over the forced resignation of United Nations Ambassador Andrew Young led to conflicts between blacks and Jews in numerous cities. Only in Los Angeles was the preexisting leadership group able to find a way to defuse the controversy.[16]

The role of Latinos in the Bradley coalition was more ambiguous. Courted by Yorty, Latinos instead crossed over to the Bradley coalition in his 1973 victory. Over the years, they strongly backed Bradley's reelection and were well rewarded with commission posts. But it was twelve years into Bradley's mayoralty before Latinos regained council representation with Richard Alatorre's election in the east side Fourteenth District. The next year, Gloria Molina was elected in the neighboring First District, created only after a lawsuit was filed against the city by Latino activists. In 1993, Richard Alarcón was elected in the Seventh District. By the time Tom Bradley left office in 1993, the council was 40 percent black and Latino, half from each group.[17]

Asian Americans also gained greater political representation through the Bradley coalition, especially in appointments to city commissions. The first Asian American city council member, Michael Woo, was elected in 1985 and became a Bradley ally. In fact, when the city council tried to redistrict Woo

TABLE 1. Minority Representation among Los Angeles City Commissioners

	Yorty		Bradley					
	1973		1973		1984		1991	
	No.	%	No.	%	No.	%	No.	%
Blacks	11	6	21	15	23	19	42	20
Latinos	12	9	13	9	19	16	34	16
Asian Americans	5	1	10	7	11	9	28	13
Women	23	17	45	32	40	33	99	47

out of office in 1986, Bradley saved Woo's seat by his veto of the ordinance and by working out an alternative plan.[18]

African Americans gained important benefits from the political incorporation they enjoyed during the heyday of the biracial coalition. Those benefits came in four main areas: representation, city hiring, federal aid, and police accountability. Bradley brought an entirely new body of personnel into Los Angeles city government. Whereas Yorty's appointees had tended to be older white businessmen, apolitical minorities, and wives of prominent politicians, Bradley appointed a diverse array of politically active men and women from minority and white communities. Table 1 shows Bradley's influence in increasing appointments of minorities and women to city commissions. On key commissions, such as public works and civil service, the Bradley appointees aggressively pursued an agenda favorable to minority interests.[19]

With the help of his appointed civil service commissioners, Bradley vigorously increased minority hiring at city hall, both in overall percentage and in the higher ranks of job categories. As table 2 shows, significant gains in city hiring were obtained by blacks, Latinos, Asian Americans, and women. Equally impressive were the solid gains registered by all four groups in the positions of officials/administrators and professionals, as can be seen in table 3.[20]

Even though African Americans were declining as a share of the city's population, from 18 percent in 1970 to 14 percent in 1990, they more than held their own in city hiring. Despite a lesser degree of political power, Latinos and Asian Americans began improving their positions. In a quiet way, the Bradley regime did a respectable job of developing a secure and upwardly mobile occupational base in local government for some elements of minority communities.

TABLE 2. Composition of Los Angeles City Government
Workforce, 1973 and 1991

	1973		1991	
	No.	%	No.	%
Whites	26,681	64.1	21,088	46.0
Blacks	9,135	21.9	10,286	22.4
Latinos	3,879	9.3	9,112	19.9
Asian Americans	1,659	4.0	3,452	7.5
Women	6,660	16.0	11,705	25.5

TABLE 3. Percentage of Minorities in Top-Level City Jobs, 1973 and 1991

	Officials and Administrators		Professionals	
	1973	1991	1973	1991
Whites	94.7	70.9	81.4	54.9
Blacks	1.3	10.5	5.0	12.0
Latinos	2.6	7.5	4.6	11.1
Asian Americans	1.3	8.0	8.0	15.4
Women	3.0	14.9	11.9	29.9

Again in contrast to Yorty, Bradley sought to improve city services through a search for federal and state assistance. He won an outstanding number of mayoral grants, bringing tens of millions of dollars into the city for physical improvements and social services.[21] The pressure to raise taxes on the middle class to help the poor was eased by an emphasis on increasing overall resources. The federal funding boom of the 1970s supported that goal significantly, enabling the city to initiate many social service programs while hardly tapping the city treasury.

The effect of these programs on the African American community in Los Angeles was mixed. A study of grants in the Bradley era indicated that, overall, they redistributed resources downward. But during the 1980s especially, the administration used private dollars and a greatly increased share of federal funds primarily to pursue a downtown economic development program.[22]

Meanwhile, progress was painfully slow in reforming the entrenched Los Angeles Police Department (L A P D). While Bradley's police commissioners were often perceived as antagonists by police officials, reformers often felt they were too cautious. Even so, the Bradley forces won some important battles, including a tighter rein on police shootings, the department's budget, and its pension fund. Through the city council and police commission, Bradley also secured a moratorium on the controversial choke-hold tactic used by the L A P D.[23]

But it was the videotaped beating of black motorist Rodney King in 1991 that set off the climactic battle between the biracial Bradley coalition and the police department. From March 1991 until the summer of 1992, liberal and conservative forces were locked in combat. Bradley's allies on the police commission tried to remove Chief Daryl Gates but were overruled by the city council. The city charter provided civil service protection for the chief of police, and Gates took every advantage. Bradley responded by appointing a commission headed by Warren Christopher to examine the conduct of the L A P D. The Christopher Commission's report was released in July 1991, and the City Council placed most of its reform recommendations on the June 1992 ballot, including the proposal that the police chief no longer have civil service protection.[24] The commission also called for Gates's resignation, but the chief did not formally retire until 26 June 1992, after the police commission hired a new chief, Willie Williams, an African American from Philadelphia. Williams arrived to wide acclaim and was credited with helping restore frayed relations between the L A P D and the community. After several years in office, Williams saw the approval rating of the L A P D double. But he was later to develop irreconcilable differences with Mayor Richard Riordan and was not rehired when his contract came up for renewal.[25]

Perhaps the greatest victory achieved by the Bradley coalition was the voters' approval of Proposition F, which limited the tenure of the police chief and made the department more subject to civilian control. It was passed in June 1992, despite the civil disorder two months earlier. The biracial coalition rose to the occasion one more time, as black voters joined white liberals and Latinos to carry Proposition F by a margin of two to one. This victory ended decades of frustrating efforts by the African American community to create a mechanism that would make the L A P D more accountable.[26]

The Bradley forces had won a great victory, but the political damage was fatal. Bradley's support among white voters fell so dramatically during the battle over Gates that the mayor's biracial base could no longer deliver for him. The civil unrest after the acquittal of the four white police officers charged with beating Rodney King tarnished Bradley's image as a racial healer, and he decided not to seek a sixth term.[27] And Bradley's loss of white support was not only due to the Gates situation. He also had been in trouble with Jews, his most loyal white supporters, over a financial scandal in which he was charged with receiving a stipend from two banks in return for depositing city funds with them. This event injured Bradley's reputation for personal integrity and led nearly a quarter of African American voters polled to disapprove of him.[28]

Minorities were also becoming upset by the mixed benefits they received from the biracial alliance in neighborhood economic development. In the area of economic policy, the Bradley coalition was unquestionably committed to a downtown development strategy. With the close ties between the mayor and the Community Redevelopment Agency (CRA), the administration embarked in 1975 on one of the grandest downtown building programs of any American city. Within the next decade, the Los Angeles skyline grew dramatically, and downtown was soon filled with gleaming skyscrapers. Tax increment financing made the massive project self-sustaining, as the increased property values generated tax revenue that was plowed back into development.[29] This building boom helped cement the economic alliance between the Bradley regime and downtown business and labor in an uneasy coexistence with the minority-liberal coalition that sustained the regime's electoral success. But the building boom also increased the alienation of poor, minority neighborhoods that continued to deteriorate as Los Angeles became a global city. Only near the end of his mayoralty did Bradley invest substantial political capital in programs to ease bank lending practices in poor and minority neighborhoods. He used redevelopment funds to provide after-school care in the city schools and supported council efforts to push banks to increase their lending in the inner city.[30]

Bradley's pro-business policies, coupled with his quiet style of leadership, drew criticism from within the African American community in his later years. His early ally Maxine Waters became his strongest critic, and a new battle emerged between Waters's forces and Bradley's supporters. As a member of the state assembly and later of Congress, Waters became an energetic advocate of the poor and marginalized. Overall, however, the issues within the African American community were more complex than the class divisions between Bradley's and Dymally's groups. One opponent of Bradley set forth the paradox of his economic policy: "Critics who accuse the Bradley administration of 'killing Southcentral L.A.' usually ignore its achievements in integrating the public workforce. . . . It may be equally true that Black political leadership in Los Angeles County has sponsored significant economic advance and contributed to the community's benign neglect at the same time."[31]

Waters began to challenge Bradley's approach, setting off a dramatic exchange of words between her and Bradley's African American associates in the opinion-editorial pages of the *Los Angeles Times*. Waters and Bradley began running city council candidates against each other in 1991, in a struggle reminiscent of the old Bradley-Dymally feud.[32] Bradley's candidates in 1991 were Mark Ridley-Thomas in the Eighth District and Rita Walters in the Ninth District. Waters backed Roderick Wright in the Eighth and Bob Gay in the Ninth. In narrow races, both Bradley candidates were victorious.[33]

The remarkable success of the Bradley coalition provided evidence once again of the distinctiveness of the African American experience in Los Angeles and by extension in California and the West. But it was somewhat less distinctive than the ability of African Americans to amass capital and own homes that had marked the first phase of their experience in the city. Bradley's coalition was powerfully unique and stands out among the biracial coalitions that elected African American mayors, but it was similar in its ability to link minority aspirations with liberal politics. And his extraordinary success had echoes elsewhere.

While Tom Bradley's five terms as mayor of Los Angeles constitute the most impressive African American political victory in California, years of organizing also paid off in other communities. In three Bay Area cities— Oakland, Richmond, and Berkeley—blacks joined city councils in the early 1960s. In Richmond and Oakland, they soon duplicated the Los Angeles feat of gaining multiple council seats. African Americans had brief stints as mayor as early as 1964 in Richmond, and with the election of Lionel Wilson as mayor of Oakland in 1977, all three East Bay cities had black mayors. Oakland and Richmond retained them into the 1990s, with Wilson serving three terms before being replaced by Elihu Harris. From the 1970s on, African Americans also served as mayors of several smaller California cities. Their local successes were capped in 1995 by the election of former Speaker of the Assembly Willie L. Brown as the first black mayor of San Francisco.[34]

These electoral victories soon fell into two demographic categories. Richmond, Oakland, and some smaller cities like Compton, just south of Los Angeles, represented municipalities in which African Americans by 1980 constituted 40 percent or more of the population and represented, or soon became, the largest racial segment. Openly racial national organizations, particularly the Black Panthers in Oakland, played a major role in attaining and keeping political power. But Los Angeles blacks never constituted more than 18 percent of that city's population, and they represented a declining portion after 1980. The long tenure of Bradley, like the later election of Brown, was partly the work of charismatic leadership, partly of multiracial coalition building.[35] Since cities with near majorities of blacks, like Oakland, are rare in California, the coalition alternative has become the more feasible model for continued African American political success. Its fate in Los Angeles after 1992 is therefore of particular interest.

The decline of the Bradley regime came in spite of the fact that it had generated substantial political and social benefits for minority communities. At great political cost, some police accountability was achieved. Even in South Central Los Angeles, many families owed their livelihoods to affirmative action programs in city hiring and to federally funded projects pursued aggressively by Bradley. Yet amid these gains, several factors were working to undermine the liberal white-black coalition. One was uneven economic conditions, which were at the root of the 1992 unrest. As thousands of young men roamed the streets without work, the potential for civil violence was plain to see. The steady obliteration of the industrial base, bringing the loss of many manufacturing jobs, and the rise of a globally based service economy sustained by massive immigration ultimately changed the foundations of city life. The political effects of this new economy were not immediately felt, but they helped seal the doom of the biracial coalition and ended the central role of blacks at Los Angeles's city hall.[36] Ironically, Tom Bradley's dream to create a world-class city was coming true but with consequences for African Americans and his own interracial coalition he would never have imagined.

The changing economy alone did not spell the end of the coalition; there were political factors as well. Increasing conflict between blacks and Jews had a chilling effect on the elite ties that had been essential to the coalition's success. When Louis Farrakhan visited Los Angeles in 1985, the leaders of the Bradley coalition were unable to surmount the resulting divisions between the two groups. Middle-class whites' increasing fear of crime also made it difficult for progressive candidates to build majority coalitions crossing race and class lines.[37]

Economic changes also made a difference. The downtown growth boom sustained by the Bradley coalition alienated disparate groups. Inner-city blacks and Latinos felt that their areas had been shortchanged in the midst of an economic boom. At the same time, many whites in West Los Angeles and the San Fernando Valley felt that there had been too much growth in their areas—too much traffic, too many stores, too big a jump in home costs. Few in either area felt that the quality of their lives had been improved by Los Angeles's growth. The divergent complaints provided little ground for coalition building.[38]

The immigration issue also significantly weakened coalition politics. In this diverse city, there were increasing conflicts at the street level. In South Central Los Angeles, citywide issues between blacks and whites were replaced by localized conflicts between African Americans and immigrant Latinos over construction jobs and between blacks and Korean American store owners.[39] South Central Los Angeles, once the home of the African American community, was becoming the main site of Latino in-migration. Some sections of South Central remained largely black, but others became overwhelmingly Latino. The area lost over 18 percent of its African American population and increased to 44 percent Latino between 1980 and 1990. As South Central became more diverse, the black community continued to move westward, epitomized by the *Los Angeles Sentinel*'s decision to move its headquarters to Crenshaw Boulevard, on the western and more affluent end of the area.[40]

Less visibly, but crucially, the immigration issue was leading to a wide concern among whites (and many blacks) that the city was changing in unpredictable and uncomfortable ways. The strands came together in 1994, when white conservatives supported and blacks were split on Proposition 187, which would make undocumented residents ineligible for social services, while Latinos and white liberals voted against it. The economic effects of the immigration issue further fractured the potential for minority coalition. The new global economy was not creating the sorts of jobs that had sustained the political activism of an up-and-coming African American community after World War II. While immigrant Latinos in South Central Los Angeles were sometimes employed at high levels, they were not earning high wages. Most were not citizens and were struggling to make ends meet, while many who were better off seemed politically invisible.[41]

In this context, the 1992 civil disturbance and the 1993 election of Mayor Richard Riordan represented two sides of a familiar coin: the appearance or reappearance of central characters in the drama of Los Angeles politics. The

TABLE 4. Population of Los Angeles
by Race and Ethnicity, 1990

	Number	Percentage
White	1,299,604	36.9
Black	487,674	13.9
Latino	1,391,411	39.5
Asian American	341,807	9.7
Total	3,520,496	

violence came from the poor and unaffiliated to a far greater degree than the more political Watts uprising of 1965. Alienated poor people had not been much of a presence in the middle-class biracial coalition, and in 1992 they were out in unorganized force, even burning down such landmarks of the minority movement as the Watts Labor Community Action Center. While Latinos on the more established east side displayed little inclination to participate, Latinos in South Central and Koreatown represented a core component of the violence.[42] A year later, white conservatives, long marginalized under the Bradley regime, burst back into the political arena they had dominated in the era of Sam Yorty. They voted in a large bloc, with a very high turnout, for a Republican candidate who promised a businesslike approach to governing Los Angeles. Former Bradley ally and City Councilman Michael Woo, a Chinese American associated with the progressive ideal of multiracial politics and strongly supported by blacks, was soundly defeated by white Republican businessman Richard Riordan.

How did this happen in a city where two-thirds of the registered voters were Democrats and where whites represented less than 40 percent of the population? How did a Woo aide's confident prediction that "Los Angeles will never elect an old, rich, white Republican" ironically turn out to be 1993's epitaph for Los Angeles liberalism? And how did African Americans, so critical to the political life of the city for twenty years, suddenly find themselves once again on the outside looking in?

The answers lie in the changing demography of Los Angeles. Until the 1980 census, whites had constituted a majority of the city's population. By 1990, whites represented less than 40 percent of the city's nearly 3.5 million people. The single largest group was Latinos, who had jumped significantly from 1980, as can be seen in table 4.[43] This increasing diversity suggested the

TABLE 5. Percentage of Select Groups in Los Angeles Population
in 1990 versus Registration and Voting in 1993

	Population	*Percent of* Registration	*Votes for Mayor (%)* 1993 Primary	1993 General
Whites	37.3	70	68	72
Jews*	7.0 (est.)	15	16	19
Blacks	14.0	15	18	12
Latinos	39.9	11	8	10
Asian Americans	9.2	4	4	4

*Jews are a subset of whites and are counted with them in the column totals.

end of the central role of African Americans in the political life of Los Angeles, and several postelection analyses emphasized the point. One commentator remarked in 1995 that it was not a question of if but when the city would have fewer black than Latino elected officials. A black scholar interpreted the steady decline of the African American population and the growth of the Latino as "the last gasp of moral and political authority for blacks in the sociopolitical arena."[44]

In one sense, these comments were valid. For decades, politics in Los Angeles could be described as black and white. While this meant a cycle of exclusion and inclusion for African Americans, it also meant that when minority issues were on the table, blacks could be certain of receiving attention. That situation changed so much in the Los Angeles of the 1990s that it has become difficult to discuss the racial lines that defined Los Angeles politics for a generation. "Multiracialism" has obscured the continuing role of race and has made it hard for blacks to define their own role in the new Los Angeles.

Simple demographic change, however, is not a complete explanation of the collapse of the Bradley coalition. Even as the city's population shifted, its politics continued to be dominated by blacks and whites. Table 5 contrasts the population of the city in 1990 with the number of people who were politically eligible and active.[45]

In the 1993 mayoral runoff, 84 percent of all votes were cast by blacks and whites. Blacks and Jews, the core groups of the biracial alliance, cast nearly one-third of the runoff votes. The gap between the Latino population and its voter participation was truly astonishing—the group had four times as

many people as its share of the vote.46 It was not until the 1997 mayoral election that Latino political participation began to catch up to the changes in
demographics.

The second, and stronger, reason for the collapse of the Bradley forces
lies in the factionalism that had built up within his "rainbow coalition" after
it had experienced five successive victorious elections. As an Asian American drawing on a multicultural constituency, Woo came to symbolize for
most voters the uncertain future of a city becoming more diverse but also
more confusing and even threatening. The declining popularity of the
Bradley coalition, combined with the gloomy outlook held by a majority of
the city's electorate, made Woo's chances slim, particularly since he found
himself positioned on the left, with little appeal to the center.47

New conflicts had arisen among the groups likely to form a progressive
multiracial coalition. Some, such as the interminority battles in an increasingly diverse South Central, were neighborhood based, while others concerned the distribution of resources and power between the inner city and
more affluent parts of the community. Such conflict became more evident
in 1997 and 1998, when the predominantly white San Fernando Valley
threatened to separate from the rest of the city. Compared to the Bradley
coalition in its heyday, the leadership capabilities of the liberal forces also
declined.

In the 1993 election, the traditional patterns of the city's coalitions held
firm. Woo had the great share (86 percent) of the African American vote,
largely because of his prominent opposition to Chief Gates. He won hand-
ily among white liberals and carried the great majority of Asian American
votes. In a city that only a year before had witnessed black and Latino riot-
ers looting and burning stores owned by Asian Americans, Woo managed
to craft a surprisingly strong rainbow coalition. But he was crushingly defeated among white non-Jews, and his support among Jews and Latinos was
well below the levels enjoyed by Bradley. The turnout of African Americans
was also smaller than in Bradley's victories, either a reflection of their lower
enthusiasm for an Asian American candidate or their resentment over the
uneven economic conditions in the city. Most remarkably, Riordan won a
solid majority in the most liberal and Jewish council district, the Fifth,
which had the highest rate of voting and had long been a pillar of the
Bradley coalition.48

Riordan's election and the marginalization of the African American political community were hardly distinctive at all in the evolution of American

cities. While Bradley's coalition pioneered new forms of interracial politics, the decline and replacement of his regime by a white moderate opposed by African Americans was a rather common tale around the nation. Los Angeles was not the only city in which blacks were facing political defeat. In 1993, white Republican Rudolph Giuliani defeated African American Mayor David Dinkins in New York City, while Mayor Richard Daley cemented himself as the white replacement of Harold Washington in Chicago. White mayors once again presided over the nation's three largest cities.[49]

The election of 1993 changed African Americans in Los Angeles from being the most enthusiastic backers of the mayor to the group most hostile to the new incumbent. And unlike the days of opposition to Yorty, blacks were largely alone in their alienation. Riordan's power-brokering style allowed him to isolate and marginalize African American opposition. Three blacks and three Latinos continued to serve on the fifteen-member council, but their influence became uncertain. Among African Americans, both Rita Walters and Mark Ridley-Thomas frequently criticized the mayor, but Nate Holden was relatively supportive. Whites on the council became less liberal than before and were unlikely to form a coalition with minority members against Riordan.[50]

While African American council members frequently and openly feuded with Riordan, the new administration was not without some benefits for black Angelenos. As a private citizen, Riordan had supported Proposition F for police reform, although his mayoral campaign received help from the Police Protective League, a largely white union profoundly hostile to reform. As mayor, he continued Bradley's affirmative action policy in city hiring and recruited such black celebrities as basketball star Earvin "Magic" Johnson to meet with African American leaders. His campaign promise to hire 3,000 new police officers was welcome news to South Central residents who had long requested greater protection against gangs, but it was at odds with the equally costly and popular policy of community-based policing championed by Chief Williams. Some of Riordan's police commissioners were committed to reform, but the mayor himself seemed to define reform as manpower expansion.[51]

Yet African Americans weighed these features against two more celebrated events: the dismissal of Chief Williams and the murder case involving former football star O. J. Simpson. Riordan's early support for Williams evaporated, in part due to a series of embarrassing incidents that eroded the chief's image. In 1997, the Police Commission decided not to rehire him. Riordan subsequently approved of Bernard Parks, a veteran African American L A P D officer, as the new chief of police. More damaging by far were the Simpson murder trials, which reopened wounds between blacks and whites and revealed Riordan's limited abilities at resolving racial dilemmas. In October 1995, a predominantly African American jury in a criminal trial in downtown Los Angeles acquitted Simpson of the 1994 slayings of his former wife, Nicole Brown Simpson, and her friend Ron Goldman. In an October 1997 civil trial in Santa Monica, however, a predominantly white jury held Simpson liable for their deaths. In both cases, opinions on Simpson's guilt split along racial lines, in the juries and the nation at large. Whites overwhelmingly believed Simpson to be guilty, while there was a strong belief in the black community that Simpson either was innocent or had been framed by the L A P D. The Mark Fuhrman tapes, which revealed virulent racism on the part of the investigating detective, strengthened this belief. The perception crystallized among blacks and whites, in the city and across the country, that members of the other group placed race above justice. In Los Angeles, these opposing racial reactions further divided west side liberals from African Americans by exhausting much of the moral authority that blacks had derived from the civil rights movement and the Bradley campaigns.[52]

The difficulty of reviving the Bradley coalition and the increasingly marginal position of blacks in Los Angeles politics were evident in the 1997 mayoral campaign, in which Riordan was easily reelected over white liberal Democrat Tom Hayden. Jews voted heavily for Riordan, and 60 percent of Latinos supported him. With only 19 percent supporting Riordan, blacks were even more conspicuously the lone opposed group than in 1993. The editor of the African American *Watts Times* summarized their feelings: "Middle-class blacks complain about loss of power; they have a feeling of helplessness and think their votes don't count."[53] The most striking aspect of the 1997 election was an upsurge of Latino participation. Roughly 15 percent of all votes were cast by Latinos, nearly double their participation in 1993. Half of them were voting for the first time. The media quickly reacted with headlines like "Latino Turnout a Breakthrough" and predicted a "white-brown coalition" that could "portend new political alignments in the city."[54]

But the extent to which African American incorporation in Los Angeles politics has been rolled back since this election remains uncertain. The black share of the vote was proportionate to the group's population, and commentators noted that the African American community remained "well organized, vigorously represented and highly politicized." Blacks were on the winning side in two crucial elements of the 1997 election. In the battle for city attorney, African Americans, Latinos, and Jews backed the winner, James K. Hahn, against Riordan's choice. And the most remarkable ballot measure in years, Proposition BB, which provided billions of dollars for school repairs, passed by more than a two-thirds majority with the support of Riordan, Latinos, Jews, and blacks.[55]

Crucial to African American political power in Los Angeles and most other California cities is the re-creation of a multiracial coalition, at the heart of which would be the potential role that both blacks and whites might play in the future of minority politics in the city. If black activists choose to go it alone, they will be consistently outvoted. If they choose a white-oriented strategy, their ability to bring about serious changes in the city's life will be compromised. Once again, the dilemma is how to pursue an activist agenda for racial equality while responding to the legitimate needs and interests of whites.

Prior to the 1990s, the city was divided into two main groups: those who sided with blacks and those who opposed them. Such hostility was assumed to extend to all minorities. That is no longer the case. The issues that once defined black progress were well known: affirmative action in city hiring, the obtaining of federal funds, and police accountability. Nothing like that clarity exists now in Los Angeles, where the old biracial alliance shares space with angry conservatives, assertive minorities, and the often disparate demands of the urban poor.

Some have wondered how viable a community African Americans constitute in Los Angeles. Middle-class blacks have been moving out of the city since 1980 in unprecedented numbers, some going to nearby cities in Los Angeles county, others to adjacent counties, while still others have returned to the South. Other writers have seen class differences among African Americans making the creation of a "black interest" impossible.[56] But the evidence remains strong that African Americans are still tightly unified in the political arena. There has been virtually no change in black voting patterns along class lines in recent elections. Even in the face of citywide consensus supporting Riordan, blacks remained defiant and relatively united in opposition. As long as racial equality remains a dream, African Americans are likely to maintain their outward unity, despite internal differences of class and politics.[57]

Any viable coalition in Los Angeles, or most any other California city, must now include at least Latinos as well as whites. A thorny issue African

Americans need to address with Latinos is the question of immigration. It has deeply divided progressive forces, whose tradition of openness to the "other" moves them to resist limits on immigration, especially in the face of conservative exploitation of nativist sentiment. But the impact of massive immigration on the wage scale of working-class Angelenos and its potential for reducing the effectiveness of unionization efforts among low-wage workers has created substantial hostility to recent immigrants among black communities statewide.

It is at the neighborhood level in Los Angeles at the beginning of the new millennium that one begins to find efforts underway to resolve interminority issues. In South Central Los Angeles, the three-cornered conflict among longtime black residents, new Latino immigrants, and Korean American owners over liquor stores has led to serious attempts to channel the dispute in ways that de-emphasize the racial and ethnic polarization that could undermine community progress. Little of this work has transferred to political coalitions, but the potential for doing so clearly exists.[58]

Whatever challenges arise in the future, important lessons can be learned from the experience of the Bradley coalition in Los Angeles. Those who care about racial equality, disappointed that more was not accomplished, often fail to note the magnitude of African American political achievement in the city. A black community that constituted a smaller percentage of the population than in any other major American city built internal unity despite factional differences. African Americans had been isolated and marginalized in a city with a conservative civic culture. Without the help of the party organizations and labor groups that built Black Power in other cities, they forged an alliance with liberal whites, especially Jews, to wrest power from a hostile establishment. With that power, African Americans moved to the head table in a city hall long indifferent to their aspirations. Tom Bradley, whose quiet demeanor belied an enormous determination to succeed, used that power to bring important benefits to the black community, most remarkably ending the regime of an unaccountable L A P D. While much was left undone during the Bradley years, the legacy of political unity among African Americans and the search for coalition partners remain critical to political success and, through it, to social change.

In Los Angeles, where diversity serves as the key metaphor of civic debate, race remains a central reality. It does not go away because of changing demographics or because people find it hard to discuss. Keeping race in the debate is crucial, but fostering a racial dialogue that recognizes how much

Los Angeles continues to change will be essential for the future, especially for the future of African Americans in local politics.

The African American journey in Los Angeles began with the thrilling hope that the world could be different, that blacks could have the opportunity, unmatched elsewhere in the nation, to have a stake and make it grow. Despite numerous setbacks and the continuing threat that paradise could become purgatory, African Americans forged a remarkable biracial coalition that represented a model for how minority and majority groups could work in alliance. But the distinctiveness of the experience of blacks in Los Angeles seemed to erode as the new millennium approached, as they once again found themselves on the outside looking in, along with their fellow African Americans in a number of other cities around the nation.

The fluidity of Los Angeles politics, economics, and society may yet recreate a distinctive black experience. This western metropolis has reinvented itself more than once, and each reinvention has had major consequences for African Americans. It may yet be that in Los Angeles, as in California and the West, the often-frustrated hopes of African Americans for a new day with fresh opportunities will rise once again.

NOTES

1. Robert M. Fogelson, *The Fragmented Metropolis: Los Angeles, 1850-1930* (Cambridge, MA: Harvard University Press, 1967), 20–21, 56, 78–79, chap. 4.

2. Charles R. Adrian, "A Typology for Nonpartisan Elections," *Western Political Quarterly* 12 (1959): 456; Charles G. Mayo, "The 1961 Mayoralty Election in Los Angeles: The Political Party in a Nonpartisan Election," *Western Political Quarterly* 17 (1964): 326–27, 330, 332–37; Francis M. Carney, "The Decentralized Politics of Los Angeles," *Annals of the American Academy of Political and Social Science* 353 (1964): 108–9, 120–27.

3. For an account of the careers of Roberts and Hawkins, see the essay by Douglas Flamming in this anthology.

4. U. S. Bureau of the Census, *U.S. Census of Population, 1950*, vol. 2, *Characteristics of Population,* part 5, *California* (Washington, DC: Government Printing Office [G P O], 1952), 84; U.S. Bureau of the Census, *Census of Population, 1960,* vol. 2, *Characteristics of Population,* part 6, *California* (Washington, DC: G P O, 1961), 136.

5. Raphael J. Sonenshein, *Politics in Black and White: Race and Power in Los Angeles* (Princeton: Princeton University Press, 1993), 30, 36, 56, 58.

6. Ibid., 58–66. See also Beeman Patterson, "The Politics of Recognition: Negro Politics in Los Angeles, 1960–1963" (Ph.D. diss., University of California, Los Angeles, 1967).

7. Beeman Patterson, "Political Action of Negroes in Los Angeles: A Case Study in the Attainment of Councilmanic Representation," *Phylon* 30 (1969): 170–83; Sonenshein, *Politics in Black and White*, chap. 3.

8. Sonenshein, *Politics in Black and White*, chap. 5. For an alternative interpretation that attributes much of the post-1960 success of all minorities in California to the Democratic Party, see Fernando J. Guerra, "The Emergence of Ethnic Officeholders in California," in *Racial and Ethnic Politics in California*, Byran O. Jackson and Michael B. Preston, eds. (Berkeley: Institute of Governmental Studies, 1991), 117–31.

9. See David O. Sears and John B. McConahay, *The Politics of Violence: The New Urban Blacks and the Watts Riot* (Boston: Houghton Mifflin, 1973).

10. Max Vorspan and Lloyd P. Gartner, *History of the Jews of Los Angeles* (San Marino, CA: Huntington Library, 1970), 117–19, 203–4, 225–28, 233–35; Mike Davis, *City of Quartz: Excavating the Future in Los Angeles* (New York: Vintage Books, 1990), 119–20, 124–25.

11. Vorspan and Gartner, *Jews of Los Angeles*, 136–38. The thesis that blacks and Jews in Los Angeles were drawn into coalition by a mix of ideology and vested interest is especially brought out in Sonenshein, *Politics in Black and White*.

12. Carney, "Decentralized Politics," 1.

13. Harlan Hahn, David Klingman, and Harry Pachon, "Cleavages, Coalitions, and the Black Candidate: The Los Angeles Mayoralty Elections of 1969 and 1973," *Western Political Quarterly* 29 (1976): 513–14; Robert M. Halley, Alan C. Acock, and Thomas Greene, "Ethnicity and Social Class: Voting in the Los Angeles Municipal Elections," *Western Political Quarterly* 29 (1976): 507–20.

14. Sonenshein, *Politics in Black and White*, 103–9, chap. 8.

15. For the Black Power view, see Stokely Carmichael and Charles V. Hamilton, *Black Power* (New York: Random House, 1967). The case for the equal or greater importance of ideology in coalitions is made in Rufus P. Browning, Dale Rogers Marshall, and David H. Tabb, *Protest Is Not Enough: The Struggle of Blacks and Hispanics for Equality in Urban Politics* (Berkeley: University of California Press, 1984).

16. Sonenshein, *Politics in Black and White*, 187–89. On the importance of

trust in coalitions, see Barbara Hinckley, *Coalitions and Politics* (New York: Harcourt Brace Jovanovich, 1981), 74.

17. Sonenshein, *Politics in Black and White*, 181, 207; Guerra, "Ethnic Officeholders," 124, 126.

18. *Los Angeles Times*, 22 July 1986, B1, 6; 30 August 1986, B1, 3.

19. Sam Yorty, interview with Raphael Sonenshein and Alan L. Saltzstein, 1986; analysis of city council files for individual commissioners, Los Angeles City Archives; Tom Bradley, interview with Raphael Sonenshein, 29 November 1988; *Los Angeles Times*, 8 August 1973; 2–3 August 1984. Table 1 is drawn from the Los Angeles City Council Files, individual commission files, Los Angeles City Archives.

20. The comparative analysis of data in tables 2 and 3 derives from City of Los Angeles, "Reports on Numerical Progress [on Affirmative Action], 1973–1991," Los Angeles City Archives.

21. Alan Saltzstein, Raphael Sonenshein, and Irving Ostrow, "Federal Aid to the City of Los Angeles: Implementing a More Centralized Local Political System," in *Research in Urban Policy*, Terry Clark, ed., 2 vols. (Greenwich, CT: JAI Press, 1986), vol. 2, 55–76.

22. Sonenshein, *Politics in Black and White*, 164–71; Grieg Smith, chief deputy to city councilman Hal Bernson, interview with Raphael Sonenshein and Alan Saltzstein, 1985. For a detailed study of federal grants during the early Bradley years, see Ruth Ross, *The Impact of Federal Grants on the City of Los Angeles*, Federal Aid Case Studies Series, Paper No. 8 (Washington, DC: Brookings Institution, 1980).

23. Sonenshein, *Politics in Black and White*, 156–60; Lou Cannon, *Official Negligence: How Rodney King and the Riots Changed Los Angeles and the LAPD* (New York: Times Books, 1997), 100–4.

24. A thorough narrative of the issues evolving from the Rodney King incident is provided in Cannon, *Official Negligence*. For the recommendations of the Christopher Commission, see Independent Commission on the Los Angeles Police Department, *Report*, 9 July 1991.

25. Cannon, *Official Negligence*, 356, 562–63.

26. Ibid ., 300, 356; Sonenshein, *Politics in Black and White*, 224–26.

27. For an analysis of the 1992 uprising, see the essay by Gerald Horne in this anthology.

28. Sonenshein, *Politics in Black and White*, 224–26; *Los Angeles Times*, 12–13 May; 14 September 1989.

29. Sonenshein, *Politics in Black and White*, 167–71.

30. James Regalado, "Organized Labor and Los Angeles City Politics: An Assessment in the Bradley Years, 1973–1989," *Urban Affairs Quarterly* 27 (1991): 87–108; Davis, *City of Quartz*, 128, 309; *Los Angeles Times*, 9 November 1991.

31. Davis, *City of Quartz*, 304.

32. Roderick Wright Interview with Raphael Sonenshein, 1986.

33. Sonenshein, *Politics in Black and White*, 216–17.

34. Lawrence P. Crouchett, Lonnie G. Bunch III, and Martha Kendall Winnacker, *Visions toward Tomorrow: The History of the East Bay Afro-American Community, 1852–1977* (Oakland: Northern California Center for Afro-American History and Life, 1989), 57–61; Joint Center for Political Studies, *Black Elected Officials: A National Roster, 1985* (Washington, DC: UNIPUA, 1985), 61–68; Joint Center for Political Studies, *Black Elected Officials: A National Roster, 1991* (Washington, DC: Joint Center for Political and Economic Studies Press, 1992), 61–75.

35. U. S. Bureau of the Census, *Census of Population, 1980*, vol. 1, *General Social and Economic Characteristics*, part 6, *California* (Washington, DC: G P O, 1983), table 15; U.S. Bureau of the Census, *Census of Population, 1990, General Population Characteristics*, California (Washington, DC: G P O, 1993), table 6. For an analysis of the liberal coalition in San Francisco that preceded Brown's victory, see Richard DeLeon, "The Progressive Urban Regime: Ethnic Coalitions in San Francisco," in Jackson and Preston, eds., *Racial and Ethnic Politics*, 157–91.

36. Peter A. Morrison and Ira S. Lowry, "A Riot of Color: The Demographic Setting," in *The Los Angeles Riots: Lessons for the Urban Future*, Mark Baldassare, ed. (Boulder, CO: Westview Press, 1994), 19–46. For an analysis of the impact of the global economy in restructuring the Los Angeles economy, see Edward Soja, Rebecca Morales, and Goetz Wolff, "Urban Restructuring: An Analysis of Social and Spatial Change in Los Angeles," *Economic Geography* 59 (1983): 195–30.

37. *Los Angeles Times*, 13, 15 September 1985; Richard Giesberg, Jewish community leader associated with the Bradley coalition, interview with Raphael Sonenshein, 1985.

38. Davis, *City of Quartz*, 205–6.

39. Melvin L. Oliver and James H. Johnson Jr., "Inter-ethnic Conflict in an Urban Ghetto: The Case of Blacks and Latinos in Los Angeles," *Research in Social Movements, Conflict, and Change* 6 (1984): 57–94; James H. Johnson, Jr. and Melvin L. Oliver, "Interethnic Minority Conflicts in Urban America: The Effects of Economic and Social Dislocations," *Urban Geography* 10 (1989): 449–63; Raphael J. Sonenshein, "The Battle over Liquor Stores in South Central Los An-

geles: The Management of an Interminority Conflict," *Urban Affairs Review* 31 (1996): 715–21.

40. Edward J. Boyer, "Changing the Political Guard," *Los Angeles Times*, 24 October 1995, B2; David M. Grant, Melvin L. Oliver, and Angela D. James, "African Americans: Social and Economic Bifurcation," in *Ethnic Los Angeles*, Roger Waldinger and Mehdi Bozorgmehr, eds. (New York: Russell Sage Foundation, 1996), 384.

41. Manuel Pastore Jr., "Economic Inequality, Latino Poverty, and the Civil Unrest in Los Angeles," *Economic Development Quarterly* 9 (1995): 238–58.

42. David O. Sears, "Urban Rioting in Los Angeles: A Comparison of 1965 with 1992," in Baldassare, ed., *Los Angeles Riots*, 237–54.

43. Table 4 is drawn from U.S. Bureau of the Census, *Census of Population, 1990, Population Characteristics, California*, table 6.

44. Boyer, "Changing the Political Guard."

45. U.S. Bureau of the Census, *Census of Population, 1990, Registration*: summary of various estimates; vote in 1993: *Los Angeles Times* exit polls.

46. Sonenshein, *Politics in Black and White*, 291; *Los Angeles Times*, 10 June 1993.

47. Sonenshein, *Politics in Black and White*, 287, 289–91.

48. Ibid., 290–93; Cannon, *Official Negligence*, 532.

49. Raphael J. Sonenshein, H. Eric Schockman, and Richard DeLeon, "Urban Conservatism in an Age of Diversity," paper presented at the annual meeting of the Western Political Science Association, 1996.

50. Sonenshein, *Politics in Black and White*, 304–5.

51. *Los Angeles Times*, 31 October 1995, B1, 6.

52. Cannon, *Official Negligence*, 560–63, 590–91, 595–96; Boyer, "Changing the Political Guard."

53. Cannon, *Official Negligence*, 586–87; *Los Angeles Times*, 10 April 1997, A26, A27; quote is found in Lou Cannon, "Scars Remain for Years After the Los Angeles Riots," *Washington Post*, 28 April 1997.

54. *Los Angeles Times*, 10 April 1997, A1, A27.

55. Ibid.

56. Boyer, "Changing the Political Guard." The migration of African Americans to California suburbs, and its implications, are explored in Lawrence B. de Graaf's essay in this anthology.

57. Raphael J. Sonenshein and Nicholas Valentino, "A New Alignment in City Politics? Evidence from the 1993 Los Angeles Mayoral Election," paper presented at the Annual Meeting of the Western Political Science Association, 1995.

58. Sonenshein, "The Battle over Liquor Stores," 727–35.

Suggested Readings

COMPILED BY ELIZABETH FORTSON ARROYO

This list focuses mainly on published secondary works, usually in print or easily accessible in academic or public libraries. Most of the titles have appeared within the last twenty years. For primary sources and more extensive readings, see the works cited in the endnotes accompanying each essay in this anthology.

ARTICLES

Allswang, John M. "Tom Bradley of Los Angeles." *Southern California Quarterly* 74 (1982): 55–105.

Aubry, Larry. "Black-Korean Relations: An Insider's Viewpoint." *Amerasia Journal* 19 (1993): 149–56.

Bailey, Beth, and David Farber. "The 'Double-V' Campaign in World War II Hawaii: African Americans, Racial Ideology, and Federal Power." *Journal of Social History* 26 (1993): 831–35.

Bragg, Susan. "Knowledge Is Power: Sacramento Blacks and the Public Schools, 1854–1860." *California History* 75 (1996): 214–21.

Broussard, Albert S. "McCants Stewart: The Struggles of a Black Attorney in the Urban West." *Oregon Historical Quarterly* 89 (1988): 157–79.

———. "Slavery in California Revisited: The Fate of a Kentucky Slave in Gold Rush California." *Pacific Historian* 29 (1985): 17–21.

Bunch, Lonnie G. III. "Allensworth: The Life, Death, and Rebirth of an All-Black Community." *Californians* 5 (1987): 26–33.

———. "A Past Not Necessarily Prologue: The Afro-American in Los Angeles since 1900." In *20th Century Los Angeles: Power, Promotion, and Social Conflict.*

Norman M. Klein and Martin J. Schiesl, eds. Claremont, CA: Regina Books, 1991.

Caesar, Clarence. "The Historical Demographics of Sacramento's Black Community, 1848–1900." *California History* 75 (1996): 198–213.

Caldwell, Dan. "The Negroization of the Chinese Stereotype in California." *Southern California Quarterly* 53 (1971): 123–31.

Carlton, Robert L. "Blacks in San Diego County: A Social Profile, 1850–1880." *Journal of San Diego History* 2 (1975): 7–20.

Chamberland, Carol P. "The House That Bop Built." *California History* 75 (1996): 272–83.

Chandler, Robert J. "Friends in Time of Need: Republicans and Black Civil Rights in California during the Civil Rights Era." *Arizona and the West* 24 (1982): 319–40.

Chang, Edward T. "Jewish and Korean American Merchants in African American Neighborhoods." *Amerasia Journal* 19 (1993): 5–17.

Cho, Sumi K. "Korean Americans vs. African Americans: Conflict and Construction." In *Reading Rodney King/Reading Urban Uprising*. Robert Gooding Williams, ed. New York: Routledge, 1993.

Clark, William A. V., and Julian Ware. "Trends in Residential Integration by Socioeconomic Status in Southern California." *Urban Affairs Review* 32 (1997): 825–43.

Cole, Olen Jr. "Black Youth in the National Youth Administration in California, 1935–1943." *Southern California Quarterly* 73 (1991): 385–402.

Coray, Michael S. "Negro and Mulatto in the Pacific West, 1850–1860: Changing Patterns in Black Population Growth." *Pacific Historian* 29 (1985): 18–27.

Crouchett, Lawrence P. "Assemblyman W. Byron Rumford: Symbol for an Era." *California History* 66 (1987): 13–23, 70–71.

de Graaf, Lawrence B. "California Blacks." In *A Guide to the History of California*. Doyce B. Nunis Jr. and Gloria Ricci Lothrop, eds. New York: Greenwood Press, 1989.

———. "City of Black Angels: Emergence of the Los Angeles Ghetto, 1890–1930." *Pacific Historical Review* 39 (1970): 323–52.

———. "Race, Sex, and Region: Black Women in the American West, 1850–1920." *Pacific Historical Review* 49 (1980): 285–313.

———. "Significant Steps on an Arduous Path: The Impact of World War II on Discrimination against African Americans in the West." *Journal of the West* 35 (1996): 24–33

DeLeon, Richard. "The Progressive Urban Regime: Ethnic Coalitions in San Francisco." In *Racial and Ethnic Politics in California,* 2 vols. Vol. 1. Bryan O. Jackson and Michael B. Preston, eds. Berkeley: Institute of Governmental Studies, 1991.

Eastman, Ralph. "Central Avenue Blues: The Making of Los Angeles Rhythm and Blues, 1942–1947." *Black Music Research Journal* 9 (1989): 19–32.

Edwards, Malcolm. "The War of Complexional Distinction: Blacks in Gold Rush California and British Columbia." *California Historical Quarterly* 66 (1977): 34–45.

Flamming, Douglas. "African Americans and the Politics of Race in Progressive-Era Los Angeles." In *California Progressivism Revisited.* William Deverell and Tom Sitton, eds. Berkeley: University of California Press, 1994.

Forbes, Jack D. "Black Pioneers: The Spanish-Speaking Afroamericans of the Southwest." *Phylon* 27 (1966): 233–46.

Fried, Michael. "W. Elmer Keeton and His w pa Chorus: Oakland's Musical Civil Rights Pioneers of the New Deal Era." *California History* 75 (1996): 236–49.

Gill, Gerald R. "'Win or Lose—We Win': The 1952 Vice-Presidential Campaign of Charlotta A. Bass." In *The Afro-American Woman: Struggles and Images.* Sharon Harley and Rosalyn Terborg-Penn, eds. Port Washington, NY: Kennikat Press, 1978.

Grant, David M., Melvin L. Oliver, and Angela D. James. "African Americans: Social and Economic Bifurcation." In *Ethnic Los Angeles.* Roger Waldinger and Mehdi Bozorgmehr, eds. New York: Russell Sage Foundation, 1996.

Grigsby, J. Eugene III, and Mary L. Hruby. "Recent Changes in the Housing Status of Blacks in Los Angeles." *Review of Black Political Economy* 19 (1991): 211–40.

Guerra, Fernando Javier. "The Emergence of Ethnic Officeholders in California." In *Racial and Ethnic Politics in California,* Vol. 1. Byran O. Jackson and Michael B. Preston, eds. Berkeley: Institute of Governmental Studies, 1991.

Gutiérrez, Henry J. "Racial Politics in Los Angeles: Black and Mexican American Challenges to Unequal Education in the 1960s." *Southern California Quarterly* 78 (1996): 51–86.

Hahn, Harlan, David Klingman, and Harry Pachon. "Cleavages, Coalitions, and the Black Candidate: The Los Angeles Mayoralty Elections of 1969 and 1973." *Western Political Quarterly* 29 (1976): 507–20.

Hayden, Dolores. "Biddy Mason's Los Angeles, 1856–1891." *California History* 68 (1989): 86–99.

Hendrick, Irving G. "Approaching Equality of Educational Opportunity in California: The Successful Struggle of Black Citizens, 1880–1920." *Pacific History* 25 (1981): 22–29.

Hudson, Lynn M. "A New Look, or 'I'm Not Mammy to Everybody in California': Mary Ellen Pleasant, a Black Entrepreneur." *Journal of the West* 32 (1993): 35–40.

Hunt, Matthew O. "The Individual, Society, or Both? A Comparison of Black, Latino, and White Beliefs about the Causes of Poverty." *Social Forces* 75 (1996): 293–322.

Johnsen, Leigh Dana. "Equal Rights and the 'Heathen Chinee': Black Activism in San Francisco, 1865–1875." *Western Historical Quarterly* 11 (1980): 57–68.

Johnson, James H. Jr., and Walter C. Farrell Jr. "The Fire This Time: The Genesis of the Los Angeles Rebellion of 1992." *North Carolina Law Review* 71 (1993): 1403–20.

Johnson, James H., Jr., and Curtis C. Roseman. "Increasing Black Outmigration from Los Angeles: The Role of Household Dynamics and Kinship Systems." *Annals of the Association of American Geographers* 80 (1990): 205–22.

Langellier, John Phillip. "Chaplain Allen Allensworth and the 24th Infantry, 1886–1906." *Smoke Signal* (Tucson Corral of Westerners International) 40 (1980): 190–208.

Leonard, Kevin Allen. "Migrants, Immigrants and Refugees: The Cold War and Demographic Change in the West." In *The Cold War American West, 1945-1989*. Kevin J. Fernlund, ed. Albuquerque: University of New Mexico Press, 1998.

———. "The Power of Race: The Federal Government and Race Relations in Los Angeles during World War II." In *Power and Place in the North American West*. Richard White and John M. Findlay, eds. Seattle: Center for the Study of the Pacific Northwest in Association with the University of Washington Press, 1999.

Madyun, Gail. "In the Midst of Things: Rebecca Craft and the Women's Civic League." *Journal of San Diego History* 34 (1988): 29–37.

Madyun, Gail, and Larry Malone. "Black Pioneers in San Diego, 1880–1920." *Journal of San Diego History* 27 (1981): 91–109.

Marmorstein, Gary. "Central Avenue Jazz: Los Angeles Black Music of the Forties." *Southern California Quarterly* 70 (1988): 415–26.

Massey, Douglas S., and Eric Fong. "Segregation and Neighborhood Quality: Blacks, Hispanics, and Asians in the San Francisco Metropolitan Area." *Social Forces* 69 (1990): 15–32.

Montesano, Philip M. "San Francisco Black Churches in the Early 1860s: Political Pressure Group." *California Historical Quarterly* 52 (1973): 145–52.

Moore, Joe Louis. "In Our Own Image: Black Artists in California, 1880–1970." *California History* 75 (1996): 264–71.

Moore, Shirley Ann Wilson. "African Americans in California: A Brief Historiography." *California History* 75 (1996): 194–97.

———. "Getting There, Being There: African American Migration to Richmond, California, 1910-1945." In *The Great Migration in Historical Perspective: New Dimensions of Race, Class, and Gender.* Joe William Trotter Jr., ed. Bloomington: Indiana University Press, 1991.

———. "'Her Husband Didn't Have a Word to Say': Black Women and Blues Clubs in Richmond, California, during World War II." In *American Labor in the Era of World War II.* Sally M. Miller and Daniel A. Cornfort, eds. Westport, CT: Praeger, 1995.

———. "'Not in Somebody's Kitchen': African American Women Workers in Richmond, California, and the Impact of World War II." In *Writing the Range: Race, Class, and Culture in the Women's West.* Elizabeth Jameson and Susan Armitage, eds. Norman: University of Oklahoma Press, 1997.

Morrison, Peter A., and Ira S. Lowry. "A Riot of Color: The Demographic Setting." In *The Los Angeles Riots: Lessons for the Urban Future.* Mark Baldassare, ed. Boulder, CO: Westview Press, 1994.

Moss, Rick. "Not Quite Paradise: The Development of the African American Community in Los Angeles through 1950." *California History* 75 (1996): 222–35.

Murphy, Larry G. "The Church and Black Californians: A Mid-Nineteenth-Century Struggle for Civil Justice." *Foundations* 18 (1975): 165–83.

Nash, Gary B. "The Hidden History of Mestizo America." *Journal of American History* 82 (1995): 841–64.

Navarro, Armondo. "The South Central Los Angeles Eruption: A Latino Perspective." *Amerasia Journal* 19 (1993): 69–85.

Odell, Thurman A. "The Negro in California before 1890." *Pacific Historian* 19 (1975): 321–46; 20 (1976): 67–72, 177–88.

Oliver, Melvin L., and James H. Johnson, Jr. "Inter-ethnic Conflict in an Urban Ghetto: The Case of Blacks and Latinos in Los Angeles." *Research in Social Movements, Conflict, and Change* 6 (1984): 57–94.

Riley, Glenda. "American Daughters: Black Women in the West." *Montana* 38 (1988): 14–27.

Sears, David O. "Urban Rioting in Los Angeles: A Comparison of 1965 with 1992." In *The Los Angeles Riots: Lessons for the Urban Future.* Mark Baldassare, ed. Boulder, CO: Westview Press, 1994.

Sides, Josh. "Battle on the Home Front: African American Shipyard Workers in World War II Los Angeles." *California History* 75 (1996): 250–63.

———. "'You Understand My Condition': The Civil Rights Congress in the Los Angeles African-American Community, 1946–1952." *Pacific Historical Review* 67 (1998): 233–57.

Smith, Alonzo, and Quintard Taylor. "Racial Discrimination in the Workplace: A Study of Two West Coast Cities [Portland and Los Angeles] during the 1940s." *Journal of Ethnic Studies* 8 (1980): 35–54.

Snorgrass, J. William. "The Black Press in the San Francisco Bay Area, 1856–1900." *California History* 60 (1981–82): 306–17.

Sonenshein, Raphael J. "The Battle Over Liquor Stores in South Central Los Angeles: The Management of an Interminority Conflict." *Urban Affairs Review* 31 (1996): 710–37.

Spickard, Paul R. "Work and Hope: African American Women in Southern California during World War II." *Journal of the West* 32 (1993): 70–79.

Spoehr, Luther. "Sambo and the Heathen Chinee: Californians' Racial Stereotypes in the Late 1870s." *Pacific Historical Review* 42 (1973): 185–204.

Stanley, Gerald. "Slavery and the Origins of the Republican Party in California." *Southern California Quarterly* 60 (1978): 1–16.

Steward, Ella. "Communication between African Americans and Korean Americans: Before and after the Los Angeles Riots." *Amerasia Journal* 19 (1993): 23–53.

Taylor, Quintard. "From Esteban to Rodney King: Five Centuries of African American History in the West." *Montana* 46 (1996): 2–23 (includes "Bibliographic Essay on the African American West").

Tolbert, Emory J., and Lawrence B. de Graaf. "'The Unseen Minority': Blacks in Orange County." *Journal of Orange County Studies* 3/4 (1989/90): 54–61.

Tyler, Bruce. "The Rise and Decline of the Watts Summer Festival, 1965 to 1986." *American Studies* 31 (1990): 61–81.

———. "Zoot-Suit Culture and the Black Press." *Journal of American Culture* 17 (1994): 21–33.

Vincent, Ted. "Black Hopes in Baja California: Black American and Mexican Cooperation." *Western Journal of Black* Studies 21 (1997): 204–13.

Watts, Jill. "This Was the Way: Father Divine's Peace Mission Movement in Los Angeles during the Great Depression." *Pacific Historical Review* 60 (1991): 475–96.

Weber, David J. "A Black American in Mexican San Diego: Two Recently Discovered Documents." *Journal of San Diego History* 20 (1974): 29–32.

Wollenberg, Charles. "James v. Marinship: Trouble on the New Black Frontier." *California History* 60 (1981): 262–79.

Zubrinsky, Camille L., and Lawrence Bobo. "Prismatic Metropolis: Race and Residential Segregation in the City of the Angels." *Social Science Research* 25 (1986): 335–74.

BOOKS

Allen, James P., and Eugene Turner. *The Ethnic Quilt: Population Diversity in Southern California.* Northridge, CA: The Center for Geographical Studies, 1997.

Allen, Robert L. *The Port Chicago Mutiny: The Story of the Largest Mass Mutiny Trial in U.S. Navy History.* New York: Warner Books, 1989.

Almaguer, Tomás. *Racial Fault Lines: The Historical Origins of White Supremacy in California.* Berkeley: University of California Press, 1994.

Anderson, E. Frederick. *The Development of Leadership and Organization Building in the Black Community of Los Angeles from 1900 through World War II.* Saratoga, CA: Century Twenty One Publishing 1980.

Baldassare, Mark, ed. *The Los Angeles Riots: Lessons for the Urban Future.* Boulder, CO: Westview Press, 1994.

Bing, Léon. *Do or Die.* New York: HarperPerennial, 1992.

Bluestone, Barry, and Bennett Harrison. *The Deindustrialization of America.* New York: Basic Books, 1982.

Brooks, Gordon, comp. *Blacks in Los Angeles in the Twentieth Century: A Bibliography.* Los Angeles: Southern California Answering Network, 1986.

Broussard, Albert. *African American Odyssey: The Stewarts, 1853–1963.* Lawrence: University Press of Kansas, 1998.

———. *Black San Francisco: The Struggle for Racial Equality in the West.* Lawrence: University of Kansas Press, 1993.

Bullard, Robert D., Eugene Grigsby III, and Charles Lee, eds. *Residential Apartheid: The American Legacy.* Los Angeles: UCLA Center for Afro-American Studies, 1994.

Bunch, Lonnie G. III. *Black Angelenos: The Afro-American in Los Angeles, 1850–1950.* Los Angeles: California Afro-American Museum, 1988.

Cannon, Lou. *Official Negligence: How Rodney King and the Riots Changed Los Angeles and the LAPD.* New York: Times Books, 1997.

Central Avenue Sounds Editorial Committee, eds. *Central Avenue Sounds: Jazz in Los Angeles.* Berkeley: University of California Press, 1998.

Chan, Sucheng, Douglas Henry Daniels, Mario T. García, and Terry P. Wilson, eds. *Peoples of Color in the American West*. Lexington, MA: D. C. Heath, 1994.

Chang, Edward T., and Russell C. Leong, eds. *Los Angeles: Struggles toward Multiethnic Community: Asian American, African American and Latino Perspectives*. Seattle: University of Washington Press, 1994.

Collins, Keith. *Black Los Angeles: The Maturing of the Ghetto, 1940–1950*. Saratoga, CA: Century Twenty One Publishing, 1980.

Cox, Bette Yarbrough. *Central Avenue—Its Rise and Fall (1890-c. 1955), Including the Musical Renaissance of Black Los Angeles*. Los Angeles: BEEM Publications, 1996.

Crouchett, Lawrence P. *William Byron Rumford: The Life and Public Service of a California Legislator*. El Cerrito, CA: Downey Place Publishing House, 1984.

Crouchett, Lawrence P., Lonnie G. Bunch III, and Martha Kendall Winnacker. *Visions toward Tomorrow: The History of the East Bay Afro-American Community, 1852–1977*. Oakland, CA: Northern California Center for Afro-American History and Life, 1989.

Crouchett, Lorraine Jacobs. *Delilah Leontium Beasley: Oakland's Crusading Journalist*. El Cerrito, CA: Downey Place Publishing House, 1990.

Daniels, Douglas H. *Pioneer Urbanites: A Social and Cultural History of Black San Francisco*. Philadelphia: Temple University Press, 1980.

De Graaf, Lawrence B. *Negro Migration to Los Angeles, 1930 to 1950*. San Francisco: R and E Research Associates, 1974.

Diver-Stamnes, Ann. *Lives in the Balance: Youth, Poverty, and Education in Watts*. Albany: State University of New York Press, 1995.

DjeDje, Jacqueline Cogdell, and Eddie S. Meadows. *California Soul: Music of African Americans in the West*. Berkeley: University of California Press, 1998.

Forbes, Jack D. *Africans and Native Americans: Color, Race, and Caste in the Evolution of Red-Black Peoples*. 2d ed. Urbana: University of Illinois Press, 1993.

———. *Afro-Americans in the Far West*. Berkeley: Far West Library, 1967.

George, Lynell. *No Crystal Stair: African Americans in the City of Angels*. New York: Anchor Books, 1992.

Gioia, Ted. *West Coast Jazz: Modern Jazz in California, 1945–1960*. New York: Oxford University Press, 1992.

Goode, Kenneth G. *California's Black Pioneers: A Brief Historical Survey*. Santa Barbara: McNally and Loftin Publishers, 1974.

Gooding-Williams, Robert, ed. *Reading Rodney King, Reading Urban Uprising*. New York: Routledge, 1993.

Gordon, Robert. *Jazz West Coast: Los Angeles Jazz Scene of the 1950s*. London: Quartet Books, 1986.

Hamilton, Kenneth Marvin. *Black Towns and Profit: Promotion and Development in the Trans-Appalachian West, 1877–1915.* Urbana: University of Illinois Press, 1991.

Hendrick, Irving G. *The Education of Non-Whites in California, 1849–1970.* San Francisco: R and E Research Associates, 1977.

Hilliard, David. *This Side of Glory: The Autobiography of David Hilliard and the Story of the Black Panther Party.* Boston: Little, Brown, 1973.

Hine, Darlene Clark, ed. *Black Women in America: An Historical Encyclopedia.* 2 vols. Brooklyn: Carlson Publishing, 1993.

————, ed. *Black Women in United States History.* 17 vols. Brooklyn: Carlson Publishing, 1990–95.

Horne, Gerald. *Fire This Time: The Watts Uprising and the 1960s.* Charlottesville: University Press of Virginia, 1995.

Jensen, Joan M. and Gloria Ricci Lothrop. *California Women: A History.* San Francisco: Boyd and Fraser Publishing Company, 1987.

Johnson, Marilynn S. *The Second Gold Rush: Oakland and the East Bay in World War II.* Berkeley: University of California Press, 1993.

Klein, Norman M., and Martin J. Schiesl, eds. *20th Century Los Angeles: Power, Promotion, and Social Conflict.* Claremont, CA: Regina Books, 1991.

Lapp, Rudolph M. *Afro-Americans in California.* 2d ed. San Francisco: Boyd and Fraser Publishing Company, 1987.

————. *Archy Lee: A California Fugitive Slave Case.* San Francisco: Book Club of California, 1969.

————. *Blacks in Gold Rush California.* New Haven: Yale University Press, 1977.

Lemke-Santangelo, Gretchen. *Abiding Courage: African American Migrant Women and the East Bay Community.* Chapel Hill: University of North Carolina Press, 1996.

Lortie, Francis N. *San Francisco's Black Community, 1870–1890.* San Francisco: R and E Research Associates, 1973.

Lotchin, Roger. *Fortress California, 1910–1961: From Warfare to Welfare.* New York: Oxford University Press, 1992.

Mason, William M. *The Census of 1790: A Demographic History of Colonial California.* Menlo Park, CA: Ballena Press, 1998.

McBroome, Delores Nason. *Parallel Communities: African-Americans in California's East Bay, 1850–1963.* New York: Garland, 1993.

Modarres, Ali. *The Racial and Ethnic Structure of Los Angeles County: A Geographic Guide.* Los Angeles: Edmund G. "Pat" Brown Institute of Public Affairs, California State University, Los Angeles, 1994.

Moore, Shirley Ann Wilson. *To Place Our Deeds: The African American Community in Richmond, California, 1910–1963*. Berkeley: University of California Press, 2000.

Morrison, Toni, and Claudia Brodsky Lacour, eds. *Birth of a Nation'hood: Gaze, Script, and Spectacle in the O.J. Simpson Case*. New York: Pantheon Books, 1997.

Otis, Johnny. *Upside Your Head! Rhythm and Blues on Central Avenue*. Hanover, NH: University Press of New England, 1993.

Owens, Tom, with Rod Browning. *Lying Eyes: The Truth Behind the Corruption and Brutality of the LAPD and the Beating of Rodney King*. New York: Thunder's Mouth Press, 1994.

Pastor, Manuel. *Latinos and the Los Angeles Uprising: The Economic Context*. Claremont, CA: Tomás Rivera Center, 1993.

Payne, J. Gregory, and Scott C. Ratzan. *Tom Bradley, the Impossible Dream: A Biography*. Santa Monica: Roundtable Publishing, 1986.

Pearson, Hugh. *The Shadow of a Panther: Huey Newton and the Price of Black Power in America*. Reading, MA: Addison-Wesley, 1994.

Peretti, Burton W. *The Creation of Jazz: Music, Race, and Culture in Urban America*. Urbana: University of Illinois Press, 1992.

Racial and Ethnic Politics in California. Vol. 1., Byran O. Jackson and Michael B. Preston, eds. Vol. 2, Michael B. Preston, Bruce E. Cain, and Sandra Bass, eds. Berkeley: Institute of Governmental Studies, 1991, 1998.

Reed, Tom. *The Black Music History of Los Angeles—Its Roots*. Los Angeles: Black Accent on L.A. Press, 1992.

Richardson, James. *Willie Brown, a Biography*. Berkeley: University of California Press, 1996.

Roseman, Curtis C., Hans Dieter Laux, and Gunter Thieme, eds. *EthniCity: Geographic Perspectives on Ethnic Change in Modern Cities*. London: Rowman and Littlefield, 1996.

Ruiz, Vicki L., and Ellen Carol DuBois, eds. *Unequal Sisters: A Multi-Cultural Reader in U.S. Women's History*. 2d ed. New York: Routledge, 1994.

Skinner, Byron Richard. *Black Origins in the Inland Empire*. San Bernadino, CA: Book Attic Press, 1983.

Sonenshein, Raphael J. *Politics in Black and White: Race and Power in Los Angeles*. Princeton: Princeton University Press, 1993.

Steinberg, James, David W. Lyon, and Mary E. Vaiana, eds. *Urban America: Policy Choices for Los Angeles and the Nation*. Santa Monica: Rand, 1992.

Taylor, Quintard. *The Forging of a Black Community: A History of Seattle's Central

District, 1870 through the Civil Rights Era. Seattle: University of Washington Press, 1994.

———. *In Search of the Racial Frontier: African Americans in the American West, 1528–1990*. New York: W. W. Norton, 1998.

Templeton, John. *Our Roots Run Deep: The Black Experience in California*. San Jose, CA: Aspire Books, 1991.

Tolbert, Emory J. *The UNIA and Black Los Angeles: Ideology and Community in the American Garvey Movement*. Los Angeles: UCLA Center for Afro-American Studies, 1980.

Trotter, Joe William, ed. *The Great Migration in Historical Perspective: New Dimensions of Race, Class, and Gender*. Bloomington: Indiana University Press, 1991.

Tyler, Bruce. *From Harlem to Hollywood: The Struggle for Racial and Cultural Democracy, 1920–1943*. New York: Garland, 1992.

Urban Institute. *Confronting the Nation's Urban Crisis: From Watts (1965) to South Central Los Angeles (1992)*. Washington, DC: The Institute, 1992.

Waldinger, Roger, and Mehdi Bozorgmehr, eds. *Ethnic Los Angeles*. New York: Russell Sage Foundation, 1996.

Weber, David J. *The Spanish Frontier in North America*. New Haven: Yale University Press, 1992.

Wheeler, B. Gordon. *Black California: The History of African-Americans in the Golden State*. New York: Hippocrene Books, 1993.

Wollenberg, Charles. *All Deliberate Speed: Segregation and Exclusion in California Schools, 1855–1975*. Berkeley: University of California Press, 1976.

DISSERTATIONS AND THESES

Caesar, Clarence. "An Historical Overview of Sacramento's Black Community, 1850–1980." Master's thesis, California State University, Sacramento, 1985.

Crowe, Daniel Edward. "The Origins of the Black Revolution: The Transformation of San Francisco Bay Area Black Communities, 1945–1969." Ph.D. diss., University of Kentucky, 1998.

DeKam, Elizabeth. "'A Home to Call Our Own': Textual Analysis of the Story of Residential Race-Restrictive Covenants in the *California Eagle* and *Los Angeles Sentinel*." Master's thesis, California State University, Northridge, 1993.

Fisher, James Adolphus. "A History of the Political and Social Development of the Black Community in California, 1850–1950." Ph.D. diss., State University of New York at Stony Brook, 1972.

Garcia, Mikel Hogan. "Adaptation Strategies of the Los Angeles Black Community, 1883–1919." Ph.D. diss., University of California, Irvine, 1985.

Guerra, Fernando Javier. "Ethnic Politics in Los Angeles: The Emergence of Black, Jewish, Latino, and Asian Officeholders, 1960–1989." Ph.D. diss., University of Michigan, 1990.

Hudson, Lynn M. "When 'Mammy' Becomes a Millionaire: Mary Ellen Pleasant, an African American Entrepreneur." Ph.D. diss., Indiana University, 1996.

Leonard, Kevin Allen. "The Impact of World War II on Race Relations in Los Angeles." Ph.D. diss., University of California, Davis, 1992.

Montesano, Philip M. "The San Francisco Black Community, 1849–1890: The Quest for 'Equality' before the Law." Ph.D. diss., University of California, Santa Barbara, 1974.

Ramsey, Eleanor Mason. "Allensworth: A Study in Social Change." Ph.D. diss., University of California, Berkeley, 1977.

Rhomberg, Christopher David. "Social Movements in a Fragmented Society: Ethnic, Class, and Racial Mobilization in Oakland, California, 1920–1970." Ph.D. diss., University of California, Berkeley, 1997.

Sandoval, Sally Jane. "Ghetto Growing Pains: The Impact of Negro Migration in the City of Los Angeles, 1940–1960." Master's thesis, California State University, Fullerton, 1973.

Smith, Alonzo Nelson. "Black Employment in the Los Angeles Area, 1938–1948." Ph.D. diss., University of California, Los Angeles, 1978.

Strohm, Susan Mary. "Black Community Organization and the Role of the Black Press in Resource Mobilization in Los Angeles from 1940 to 1980." Ph.D. diss., University of Minnesota, 1989.

Sweeting, Anthony Charles. "The Dunbar Hotel and Central Avenue Renaissance, 1781–1950." Ph.D. diss., University of California, Los Angeles, 1992.

Wilson, Leslie E. "Dark Spaces: An Account of Afro-American Suburbanization, 1890–1950." Ph.D. diss., City University of New York, 1992.

Contributors

ELIZABETH FORTSON ARROYO is a former research associate at the Autry Museum of Western Heritage. Her article "Poor Whites, Slaves, and Free Blacks in Tennessee, 1796–1861" appeared in *Tennessee History: The Land, the People, and the Culture* (1998).

ALBERT S. BROUSSARD is associate professor of history at Texas A & M University. He is the author of *Black San Francisco: The Struggle for Racial Equality in the West, 1900–1954* (1993) and *African American Odyssey: The Stewarts, 1853–1963* (1998). He is also former president of the Oral History Association.

LONNIE G. BUNCH III is associate director for curatorial affairs at the Smithsonian Institution's National Museum of American History. His many publications include *The Black Olympians: The Afro-American in the Olympic Games, 1904–1984* (1984), *Black Angelenos: The Afro-American in Los Angeles, 1850–1950* (1988), and he is coauthor of *Visions toward Tomorrow: The History of the East Bay Afro-American Community, 1852–1977* (1989).

WILLI COLEMAN is associate professor of history and Asian, Latina, African American, and Native American Studies at the University of Vermont. She has contributed chapters to *Double Stitch: Black Women Write about Mothers and Daughters* (1991) and *Black Women in United States History* (1990–1995).

BETTE YARBROUGH COX, a pioneer musicologist, is the author of *Central Avenue—Its Rise and Fall (1890–c. 1955), Including the Musical Renaissance of Black Los Angeles* (1996). She has served as commissioner of cultural affairs for Los Angeles and is founder and president of the BEEM Foundation for the Advancement of Music.

LAWRENCE B. DE GRAAF is professor of history, emeritus, at California State University, Fullerton. He has authored a number of articles on black history in the West, including the pioneering "The City of Black Angels: Emergence of the Los Angeles Ghetto, 1890–1930" (1970), which won the Koontz and Western Historical Association awards for best article, "Race, Sex, and Region: Black Women in the American West, 1850–1920" (1980) and "Significant Steps on an Arduous Path: The Impact of World War II on Discrimination against African Americans in the West" (1996).

DOUGLAS FLAMMING is associate professor of history at the Georgia Institute of Technology, where he serves as director of the Center for the Study of Southern Industrialization. His first book, *Creating the Modern South: Millhands and Managers in Dalton, Georgia, 1884–1984* (1992), won the 1992 Philip Taft Labor History Prize. His essays include "African-Americans and the Politics of Race in Progressive-Era Los Angeles" (1994). His current book project is titled *A World to Gain: African Americans and the Making of Los Angeles, 1890–1940*.

JACK D. FORBES is professor of Native American Studies at the University of California, Davis. His many publications include *Apache, Navajo, and Spaniard* (1960); *Aztecas del Norte: The Chicanos of Aztlán* (1973) (compiler), and *Africans and Native Americans* (1993). He won the American Book Award for Lifetime Achievement in 1997.

GERALD HORNE, professor of African American Studies and director of the Institute of African American Research at the University of North Carolina, Chapel Hill, is the author of *Fire This Time: The Watts Uprising and the 1960s* (1995) and the forthcoming *Class Struggle in Hollywood: Moguls, Mobsters, Stars, Trade Unionists, and Reds, 1945–50*.

GRETCHEN LEMKE-SANTANGELO is associate professor of history at Saint Mary's College of California. Her book *Abiding Courage: African*

American Migrant Women and the East Bay Community (1996) received the American Historical Association's Wesley-Logan Prize.

KEVIN ALLEN LEONARD is assistant professor of history at Western Washington University. His essays include "Migrants, Immigrants, and Refugees: The Cold War and Demographic Change in the West" (1998), and "The Power of Race: The Federal Government and Race Relations in Los Angeles during World War II" (1999). His forthcoming book is titled *The Battle for Los Angeles: Race, Politics, and World War II.*

DELORES NASON MCBROOME is professor of history at Humboldt State University, California. She is the author of *Parallel Communities: African Americans in California's East Bay, 1850–1963* (1993). She is currently working on a study of African American migrations to British Columbia during the nineteenth century.

SHIRLEY ANN WILSON MOORE is professor of history at California State University, Sacramento. She is the author of *To Place Our Deeds: The African American Community in Richmond, California, 1910–1963* (2000) and coeditor (with Quintard Taylor) of the forthcoming anthology *African American Women in the American West, 1600 to 1990.*

KEVIN MULROY is director of the research center at the Autry Museum of Western Heritage. He is the author of the award-winning *Freedom on the Border: The Seminole Maroons in Florida, the Indian Territory, Coahuila, and Texas* (1993).

RAPHAEL J. SONENSHEIN is executive director of the City of Los Angeles Charter Reform Commission and professor of political science at California State University, Fullerton. Long active in Los Angeles politics and government, he has published widely on the subject of interracial coalitions, with particular attention to black-Jewish relations and Los Angeles politics. His book *Politics in Black and White: Race and Power in Los Angeles* (1993) won the Ralph J. Bunche Award from the American Political Science Association.

QUINTARD TAYLOR is Bullitt Professor of History at the University of Washington. His publications include *The Forging of a Black Community: A*

History of Seattle's Central District, from 1870 through the Civil Rights Era (1994), *In Search of the Racial Frontier: African Americans in the American West, 1528–1990* (1998), and the forthcoming anthology *African American Women in the American West, 1600 to 1990* (coeditor with Shirley Moore).

Acknowledgments

The editors would like to thank several individuals for their contributions to *Seeking El Dorado*. At the Autry Museum of Western Heritage, Joanne Hale, president, John Gray, chief executive officer and executive director, and James Nottage, vice president and chief curator, showed remarkable patience and fortitude in seeing this lengthy project through to fruition. Suzanne G. Fox, publications director, critiqued the essays and worked closely with University of Washington Press in bringing the manuscript to print. Elizabeth (Leah) Fortson Arroyo, former research associate, did a magnificent job of managing revisions to the essays. In addition, she compiled the suggested readings, organized data for the maps, listed the contributors, and generally helped to improve the manuscript through her own substantial insights and expertise. For her efforts, the editors express their sincere appreciation. Chris Keledjian edited the entire manuscript with vigor and skill and did so in a remarkably short time. Sandra Odor, assistant to the publications director, prepared the final manuscript for the press.

At the library of California State University, Fullerton, Tuyet Tran and the staff of the government documents section provided valuable assistance with statistical research for the project. At the University of Washington Press, Pat Soden, director, and Julidta Tarver, managing editor, provided wise and encouraging advice based on their many distinguished years of service in scholarly publishing.

Lastly, for their support through the many long evenings and lost weekends this project demanded, the editors thank their families and loved ones, especially Marcine Anderson, Shirley de Graaf and Kieran and Sara Mulroy.

Index

Abbott, Robert, 131

Abdul-Jabbar, Kareem (Lew Alcindor), 43

abolitionists, white, 9

accountability, police, 392, 403n.37, 457, 467

Acquired Immune Deficiency Syndrome (AIDS), 237–238

activism, antidiscrimination: and defeats, 35, 220; direct or militant, 38; leaders of, 9, 131; legislative, 37, 40, 297–300; political, 35–36, 218–219; postwar era, 360; World War II era, 199–200. *See also* elective office, African Americans in; lawsuits against segregation

activism by women, 104; 19th century role models, 9, 210; club movement, 215–219; clubs and collective, 215–217, 218–219, 220, 361; and future civil rights campaigns, 219, 229; individual, 219–222, 225–229; and march on USES, 28, 31; and political gains, 229–232; for rights in streetcars, 56n.25, 104–105, 108; tradition

of, 229–230, 239–240. *See also* women, African American

actors, African American, 22–23. *See also* films

actresses, African American, 23, 26, 44, 213–214, 233–234. *See also* films

Adams, Lorraine, 382–383

adult education. *See* job training

affirmative action, 41–42, 422, 426; broadening scope of, 445n.61; in city government, 455–456, 465, 467; future of, 50, 239; opposition to, 49, 239

African American Musicians Union, 256

African Methodist Episcopal (AME) churches, 12; in Los Angeles, 18, 52, 107, 215, 253; Saint Andrews, Sacramento, 10; in San Francisco, 17–18, 106, 109. *See also* churches, African American; religious community

age differentials: and low-wage jobs, 358; postmigrant generation, 363, 364, 369; and unemployment, 347, 363

cities with significant African American populations: African American proportion in, 448n.82; and a black majority, 411, 430; definitions of, 435, 448n.82; fastest-growing *(tables)*, 413, 420; growth in, 435, 448n.82. *See also* urban communities, African American; *specific city names*

Citizens' Committee for the Defense of Mexican American Youth, 322–323

citizenship: and black homeownership, 139; and the Double V movement, 30, 200, 225–226, 292

Citrus Heights, CA, 442n.40, 444n.50

Civil Rights Act of 1964, 299

Civil Rights Act of 1968, Title VIII, 415

Civil Rights Commission, 228

Civil Rights Congress (CRC), East Bay, 360–361

civil rights legislation: 1940s efforts to secure, 293–296, 339n.61; 1950s California, 37, 297–299, 413–414; 1960s federal, 298, 299; antidiscrimination, 37, 40, 48; coalition building for, 293–299, 307n.53, 308n.64, 339n.61, 360–361, 367; Hawkins's and Rumford's struggles for, 293–298, 307n.53, 308n.64, 339n.61; "Second Reconstruction" mid-1960s, 279; success and failures of, 432, 436. *See also* fair housing acts; lawsuits against segregation

civil rights, minority, 394–396, 416; legal limitations on, 104–105, 133; as triumph or overdue, 436–437

civil rights movement: and anticommunism, 395; in California, 37–38, 230, 297–299; collapse of, 299; and the gap between classes, 393–394; and the liberal agenda, 279, 360, 395;

postwar, 219, 228, 294, 360–361; sit-in campaigns, 38; in the South, 234; and welfare rights, 363, 364–366; women's club movement foundation for, 219

civil rights organizations, 433; ad hoc protest and, 30–31; in Los Angeles, 20; in Oakland, 360–361, 367. *See also* interracial organizations

Civil Works Administration (CWA), 224, 225, 290

Civilian Conservation Corps (CCC), 290, 305n.41

class stratification: and factional politics, 451–452, 467; into separate neighborhoods, 269, 284, 381, 393–394, 452; intraracial, 47–48, 211, 219, 272–273, 381–382, 432, 460; and suburbanization, 416, 432; and voting patterns, 467

Clay, William "Sonny," 259

Cleaver, Eldridge, 39, 40, 382

Cleveland, OH, population statistics, 185

closed-shop union, 201

club members, African American women, names of, 216

club movement, black women's, 215–219. *See also* women's clubs, African American

clubs, music. *See* nightclubs

coaches and managers, sports, 43, 44

coalition building, African American, 450–469; achievements of, 468; among civil rights organizations, 360–361, 367; by Hawkins in 1930s, 286–289; for civil rights legislation, 297–299, 360–361, 367; consequences of failure of, 332; for dealing with interracial problems, 326–329; forces against, 294–295, 385–386, 460–464;

domestic help (*cont.*)
away from, 237; roles in movies, 23,
214; servants, 213, 237; women work-
ing as, 22, 112–113, 114, 195, 207n.42,
213, 225, 410. *See also* occupational
opportunities, African American
Dominguez, Juan José, 82
Dones, Bessie (Bessie Williams), 254, 256
Dones, Sidney P., 25, 285, 302n.16,
304n.35
Dorsey, Tommy, 270
Double V movement. *See* fascism in
Europe and racism in America,
combating
Douglas, Frederick, 151
Douroux, Margaret Pleasant, 234
draft evasion, 160
Drake, Francis, 53n.1
Dream, the American. *See* American
Dream
Du Bois, W.E.B., 129, 144n.1, 156, 160,
232–233, 259
DuBois, Ellen Carol, 229, 279
Dunbar Hotel, 22, 259, 275n.31
Dymally, Mervyn M., 46, 298, 333, 452

Eagle, the. *See California Eagle* (newspaper)
earthquake and fire of 1906, San Francisco, 18, 130, 184
East Bay cities. *See* Bay Area, San Francisco; *specific city names*
East Bay Civil Rights Congress (CRC),
360–361
East Bay Women's Welfare Club, 220,
223
East Palo Alto, CA, 421, 440n.19
Ebonics (Black English), 41
Eckstine, Billy, 259, 266
Economic Development Administration (EDA), 354–355, 362

economic development, urban, 348; divergence of complaints about, 461;
downtown Los Angeles, 42, 456, 458;
Oakland, 42, 362, 363; social consequences of, 353–354
Economic Opportunity, Office of. *See*
Office of Economic Opportunity
(OEO)
Edmonds, Jefferson Lewis, Jr., 20,
129–144; black advancement strategies of, 130–131, 135, 140–142 143–144;
impact of, 143–144; and the *Liberator* (news magazine), 134–138,
141–142, 143; life of, 131–132, 142
Edmonds, Kenneth "Babyface," 45
education: and affirmative action, 239;
African American opposition to all-
black, 146n.17, 155; and cultural differences, 238–239; of girls, 118, 239;
NYA-assisted, 24; vocational,
146n.17, 155; of youth for citizenship,
353. *See also* schools, public
educational opportunities: campaign
for equal, 14; integrated, 137,
435–436; as migration motivation,
186, 188–189, 419; in suburban communities, 435–436. *See also* school
segregation
Educational Opportunity Programs
(EOP), 41
Edwards, Harry, 43
Edwards, J. E., 19–20
Edwards, Malcolm, 9
El Cajon, CA, 444n.50
El Monte, CA, 440n.19
El Toro, CA, 442n.40
elective office, African Americans in, 5,
45–46; and appointive office, 46,
455; city commissioners, 455; city
council positions, 37, 45, 46, 230,
299, 329, 451, 452, 459, 465; congress-

health insurance, 307n.53

Hearst, William Randolph, 26, 322

Heisman trophy winners, 43–44

Henderson, Fletcher, 263, 267

Henderson, J. Raymond, 320

Henderson, Miles, 165

Heritage Music Foundation, 234

Herndon, Larena Frances, 188

Hewes, Laurence, 33

higher education: access of African Americans to, 24, 41–42, 421, 435–436; black studies programs, 40

Hightower, Alma, 262–263

highway project, Baja California, 161–162

Hill, Betty, 220

Hilliard, Flora M., 226

Himes,Chester, 324–325, 333n.2; *If He Hollers Let Him Go* (novel), 309, 317; on Japanese American internment, 317–318; *Lonely Crusade* (novel), 309–311, 325, 337n.42

Hinds, Wiley, 152

Hine, Darlene Clark, 188

Hispanics, 425; in the Bradley coalition, 454; discrimination against, 10; education of, 239; elected officials, 47, 329, 451; electoral power of, 452, 463–464, 466, 468; employment opportunities for, 237, 367, 393; interminority cooperation with, 467–468; population growth by, 46, 191, 394, 421, 461–462

historical gaps and omitted subjects: African heritage, 27, 74; black women of the West, 98–99; interracially mixed population, 74, 90n.3

History Parade, Black, 433

Hite, Les, 259

Holden, Caleb, 142

Holden, Nate, 465

Holliday, Billie, 265

Holliday, George, 380

Hollingsworth, Joseph, 452

homeownership: cost inflation and median income, 423; importance of, 139, 405; pre-World War II, 24–25, 139; or rentals, 416, 421; restricted, 409. *See also* real estate

Hoover, Herbert, 283, 285

hopelessness and despair: African American communities feeling, 368–369, 379–380; and drug abuse, 387

Hopkins, Mark, 9

Horne, Lena, 23, 26, 259, 265, 323

Horowitz, David, 40

housing. *See* homeownership; real estate

Housing Act (1968), 415

housing authorities, 194, 423–424. *See also* public housing projects, government

Housing and Community Development Act of 1974 (HCDA), Section 8 funds, 423–424

housing developments: racial exclusion from, 350–351. *See also* public housing projects, government; suburbs, the

housing discrimination. *See* fair housing acts; residential segregation

housing shortages: and inflation, 423–424; migrants influx and, 115, 196, 293; postwar, 34–35, 293; and urban crisis, 417, 423–424; wartime, 29–30, 193, 195, 196, 226, 227, 313. *See also* residence patterns, African American

Housing and Urban Development (HUD), Department of, 422

Houston, Norman O., 35, 339n.66

Howard, Paul, 254
Hubbard, E. T., 282
Hudlin, Julia, 213
Hudson, H. Claude, 22, 36
Hughes, Langston, 259, 261
human relations commissions, local, 31, 36, 422
Huntington Beach, CA, 413, 428, 429, 440n.19
Hyer, Anna and Emma, 116

immigration: Hispanic, 421, 461; and interracial conflict, 48, 461; into Mexico, 163–164; Japanese, 152; Mexican, 48, 386; openness or hostility to, 468; of undocumented residents, 393, 461. *See also* minority groups, other
Imperial Valley, CA, 159, 164, 171
inclusion, politics of, 328–329, 361–362
income: intraracial gap in, 47; median, 423, 447n.69; parity of African American and white women, 50; racial gap in, 17, 37, 430–431; of sports stars, 43; for women, equality of, 228, 237
indigenous people. *See* Native Americans
industrial restructuring and relocation: and chronic job loss, 350–354, 356–358; effects on inner cities, 392–393; effects on national economy, 357–358; to the suburbs, 348–349, 350–351. *See also* opportunity structure
inflation in housing costs, 423–424
Inglewood, CA, 25, 412, 413, 428, 430, 440n.19, 443n.41
Inland Empire, 50, 417
inner cities: African Americans not just in, 436; alienation of, 458, 461; black

flight from, 47, 296, 419, 421; confinement in, 408–410, 416; explaining the decline of, 345–346, 419; impact of deindustrialization of, 357–358, 392–393; marginalization within, 345; slum neighborhoods, 30, 353–354; and "urban pathology," 346, 368, 370, 408. *See also* ghettos, urban; *specific city names*
integrated neighborhoods. *See* communities, integrated; mixed neighborhoods
integration, racial: black-white, 273; hope for postwar, 361–362; New Deal programs and, 224–225, 290–292, 305n.41; Oakland the city with the most, 366; promise of school, 137; and social isolation, 432–433, 437; as a spatial construct, 50, 436; success or failure of, 52, 422, 432, 436; token, 270; World War II era changes and, 28. *See also* residence patterns, African American
intermarriage. *See* marriage, interracial
International Brotherhood of Boilermakers, 30, 198–200, 226, 313
interracial conflict: ethnic and, 394–396; and gangs, 386–387, 397; and immigration, 461
interracial cooperation: ambivalence toward, 330–331, 388; during World War II, 160, 199–200, 319–320, 324–329, 332–333; early, 11; future of, 467–468; groups supporting, 319–320, 324, 326–327; in Los Angeles, 160, 319–320, 324–329, 332–333, 454, 467; in Mexico, 163–164; in Oakland, 367, 385, 397; postwar, 330–331, 350, 360–361; in San Francisco, 11; seen as futile, 388. *See also* coalition building, African American

organizations and institutions, African
American community, 106; all-
black, 16, 280, 314, 361; and class
stratification, 219, 451–452; founded
by women, 216, 219–220, 226, 232,
361; grassroots, 232, 361, 363, 426;
Los Angeles, 19, 31, 36, 133, 134; reliance on, 16, 50, 280, 359–360, 361,
369, 433–434; rivalry between, 361,
451–452; in the suburbs, 433–434;
women's clubs and committees,
111–112, 215–216, 361. *See also* social
services and institutions, African
American
organizations, religious. *See* churches,
African American; *specific denomi-
nations*
organizations, women's. *See* women's
clubs, African American
Original Americans. *See* Native
Americans
Ory, Edward "Kid," 26, 255, 257
other minority groups. *See* minority
groups, other; racial discrimination
against other Californians
Otis, Harrison Gray, 158
Otis, Johnny, 271
out-migration: after Watts uprising,
412, 416; by middle-class African
Americans, 416, 467; from Los Angeles, 411, 416, 417, 419; from Oakland, 419; from San Francisco, 411,
419. *See also* black flight; migration
by African Americans
Overr, Oscar, 156
Overton, Sarah, 221
Owen, Chandler, 21–22
Owens, Robert C., 13, 18, 129, 133, 138,
158
Owens-Bynum, Harriet, 115
Oyama, Mary, 318

Pacific Coast Negro Improvement Association, 219–220
Pacific Gas and Electric Company, 198
Palm Springs, CA, 428
Palmdale, CA, 396, 421
Palo Alto, CA, 421, 422
Panthers, Black. *See* Black Panther
Party (BPP)
pardos. See mixed bloods
Parker, Charlie "Bird," 266, 267
Parker, William, 390, 452
Parks, Bernard, 466
part-Africans. *See* mixed bloods
parties, political: cross-filing in primaries of, 289, 298, 304n.34, 307n.58;
and homogeneous nonpartisanship,
451; racial integration in, 388; re-
alignment between, 279. *See also
names of parties*
Pasadena, CA, 25, 37, 412, 429, 440n.19,
443n.41
Patterson, Eva Jefferson, 232
Peace and Freedom Party, 39
Peace and Justice Organization, 367
Pentecostal churches, 20–21
people of color. *See* minority groups,
other; mixed bloods; *names of spe-
cific groups*
Perkins, Robert and Carter, 9
philanthropy, by African American
women, 107, 111
Phyllis Wheatly Club of the East Bay,
216–217
Pico, Andres, 6–7, 84, 100
Pico, Antonio María, 88
Pico, José Dolores, 83
Pico, José María, 83
Pico, Pio, 6, 83, 84, 96n.20, 100
Pico, Santiago de la Cruz, 80, 83
Pico family, 83, 84, 100
Pindell, Anna, 116

pioneers and overlanders: black, 86–87;
gaps in history of, 98–99
Pittman, Tarea Hall, 23, 197, 218; activism by, 228
Pittman, William, 23
Pittsburgh, C A, 440n.19
Placerville, C A, 12
Pleasant, Earl Amos and Olga
Williams, 234
Pleasant, Mary Ellen (Mammy), 5, 9,
17, 183, 210; life of, 107, 115; in streetcar access cases, 56n.25, 108
Pleasanton, C A, 442n.40, 444n.50
Poitier, Sidney, 44, 262
police departments: African Americans
in, 41, 426; allowing racial violence
incidents, 383; reforms recommended for, 392, 403n.37, 457, 465
police, treatment of African Americans
by: brutality in, 34, 48, 379, 390–391,
452–453, 457; harassment and racial
profiling, 268, 271, 419, 432, 437; improvements in, 425; and Mexican
Americans, 323; not solving their
murders, 384; and racism, 268, 271,
383, 384, 390–391, 466; and shootings, 29, 38, 379, 391, 434, 457
political action. *See* activism, antidiscrimination; activism by women
political campaigns. *See* electoral campaigns, African American
political parties. *See* parties, political;
names of parties
political power. *See* coalition building,
African American; electoral
strength, African American
politicians. *See* elective office, African
Americans in
politics: achieving control of local, 360,
363–364, 366; of African American
community marginalization,

464–465; African American political
defeats in, 465; Black Power in, 232,
387, 389; of interracial cooperation,
329, 453–454, 467–468; new multiracial or old biracial, 332, 367, 396,
459–460, 463–464, 467–468; Red
Scare anticommunist, 294, 385, 388,
395; right-wing, 388; suburbanization and less power in, 396; and
trust among leaders, 454; white
backlash power in, 389–390, 462. *See
also* coalition building, African
American; liberal politics
politics, city. *See specific city names*
Polk, James K., 7
Pomona, C A, 407, 412, 415, 424, 430,
440n.19
Poole, Cecil, 36
population in California, the African
American: gender ratio, 102; Gold
Rush-era, 10, 106; largest decennial
increase in, 381; tables of, 15, 33,
103. *See also* migration by African
American
population statistics. *See* residence patterns, African American; statistics
on African American populations
in California
Port Chicago Mutiny, 29, 62n.67
Porter, Roy, 270
poverty: and A I D S, 237–238; and antipoverty programs, 353, 354–355,
362; and black flight, 296; and destructive survival strategies, 369;
feminization of (concept), 211, 231;
and loss of opportunity structure,
345, 353, 356–358, 369–370; myths of
responsibility for, 345–346, 359, 365,
369–370; national full-employment
movement against, 367; question of
subsidizing black, 369–370; racial

White, Walter, 324

white women: employment of, 112, 225; income parity of African American and, 50; suffrage and temperance campaigns, 221–222, 231–232

white-collar jobs, 366, 448n.80; exclusion of blacks from, 410; highest numbers in newer suburbs, 428–429; increase in, 427–428; race-related, 422, 434; in San Francisco, 187, 197–198, 202; statistics, 410, 427; stereotypes, 446n.65. *See also* middle-class African Americans; occupational opportunities, African American

whitening. *See* mobility, social

Whitlock, Mark, 52

Wilkins, Roy E., 339n.66

Wilkins, William, 253

Williams, A. O., 168

Williams, Cecil, 51

Williams, Fred, 285, 302n.17

Williams, Mrs. Fred, 216

Williams, Paul, 22

Williams, Richard, 236

Williams, Serena, 236

Williams, Sherley Anne, 233

Williams, Slina, 115

Williams, Venus, 236

Williams, Walter "Dootsie," 265

Williams, Willie, 457, 465

Willis Petroleum Company, 170

Wilson, Beth Pierre, 223

Wilson, Lionel, 46, 230, 364, 366, 459

Wilson, Teddy, 270

Wilson, William Julius, 429

Winfrey, Oprah, 45

"womanist" or "feminist," 232

women activists. *See* activism by women; elective office, African Americans in

women, African American, 210–240; and AIDS, 237–238; in the arts, 233–236; athletes, 236; and church committees, 12, 111, 361; clubs and organizations led by, 19, 111, 191, 361; and community development, 17, 98–118, 226, 361; defense industry employment of, 195; domestic service jobs of, 22, 112–113, 114, 195, 207n.42, 348; economic roles of, 113–116; in elective office, 229–230, 237, 455; employed, proportion of, 112, 237, 431, 432; employment patterns of, 22, 112, 113, 114, 186, 213, 222–223, 225–228, 236–237, 348, 352, 431, 432, 455, 456; government employment of, 352, 455, 456; income of, 50; invisibility of, historical, 98–99; issues and concerns of, 231–232, 237–239, 361, 364; leadership tradition of, 106, 218–219, 225–226, 228–232; literacy of, 102; mass mobilization of, postwar, 228; media images of, 23, 213, 235; middle-class, 50, 211, 215–217, 219; migration by, 188–189, 194; musicians and music teachers, 234, 252, 254, 256–257, 258, 259, 262–263, 265; political gains by, 229–230; population statistics, 102, 103; and poverty, 211, 231; professional, 50, 237, 436; recent historical study of, 99, 229; sexual and racial discrimination against, 224–225, 226, 232–233; sororities of, 189, 222, 243n.25; in the suburbs, 431, 432; on welfare, 364; working, 19, 188–189, 194, 217–218, 361; working mothers, 195; World War II-era changes for, 225–228. *See also* gender

Women of Color Resource Center, 232

women leaders. *See* activism by

Library of Congress Cataloging-in-Publication Data

Seeking El Dorado : African Americans in California /
edited by Lawrence B. de Graaf, Kevin Mulroy, and Quintard Taylor.
p. cm.
Includes bibliographical references and index.
ISBN 0-295-98082-6 (cloth : alk. paper)
ISBN 0-295-98083-4 (pbk. : alk. paper)
1. Afro-Americans—California—History.
2. Afro-Americans—California—Social conditions.
3. California—History.
4. California—Social conditions.
I. De Graaf, Lawrence Brooks.
II. Mulroy, Kevin.
III. Taylor, Quintard.
IV. Autry Museum of Western Heritage.
F870.N4S44
2001
979.4'00496073—DC21
00-051158